Network Monitoring and Analysis

A Protocol Approach to Troubleshooting

Ed Wilson

Prentice Hall PTR
Upper Saddle River, New Jersey 07458
www.phptr.com

ISBN 0-13-026495-4

9 780130 264954

90000

Acquisitions editor: *Mike Meehan*
Editorial/production supervision: *Patti Guerrieri*
Cover design director: *Jayne Conte*
Cover design: *Bruce Kenselaar*
Manufacturing manager: *Maura Goldstaub*
Editorial assistant: *Julie Okulicz*
Marketing manager: *Bryan Gambrel*

Prentice Hall books are widely used by corporations and
government agencies for training, marketing, and resale.
The publisher offers discounts on this book when ordered in bulk quantities.
For more information, contact Corporate Sales Department, Phone: 800-382-3419;
FAX: 201-236-7141; E-mail: corpsales@prenhall.com
Prentice Hall PTR, One Lake Street, Upper Saddle River, NJ 07458.

Printed in the United States of America
10   9   8   7   6   5   4   3   2   1

ISBN 0-13-026495-4

Prentice-Hall International (UK) Limited, *London*
Prentice-Hall of Australia Pty. Limited, *Sydney*
Prentice-Hall Canada Inc., *Toronto*
Prentice-Hall Hispanoamericana, S.A., *Mexico*
Prentice-Hall of India Private Limited, *New Delhi*
Prentice-Hall of Japan, Inc., *Tokyo*
Pearson Education Asia Pte. Ltd.
Editora Prentice-Hall do Brasil, Ltda., *Rio de Janeiro*

Dedicated to my wife and friend, Teresa

Contents

Chapter 2   43

The TCP/IP Protocol Suite

Chapter 3   84

The SPX/IPX Protocol

Chapter 4   103

Server Message Blocks   103

Chapter 6   168

A Look at Server Traffic

Chapter 7   194

A Look at Application Traffic

Part 4   271

Troubleshooting Scenarios: A Look at Common Problems

Chapter 10   273

Troubleshooting Issues

Foreword

Full Service Networking sells and supports computer networks to a wide range of customers. A major part of our business is maintaining mission critical LANs and WANs for a growing base of customers. Key to providing this service is the ability to respond quickly to a wide variety of network problems—often with an anxious customer demanding answers as we seek the solution.

Further complicating matters is the rapid change to core networking technology deployed in the network. This requires both specialization and extensive training for our technical staff to understand the implications of new technologies.

Microsoft® updates its networking products on a regular basis, as does every other company in this industry. We work in an industry that is constantly releasing new products to take advantage of the "possible," which grows exponentially as the technology continues to advance.

How do you deal with this situation and still guarantee the service level that network users demand? The pressure is on the on-site network technician. They have to work more intelligently and more efficiently.

The network engineer who has a good understanding of the procedures and tools to monitor and analyze a complex network is able to identify and resolve problems quickly and efficiently. In addition, the same tools are invaluable for proactively managing a network to identify potential problems before they become critical. *Network Monitoring and Analysis: A protocol approach to troubleshooting* should give the network engineer the tools to work smarter.

James Naramore
President
Full Service Networking

xv

Introduction

Did you ever wonder what in the world was happening under the hood of your network? Why things are running slowly, what causes print jobs to suddenly fail, or programs to unexpectedly terminate? Are you looking for something to do when users call up complaining that the server is slow? Do you want to get a better feel for how much traffic is actually getting through? If so, then this book is for you because it is about network monitoring and analysis—perhaps the least understood of all administrator activities.

For many, the question is not, why should I perform network monitoring; indeed, it seems a rather intuitive thing. The question is, when do I find time? Couple this with the fact that there is a learning curve, which must be met before the most useful information can be gleaned, and you have lots of resistance. In some respects it is like changing the oil in your car. You know it needs to be done; however, you do not want to get dirty.

The time to learn how to use the tool is not when the network is down, but when things are running well. Network monitoring throws open the door to your data communication stream allowing you to seize new vistas of understanding. We will share many insights with you and hint at possibilities for further exploration. In fact, you will find many ideas for setting up a regular monitoring and analysis program inside these covers. Some of the areas that will pay the greatest dividends are troubleshooting, optimization, and security concerns, each of which commands considerable attention.

In this book, we look at the protocols likely to be present on your network and describe many of the sources of traffic. Through this understanding, we arrive at a plan for fine-tuning our communication scenarios, and we offer solutions that work in real life settings. Once the traffic is characterized, we can reasonably predict the effect of adding additional services or computers onto the network. This gets us out of the reactive mode of chasing phantoms and goblins and allows us to take a proactive, balanced approach to network management. Through traffic prediction, we are able to determine infrastructure requirements and implement solutions before their need even becomes apparent to the users.

WHY USE NETWORK MONITORING

Networks are noisy places. As you look at network traces, one thing that stands out is the sheer volume of data that passes along the wire every second. It is amazing that more data is not lost. We will see several areas to reduce some of the noise. However, in network optimization, the mantra "nothing is free" holds especially true. As we tweak the operating system, we need to see what we are giving up in order to reduce some of the traffic. In many instances, we can make changes without giving up anything significant. At other times, it must be a carefully weighed decision, rooted firmly in a thorough understanding of your particular network configuration and the functionality provided by the specific service or setting. We offer advice and guidance with this determination, and thereby empower you to make the decisions needed to draw order from the ethereal chaos. This analysis is our task as we optimize the network.

Network Optimization

Armed with a thorough understanding of the protocols, we can pick up ideas to reduce the traffic. One of the first things we learn is to eliminate superfluous services. As we will learn in this overview of the protocols, the traffic associated with additional protocols is not just the transport, but the services associated with the protocol. Each service talks to other services, advertises its presence, or in other ways makes itself known on the network. It is conceivable that by simply removing one or two services, a 5 to 10 percent reduction in network traffic can be achieved.

In order to use only the protocols needed on the network, we need to know what the protocols are and where they fit into the scheme of things. Therefore, in the first section of the book, we examine some of the common protocols in use, and look in depth at them to see how they work. With this insight, we can develop our optimization methodology. We see which ones we need, and which ones we do not. We will gain the confidence to run with only one protocol and avoid the temptation to "keep one for a backup." In addition to the flood of extraneous traffic, network communication slows to a crawl as programs make numerous attempts to find a shared protocol.

Although we cannot perform true baselining with the Microsoft Network Monitor tool (some of the other products currently available do this for us), we can get a good idea of our network utilization and thereby manually trend the pertinent statistics in a spreadsheet or database. As we turn off services, reduce protocols, and optimize all that remains, we can chart our progress. We will see the utilization percentages, broadcasts, and CRC errors all fall away like autumn leaves after the first rain. Armed with documentation collected in this step, we are in a good position to plan for expansion.

Expansion Planning

Whenever we add additional workstations, printers, servers, or services to our network we need to have a clear understanding of how the computing environment will be affected. As we plan for expansion, we need an idea of what and where the impact will be on the network itself. The traffic burden is likely to be far greater than a new machine simply talking to a server. If the new machine is performing file-sharing services, then it will be advertising its presence in some manner. When this computer hangs out an open-for-business shingle, how much traffic is going to be generated? What effect does it have on the rest of the segment? If this is a single segment, then what about the other machines sharing the wire? What will the impact be across the router, or at the switch? These are the things we need to look at and the kind of things we talk about in this section.

Security Concerns

Network monitoring can be tremendously helpful as we fight the battle against hacker insurgents. Although it may be possible for them to slip into the network undetected—either through stealing passwords, or bypassing security altogether—it is impossible for them to hide their activities once inside. From this vantage point, the low-level network monitor can see everything. So how do we detect the hackers in our network neighborhood?

A rogue DHCP server is particularly nasty. The DHCP server sits on your network, receives the client request for an IP address, and then proceeds to hand out addresses on its own. They may or may not be legitimate for your network, or they may even hand out duplicate addresses causing no end of grief and heartache. In reality, Network monitoring is the best way to find a rogue DHCP server. Microsoft Network Monitor version 2 makes this sabotage even easier to detect.

Many years ago, the U.S. Navy realized that the best way to catch a submarine was to use another submarine. These silent deadly devices were purposefully designed to avoid detection and thus was born the class of submarines called the fast attack. In the same way, the only way to detect unauthorized sniffing is to use a network monitor. Nearly all tools in this class will assist you in finding clandestine sniffing. Network Monitor version 2 can even shut down unauthorized sniffers.

IP spoofing is a favorite hacker trick in which one computer masquerades as another by using the IP address of another machine and then responding to queries addressed to someone else. We can detect spoofing by firing up our favorite Network Monitoring tool. IP spoofing can also happen if routers are improperly configured. In this situation, a machine answers requests directed to a different machine with the same IP address. This can absolutely drive you crazy until you detect the spoofing.

Troubleshooting

Obviously, a bad Ethernet card is easy to detect. It just lies there, doing nothing but collecting dust—or you look for smoke. However, a card that thinks it is good, and that actually transmits and receives information from time to time, can be far more difficult to find. This is called chattering. The Ethernet card floods the network with bogus information causing all communication to bog down worse than I-75 in Cincinnati during rush hour. This can be detected using Network monitoring tools.

The old song "One bad app don't spoil a whole bunch of good" is not necessarily true. One bad app can affect every other program running on the network. Bad applications can manifest themselves in many different ways. They can look for support files that are not there, cause excessive lookups on the server, or even generate unnecessary traffic. We will look at several somewhat typical scenarios and develop a template you can use to look for other problems in this area.

Network monitoring excels at helping to solve perplexing connectivity problems. Obviously, if you are running TCP/IP, then you use ping to test basic communication between machines. But that is only the first step. When ping works and you still cannot talk to the server is the subject of this section.

INTENDED AUDIENCE

The target audience is network administrators, system architects, technicians, and others who support Windows NT (although the book is useful to those not directly supporting a Windows NT network because the protocols are essentially the same no matter what platform they are running on). The book is also useful for those wishing to do supplemental reading while preparing for their MCSE, Cisco CCNA, or Comptia Network Plus certifications. It is therefore a moderately advanced book. We make no real assumptions either about knowledge of the protocols or experience with the products, as we will be discussing them. Exposure to the OSI model will help make the protocol sections go quicker, but we cover it as well. A basic knowledge of TCP/IP, DHCP, DNS, and WINS is helpful because they show up in some of the examples. If you want to perform network monitoring and analysis and/or wish to be able to troubleshoot and optimize your network communications, then this book is definitely for you.

ORGANIZATION OF THE BOOK

In this book we approach Network Monitoring and Analysis from a protocol point of view. The tool we will use the most in our troubleshooting examples is Microsoft's Network Monitor (AKA Netmon). There are currently four different versions of this tool, and we compare each of them. Originally code-named bloodhound, Netmon has actually changed little since its initial release. To complicate matters, the interface is less than intuitive, and the online help files provide little about how to actually use the product.

We will close this gap and show you how to get the most out of this powerful tool. To this end, we illustrate typical usage scenarios, point out potential pitfalls, and then dive into real-world examples to drive home the utility of this program. Next, fresh from our review of the OSI model and the protocols themselves, we use our knowledge of protocol interlocking to release the full unbridled power of Network Monitor. Finally, we look at how the protocols talk to each other. With this information at our fingertips, we are able to understand what we are looking at in the frame fields. We become one with the network as we speak the language of our machines.

We show you how to use Network Monitor to analyze your network traffic, and how to troubleshoot utilizing this tool. We look at various optimization scenarios and give you lots of food for thought. After reading this book, you will look at your network in a new light. Of course, our end result is to be able to utilize existing tools to troubleshoot complex networks and shed light on these somewhat erstwhile entities.

Our approach is to an extent governed by our task, that is, we will move from the general to the specific. Our path will take us into some turbulent seas, but they are not uncharted waters. Indeed, with the foundation laid down in part one, we will have smooth sailing.

Part 1. Protocol Analysis: A Look at the Players

In order to properly perform network monitoring and analysis, we need to know what we are looking at. This is part of what keeps many of us from using these important tools. However, by looking at everyday protocols and examining the characteristics associated with them, we will be able to understand what it is we are looking at, and therefore be able to more effectively troubleshoot our networks. Chapters in this section include the following:

Chapter One: *Basic Network Models* begins with the Open Systems Interconnection Model and the modifications made by the IEEE 802 project. We also look at how packets are formed and the way in which protocols work with all this.

Chapter Two: *The TCP/IP Protocol Suite* provides an introduction to the senior protocol on the block. We will spend much of the book working with the transmission control protocol, the internet protocol, and all their relatives.

Chapter Three: *The IPX/SPX Protocol Suite* introduces both the Internet packet exchange protocol and the sequenced packet exchange protocol. We will look at how the packets are formed, as well as the role of the service advertising protocol and how it performs name resolution.

Chapter Four: *The Server Message Block Protocol* is central to network computer communications. We examine many of the commands as we prepare to interpret our traces. When we complete that task, we close out part one of our book.

Part 2. Network Traffic Analysis and Optimization: A Look at the Issues

In Part Two, we look at traffic from four different perspectives, and once this is done, we glean suggestions for reducing this traffic in each of the cases.

Chapter Five: *Client Traffic* looks at some of the sources of client traffic including that of browsing and attempting name resolution in order to communicate with other machines.

Chapter Six: *Server Traffic* discusses some of the sources of server traffic including that of directory replication, and responding to DNS queries.

Chapter Seven: *Application Traffic* discusses traffic related specifically to applications such as file and print, internet browsing, and even email programs.

Part 3. Common Network Monitors: A Look at the Tools

Now we get to the fun stuff—a look at the tools of the trade. Microsoft has some good ones that are obtained in various ways, and in many respects are quite powerful. We begin our look at the tools by focusing on the Microsoft entry into this arena.

Chapter Eight: *Microsoft's Network Monitor Family* points out at least three different Microsoft Network Monitor tools out there—all called Netmon, and all a little different. In this section, we look at the tool, and the issues surrounding the tools, as well as hints for making the most out of these raw tools.

Part 4. Troubleshooting Scenarios: A Look at Common Problems

Ok, let's roll up our sleeves and apply our fine-tuned knowledge of protocols, and network monitoring tools to some real world problems. Armed with powerful network monitoring tools, we can solve complex problems in a single bound. Let's go troubleshooting.

Chapter Nine: *Connectivity Problems* looks at the age-old scenario, "I can't get logged in!" There are, of course, many permutations to this and we may occasionally see a workstation that cannot find the domain controller, obtain a DHCP lease, or maybe it just simply cannot connect to the server. Perhaps it is a password problem or other login issue. These issues simply cannot go undetected from a well-tuned network monitor. Unfortunately, some applications are not perfect on their ship date, and therefore get released to manufacturing prematurely. In many instances, these undocumented features are solved in later revisions of the code. But how are they detected? What are some of the clues that get you looking for fixes in the first place? Excessive broadcasts, slow network performance, and unallocated pages are all candidates for the probing ears of Netmon.

Chapter Ten: *Security Issues* can be looked at with our favorite sniffer. Rogue DHCP servers, unauthorized sniffing, and the like are discussed in this chapter.

On the CD-ROM

On the CD-ROM we have copies of the capture files mentioned in the book to allow you to follow along with the examples and to delve more deeply into the ethereal abyss. We have created filters you can load into your Microsoft Network Monitor that you can use for different troubleshooting scenarios. In addition, there are sample batch files you can use to assist you in triggering unattended Netmon sessions using the Microsoft Windows NT scheduler service. These items are referred to in the text along with hints to allow you to obtain the full benefit from them.

ACKNOWLEDGMENTS

Many people have assisted with this project. In particular, the technicians at Full Service Networking have read and offered comments about most of the book. David Martin read the entire book several times and offered great recommendations. Mark Groce and Jason Webber contributed several weekends to make nearly all the network capture files that are included on the CD-ROM. Teresa Wilson made several of the drawings.

About the Author

Ed Wilson, MCSE + I, MCT, Master ASE, CCNA is a Senior Networking Specialist with Full Service Networking, a Microsoft Solution Provider Partner in Cincinnati, Ohio. His previous publications include chapters on Performance Monitoring, and Network Monitor in the MCSE for Dummies book NT Server in the Enterprise, Osborne McGraw Hill MCSE study guide for the Windows NT Workstation book chapters on troubleshooting and the registry, Osborne McGraw Hill MCSE study guide for Windows 98 chapter on troubleshooting, and the New Riders MCSE Training guide chapters on Setup, Installation, Troubleshooting and Exam Tips.

PROTOCOL ANALYSIS: A LOOK AT THE PLAYERS

In order to properly perform network monitoring and analysis, we need to understand what we are looking at. This is part of what keeps many from using these important tools. However, by looking at the more common protocols we are likely to run into and the common things associated with them, we will be able to understand what it is we are in fact looking at, and therefore be able to more effectively troubleshoot our networks.

Basic Network Models

$\mathbf{I}$n this chapter we will look at the Open Systems Interconnection (OSI) Model and see how we can use it in our network monitoring activities. We will also look at modifications made to the OSI model by the IEEE 802 group. Then, we will look at how data makes it onto the wire, and finally, we will conclude with the role of Protocols in all this.

Network Models assist us in visualizing the way that computers talk to one another with our network monitoring tools. We will use them in our efforts to first understand the protocols and the data flow, and we will revisit them as we examine network optimization and the troubleshooting scenarios.

THE OSI MODEL

Our first step in network monitoring is to look at the OSI model. This will provide a framework for understanding the way protocols work. The OSI model was developed in 1984 by the International Standards Organization (ISO) to serve as a guide for network communication. It updated a 1978 specification the organization had developed to allow dissimilar equipment to talk back and forth to exchange data while using similar protocols. The 1984 OSI model is an international "classic" to which nearly all network architectures answer. While most implementations do not necessarily lay out cleanly like the OSI model does, the functions described by the model must be performed (or at least taken into consideration) in some manner. It is the description of activities, or functions, that make the OSI model so valuable as a troubleshooting tool. For instance by describing what a scenario is doing, "yes I can do this, this and this, but not that," you can isolate where exactly the problem is occurring.

The OSI model clearly describes functions and is often used by hardware manufactures as guidelines to incorporate features into their designs. In this manner we see how hardware and software work together to provide for reliable and efficient communication between devices. We will be referring back to this model again and again during the course of the book.

The OSI model is a layered approach to communication, and each layer provides services to the layer below and above it in the hierarchy. Figure 1–1 lists the seven layers of the OSI model.

The highest layer, layer 7, is normally depicted on top because it is where the applications reside and where the interface to the user may be. The lowest two layers, layers 1 and 2, are where the wire and network adapters reside.

We can use the telephone system as an analogy to the way data communication takes place in a networked environment. When I pick up the telephone and call the office, I am using services provided by the telephone company. The telephone uses the wire in my house, and goes out onto the local and, eventually, long-distance carriers. Neither the people in my office nor I am aware of the wires and equipment involved. It is as if we're talking di-

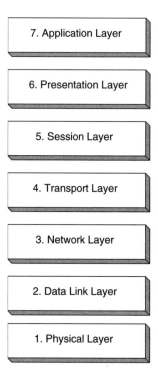

Fig. 1–1 The seven-layer Open Systems Interconnection model is the basis for both understanding and troubleshooting modern computer networks.

rectly to each other. The OSI model works in the same way. The application layer on one machine establishes a virtual conversation with the application layer at the other machine, and each does not know that the other layer is involved.

Figure 1–2 illustrates that each layer in the OSI model thinks it is talking to its counterpart on the other machine. In reality, each layer talks only to the layer above or below it in the hierarchy. Each layer is responsible for performing certain functions according to the protocol involved.

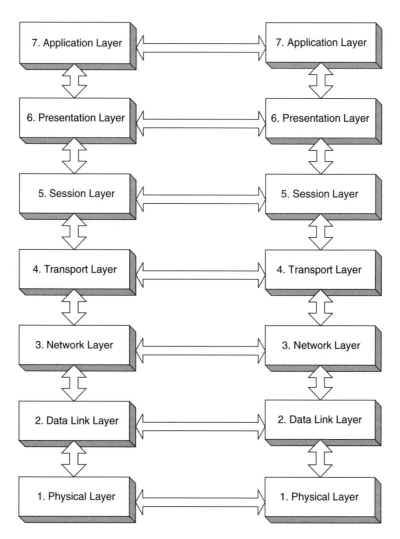

Fig. 1–2 The perceived communication, and the actual path of communication.

When an application wants to send data to another application, the data is passed from one layer to the next down the entire protocol stack. Each layer will add header information to assist it in performing its specific function. In some instances the layer may also add trailer information as well. The data is broken into pieces to assist it in its journey across the network. Data received from the TCP layer is called a segment, but as the data passes to the IP layer and its header information is added, it is called a packet or a datagram. Once the unit of data is on the wire flowing towards its destination, it is called a frame. The terms packet and frame are sometimes (although technically incorrect) used interchangeably. To be completely accurate, data received from the network layer should be referred to as a packet, and data received from the wire should be referred to as a frame. The data then passes from layer to layer, and each layer will add something or take something away from the packet according to where it is in the process. On the receiving end of the communication, the process occurs in the reverse; therefore, it is taken off the wire at the physical layer and moves back up the different layers until arriving at the application layer as it is sent by the other application. Only the physical layer talks to its counterpart on the other machine. Interaction between adjacent layers occurs through an interface that defines which services it will provide to the layer above or below in the hierarchy. With this basis of understanding, let us look in more detail at the services provided by each layer of the OSI model.

Application Layer

Layer seven, the application layer, is the highest level in the OSI model, and it serves as the window for applications to access network services. This layer directly supports user applications, but it is not where applications such as Word or Excel reside. They are not part of the OSI model. Applications that do reside here are Telnet, FTP, and the like. This layer handles general network access, flow control, and error recovery.

The application layer interacts with software applications that implement or support the communicating component of the network application. These network applications are things such as file transfer, e-mail, network management, remote access, and the like. Application layer functions typically include the following:

- Identifying communication partners—The application layer identifies and determines the availability of communication partners for an application with data to transmit.
- Determining resource availability—The application layer must determine whether sufficient network resources for the requested communication are available.

- Synchronizing communication—Communication between applications requires cooperation that is managed by the application layer.

The application layer is the OSI layer closest to the end user. That is, both the OSI application layer and the user interact directly with the software application. Some examples of application layer implementations:

- TCP/IP applications—TCP/IP applications are protocols in the Internet Protocol suite, such as Telnet, File Transfer Protocol (FTP), and Simple Mail Transfer Protocol (SMTP).
- OSI applications—OSI applications are protocols in the OSI suite such as File Transfer, Access, and Management (FTAM), Virtual Terminal Protocol (VTP), and Common Management Information Protocol (CMIP).

Presentation Layer

Layer six, the presentation layer, determines the format used to send data among computers. It can be called the network translator because it is involved in translating data from the format sent down from the application layer into a commonly recognized intermediate format. At the receiving computer, the presentation layer translates data back into the format in which the Application layer on the other computer had sent it. Some of the common activities performed by the presentation layer include protocol conversion, translating the data, encrypting the data, changing or converting the character set, and expanding graphics commands. The presentation layer also manages data compression to reduce the number of bits needed to transmit the data. The redirector, who is responsible for deciding where to obtain data for input or output operations to resources on a server, resides at the presentation layer.

The presentation layer provides a variety of coding and conversion functions that are applied to application layer data. These functions ensure that information sent from the application layer of one system will be readable by the application layer of another system. Some examples of presentation layer coding and conversion schemes follow:

- Common data representation formats—The use of standard image, sound, and video formats allow the interchange of application data between different types of computer systems (JPEG, MPEG, GIF, . . .).
- Conversion of character representation formats—Conversion schemes are used to exchange information with systems using different text and data representations (such as EBCDIC, ASCII and the ever popular Hypertext Markup Language (HTML) that describes how information

should appear when viewed by a web browser such as Internet Explorer or Opera).

- Common data compression schemes—The use of standard data compression schemes allows data that is compressed at the source device to be properly decompressed at the destination.
- Common data encryption schemes—The use of standard data encryption schemes allows data encrypted at the source device to be properly decrypted at the destination.

Presentation layer implementations are not typically associated with a particular protocol stack. Some well-known standards follow:

- Data: ASCII, EBCDIC, Encryption
- Visual Imaging: PICT, TIFF, GIF, JPEG
- Audio and Video: MIDI, MPEG, QuickTime

Session Layer

Layer five, the session Layer, allows applications on different computers to set up, manage, and conclude a conversation, called a session. This layer provides some of the things you would naturally think of as being needed at this level, such as name recognition and security. We need security to prevent anyone from being able to connect to the computer across the network. Some of the other things we would expect to see at this layer are tools to control how the machines communicate during the session. We also find data recovery options such as checkpoints between the communicating applications. This allows the machine to know what was sent and when. It is crucial this function is performed—particularly on unreliable networks (such as the Internet). In this way, if data is lost, then the only thing that must be retransmitted is the data lost since the last checkpoint. This layer also implements dialog control between the communicating processes. This regulates which side transmits, when, and for how long. Thus the session is in charge of managing all service requests and responses that occur between the applications running on two separate computers.

The session layer establishes, manages, and terminates communication sessions between presentation layer entities. Communication sessions consist of service requests and service responses that occur between applications located in different network devices. These requests and responses are coordinated by protocols implemented at the session layer. Some examples of session layer implementations are the following: AppleTalk Session Protocol, DEC SCP, NFS, SQL, RPC, and X Windows implementations.

Transport Layer

Layer four is the transport layer, which provides an additional connection level beneath the session layer and thereby defines end-to-end connectivity between host applications. The transport layer is responsible for ensuring that the packets are delivered error free, in sequence, and with no loss or duplication. This layer repackages messages received from the upper layers, dividing long messages into smaller packets when required, and gathering up several small messages and putting them into larger packages. This repackaging allows the packets to be transmitted more efficiently across the network. At the receiving end, the Transport layer reassembles the original messages and typically sends an acknowledgement back to the originator.

The transport layer is responsible for establishing end-to-end operations. This is a logical relationship. The functions provided by the transport layer are flow control, error handling, and problem solving related to the transmission and reception of packets. This is where we find the TCP (Transmission Control Protocol) part of TCP/IP. The transport layer implements reliable internetwork data transport services that are transparent to upper layers. Transport layer functions typically include the following:

- Flow control—Flow control manages data transmission between devices so that the transmitting device does not send more data than the receiving device can process. This is especially important on busy networks where many machines could flood the network with information destined for the same host. It would be very easy for packets to be dropped if there were not some way to control the congestion. When datagrams arrive, they are stored in memory in a buffer. If this gets overloaded before the data can be processed, TCP has the ability to send a not-ready indicator. This acts like a red light to allow the computer time to catch up. Once able to handle additional segments, the receiver sends a ready indicator and the senders can again resume transmitting.

- Multiplexing—Multiplexing allows data from several applications to be transmitted onto a single physical link. This is achieved through the layering approach of the OSI model. Different applications send segments on an as-received basis, and they can be directed to one or many destinations. When the data stream arrives at the destination hosts transport layer, it is reassembled and passed back up to the appropriate application. TCP uses port numbers to enable multiplexing. Since several different applications could conceivably use TCP (or UDP) at the same time, the transport layer protocols store an identifier in the header. This identifier is a 16-bit port number stored in the header. Both TCP and UDP use this to identify the source and destination port number. A list of well-known port numbers is included in Appendix A.

These well-known ports are assigned by the Internet Assigned Numbers Authority (IANA) and have the numbers between 1 and 1023 for various server services such as telnet, FTP, SMTP and the like. Numbers between 1024 and 5000 can be used for applications creating ephemeral ports (short lived ports). IPX/SPX uses a similar concept, although they are called sockets in that suite.

- Virtual circuit management—Virtual circuits are established, maintained, and terminated by the transport layer. This is a connection-oriented session. In order for data transfer to occur, both the sending and the receiving machine are involved. You cannot send data to a machine at this layer without the involvement of both machines. The initiating machine will send a synchronization message to begin the transfer, the receiving machine acknowledges the synchronization message and includes a synchronize sequence request, and once this is acknowledged the data transfer begins.

- Error checking and recovery—Error checking involves various mechanisms for detecting transmission errors. Error recovery involves taking an action (such as requesting that data be retransmitted) to resolve any errors that occur. TCP and SPX require a positive acknowledgment of the receipt of the data that has been transmitted. When data is transmitted, a timer is started. If an ACK is not received before the timer expires, then the segment is resent.

Network Layer

Layer three is the network layer, which is responsible for addressing messages and translating logical addresses and names into physical addresses. This layer also decides the route from the source to the destination computer. It determines which path the data takes in order to arrive at the destination computer, based on such factors as traffic congestion, priority of service, routing and the like. In addition to these functions, if the network adapter on the router cannot transmit a data chunk as large as the source computer sends, then it will compensate for it by breaking the data into smaller units. On the destination end, the receiving computer will reassemble the data as required. The Network layer manages device addressing and tracks the location of devices on the network. As a result, at this layer we typically find routers. The IP (Internetwork Protocol) performs Layer 3 functions.

The network layer provides routing and related functions that allow multiple data links to be combined into an internetwork. This is accomplished by the logical addressing (as opposed to the physical addressing) of devices. The network layer supports both connection-oriented and connectionless service from higher-layer protocols.

Data Link Layer

Layer two is the data link layer, which is responsible for sending data frames from the network layer to the physical layer. On the receiving end, it packages the raw bits received from the physical layer into data frames. A data frame is an organized, logical structure in which data can be placed. Figure 1–3 shows a typical data frame. In it we see the destination address, the sender address, the frame type, length of both the frame and data, as well as how much information is remaining.

The data link layer is responsible for providing the error-free transfer of these frames from one computer to another through the physical layer. One method it uses is the CRC (Cyclical Redundancy Check) that represents error correction and verification information to ensure that the data frame is received properly. It is in effect a magic number that lets the receiving computer know the packet is valid. This allows the network layer to assume virtually error-free transmission over the network connection. In general, the data link layer sends a frame and then waits for an acknowledgement from the recipient. The recipient's data link layer detects any problems with the frame that may have occurred during transmission. Frames that are not ac-

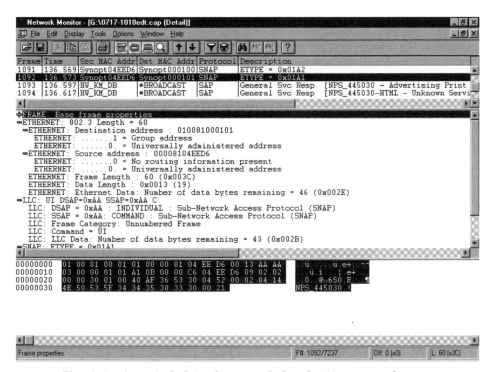

Fig. 1–3 A typical data frame includes destination- and error-checking information added at the data link layer.

knowledged, or frames that are damaged, are retransmitted. Thus the data link layer is responsible for notification, network topology, and flow control.

The data link layer provides access to the physical media and ensures reliable transit of data across a physical network link. This is where Ethernet, Token Ring, and FDDI media access methods are defined. Each of the different data link layer specifications define different network and protocol characteristics, including the following:

- Physical addressing—Physical addressing (as opposed to network addressing) defines how devices are addressed at the data link layer.
- Network topology—Data link layer specifications often define how devices are to be physically connected (such as in a bus or a ring topology).
- Error notification—Error notification involves alerting upper layer protocols that a transmission error has occurred.
- Sequencing of frames—Sequencing of data frames involves the reordering of frames that are transmitted out of sequence.
- Flow control—Flow control involves moderating the transmission of data so that the receiving device is not overwhelmed with more traffic than it can handle at one time.

Some of the physical devices that typically operate at layer two include bridges and switches (although some of the more intelligent switches now are capable of operating at layer three).

Physical Layer

Layer one is the physical layer that transmits the data stream between the machines. As the name implies, this layer incorporates the means to connect the two machines together. It is related to the electrical, optical, mechanical media, procedural, or the interfaces required to make the connection whether it is physical wiring, infrared, laser, or other methods. The physical layer is responsible for carrying the data that has been generated by the higher layers.

This layer also defines how the cable is attached to the network adapter card, for instance, the number of wires used and the like. It is responsible for carrying the bits (the ones and zeros) from one computer to another. The bits do not have any meaning at the physical layer; instead they are merely ones and zeros, electrical pulses, or flashes of light. Layer one is responsible for ensuring that when a one is transmitted, it is received as a one and not as a zero. This layer also defines what a one is, how long the pulse lasts, how long it has to be, how strong, and the like and so pays attention to the voltage levels, timing of voltage changes, physical data rates, and maximum distances each can travel. This is where we find devices such as repeaters.

THE IEEE 802 PROJECT

Around the same time the ISO was working on the OSI model, the Institute of Electrical and Electronics Engineers (IEEE) worked on LAN standards as well. These standards became known as the 802 project named from the year and month it began (February 1980). As these models were emerging at around the same time, and since the two organizations shared information between them, the two standards are compatible. The 802 project defines the standards for the physical components of a network—the interface cable and the cabling—that are contained in the first two layers of the OSI model, the physical and the data link layers. These standards contain specifications for Network Interface Cards, Wide Area Network components, and components used to create both coaxial and twisted pair networks. There are twelve categories in the 802 project, which are listed in Table 1–1.

Enhancements Made to the OSI model

The 802 project split the data link layer into two parts: the Logical Link Control (LLC) layer and the Media Access control layer. In Figure 1–4, we can see how the 802 project achieves a more granular approach to the standards by implementing the data link layer subsections.

Logical Link Control Layer (LLC)

The LLC sub layer manages data-link communication between devices on a single network link. The LLC defines the use of logical interface points,

Table 1–1   802 Project

802 number	Title
802.1	Internetworking
802.2	Logical Link Control
802.3	Carrier-sense Multiple Access with Collision Detection (CSMA/CD) LAN (Ethernet)
802.4	Token Bus LAN
802.5	Token Ring LAN
802.6	Metropolitan Area Network (MAN)
802.7	Broadband Technical Advisory Group
802.8	Fiber-Optic Technical Advisory Group
802.9	Integrated Voice/Data Networks
802.10	Network Security
802.11	Wireless Networks
802.12	Demand Priority Access LAN, 100BaseVg-AnyLan

which are called service access points (SAPs) that allow higher-level protocols to use the data link. Other computers can also refer to and use SAPs to transfer information from the LLC sublayer to the upper OSI layers.

Because the LLC resides on top of the other 802 protocols, we have great flexibility in that upper level protocols can now operate without worrying

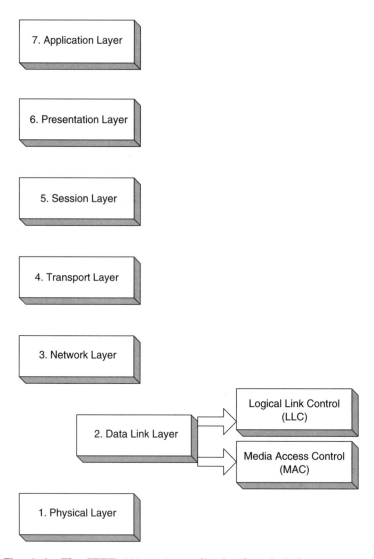

Fig. 1–4 The IEEE 802 project split the data link layer into two sublayers to provide a finer definition of media access methods.

about what type of media we have below. The media access control layer, however, is media-dependent and tied to specific 802 types.

Two service access points (SAPs) are defined in 802.2: the Destination Service Access point (DSAP) and the Source Service Access Point (SSAP). LLC provides support between applications for flow control, through the use of ready-or-not bits and sequence control bits. Figure 1–5 illustrates how these two service access points show up in a trace in Network Monitor.

Media Access Control Layer (MAC)

The lower layer of the two sublayers is the MAC layer, which provides access for the computer's network adapter card to the physical layer. The media access control layer communicates directly with the network adapter card and is responsible for delivering error-free data between computers on a network. Specific media access methods are detailed in 802.3,4,5 and 802.12. In this book we will focus on the access method detailed in 802.3, the Carrier-sense Multiple Access with Collision Detection (CSMA/CD) LAN (Ethernet).

In order for multiple machines to share access to the physical layer in an efficient manner, they need to be able to identify each other with unique addresses. The most important functionality provided by the MAC layer is the unique hardware address, called the MAC address. Every LAN interface must have a MAC address. The MAC address is a 48-bit address comprised of 12 hexadecimal digits. The first six hex numbers are the vendor code (also known as the organizational unique identifier (OUI)). These numbers are administered by the IEEE and can be very useful to network administrators trying to find drivers for a generic Ethernet card, or when sniffing the network. The last six hexadecimal numbers are generally assigned by the manufacturer, and are often burned into the ROM of the device.

A LOOK AT HOW DATA MAKES IT ONTO THE WIRE

In order to transmit large files in a reliable manner across networks, the files must be broken into pieces called packets. Packets are the basic unit of net-

```
✛LLC: UI DSAP=0xE0 SSAP=0xE0 C
✛IPX: SAP Packet - 3.0008C7B91A29.4058 -> 3.FFFFFFFFFFFF.452 - 0 Hops
✛SAP: General Svc Resp  [JWH1364 - RPC Server]
```

Fig. 1–5 The two service access points defined in 802.2 are clearly visible in Network Monitor.

work communication. Because data is divided up into packets, traffic congestion is reduced, and communication speed is increased as more computers have greater opportunities to access the wire. Special information is entered into each packet that enables the computer to break the data into pieces, put it back together, and check for errors once reassembled. In fact, packets may contain many different types of data such as messages, files, control data, commands or service requests, session control codes, or error messages.

All packets, regardless of the protocol, contain basically the same kinds of information in order to transmit from one computer to another. These are the source address of the sending machine, the destination address of the intended recipient (or recipients), the data itself, the instructions to various networking components it may meet along the way, and some kind of error checking and sequencing information.

Because of this need to contain basic kinds of information, all packets are comprised of at least three basic sections. These sections are the header, the data, and the trailer. In the header you will find information such as the source address, the destination address, what type of frame it is, and how much data it contains. The next section contains the actual data itself, the size of which varies depending on the type of network and the communication protocols being used. For instance, an Ethernet frame has a data load with a minimum size of 46 bytes and a maximum size of 1500 bytes, but that includes the TCP header and the IP header. When you remove the overhead, you are left with a maximum data size of 1460 bytes. The trailer contents will vary depending again on the protocol used, and the access method; however, you will typically see some kind of cyclical redundancy check (CRC) error-checking information. The CRC is one of those magic numbers that is computed by looking at the size of the packet and running it through some algorithm. This is a repeatable calculation, so when the packet arrives at the destination, the receiving computer can look at the CRC number, perform the calculation on the packet, and then compare the CRC number it obtains from its calculation with the one reported in the trailer of the packet. If they match, then the packet is presumed good and passed along up the OSI model to the next layer. If the CRC number computed by the receiving computer does not match the one reported in the packet, then the protocol will report the packet as bad and send a request for a retransmission of the packet.

The Packet Creation Process

How do our network models fall into this process, and what role do they play? Each layer of the OSI model will make its contribution to the format of the packet in the following manner. The packet creation process begins at the application layer. When data generated there needs to be transmitted to another machine on the network, the application layer will add a little header information. From there it goes to the presentation layer, which will add some header information and then pass the packet to the session layer, which also adds some header information. It then goes to the transport layer, where the original data gets broken into the actual packet. Therefore, the actual format of the packet is dependant on the type of transport protocol being used. For instance, the transport protocol used in the TCP/IP protocol stack is the transmission control protocol. The transport control used in the IPX/SPX protocol is the sequenced packet exchange protocol. Each of these transport protocols handles packets a little differently, and we will look at them in more detail in later chapters. Basically, though, after the transport protocol breaks the data into packets, it must add some kind of sequence number to let the receiving computer know how to put the packets back together to reassemble the data. This will happen at the transport level of the receiving computer.

After the transport protocol has broken the data into packets, it is passed down to layer three in the OSI model, the network layer. Here again, specific actions are dependant on the protocol stack being utilized. In the TCP/IP stack, the network protocol is the Internetwork Protocol, and in IPX/SPX, it is the internetwork packet exchange protocol. In general, however, the network layer is responsible for adding routing information, protocol specific source and destination information, checksum information, and timing information as well.

The data link layer also will add its header and a CRC trailer. Finally, the packet arrives at the physical layer ready to make its journey to its destination, and it has not only the data payload, but also the header and trailer information added by the six upper layers to ensure timely and accurate delivery of the data.

On the receiving end, the packet proceeds from the physical layer, up to layer seven—the application layer—with each layer stripping away the information added by the corresponding layer from the sending computer.

Packets are addressed to a specific destination. In most instances, the destination is a particular computer, either a server, or a client machine. Although all the traffic on the wire is visible to each network adapter card, the computer does not pull the data off the wire if it is not addressed to it. There are times when this is not the case. For instance, certain types of information are broadcast that are transmitted to everyone. In this case every network adapter will pull the broadcast off the wire and look at the packet. This is one reason we will look at ways to control broadcast traffic in Chapters 5 and 6.

There are other occasions when a network adapter may pull traffic not destined to itself off the wire, such as in the case of a router. In our examination of network traffic, several of our capture files have routers in them. In these packets, we must look closely to see what the real destination and origination actually are. Of course all of this has a particular implantation in an Ethernet network, and that leads us into our next section.

ETHERNET COMMUNICATION SPECIFICS

The MAC layer (lower level of OSI layer 2) defines how the computer will gain access to the wire and how it will transmit and receive data. In order to do this, it communicates with the physical layer (OSI layer 1) through a common interface. This interface is composed of basic services or functions that control the exchange of data between the MAC layer on two different machines. By working through the interfaces, the MAC layer is essentially independent of the underlying physical media. It can be copper, fiber, radio, laser, or infrared. The first of these helper interfaces is the physical line signaling. This is a sublayer of the MAC layer, and its main function is to control access to the wire.

Because this is Ethernet, the method used is carrier sense—that is, the computer will sense when the line is free. Before every transmission, a check is made to see whether the line is currently in use. However, there is no carrier signal present on an Ethernet network. So how does it sense activity? It detects that the line is not busy by a timing mechanism between frames of data. This is called the interframe gap, and it is 96-bit periods long (9.6 microseconds). The interframe gap is therefore the smallest permissible space between frames of data on an Ethernet network. The physical line signaling will also detect when the line is occupied, and whether a collision has occurred. These functions are implemented into a part of the Ethernet card called the transceiver. In the old days the transceiver was a separate device, but it has long (thankfully) been implemented as a chip on the Ethernet card. At times this device is referred to as a media access unit (MAU). The transceiver is responsible for four basic functions. These are the transmission of the electrical signals onto the wire, the reception of the signals from the wire, the determination as to whether the wire is busy, or free, and the observation of the data for collisions.

Data is placed onto the wire through a process called the Manchester code. In this process, the first half of the bit value contains the complementary value, while the second half contains the actual value. In this way, each signal placed onto the wire is unique. This even works when transmitting several packets of essentially identical information. In Figure 1–6 we see the period of time used to transmit the information on the wire. The amount of time it would take to change from 1 to 0 on the wire is referred to as a bit period.

Since there is no external clock on an Ethernet network, the Manchester encoding enables the transmitters and receivers to synchronize with one an-

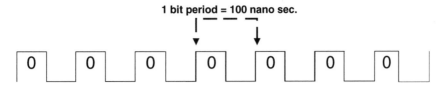

Fig. 1–6 The bit period for Ethernet is 100 nanoseconds.

other. The voltage on the Ethernet cable is between –2.2 volts and 0 volts, and it has a current between –90 mA and 0 mA.

The physical medium attachment performs several important tasks such as the transmitting and receiving data, identifying collisions, and controlling jabber. We will look at several of these briefly.

The Ethernet card must be able to take a parallel data stream and transmit it as a serial stream of data onto the wire. This is like driving down a multilane highway and coming upon a one-lane bridge. The transmit function cannot lose more than two complete bit cells. The delay between bit cells must be less than 50 nanoseconds. When the physical medium attachment receives the bit stream, it cannot lose more than five bit cells. So how does the MAC layer transmit data? Let's look at it in a little more detail.

First, the MAC layer receives the packet form the LLC. Next it adds the following information onto the packet: the preamble, start frame delimiter, destination address, source address, type field (for Ethernet), the length field, and data field with the protocol information form the higher layers. This is illustrated in Figure 1–7 below. If the data is less than 48 bytes, then the data field is padded with zeros to the minimum length.

After the data packet is generated, the transmission module calculates the CRC and puts this into the CRC field. The entire packet is transferred to the transmission MAC module. At this point the wire is checked for activity. If the wire is free, then MAC module waits for the interframe gap (9.6 microseconds) and then transmits. While transmitting, the MAC module checks to see whether a collision is detected. If there are no collisions, then transmission completes, and the next frame can be sent. If a collision is detected, then the collision function is called.

The collision function is used to detect collisions on the wire. When two computers transmit at the same time, the combined voltage of the resulting collision exceeds the amount normally on the wire, and the detecting machine will generate a collision signal. This will last for nine bit periods, or 900 nanoseconds, at which time, the machines attempting to use the wire will retransmit their packets at a random interval to avoid an additional collision. If this fails 16 times in a row, then an error is returned to the higher-level protocols.

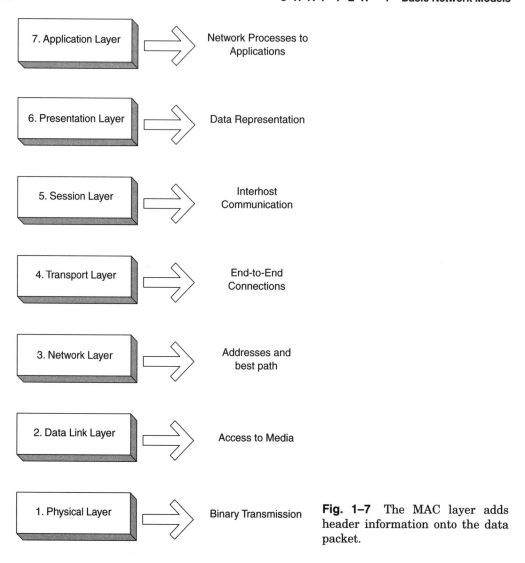

Fig. 1–7 The MAC layer adds header information onto the data packet.

The jabber function was put into the 802.3 standard to prevent one machine from monopolizing the wire. Each machine can use the wire for no more than 30 milliseconds at a time before it must allow another machine the chance to use the wire. If the machine does not cease transmitting during that period, the card assumes it is jabbering, and it should cease transmitting.

The MAC layer is also in charge of receiving data from the wire. All traffic is visible on the wire, but only packets addressed to the local machine are processed by the MAC layer. If it is not addressed to the local machine, then the data packet is simply discarded by the machine. However, once it is received off the wire, then the first thing to do is to check it for errors. This is done by the MAC module verifying the CRC value. If the packet fails this initial check, then it is discarded as trash. Once the packet has passed the CRC check, the MAC layer begins the process of stripping off the preamble, the start frame delimiter, the destination address, the source address, the type field, and any padding that may have been added to the data field to make the packet meet the minimum size requirement. After this has been done, two more checks are performed against the packet. First the MAC layer will check to make sure the data field has the correct length and is a multiple of eight bits. If both of these additional checks are passed, the data is declared intact, and passed up the protocol layers. If the packet fails either of these checks, it is declared trash, discarded into the bit rubbish heap, and the process has to start over again.

What Is the Role of Protocols in All This?

You can think of protocols as languages. For instance, if I went to France and spoke French, I would get along just fine. But if I went to France and spoke Greek, I might have problems communicating unless I found someone who also spoke Greek. In the same way, protocols need to match between two computers wishing to communicate. Just as there are rules for the way in which languages function—for example subject and verb agreement, each of which must match the language—there are rules for the way that protocols work.

There are commands that the protocols support, and each also has a specific purpose. Just as with the English language, in which there is a difference between spoken English and written English, there are also differences in the way the protocols function. As there are many different languages, there are many different protocols. As certain languages work in certain countries, certain protocols work at different levels of the OSI model and are used for certain purposes. When several protocols work together at various levels of the OSI model, then they are referred to as a protocol stack. A network works at all levels of the OSI model. In the same way, a protocol stack will have protocols that work at different levels of the OSI model as well.

Protocol Stack

Protocols govern how communication takes place over the network between two or more computers. There are many different protocols that can be used to manage the exchange of information between machines on a network. The protocols define how they are going to interact, such as how and when a user is allowed to send, how errors are reported, and how much information can be sent at one time. If it were not for these rules, communication across a network would be impossible. Depending on which layer of the OSI model the protocol is designed to operate, it may be tasked with breaking down data into small enough pieces to transmit over the wire to another computer. In doing this, it will have to know into how many pieces to break the data, in which order to transmit them, how to put them back together, and how to make sure they arrive in the correct order and in the same shape as when they were transmitted. It will also need to know the location of the machine where the data is supposed to go to, and how to get to the machine with the data. It then needs to know how to talk to the Ethernet card to get it actually put on the wire.

On the receiving computer, the protocol does some of the same things as the sending computer does, only in reverse. First, it must recognize the packet as addressed to the computer. Next it has to pull the data off of the wire and on into the computer through the Ethernet card. The protocols have to put the data back together in the same order they were in originally, and finally present the information to the application so that it can act on the information contained in the packet.

As we can see from the example above, there were many levels of the OSI model involved in this simple transaction. The application layer protocol talks to the application layer protocol on the other machine, the presentation layer talks to the presentation layer on the other machine, the session is responsible for establishing a session, the transport is responsible for getting the data to the other machine, and the internet layer finds the route to the destination and the LLC and physical layers.

As you might imagine, in order to be able to perform its tasks, each layer adds information to the basic packet of information for tracking purposes, so to speak. The sending machine adds as the information flows to layer one from the layer seven applications. As the receiving machine picks the data off the wire, at layer one, it will strip the added information off each layer on its way back up to the application layer. The presentation layer then presents the reassembled data back to the application layer in a reusable format.

One thing to keep in mind about protocols is that they have to be designed to route. While nowadays that is not really an issue, in the past it was. For instance, NETBEUI is a fast protocol good for small workgroups, but it does not route, and therefore is not suited very well for an Enterprise solution. Of course, there are other reasons one would not want to use NETBEUI on a WAN, but we will look at those reasons later. When data has to travel from one LAN to another LAN across a router that ties them together, there may be several ways to get there. Determining how to get there is the function of layer three protocols.

A Layered Approach

There are many tasks that must be performed in order for network communication to take place. As we see many of these activities take place on the network, it is important to understand what is going to aid our troubleshooting efforts. Our protocol stack is a layered approach. There are at least four reasons for using a layered approach. They reduce complexity, standardize interfaces, facilitate modular engineering, and ensure interoperable technology.

The information has to be prepared, transferred, received, and acted upon. The different protocols that handle these chores form the discussion for the rest of the chapter. The way they work together to handle the task of transferring data from one machine to another is called layering. A protocol stack is a combination of protocols, and each layer in the stack has a different function that is handled by a different protocol—each with rules that govern the way it behaves in various situations. Each layer has its own duties. As we see in Figure 1–8, each layer performs certain duties, tasks and responsibilities.

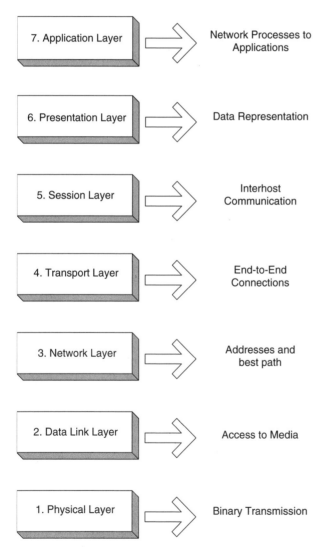

7. Application Layer ⟹ Network Processes to Applications

6. Presentation Layer ⟹ Data Representation

5. Session Layer ⟹ Interhost Communication

4. Transport Layer ⟹ End-to-End Connections

3. Network Layer ⟹ Addresses and best path

2. Data Link Layer ⟹ Access to Media

1. Physical Layer ⟹ Binary Transmission

Fig. 1–8 Each layer does its own job, blithely ignoring the existence of the other protocols on the team.

Each layer talks to the protocol in the layer above and below it in the stack but does not know about the other protocols. In this way, protocols are able to achieve virtual communication between layers on different machines. For instance, the application thinks it is talking to the application layer on another machine. Little does it know it is only talking to its own presentation layer. Who says computers are so smart?

The lower layers of the model specify how equipment manufacturers enable their products to connect to the network and to the computers with which they are associated. The upper layers determine how applications will talk to each other, the rules for their communication, and error correction. The higher in the protocol stack, the more sophisticated the tasks and protocols become.

So How do I Tie All This Together?

All these things get tied together in a process called binding. This gives us a great deal of flexibility in that now the protocol and the network card adapter are independent, and therefore we can change a protocol stack without also having to change a driver for the network adapter. We can also change media access methods without having to change protocols as well. Therefore, we can run TCP/IP over Ethernet, token-ring, or whatever method we choose to implement. In addition to the above, if there are multiple network adapters, we can bind the protocol to one or all of the network adapters as we see fit. It simply does not matter how we do it, at least not from the protocol stack point of view. We may, however, need to pay attention to the binding order of the protocols, and we will look at that next.

The binding order is the order in which the computer will try a protocol in an attempt to communicate with other machines on the network, or in the world. Thus the order in which the protocols are bound to the network adapter card determines the order in which they will attempt to communicate with others. This order can be manually determined in Windows NT as seen in Figure 1–9.

The binding process also carries over to more than just the protocol stack to the network adapter; for instance, the Ethernet card driver must be bound to the Ethernet card, and the transport protocol must also be bound to the NetBIOS session layer above it in the stack.

There are several protocol stacks that have been developed over the years, some of which are listed below:

1. The ISO/OSI protocol suite
2. IBM Systems Network Architecture (SNA)
3. Digital DECnet

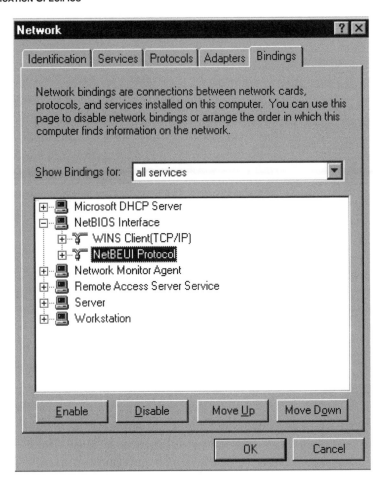

Fig. 1–9 On Windows NT machines, the binding order can be manually configured for optimal performance.

4. Novel Netware
5. Apple AppleTalk
6. The Internet protocol suite, TCP/IP

In each of these stacks, there are specific protocols that reside at the different layers in the OSI model. They may overlap one or more layers in the suite, but their functionality will be present. It may be helpful for us at this time to group some of these levels of functionality together into areas of service as seen in Table 1–2. There are three areas of function: application, transport and network.

Table 1–2   The OSI model provides three essential services

Layer	OSI layer	Functionality provided
Seven	Application	Application level, network services
Six	Presentation layer	Application level, network services
Five	Session layer	Application level, network services
Four	Transport layer	Transport services
Three	Network layer	Network services
Two	Data link layer	Network services
One	Physical layer	Network services

Application Protocols

Now we can talk about application level protocols, transport protocols, and network protocols. The application level protocols incorporate the top three layers of the OSI model, that is, the application, presentation, and session layers. They provide application to application interaction and data exchange. Some of the application level protocols we may find include those listed below:

1. APPC (advanced program-to-program communication), IBM's peer-to-peer SNA protocol, used mostly on AS/400's.
2. FTAM (file transfer access and management), an OSI file access protocol.
3. X.400, a CCITT protocol for international e-mail transmissions.
4. X.500, a CCITT protocol for file and directory services across several systems.
5. SMTP (simple mail transport protocol), an internet protocol for transferring e-mail.
6. FTP (file transfer protocol), an internet file transfer protocol.
7. SNMP (simple network management protocol), an internet protocol for monitoring networks and network components.
8. Telnet, an internet protocol for logging on to remote hosts and processing data locally.
9. Microsoft SMBs (server message blocks) and client shells or redirectors.
10. NCP (Novell Netware Core Protocol) and Novell client shells or redirectors.
11. AppleTalk and Appleshare Apples networking protocol suite.
12. AFP apples protocol for remote file access.
13. DAP (data access protocol), a DECnet file access protocol.

Transport Protocols

Transport protocols reside at the fourth or middle layer of the OSI model. They provide communication sessions between computers to ensure that data is able to move reliably between computers. Popular transport protocols include those listed below.

1. TCP (transmission control protocol), the TCP/IP protocol for guaranteed delivery of sequenced data.
2. SPX (sequential packet exchange), the transport portion of the IPX/SPX protocol suite for sequenced data.
3. NWLink, the Microsoft implementation of IPX/SPX.
4. NetBEUI (NetBIOS extended user interface) establishes communication sessions between computers and provides the underlying data transport services.
5. ATP AppleTalk transaction protocol, NBP name-binding protocol communication session and data transport protocols.

Network Protocols

Network protocols provide what are called link services and make up the bottom three layers of the OSI model. These protocols handle addressing and routing information, error checking and retransmission requests. Network protocols also define rules for communicating in a particular networking environment such as Ethernet or Token Ring. The more popular network protocols include those listed below:

1. IP (internet protocol), the TCP/IP protocol for packet forwarding routing.
2. IPX (internetwork packet exchange), NetWare's protocol for packet forwarding and routing.
3. NWLink, the Microsoft implementation of the IPX/SPX protocol.
4. NetBEUI, a transport protocol that provides data transport services for NetBIOS sessions and applications.
5. DDP datagram delivery protocol, an AppleTalk data transport protocol.

We can see how the protocols map to the OSI model, and we now have an idea of the functionality of each. We do, however, want to see how all these things map together, and after that, we will begin to explore differences in the way each behaves, and hopefully begin to see how each is used, as well as the different levels of functionality achieved by each.

Connection-Oriented Network Service

Connection-oriented service involves three phases:

- Connection establishment—During the connection establishment phase, a single path between the source and destination systems is determined. Network resources are typically reserved at this time to ensure a consistent grade of service (such as a guaranteed throughput rate).
- Data transfer—During the data transfer phase, data is transmitted sequentially over the path that has been established. Data always arrives at the destination system in the order in which it was sent.
- Connection termination—During the connection termination phase, an established connection that is no longer needed is terminated. Further communication between the source and destination systems requires that a new connection be established.

Connection-oriented service has two significant disadvantages as compared to connectionless network service:

- Static path selection—Because all traffic must travel along the same static path, a failure anywhere along that path causes the connection to fail.
- Static reservation of network resources—A guaranteed rate of throughput requires the commitment of resources that cannot be shared by other network users. Unless full, uninterrupted throughput is required for the communication, bandwidth is not used efficiently.

Connection-oriented services are useful for transmitting data from applications that are intolerant of delays and packet resequencing. Voice and video applications are typically based on connection-oriented services.

Connectionless Network Service

Connectionless network service does not predetermine the path from the source to the destination system, nor are packet sequencing, data throughput, and other network resources guaranteed. Each packet must be completely addressed because different paths through the network might be selected for different packets, based on a variety of influences. Each packet is transmitted independently by the source system and is handled independently by intermediate network devices. Connectionless service offers two important advantages over connection-oriented service:

- Dynamic path selection—Because paths are selected on a packet-by-packet basis, traffic can be routed around network failures.

- Dynamic bandwidth allocation—Bandwidth is used more efficiently because network resources are not allocated bandwidth that they are not going to use.

Connectionless services are useful for transmitting data from applications that can tolerate some delay and resequencing. Data-based applications are typically based on connectionless service.

Data Link Layer Addresses

A data link layer address uniquely identifies each physical network connection of a network device. Data link addresses are sometimes referred to as physical or hardware addresses. Data link addresses usually exist within a flat address space and have a preestablished and typically fixed relationship to a specific device. End systems typically have only one physical network connection, and thus only one data link address. Routers and other internetworking devices typically have multiple physical network connections. They therefore have multiple data link addresses.

Media access control (MAC) addresses are a subset of data link layer addresses. MAC addresses identify network entities in LANs implementing the IEEE MAC sublayer of the data link layer. Like most data link addresses, MAC addresses are unique for each LAN interface. MAC addresses are 48 bits in length and are expressed as 12 hexadecimal digits: The first six hexadecimal digits are the manufacturer identification (or vendor code), called the organizational unique identifier (OUI). The IEEE administers these six digits. The last six hexadecimal digits are the interface serial number or another value administered by the specific vendor. MAC addresses are sometimes called burned-in addresses (BIAs) because they are burned into read-only memory (ROM) and copied into random-access memory (RAM) when the interface card initializes.

Network Layer Addresses

A network layer address identifies an entity at the network layer of the OSI reference model. Network addresses usually exist within a hierarchical address space. They are sometimes called virtual or logical addresses. The relationship of a network address with a device is logical and unfixed. It is typically based either on physical network characteristics (the device is on a particular network segment) or on groupings that have no physical basis (the device is part of an AppleTalk zone). End systems require one network layer address for each network layer protocol they support. (This assumes that the device has only one physical network connection.) Routers and other internetworking devices require one network layer address per physical network connection for each network layer protocol supported. For example, a router with three interfaces, each running AppleTalk, TCP/IP, and OSI, must have three network layer addresses for each interface. The router therefore has nine network layer addresses.

Data Encapsulation

Each layer of the OSI model talks to the layer below and is dependant upon it to provide specific services and functionality. As each layer provides the service, it adds information to the data coming from the application in order to be able to transport the information to the destination machine. Of course, the specific information added depends upon the protocol stack in use, but following the general model, we see each layer add header information to the data, and in some cases also a trailer to the end of the data until we have a neatly formed packet that gets put onto the wire.

As we see in Figure 1–10, each layer adds header information to enable it to perform the service needed for the application. As data flows down the OSI model on the sending computer, this information is added. Once at the receiving computer, the header and trailer information is stripped away as the data is passed back up the OSI model.

There are five steps involved in the process of data encapsulation as it is prepared by the transport layer to be placed onto the wire. These are listed below:

1. Information from the user is received from the upper layers. It can be anything actually, from a logon request to a server, a print job, or surfing the web. Information is converted to data so that it can be transported to the destination.

2. The data is prepared for transport to the destination computer. In the case of TCP, a TCP header is added to the data that will include sequencing information to assist with keeping things in order as it is converted to Segments.

3. We are now at layer 3 in the OSI model, where the Internet protocol resides. Now we will add an IP header as we convert the TCP Segment into an IP packet. The IP header includes both source and destination IP addresses which will assist in routing (performed at this layer of the OSI model) the packet to the proper destination.

4. At the data link layer, IP packets are converted to Ethernet frames in our example. Each network device has to be able to put the packet into a frame so that the device can communicate over the local interface to another interface on the network. The frame type has to match or the devices will not be able to communicate. In our traces we will see that the Ethernet framing has been wrapped around our IP packet.

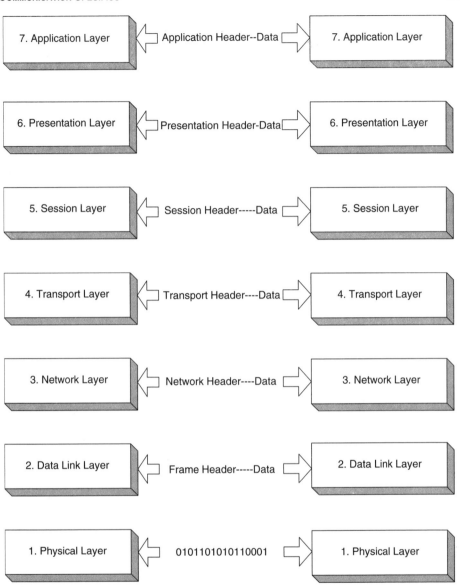

Fig. 1–10 Header information added at the sending computer is stripped off by the same layer at the receiving computer.

5. Now the Ethernet Frame is converted to ones and zeros. As we discussed earlier, these bits travel the network in a particular fashion defined by our access methods until they reach their destination.

IP over LAN Technologies

As we move forward with our troubleshooting skills, we need to be able to understand LAN encapsulations. LAN technologies encompass desktop technologies such as Ethernet, token ring, and arcnet and MAN technologies such as FDDI. In some technologies such as Ethernet, multiple encapsulations may exist, causing possible interoperability problems. In each of these technologies, the IP datagram needs to be delimited, addressed, and identified as an IP datagram.

Ethernet II   When sent over an Ethernet network, IP datagrams use either the Ethernet II or the IEEE 802.3 SNAP encapsulation. The Ethernet II encapsulation uses the 2-byte ethertype field to denote upper layer protocols. The ethertype field is set at 0x08-00 to denote IP and 0x08-06 to designate ARP.

IP datagrams sent using an Ethernet II frame have a maximum size of 1,500 bytes and a minimum size of 46 bytes. IP datagrams under 46 bytes in length are padded with zeros to 46 bytes to preserve the Ethernet minimum frame size of 64 bytes (not including the preamble).

As we see in Figure 1–11, the Ethernet II frame is comprised of the preamble, and then the destination address, the source address, the ethertype field code, the payload, and finally the frame check sequence.

IEEE 802.3 SNAP   The IEEE 802.3 SNAP encapsulation also begins with a preamble, a destination address, and source address; however, at that point the 802.3 SNAP diverges from the Ethernet II encapsulation. As we can see in Figure 1–12, we have a length field, and a sub-network access protocol (SNAP) header to encapsulate the IP datagram so that it can be sent on an IEEE 802.3 compliant network. The IEEE 802.3 header uses the defined value of 0xAA for both the destination service access point (DSAP) and the source service access point (SSAP) fields to indicate a SNAP frame. The control code is set to 0x03 to denote an unnumbered frame. The organization code field is set at 0x00-00-00 and the ethertype value of 0x08-00 for IP and 0x08-06 for ARP is the same as in the Ethernet II frame type.

IP datagrams sent using an IEEE 802.3 SNAP frame have a maximum size of 1,492 and a minimum size of 38 bytes. This is changed slightly from the Ethernet II size limitations and reflects the larger size of the 802.3 SNAP encapsulation overhead. IP datagrams under 38 bytes in length are padded

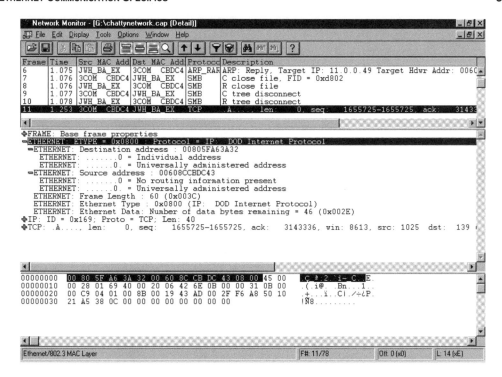

Fig. 1–11   The Ethernet II frame encapsulates an IP datagram.

with zeros to preserve the Ethernet minimum frame size of 64 bytes (not in-cluding the preamble and the start delimiter).

Ethernet II and IEEE 802.3 compared   On a normal everyday net-work, it is indeed possible that both Ethernet II and IEEE 802.3 may be pre-sent on your network. How this works is that the internet protocol standards require all hosts to be able to send and receive Ethernet II encapsulated frames. In addition, most hosts are able to receive IEEE 802.3 encapsulated packets. Some hosts on the network may be able both to send and receive IEEE 802.3 packets. If this is the case, however, the default must be the Ethernet II type. Figure 1–13 has both the IEEE 802.3 and the Ethernet II packets, so we can get a good idea of the differences between the two encap-sulation methods.

Ethernet II is the default for most networks. As we see in Figure 1–13, both frame formats have a six-byte (48 bit) destination and source address. This is the MAC address, the Ethernet address, or the hardware address of the host that is physically attached to the network. These addresses are re-solved to the four-byte (32 bit) IP address by the address resolution protocol (ARP) that we will look at in the next chapter.

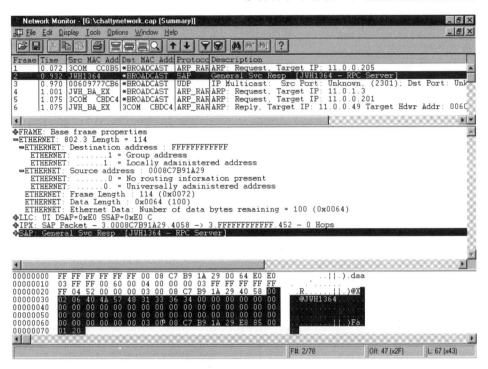

Fig. 1–12 The IEEE 802.3 SNAP encapsulation includes slightly more overhead than the Ethernet II frame.

In the Ethernet II header, the next two bytes are used to indicate the type (0x08-00 for IP, 0x08-06 for ARP). This is the same field that is found later in the 802.3 frame just before the start of the data portion of the frame. The IEEE 802.3 frame has, instead of the type, a two-byte length field. This has no correlation between Ethernet II frame and enables you to distinguish these two types of frame encapsulation methods. Following the type field in the Ethernet II header is the data portion of the frame with a size between 46 and 1500 bytes.

In the IEEE 802.3 encapsulation method after the destination and source addresses, we have a two-byte length field. This field is used to indicate how many bytes follow up to, but not including the CRC at the end of the frame. After the length field, we come to the section defined by the 802.2 chapter of the IEEE project. The first three fields in this section are the LLC fields. The DSAP and the SSAP fields are always set to AA, while the control field is always set to 03. In the next five bytes of SNAP data, the organization code is set to 0x00-00-00, which takes up three bytes. The next two bytes form the type field, which is the same as the type field found in the Ethernet II type field. As a result, it will be 0x08-00 for IP or

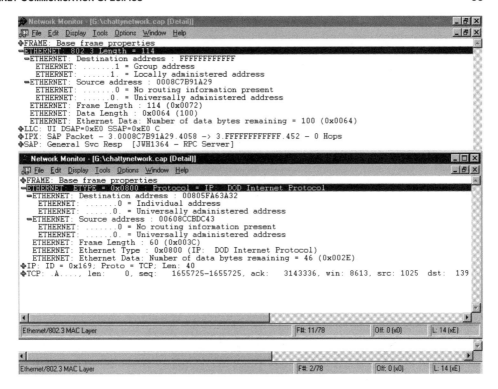

Fig. 1–13   IEEE 802.3 and Ethernet II compared.

0x08-06 for ARP or 0x08-35 for an RARP frame. Other types are listed in Appendix B.

The cyclic redundancy check (CRC) field is a checksum that is used to detect errors in the frame. This is also sometimes referred to as a frame check sequence (FRC).

The minimum size for IEEE 802.3 encapsulated frames and Ethernet II frames is the same. But because of the additional fields inserted before the data in the IEEE 802.3 type of frame (which takes up eight bytes), the minimum and maximum amounts for data load are eight bytes fewer than for the Ethernet II frame type.

Flow Control

Flow control is a function that prevents network congestion by ensuring that transmitting devices do not overwhelm receiving devices with data. There are a number of possible causes of network congestion. For example, a high-speed computer might generate traffic faster than the network can transfer it, or faster than the destination device can receive and process it. There are three commonly used methods for handling network congestion:

1. Buffering is used by network devices to temporarily store bursts of excess data in memory until they can be processed. Occasional data bursts are easily handled by buffering. However, excess data bursts can exhaust memory, forcing the device to discard any additional datagrams that arrive.

2. Source quench messages are used by receiving devices to help prevent their buffers from overflowing. The receiving device sends source quench messages to request that the source reduce its current rate of data transmission for several reasons. Perhaps the most common occurs when the receiving device begins discarding received data due to overflowing buffers. When this happens, the receiving device begins sending source quench messages to the transmitting device at the rate of one message for each packet dropped. When these begin arriving at the source device, as each receives the source quench messages, it will begin lowering the data rate until it stops receiving the messages. Once the receiving device is no longer sending the source quench messages, the source device will gradually begin increasing the data rate as long as no further source quench requests are received.

3. Windowing is a flow-control scheme in which the source device requires an acknowledgement from the destination after a certain number of packets have been transmitted. With a window size of three, the source requires an acknowledgment after sending three packets. Let's look at how this works. The source device sends three packets to the destination device. After receiving the three packets, the destination device sends an acknowledgment to the source. The source receives the acknowledgment and sends three more packets. If the destination does not receive one or more of the packets for some reason (such as overflowing buffers), it does not receive enough packets to send an acknowledgment. The source, not receiving an acknowledgment, retransmits the packets at a reduced transmission rate.

Internetworking Functions of the OSI Network Layer

The internetworking functions of the network layer are responsible for selecting the best path through a network, establishing the network addresses, and communicating paths.

Routers use a routing protocol between routers, use a routed protocol to carry user packets, set up and maintain routing tables, discover networks, adapt to internetwork topology changes, use a two part address, and contain broadcasts.

WAN Services

X.25   X.25 was originally developed in the 1970's to provide dumb terminals with WAN connectivity across public data networks (PDN's). However, due to its flexibility and reliability, it has emerged as an international standard for sending data across PDN's.

A connection-oriented interface to a packet switched network (PSN) provides both error checking and guaranteed delivery of packets using either switched or virtual circuits. Due to its reliability, it is used for applications that require reliable transmission. A router would connect to a packet assembler/disassembler (PAD) on the X.25 network. The PAD is responsible for breaking down the messages into packets and then addressing them appropriately.

The X.25 specification maps to the physical, data link, and network layers of the OSI model. However, because the X.25 specification predates the OSI model, the layer names are different. For instance, the physical layer is called X.21 and specifies the electrical and the physical interfaces that can be used. Layer two is called the link access procedure-balanced (LAPB) protocol, which takes care of frame composition, flow control, and error checking. The packet layer corresponds to the network layer and is responsible for the set up and addressing of the virtual circuit.

Frame relay   Frame relay is an industry standard, switched protocol that operates at the data link layer. It handles multiple virtual circuits using HDLC encapsulation between connected devices. Frame relay uses high-quality digital techniques, making error checking and flow control methods unnecessary. It is therefore more efficient and faster than X.25, the protocol for which it is generally considered a replacement. By using a simplified framing with no error correction, frame relay can send layer information very rapidly. It was originally conceived as a protocol to use over ISDN interfaces and was therefore developed as an independent protocol.

Within the frame relay PDN, the switching is implemented using a statistical rather than a time-division multiplexing method. With statistical multiplexing, available circuits form devices that are not currently allocated. Due to this dynamic characteristic, real time networks that are bursty in nature are ideal candidates for frame relay.

The management of the link is accomplished by using the local management interface. The LMI is responsible for establishing a link and monitoring the PVC's. Because the digital links are less susceptible to errors, frame relay uses only a CRC algorithm to detect bad data but not any mechanism for correcting the bad data. Frame relay relies on upper protocols for flow control over the link.

ATM   Asynchronous transfer mode technology is a connection-oriented nonguaranteed delivery service. It scales very well and is used on both LANs and WANs. ATM is different from frame relay in that instead of breaking down messages into variably sized frames, all messages are broken into equally sized cells. Each cell has a five-byte header, and a 48-byte data field. Since all the cells are the same size, the switching can be done very fast, and therefore the need for buffering is eliminated.

Because it is an asynchronous method, we do not have the need for TDM techniques. With ATM, a station can send cells whenever it needs to, rather than waiting for the transmit turn to come up as with TDM.

Although ATM does not map directly to the OSI model, it does map basically to the data link and a network layer. As such, it can run over many different physical mediums including SONET and FDDI. The ATM adaptation layer maps to the OSI session and transport layers. It is responsible for receiving the data for the higher layer protocols such as IP and segmenting the data into the 48-byte cells to transmit over the ATM network.

ISDN   Integrated services digital network is a communication protocol offered by telephone companies that permits telephone networks to carry data, voice, and other source traffic over telephone lines. ISDN is built on two main types of communications channels. The first is the Bearer (B channel) channel, which can carry voice, data, or images at a rate of 64 Kbps, and the second is the D (Data channel) channel, which is 16 Kbps and is used for control information, signaling, and link management data. ISDN is typically implemented in two versions: the basic rate ISDN, which is two B channels and a D channel; and the primary rate ISDN, which includes 23 B channels and a D channel.

HDLC   The high-level data link control is a bit-oriented, synchronous data link layer protocol developed by ISO. Derived from SDLC, HDLC specifies a data encapsulation method on synchronous serial links using frame characters and checksums. Data is carried in frames that may contain variable amounts of data.

SLIP   The serial line IP is used as a serial line encapsulation method and is therefore a simple packet framing protocol. SLIP defines a few characters that frame the IP packets onto a serial line. It is a minimal overhead technique that provides no addressing negotiation, protocol identification, error detection, or compression mechanism. Designed to be used over slow serial lines (such as modems), it works by defining two special characters that are used to provide framing.

The first one is the END character (0xC0), which is used to define the end of the IP datagram. The second character is the ESC character (0xDB), which is used to indicate when the 0xC0 character occurs inside the

IP datagram. The SLIP ESC character is different from the ASCII ESC character (0x1B).

SLIP uses a technique called character stuffing to prevent the occurrence of the END character in the middle of the IP datagram. If the END character (0xC0) occurs inside the original IP datagram, then it is replaced with the sequence 0xDB-DC. If the ESC character (0xDB) occurs within the IP datagram, then it is replaced with the sequence 0xDB-DD. This prevents the modem from hanging up in the middle of a transmission.

The maximum size of an IP datagram over SLIP is typically limited to 1,500 bytes on newer systems, or to 1,006 bytes on Berkeley UNIX version 4.2 implementations. However, this is a common practice, although it is not specified in the standards.

To reduce the amount of overhead on potentially slow serial links, a method of compressing the IP and TCP headers into a 3- to 5-byte header is defined in RFC 1144 and is known as C-SLIP or Compressed SLIP.

PPP   The point-to-point protocol is a successor to SLIP. PPP provides router-to-router and host-to-network connections over synchronous serial lines such as ISDN or SONET, as well as asynchronous circuits such as typical dial-up phone lines. It addresses the shortcomings of SLIP.

Point-to-point protocol is a family of protocols that provides multi-protocol encapsulation, a link control protocol (LCP) for establishing, configuring and testing the datalink connection, and a family of network control protocols (NCPs) for establishing and configuring different network layer protocols.

As we see in Figure 1–14, PPP sets a flag to 0x7E (01111110) in order to signify the start and end of a PPP frame. In successive PPP frames, only a single flag character will be set. The address field is used to address the packet to the destination node. On a point-to-point link, the destination node does not need to be addressed. Therefore, in PPP the address field is set to 0xFF, the broadcast address.

In an HDLC environment, the control field is used for a data link layer sequencing and acknowledgment function; however, in PPP the control field is set to 0x03 to indicate an unnumbered information (UI) frame. This is the same as the bit we saw set in our earlier discussion of Ethernet framing methods.

The protocol field is a two-byte field used to identify the protocol in the PPP payload. If the field is set to 0x00-21, it indicates an IP datagram. The frame check sequence (FCS) is a two-byte CRC similar to the one used for Ethernet encapsulation.

As in SLIP, PPP has a method to prevent the flag character from appearing in the middle of the data. On a synchronous link such as ISDN, we use bit stuffing to insert extra bits to mark when the flag character occurs. Bit stuffing means that a byte can be encoded as more than eight bits, but the extra bits are added or removed by the synchronous link hardware.

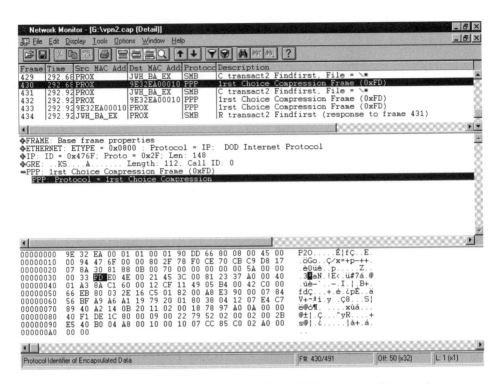

Fig. 1–14   The PPP protocol encapsulates IP for improved transmission over both synchronous and asynchronous circuits.

PPP also uses character stuffing (like SLIP) on asynchronous links to prevent the flag from appearing inside the PPP frame. If the 0x7E character occurs in the original IP datagram, it is replaced with the character string 0x7D-5E. If the ESC (0x7D) character occurs in the original IP datagram, it is replaced with the sequence 0x7D-5D back to 0x7D.

Characters fewer than 0x20 are also modified to prevent the serial drivers from interpreting them as control characters, by sending a 0x7D and then the original character with the sixth bit complemented.

The maximum receive unit (MRU) is 1,500 bytes.

PPTP   Point-to-point tunneling protocol is a way to take an existing PPP frame and encapsulate it over an IP internetwork. PPTP allows the creation of secured virtual private networks (VPN) over the Internet. PPTP can be used whether or not the Internet service provider (ISP) is VPN-enabled or not. All that is needed is a server that supports PPTP and a client capable of making a PPTP connection.

The encapsulation of PPP frames is done using the generic routing encapsulation (GRE) protocol, which uses the IP protocol ID of 47 (0x2F). To use with PPTP, the GRE protocol was enhanced to provide an acknowledgment field.

As we see in Figure 1–15, the PPTP frame has a media header and an IP header before getting to the GRE header. After the GRE header comes the PPP header, and then the PPP payload.

The GRE header begins with two bytes for flags. These flags indicate whether a GRE payload is present, and whether sequence and acknowledgment numbers are present. The protocol type field is the Ethertype value that corresponds to PPP (0x88-0B). The payload length is the size of the GRE payload in bytes. Call ID is the session identification information for this PPTP packet, followed by the sequence number, and acknowledgement number, which is the highest sequence number received by the sending peer for this session. The acknowledgment number is used for flow control, not for retransmission of lost PPTP frames.

Fig. 1–15 The PPTP frame has several headers before getting to the GRE header information.

CHAPTER REVIEW

In this chapter we have covered much territory. We began by looking at the OSI model in which we looked at the level of functionality provided by each layer in the model. Next, we looked at the modifications made to the OSI model by the IEEE 802 project, and we saw how they split layer two, the data link layer, into two sections: the logical link control layer, and the media access control layer. These changes permit a finer bit of control over the lower layers allowing the logical link control to be media-independent since it sits on top of the MAC layer.

Next, we looked at how packets are formed, and we looked at some of the terminology involved such as IP datagrams, TCP segments, as well as Ethernet frames. After that, we took a pretty good look at how Ethernet actually communicates, how the carrier sensing works with Ethernet, how the multiple access is handled, and the methods of detecting collisions.

We then looked at the role of protocols and examined the concept of the protocol stack and the layered approach to network communications. We saw how binding works to enable us to change protocols without having to change network adapter drivers, and we looked at the concept of the protocol binding order as well.

Finally, we looked at how data encapsulation works and examined many of the common methods for encapsulation that are currently in use today. This was done by examining the way in which the headers work, and looking at each field in many of the more popular network interface layer protocols.

IN THE NEXT CHAPTER

We will begin our look at the TCP/IP protocol stack. We will see how the protocol suite maps to the various layers of the OSI model, and we will examine some of the protocols commonly implemented in a standard TCP/IP protocol stack.

Next, we will begin by looking at the transmission control protocol and the methods used by it to ensure reliable connection oriented communication. We will look at flow control methods and sequencing numbers. Following our discussion of TCP, we will look at its evil twin, the IP protocol.

In our discussion of IP, we examine the way IP encapsulates data in decent detail, as well as the IP header and the like. We look at some of the common commands used with IP and find hints we will use in our troubleshooting efforts later in the book.

The TCP/IP Protocol Suite

As mentioned in the last chapter, TCP/IP is not merely one or two protocols; rather, it is commonly implemented as a suite of protocols, or, as sometimes referred to, a protocol stack. In the last chapter we saw where the major parts of the suite map to the OSI model, but now we want to look at the suite in more detail. As you can see in Figure 2–1, the TCP/IP suite consists of four layers: the application layer, the transport layer, the internet layer, and the network layer. When taken together, they provide the functionality achieved from the OSI model.

At the bottom of the stack is the network interface layer, which maps closely to the physical layer in the OSI model. This layer is responsible for putting the frames onto transmission media, and for pulling the frames off the transmission media. It should be pointed out that this is a media-independent layer. It does not matter if it is copper wire, fiber optic cable, laser, infrared, or radio. In addition, it is independent of the media-access method. Therefore, you can run TCP/IP over Ethernet, token ring, or FDDI on the local area network (LAN) side, and of course you can run it over various wide area network (WAN) technologies such as serial line using the older serial line internet protocol (SLIP) or the point-to-point protocol (PPP), which was designed as an enhancement to the older SLIP standard. PPP provides data link services, which include error detection, handling the configuration, as well as security methods. The other type of WAN technologies is packet-switched such as frame relay, or ATM as well.

The next layer from the bottom is the Internet layer, which provides functions addressed by layer two (data link layer) and layer three (network layer) in the OSI model. It is the responsibility of the Internet layer to encap-

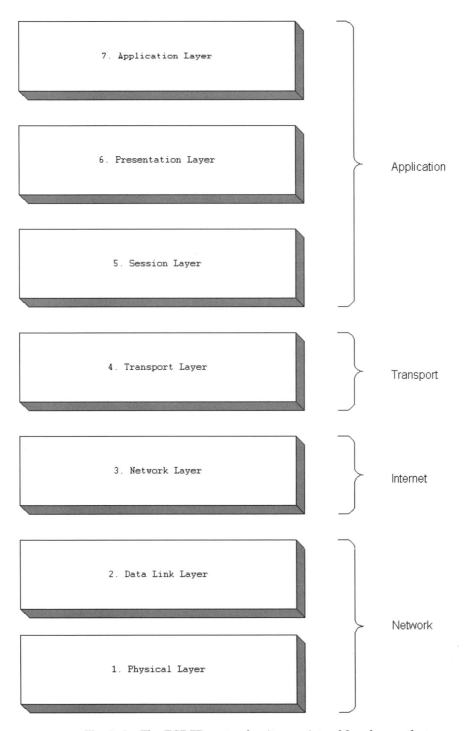

Fig. 2–1 The TCP/IP protocol suite consists of four layers that map roughly to the OSI model.

sulate the packets into Internet datagrams and run all the necessary routing algorithms. There are four Internet protocols found here: Internet control message protocol (ICMP), Internet group management protocol (IGMP), Internet protocol (IP) and, address resolution protocol (ARP). The ICMP protocol is used to send messages and report errors regarding the delivery of packets. It does this on behalf of IP. ICMP does not make IP a "reliable" protocol, but it can provide a certain amount of feedback on specific conditions. The ICMP messages themselves are carried as datagrams and hence are unreliable. The next protocol present at this layer is IGMP, which is used by computers to report their membership in a particular group in order to receive multicast transmissions from routers that support multicasting. This information is transmitted to other multicast capable routers to inform them of the group membership lists that are on the network. These transmissions are carried as datagrams and, as a result, are an unreliable form of communication. The last two Internet protocols we want to talk about are IP and ARP. Because of the importance to network communication, we will go into a bit more detail here. Let us first look at the Internet protocol.

IP is responsible for addressing and routing of packets between computers and networks. (Every device on an IP network that has an IP address is called a host, and sometimes you will see computers, routers, printers, and even managed hubs called host). This makes sense in that the address assigned to a host running the TCP/IP protocol is called an IP address. It is a connectionless protocol, which means that it does not establish a session before transmitting data. In this regard, it is an unreliable protocol because it does not guarantee delivery by requiring an acknowledgement when the data is received at the destination. The next Internet layer protocol is the address resolution protocol.

ARP is used to find the hardware address of a machine on the network. This address, sometimes called a MAC address, or an Ethernet card address is required if two computers are going to be able to talk to each other. This MAC address must be mapped to an IP address in order for hosts to communicate using the IP protocol. The way ARP resolves the address is through the use of a broadcast to all hosts on the local network. The destination computer will respond with a packet that has both the IP address and the MAC address in it. This information will then be stored into the ARP cache on the local machine. The next information is destined for the remote host; the ARP cache will be checked first before another broadcast is sent out.

The second layer from the top is the transport layer, which is responsible for providing communication sessions between computers. We have two transport protocols in our stack. They are the transmission control protocol (TCP) and the user datagram protocol (UDP). There is good reason to have two transport protocols in our stack because they work differently. TCP is a connection-oriented protocol, which means it first creates a connection with the other machine. Used when reliable communication is required, it provides for an acknowledgement of delivery for each packet. If an acknowledgement is not received, then the sending computer will retransmit the information.

UDP, on the other hand, is not a connection-oriented protocol; rather, it is connectionless and does not guarantee delivery of the packet. It is a best-effort protocol, which leaves the business of keeping track of the packets and controlling the flow of data up to the application that called the transport.

At the top of the model is the application layer. There are many utilities found at this level in a standard implementation of the TCP/IP protocol stack. Items such as file transfer protocol (FTP), Telnet, SNMP (simple network management protocol), domain name service (DNS) are all found at this level because this is where applications gain access to the network. In Microsoft's implementation of TCP/IP, there are two ways applications can gain access to the network: either through NetBIOS (network basic input output service) or through Windows Sockets. The NetBIOS interface allows TCP/IP or NetBEUI protocols to use naming and messaging services using NetBIOS naming conventions, while the Windows Sockets service provides an application programming interface (API) to transport protocols such as TCP/IP or IPX.

Transmission Control Protocol

Transmission control protocol is able to perform basic data transfer by using a continuous stream of byte-sized data. The data is packaged into segments for transmission by the Internet protocol. In general, TCP performs its own flow control and will decide when to transmit and when to hold back data as required. A push function is defined that allows the user to know when TCP has successfully transmitted all the data submitted to it by the application. A sending TCP is allowed to collect data from the sending user and to send that data in segments at its own convenience, until the push function is signaled; then it must send all unsent data. When a receiving TCP sees the PUSH flag, it must not wait for more data from the sending TCP before passing the data to the receiving process. A push causes TCP to forward and deliver data up to that point promptly to the receiver. We will see the push flag set in some of our traces.

In order to recover from data that is corrupt, lost, arrives out of order, or is otherwise damaged, TCP assigns a sequence number to each octet that is transmitted. This lets the TCP layer on the receiving machine know what order the packets need to go into in order to be reassembled properly. In addition to the sequence number, each packet properly received must also be acknowledged (ACK) from the receiving TCP. If the ACK is not received within the timeout period, the data will be retransmitted. A checksum is used to determine whether a packet has been damaged. This is added to each segment transmitted by the sending machine, and it is checked at the receiver.

Flow control is provided by using a "window" that is sent back with every ACK. This window is a range of sequence numbers that can be transmitted in the next round of communication. These are beyond the last segment successfully received. The window indicates the number of octets the sender may transmit before receiving further permission. In order for a host to allow multiple processes to communicate over TCP at the same time, ports are used. Adding the port number to the end of an IP address (for example: 123.123.123.123:29) forms a socket. A pair of sockets is used to identify a connection, so a socket could be used in more than one conversation at the same time. A connection can be used to carry data in both directions at the same time, that is, it is "full duplex."

While each host is responsible for binding the ports it uses for these connections, certain functions have been assigned to "well known ports." These services are accessed through the known addresses. A listing of these well-known ports is found in Appendix A. The combination of sockets, sequence numbers, and window sizes is called a connection. Two processes communicate by first establishing a connection. When the communication is over, the connection is closed to free the resources.

There are two interfaces supported by the transmission control protocol. These interfaces are the user interface and the Internet interface. The user interface allows five basic calls to be made to the protocol. The calls are named: Open a connection; Close a connection; Send data; Receive data; and Status. The status call will obtain information about a connection. These five calls operate just like their counterparts do from any other program. For example, you might open a file or close a file in the same manner TCP performs the same type of functions. A passive OPEN request means that the process wants to accept incoming connection requests rather than attempting to initiate a connection.

Often the process requesting a passive OPEN will accept a connection request from any caller. In this case, a foreign socket of all zeros is used to denote an unspecified socket. Unspecified foreign sockets are allowed only on passive OPENs. A service process that wished to provide services for unknown other processes would issue a passive OPEN request with an unspecified foreign socket. Then, a connection could be made with any process that requested a connection to this local socket. It would help if this local socket were known to be associated with this service.

Well-known sockets are a convenient mechanism for associating a socket address with a standard service. For instance, the "Telnet-Server" process is permanently assigned to a particular socket, and other sockets are reserved for file transfer. The Internet interface supported by TCP provides only two calls. It can send or receive datagrams addressed to TCP modules in other hosts. These calls do have a number of parameters that can be set. These are set as flags in the frame, as we will see in our traces. These parameters include such things as type of service, precedence, security, and other control information.

A Look at the TCP Header

Source and destination fields   Let us now see how the TCP header is structured as we look at Figure 2–2 and parse a TCP segment captured with network monitor. The first field we come to in the TCP header is the source port, which is a 16-bit field used to identify the source process that is sending the TCP segment to the destination machine. In Figure 2–2, this is 0x04-05 (1029 decimal). The next field (obviously) is the destination port. Like the source port, this is also a 16-bit field that is used to identify the process on the target machine. In the figure, it is the telnet port 0x17 (23).

Sequence field   Now we come to the sequence number, which is a 32 bit field that is used to identify the sequence number that corresponds to the first byte in this segment. TCP sequencing uses a byte offset in the data stream to indicate where in the stream the data falls. When the SYN (synchronize) flag is set during the connection establishment, the sequence number becomes the initial sequence number (ISN) and, as the data is sent, the ISN is incremented by 1. This tells both the sending and receiving machines where in the data stream they are working.

Acknowledgment field   The next 32 bits are the acknowledgment number field, which indicates to the sending machine that the previous segment was received intact. This field is significant only if the ACK (acknowledgment) flag is set. Once a connection is established, this field is always important.

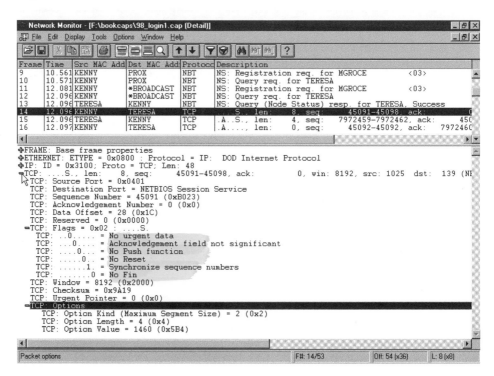

Fig. 2–2   A typical TCP header, as seen in network monitor.

Data offset field   The data offset field takes up four bits and is used to indicate where the TCP payload begins. It is also called the header length field because, once you figure out where the TCP data begins, you know how long the header is. The TCP header (including options) is always an integral number of 32 bits with a maximum size of 60 bytes. The six bits following the data offset field are reserved and must be set to 0.

The six TCP flags   There are six flags that can be set in the TCP header. These flags are listed below and are set using a 1-bit field for each of the flags available. Therefore, the flag field occupies a total of six bits in the header. If a flag is not set, then 0 is utilized.

1. Urgent field (URG) is significant. When this flag is set, the urgent pointer field contains data that is important. The urgent data is not part of the normal data stream and will be processed before any other data. Urgent data can be used to interrupt programs and notify an application of out-of-sync events. It is also used to pass a message across the network to an application that is not part of the current data stream (out-of-band data).

2. The acknowledgment field (ACK) is significant when this flag is set. Once a normal connection is established, the ACK flag will always be flying.

3. The push (PSH) flag indicates that the data in the segment and other data received is in a receiving buffer and must be passed immediately to the application. TCP will often hold incoming data in a receive buffer, and when the buffer is full, it passes the data to the application. This can cause problems for some applications such as Telnet, which needs to be able to pass keystrokes through to another machine. The pushed data does not have to be ACKed immediately; rather it can be ACKed at the next normal transmission of data.

4. The reset (RST) flag is used to abort the connection. When a reset is received on an active connection, it indicates that a failure has occurred and the connection should be forcibly closed. When you are trying to establish a connection and you receive a reset, it means the request is being rejected.

5. The synchronize sequence number (SYN) flag is used at the beginning of the connection set-up to establish the sequence and acknowledgment numbers. Before a connection is made, neither machine knows about the other machine's sequence numbers. The three-way handshake is used to pass the information about the sequence numbers at the beginning of a conversation. When they want to agree on the sequence numbers, they will fly the SYN flag.

6. The finished sending data flag (FIN) gracefully terminates a TCP connection. When one machine wants to terminate the connection, it will send a segment with the FIN flag set. When both machines have sent a

segment with the FIN set and both machines have acknowledged the flag, then the connection is terminated.

The window field   The window field uses 16 bits to indicate the number of bytes the sender of the TCP segment is willing to accept. This data must begin with the octet indicated in the acknowledgment field, or else it will be rejected. This window is an explicit indication of the size of the TCP buffer on the sending host. It can also be used to determine the maximum sequence number that can be acknowledged from this segment by adding the current acknowledgment number to the window field number.

Checksum   The checksum is the 16-bit complement of the one's complement sum of all the 16-bit words in the TCP header and the text. If the segment has an odd number of header and text octets, then the last octet is padded on the right with 0's until a 16-bit word can be formed to use for checksum purposes. It is important to note that the padding is not transmitted. While the checksum is being calculated, the checksum field is filled with zeros.

Urgent pointer   The urgent pointer field is a 16-bit field that is set to the sequence number of the last octet of the urgent data. It is used only when segments with the URG (urgent) bit are transmitted. When not in use, this field is set to zero (0x0).

Frame padding and options   The options field is a multiple of 32 bits that is used to store TCP options. If the option does not use the entire 32-bit field, then it is padded out with zeros.

A Look at the Three-way Handshake

The procedures to establish connections utilize the synchronize (SYN) control flag and involve an exchange of three messages. This exchange has been termed a three-way handshake. A connection is initiated by the rendezvous of an arriving segment containing a SYN and a waiting TCB entry, each created by a user OPEN command. The matching of local and foreign sockets determines when a connection has been initiated. The connection becomes "established" when sequence numbers have been synchronized in both directions. The clearing of a connection also involves the exchange of segments, in this case, carrying the FIN control flag.

The protocol places no restriction on a particular connection being used over and over again. A connection is defined by a pair of sockets. New instances of a connection will be referred to as incarnations of the connection. The problem that arises is, "How does the TCP identify duplicate segments from previous incarnations of the connection?" This problem becomes apparent if the connection is being opened and closed in quick succession, or if the connection breaks with loss of memory and is then reestablished.

To avoid confusion, we must prevent segments from one incarnation of a connection from being used while the same sequence numbers may still be present in the network from an earlier incarnation. We want to assure this, even if a TCP crashes and loses all knowledge of the sequence numbers it has been using. When new connections are created, an initial sequence number (ISN) generator is employed, which selects a new 32-bit ISN. The generator is bound to a (possibly fictitious) 32-bit clock whose low order bit is incremented roughly every four microseconds. Thus, the ISN cycles approximately every 4.55 hours. Since we assume that segments will stay in the network no more than the maximum segment lifetime (MSL) and that the MSL is less than 4.55 hours, we can reasonably assume that ISNs will be unique.

For each connection there is a send sequence number and a receive sequence number. The initial send sequence number (ISS) is chosen by the data sending TCP, and the initial receive sequence number (IRS) is learned during the connection establishing procedure. For a connection to be established or initialized, the two TCPs must synchronize with each other's initial sequence numbers. This is done in an exchange of connection establishing segments carrying a control bit called "SYN" (for synchronize) and the initial sequence numbers. As shorthand, segments carrying the SYN bit are also called "SYNs." Hence, the solution requires a suitable mechanism for picking an initial sequence number and a slightly involved handshake to exchange the ISNs.

The synchronization requires each side to send its own initial sequence number and to receive a confirmation of it in acknowledgment from the other side. Each side must also receive the other side's initial sequence number and send a confirming acknowledgment.

1. A --> B SYN my sequence number is X
2. A <-- B ACK your sequence number is X
3. A <-- B SYN my sequence number is Y
4. A --> B ACK your sequence number is Y

Because steps two and three are normally combined into a single message, the sequence is called the three-way handshake. Figure 2–3 shows what this looks like in real life.

A three-way handshake is necessary because sequence numbers are not tied to a global clock in the network, and TCPs may have different mechanisms for picking the ISNs. The receiver of the first SYN has no way of knowing whether the segment was an old delayed one or not, unless it remembers the last sequence number used on the connection (which is not always possible), so it must ask the sender to be sure that a TCP does not create a segment that carries a sequence number that may be duplicated by an old segment remaining in the network. The TCP must keep quiet for a maximum segment lifetime (MSL) before assigning any sequence numbers upon starting up or recovering from a crash in which memory of sequence numbers in

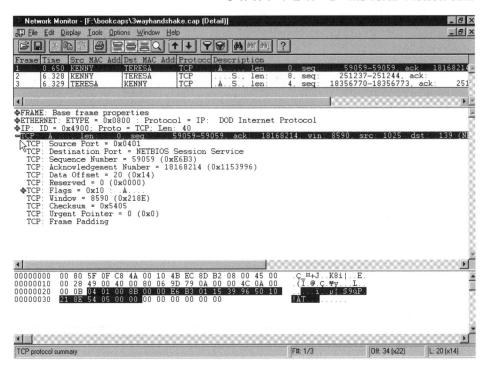

Fig. 2–3 The three-way handshake is used by TCP to establish a reliable connection.

use was lost. For this specification, the MSL is taken to be two minutes. This is an engineering choice, and may be changed if experience indicates it is desirable to do so. Note that if a TCP is reinitialized in some sense, yet retains its memory of sequence numbers in use, then it need not wait at all; it must be sure only to use sequence numbers larger than those recently used.

The TCP Quiet Time Concept

When a host crashes without retaining any knowledge of the last sequence numbers transmitted during an active (i.e., not closed) connection it will delay sending any TCP segments for at least the agreed MSL in the internet system of which the host is a part. In the paragraphs below, an explanation for this specification is given. TCP implementers may violate the "quiet time" restriction, but only at the risk of causing some old data to be accepted as new or new data rejected as old duplicated by some receivers in the Internet system.

TCPs consume sequence number space each time a segment is formed and entered into the network output queue at a source host. The duplicate detection and sequencing algorithm in the TCP protocol relies on the unique binding of segment data to sequence space to the extent that sequence numbers will not cycle through all 2^{32} values before the segment data bound to those sequence numbers has been delivered and acknowledged by the receiver and all duplicate copies of the segments have "drained" from the Internet. Without such an assumption, two distinct TCP segments could conceivably be assigned the same or overlapping sequence numbers, causing confusion at the receiver as to which data is new and which is old. Remember that each segment is bound to as many consecutive sequence numbers as there are octets of data in the segment.

Under normal conditions, TCPs keep track of the next sequence number to emit and the oldest awaiting acknowledgment so as to avoid mistakenly using a sequence number over before its first use has been acknowledged. This alone does not guarantee that old duplicate data is drained from the net, so the sequence space has been made very large to reduce the probability that a wandering duplicate will cause trouble upon arrival. At two megabits/sec. it takes 4.5 hours to use up 2^{32} octets of sequence space. Since the maximum segment lifetime in the net is not likely to exceed a few tens of seconds, this is deemed ample protection for foreseeable nets, even if data rates escalate to tens of megabits/sec. At 100 megabits/sec, the cycle time is 5.4 minutes, which may be a little short but still within reason.

The basic duplicate detection and sequencing algorithm in TCP can be defeated, however, if a source TCP does not have any memory of the sequence numbers it last used on a given connection. For example, if the TCP were to start all connections with sequence number 0, then, upon crashing and restarting a TCP might re-form an earlier connection (possibly after half-open connection resolution) and emit packets with sequence numbers identical to or overlapping with packets still in the network that were emitted on an earlier incarnation of the same connection. In the absence of knowledge about the sequence numbers used on a particular connection, the TCP specification recommends that the source delay for MSL seconds before emitting segments on the connection, to allow time for segments from the earlier connection incarnation to drain from the system. Even hosts that can remember the time of day and use it to select initial sequence number values are not immune from this problem (i.e., even if time of day is used to select an initial sequence number for each new connection incarnation).

Half-Open Connections and Other Anomalies

An established connection is said to be "half-open" if one of the TCPs has closed or aborted the connection at its end without the knowledge of the other, or if the two ends of the connection have become desynchronized owing to a crash that resulted in loss of memory. Such connections will automatically become reset if an attempt is made to send data in either direction. However, half-open connections are expected to be unusual, and the recovery procedure is mildly involved. If at site A the connection no longer exists, then an attempt by the user at site B to send any data on it will result in the site B TCP receiving a reset control message. Such a message indicates to site B TCP that something is wrong, and it is expected to abort the connection.

Assume that two user processes A and B are communicating with one another when a crash occurs, causing loss of memory to A's TCP. Depending on the operating system supporting A's TCP, it is likely that some error recovery mechanism exists. When the TCP is up again, A is likely to start again from the beginning or from a recovery point. As a result, A will probably try to OPEN the connection again or try to SEND on the connection it believes open. In the latter case, it receives the error message "connection not open" from the local (A's) TCP. In an attempt to establish the connection, A's TCP will send a segment containing SYN.

Reset Generation

As a general rule, reset (RST) must be sent whenever a segment arrives that apparently is not intended for the current connection. A reset must not be sent if it is not clear that this is the case. There are three groups of states, each of which is detailed below.

1. If the connection does not exist (CLOSED), then a reset is sent in response to any incoming segment except another reset. In particular, SYNs addressed to a nonexistent connection are rejected by this means. If the incoming segment has an ACK field, the reset takes its sequence number from the ACK field of the segment; otherwise, the reset has sequence number zero, and the ACK field is set to the sum of the sequence number and segment length of the incoming segment. The connection remains in the CLOSED state.

2. If the connection is in any nonsynchronized state (LISTEN, SYN-SENT, SYN-RECEIVED), and the incoming segment acknowledges something not yet sent (the segment carries an unacceptable ACK), or if an incoming segment has a security level or compartment that does not exactly match the level and compartment requested for the connection, a reset is sent. If our SYN has not been acknowledged and the precedence level of the incoming segment is higher than the precedence level requested, then either raise the local precedence level (if allowed by the user and the system) or send a reset; or if the precedence level of the incoming segment is lower than the precedence level requested, then continue as if the precedence matched exactly (if the remote TCP cannot raise the precedence level to match ours, this will be detected in the next segment it sends, and the connection will be terminated then). If our SYN has been acknowledged (perhaps in this incoming segment), the precedence level of the incoming segment must match the local precedence level exactly; if it does not, a reset must be sent. If the incoming segment has an ACK field, the reset takes its sequence number from the ACK field of

the segment; otherwise, the reset has sequence number zero, and the ACK field is set to the sum of the sequence number and segment length of the incoming segment. The connection remains in the same state.

3. If the connection is in a synchronized state (ESTABLISHED, FIN-WAIT-1, FIN-WAIT-2, CLOSE-WAIT, CLOSING, LAST-ACK, TIME-WAIT), any unacceptable segment (out-of-window sequence number or unacceptable acknowledgment number) must elicit only an empty acknowledgment segment containing the current send-sequence number and an acknowledgment indicating the next sequence number expected to be received, and the connection remains in the same state. If an incoming segment has a security level, or compartment, or precedence that does not exactly match the level, and compartment, and precedence requested for the connection, a reset is sent and connection goes to the CLOSED state. The reset takes its sequence number from the ACK field of the incoming segment.

RESET PROCESSING

In all states except SYN-SENT, all reset (RST) segments are validated by checking their SEQ-fields. A reset is valid if its sequence number is in the window. In the SYN-SENT state (a RST received in response to an initial SYN), the RST is acceptable if the ACK field acknowledges the SYN.

The receiver of a RST first validates it, then changes state. If the receiver was in the LISTEN state, it ignores it. If the receiver was in SYN-RECEIVED state and had previously been in the LISTEN state, then the receiver returns to the LISTEN state; otherwise, the receiver aborts the connection and goes to the CLOSED state. If the receiver was in any other state, it aborts the connection and advises the user and goes to the CLOSED state. Closing a connection (CLOSE) is an operation meaning "I have no more data to send." The notion of closing a full-duplex connection is subject to ambiguous interpretation, of course, since it may not be obvious how to treat the receiving side of the connection. We have chosen to treat CLOSE in a simplex fashion. The users who CLOSE may continue to RECEIVE until they are told that the other side has CLOSED also. Thus, a program could initiate several SENDs followed by a CLOSE, and then continue to RECEIVE until signaled that a RECEIVE failed because the other side has CLOSED. We assume that the TCP will signal a user, even if no RECEIVEs are outstanding, and that the other side has closed, so the user can terminate his side gracefully. A TCP will reliably deliver all buffers SENT before the connection was CLOSED, so a user who expects no data in return need only wait to hear the connection was CLOSED successfully to know that all his data was received at the destination TCP. Users must keep reading connections they close for sending until the TCP says no more data. There are essentially three scenarios we want to look at:

1. The user initiates by telling the TCP to CLOSE the connection.
2. The remote TCP initiates by sending a FIN control signal.
3. Both users CLOSE simultaneously.

Scenario 1: Local User Initiates the Close

In this case, a FIN segment can be constructed and placed on the outgoing segment queue. No further SENDs from the user will be accepted by the TCP, and it enters the FIN-WAIT-1 state. RECEIVEs are allowed in this state. All segments preceding and including FIN will be retransmitted until acknowledged. When the other TCP has both acknowledged the FIN and sent a FIN of its own, the first TCP can ACK this FIN. Note that a TCP receiving a FIN will ACK but not send its own FIN until its user has CLOSED the connection also.

Scenario 2: TCP Receives a FIN from the Network

If an unsolicited FIN arrives from the network, the receiving TCP can ACK it and tell the user that the connection is closing. The user will respond with a CLOSE, upon which the TCP can send a FIN to the other TCP after sending any remaining data. The TCP then waits until its own FIN is acknowledged, whereupon it deletes the connection. If an ACK is not forthcoming after the user timeout, the connection is aborted and the user is told.

Scenario 3: Both Users Close Simultaneously

A simultaneous CLOSE by users at both ends of a connection causes FIN segments to be exchanged. When all segments preceding the FINs have been processed and acknowledged, each TCP can ACK the FIN it has received. Both will, upon receiving these ACKs, delete the connection.

The Communication of Urgent Information

The objective of the TCP urgent mechanism is to allow the sending user to stimulate the receiver to accept some urgent data and to permit the receiving TCP to indicate to the receiver when all the currently known urgent data has been received by the user.

This mechanism permits a point in the data stream to be designated as the end of urgent information. Whenever this point occurs in advance of the receive sequence number (RCV.NXT) at the receiving TCP, that TCP must tell the user to go into "urgent mode"; when the receive sequence number catches up to the urgent pointer, the TCP must tell user to go into "normal mode." If the urgent pointer is updated while the user is in "urgent mode," the update will be invisible to the user. The method employs an urgent field, which is carried in all segments transmitted. The URG control flag indicates that the urgent field is meaningful and must be added to the segment sequence number to yield the urgent pointer. The absence of this flag indicates that there is no urgent data outstanding.

To send an urgent indication, the user must also send at least one data octet. If the sending user also indicates a push, timely delivery of the urgent information to the destination process is enhanced.

Managing the Window

The window sent in each segment indicates the range of sequence numbers the sender of the window (the data receiver) is currently prepared to accept. There is an assumption that this is related to the currently available data buffer space available for this connection.

Indicating a large window encourages transmissions. If more data arrives than can be accepted, it will be discarded. This will result in excessive retransmissions, adding unnecessarily to the load on the network and the TCPs. Indicating a small window may restrict the transmission of data to the point of introducing a round-trip delay between each new segment transmitted.

The mechanisms provided allow a TCP to advertise a large window and to subsequently advertise a much smaller window without having accepted that much data. This so-called "shrinking the window" is strongly discouraged. The robustness principle dictates that TCPs will not shrink the window themselves but will be prepared for such behavior on the part of other TCPs.

The sending TCP must be prepared to accept from the user and send at least one octet of new data even if the send window is zero. The sending TCP must regularly retransmit to the receiving TCP even when the window is zero. Two minutes is recommended for the retransmission interval when the window is zero. This retransmission is essential to guarantee that when either TCP has a zero window the reopening of the window will be reliably reported to the other.

When the receiving TCP has a zero window and a segment arrives, it must still send an acknowledgment showing its next expected sequence number and current window (zero). The sending TCP packages the data to be transmitted into segments that fit the current window and may repackage segments on the retransmission queue. Such repackaging is not required but may be helpful.

In a connection with a one-way data flow, the window information will be carried in acknowledgment segments that all have the same sequence number, so there will be no way to reorder them if they arrive out of order. This is not a serious problem, but it will allow the window information to be on occasion temporarily based on old reports from the data receiver. A refinement to avoid this problem is to act on the window information from segments that carry the highest acknowledgment number (that is, segments with an acknowledgment number equal or greater than the highest previously received).

The window management procedure has significant influence on the communication performance. The following comments are suggestions to implementers.

Window management suggestions   Allocating a very small window causes data to be transmitted in many small segments when better performance is achieved using fewer large segments.

One suggestion for avoiding small windows is for the receiver to defer updating a window until the additional allocation is at least X percent of the maximum allocation possible for the connection (where X might be 20 to 40).

Another suggestion is for the sender to avoid sending small segments by waiting until the window is large enough before sending data. If the user signals a push function, then the data must be sent even if it is a small segment.

Note that the acknowledgments should not be delayed or unnecessary retransmissions will result. One strategy would be to send an acknowledgment when a small segment arrives (without updating the window information), and then to send another acknowledgment with new window information when the window is larger. The segment sent to probe a zero window may also begin a breakup of transmitted data into smaller and smaller segments. If a segment containing a single data octet sent to probe a zero window is accepted, it consumes one octet of the window now available.

If the sending TCP simply sends as much as it can whenever the window is nonzero, the transmitted data will be broken into alternating big and small segments. As time goes on, occasional pauses in the receiver making window allocation available will result in breaking the big segments into a small and not quite so big pair. After a while, the data transmission will be in mostly small segments.

The suggestion here is that the TCP implementations actively attempt to combine small window allocations into larger windows, since the mechanisms for managing the window tend to lead to many small windows in the simplest minded implementations.

USER/TCP INTERFACE

The following functional description of TCP commands is somewhat generic; however, all TCPs must provide a certain minimum set of services to guarantee that all TCP implementations can support the same protocol hierarchy. This section specifies the functional interfaces found in all TCP implementations.

TCP User Commands

The following sections explain how some of the more common TCP commands work and will give us a lot better insight into our troubleshooting. The user commands described below specify the basic functions that TCP will perform to support interprocess communication. Although these commands will not necessarily be visible, we do find evidence of their work in our traces. Different implementations may change the exact format, or provide combinations or subsets of the basic functions in single calls. In particular, some implementations may wish to OPEN a connection automatically on the first SEND or RECEIVE issued by the user for a given connection. In providing interprocess communication facilities, the TCP must not only accept commands, but must also return information to the processes it serves. The latter consists of general information about a connection (e.g., interrupts, remote close, binding of unspecified foreign socket). Replies to specific user commands indicate success or various types of failure.

We assume that the local TCP is aware of the identity of the processes it serves and will check the authority of the process to use the connection specified. Depending upon the implementation of the TCP, the local network and TCP identifiers for the source address will either be supplied by the TCP or the lower-level protocol (e.g., IP). These considerations are the result of concern about security, to the extent that no TCP be able to masquerade as another one, and so on. Similarly, no process can masquerade as another without the collusion of the TCP.

If the active/passive flag is set to passive, then this is a call to LISTEN for an incoming connection. A passive open may have either a fully specified foreign socket to wait for a particular connection or an unspecified foreign socket to wait for any call. A fully specified passive call can be made active by the subsequent execution of a SEND. A transmission control block (TCB) is created and partially filled in with data from the OPEN command parameters. On an active OPEN command, the TCP will begin the procedure to synchronize (i.e., establish) the connection at once.

The timeout, if present, permits the caller to set up a timeout for all data submitted to TCP. If data is not successfully delivered to the destination within the timeout period, the TCP will abort the connection. The present global default is five minutes.

The TCP or some component of the operating system will verify the user's authority to open a connection with the specified precedence or security/compartment. The absence of precedence or security/compartment specification in the OPEN call indicates that the default values must be used.

TCP will accept incoming requests as matching only if the security/compartment information is exactly the same and only if the precedence is equal to or higher than the precedence requested in the OPEN call.

The precedence for the connection is the higher of the values requested in the OPEN call and received from the incoming request, and fixed at that value for the life of the connection. Implementers may want to give the user control of this precedence negotiation. For example, the user might be allowed to specify that the precedence must be exactly matched, or that any attempt to raise the precedence be confirmed by the user.

A local connection name will be returned to the user by the TCP. The local connection name can then be used as a shorthand term for the connection defined by the <local socket, foreign socket> pair.

Send

This call causes the data contained in the indicated user buffer to be sent on the indicated connection. If the connection has not been opened, the SEND is considered an error. Some implementations may allow users to SEND first; in that case, an automatic OPEN would occur. If the calling process is not authorized to use this connection, an error is returned.

If the PUSH flag is set, the data must be transmitted promptly to the receiver, and the PUSH bit will be set in the last TCP segment created from the buffer. If the PUSH flag is not set, the data may be combined with data from subsequent SENDs for transmission efficiency.

If the URGENT flag is set, segments sent to the destination TCP will have the urgent pointer set. The receiving TCP will signal the urgent condition to the receiving process if the urgent pointer indicates that data preceding the urgent pointer has not been consumed by the receiving process. The purpose of urgent is to stimulate the receiver to process the urgent data and to indicate to the receiver when all the currently-known urgent data has been received. The number of times the sending user's CP signals are urgent will not necessarily be equal to the number of times the receiving user will be notified of the presence of urgent data.

If no foreign socket was specified in the OPEN but the connection is established (e.g., because a LISTENing connection has become specific due to a foreign segment arriving for the local socket), then the designated buffer is sent to the implied foreign socket. Users who make use of OPEN with an unspecified foreign socket can make use of SEND without ever explicitly knowing the foreign socket address.

However, if a SEND is attempted before the foreign socket becomes specified, an error will be returned. Users can use the STATUS call to determine the status of the connection. In some implementations, the TCP may notify the user when an unspecified socket is bound.

If a timeout is specified, the current user timeout for this connection is changed to the new one. In the simplest implementation, SEND would not return control to the sending process until either the transmission was complete or the timeout had been exceeded. However, this simple method is both subject to deadlocks (for example, both sides of the connection might try to do SENDs before doing any RECEIVEs) and offers poor performance, so it is not recommended. A more sophisticated implementation would return immediately to follow the process to run concurrently with network I/O, and, furthermore, to allow multiple SENDs to be in progress. Multiple SENDs are served in first-come, first-served order, so the TCP will queue those it cannot service immediately.

We have implicitly assumed an asynchronous user interface in which a SEND later elicits some kind of SIGNAL or pseudo-interrupt from the serving TCP. An alternative is to return a response immediately. For instance, SENDs might return immediate local acknowledgment, even if the segment sent had not been acknowledged by the distant TCP. We could optimistically assume eventual success. If we are wrong, the connection will close anyway due to the timeout. In implementations of this kind (synchronous), there will still be some asynchronous signals, but these will deal with the connection itself, and not with specific segments or buffers.

In order for the process to distinguish among error or success indications for different SENDs, it might be appropriate for the buffer address to be returned along with the coded response to the SEND request. TCP-to-user signals are discussed below, indicating the information that should be returned to the calling process.

Receive

This command allocates a receiving buffer associated with the specified connection. If no OPEN precedes this command, or the calling process is not authorized to use this connection, an error is returned.

In the simplest implementation, control would not return to the calling program until either the buffer was filled, or some error occurred, but this scheme is highly subject to deadlocks. A more sophisticated implementation would permit several RECEIVEs to be outstanding at once. These would be filled as segments arrive. This strategy permits increased throughput at the cost of a more elaborate scheme (possibly asynchronous) to notify the calling program that a PUSH has been seen or a buffer filled. If enough data arrives to fill the buffer before a PUSH is seen, the PUSH flag will not be set in the response to the RECEIVE. The buffer will be filled with as much data as it can hold. If a PUSH is seen before the buffer is filled, the buffer will be returned partially filled and PUSH indicated.

If there is urgent data, the user will have been informed as soon as it arrived via a TCP-to-user signal. The receiving user should thus be in "urgent mode." If the URGENT flag is on, additional urgent data remains. If the URGENT flag is off, this call to RECEIVE has returned all the urgent data, and the user may now leave "urgent mode." Note that data following the urgent pointer (nonurgent data) cannot be delivered to the user in the same buffer with preceding urgent data unless the boundary is clearly marked for the user.

To distinguish among several outstanding RECEIVEs and to compensate for a buffer that is not completely filled, the return code is accompanied by both a buffer pointer and a byte count indicating the actual length of the data received.

Alternative implementations of RECEIVE might have the TCP allocate buffer storage, or the TCP might share a ring buffer with the user.

Close

This command causes the connection specified to be closed. If the connection is not open, or the calling process is not authorized to use this connection, an error is returned. Closing connections is intended to be a graceful operation in the sense that outstanding SENDs will be transmitted (and re-transmitted), as flow control permits, until all have been serviced. Thus, it should be acceptable to make several SEND calls, followed by a CLOSE, and expect all the data to be sent to the destination. It should also be clear that users should continue to RECEIVE on CLOSING connections, since the other side may be trying to transmit the last of its data. Thus, CLOSE means, "I have no more to send" but does not mean, "I will not receive any more." It may happen (if the user-level protocol is not well thought out) that the side is unable to get rid of all its data before timing out. In this event, CLOSE turns into ABORT, and the closing TCP gives up. The user may CLOSE the connection at any time on his own initiative, or in response to various prompts from the TCP (e.g., remote close executed, transmission timeout exceeded, destination inaccessible).

Because closing a connection requires communication with the foreign TCP, connections may remain in the closing state for a short time. Attempts to reopen the connection before the TCP replies to the CLOSE command will result in error responses. CLOSE also implies push function.

Status Abort

This command causes all pending SENDs and RECEIVEs to be aborted, the TCB to be removed, and a special RESET message to be sent to the TCP on the other side of the connection. Depending on the implementation, users may receive abort indications for each outstanding SEND or RECEIVE or may simply receive an ABORT-acknowledgment.

TCP/Lower-Level Interface

The TCP calls on a lower-level protocol module to actually send and receive information over a network. One case is that of the ARPA internetwork system where the lower-level module is the Internet Protocol (IP). If the lower-level protocol is IP, it provides arguments for a type of service and for a time to live. TCP uses the following settings for these parameters: type of service = precedence: routine; delay: normal; throughput: normal; reliability: normal; or 00000000. Time to live = one minute, or 00111100. Note that the assumed maximum segment lifetime is two minutes. Here we explicitly ask that a segment be destroyed if it cannot be delivered by the Internet system within one minute. If the lower level is IP (or other protocol that provides this feature) and source routing is used, the interface must allow the route information to be communicated. This is especially important so that the source and destination addresses used in the TCP checksum be the originating source and ultimate destination. It is also important to preserve the return route to answer connection requests.

Any lower-level protocol will have to provide the source address, destination address, and protocol fields, and some way to determine the "TCP length," both to provide the functional equivalent service of IP and to be used in the TCP checksum. The processing depicted in this section is an example of one possible implementation. Other implementations may have slightly different processing sequences, but they should differ from those in this section only in detail, not in substance. The activity of the TCP can be characterized as responding to events. The events that occur can be cast into three categories: user calls, arriving segments, and timeouts. This section describes the processing the TCP does in response to each of the events. In many cases, the processing required depends on the state of the connection.

Events That Occur: User Calls

The model of the TCP/user interface is one in which user commands receive an immediate return and possibly a delayed response via an event or pseudo-interrupt. In the following descriptions, the term "signal" means "cause a delayed response." Error responses are given as character strings. For example, user commands referencing connections that do not exist receive "error: connection not open."

Please note in the following that all arithmetic on sequence numbers, acknowledgment numbers, windows, etc. is modulo 2^{32} the size of the sequence number space. Also note that "=<" means less than or equal to (modulo 2^{32}). A natural way to think about processing incoming segments is to imagine that they are first tested for proper sequence number (i.e., that their contents lie in the range of the expected "receive window" in the sequence number space) and then generally queued and processed in sequence number order. When a segment overlaps other already received segments, we reconstruct the segment to contain just the new data, and adjust the header fields to be consistent. Note that if no state change is mentioned, the TCP stays in the same state (i.e., TCB does not exist). Create a new transmission control block (TCB) to hold connection state information. Fill in local socket identifier, foreign socket, precedence, security/compartment, and user timeout information. Note that some parts of the foreign socket may be unspecified in a passive OPEN and are to be filled in by the parameters of the incoming SYN segment. Verify that the security and precedence requested are allowed for this user; if not, return "error: precedence not allowed" or "error: security/compartment not allowed." If passive, enter the LISTEN state and return. If active and the foreign socket is unspecified, return "error: foreign socket unspecified"; if active and the foreign socket is specified, issue a SYN segment. An initial send sequence number (ISS) is selected. A SYN segment of the form <SEQ=ISS><CTL=SYN> is sent. Set SND.UNA to ISS, SND.NXT to ISS+1, enter SYN-SENT state, and return. If the caller does not have access to the local socket specified, return "error: connection illegal for this process." If there is no room to create a new connection, return "error: insufficient resources."

LISTEN STATE

If active and the foreign socket is specified, then change the connection from passive to active, and select an ISS. Send a SYN segment, set SND.UNA to ISS, SND.NXT to ISS+1. Enter SYN-SENT state. Data associated with SEND may be sent with SYN segment or queued for transmission after entering ESTABLISHED state. The urgent bit, if requested in the command, must be sent with the data segments sent as a result of this command. If there is no room to queue the request, respond with "error: insufficient resources." If foreign socket was not specified, then return "error: foreign socket unspecified."

SEND Call

- CLOSED STATE (i.e., TCB does not exist). If the user does not have access to such a connection, then return "error: connection illegal for this process". Otherwise, return "error: connection does not exist."
- LISTEN STATE If the foreign socket is specified, then change the connection from passive to active, and select an ISS. Send a SYN segment, and set SND.UNA to ISS, SND.NXT to ISS+1. Enter SYN-SENT state. Data associated with SEND may be sent with SYN segment or queued for transmission after entering ESTABLISHED state. The urgent bit (if requested in the command) must be sent with the data segments sent as a result of this command. If there is no room to queue the request, respond with "error: insufficient resources." If foreign socket was not specified, then return "error: foreign socket unspecified."
- SYN-SENT STATE SYN-RECEIVED STATE Queue the data for transmission after entering ESTABLISHED state. If no space to queue, respond with "error: insufficient resources."
- ESTABLISHED STATE CLOSE-WAIT STATE. Segmentize the buffer and send it with a piggybacked acknowledgment (acknowledgment value = RCV.NXT). If there is insufficient space to remember this buffer, simply return "error: insufficient resources." If the urgent flag is set, then SND.UP <- SND.NXT-1 and set the urgent pointer in the outgoing segments. Call CLOSED STATE (i.e., TCB does not exist). If the user does not have access to such a connection, return "error: connection illegal for this process." Otherwise, return "error: connection does not exist."
- LISTEN STATE SYN-SENT STATE SYN-RECEIVED STATE. Queue for processing after entering ESTABLISHED state. If there is no room to queue this request, respond with "error: insufficient resources."
- ESTABLISHED STATE FIN-WAIT-1 STATE FIN-WAIT-2 STATE. If insufficient incoming segments are queued to satisfy the request, queue the request. If there is no queue space to remember the RECEIVE, respond with "error: insufficient resources." Reassemble queued incoming

segments into receive buffer and return to user. Mark "push seen" (PUSH) if this is the case. If RCV.UP is in advance of the data currently being passed to the user, notify the user of the presence of urgent data. When the TCP takes responsibility for delivering data to the user, that fact must be communicated to the sender via an acknowledgment. The formation of such an acknowledgment is described below in the discussion of processing an incoming segment.

- RECEIVE Call: CLOSE-WAIT STATE. Since the remote side has already sent FIN, RECEIVEs must be satisfied by text already on hand, but not yet delivered to the user. If no text is awaiting delivery, the RECEIVE will get an "error: connection closing" response. Otherwise, any remaining text can be used to satisfy the RECEIVE.

- CLOSING STATE LAST-ACK STATE TIME-WAIT STATE. Return "error: connection closing." Call CLOSED STATE (i.e., TCB does not exist). If the user should not have access to such a connection, return "error: connection illegal for this process." Otherwise, return "error: connection does not exist."

- LISTEN STATE. Any outstanding RECEIVEs should be returned with "error: connection reset" responses. Delete TCB, enter CLOSED state, and return. SYN-SENT STATE All queued SENDs and RECEIVEs should be given "connection reset" notification, delete the TCB, enter CLOSED state, and return.

- SYN-RECEIVED STATE ESTABLISHED STATE FIN-WAIT-1 STATE FIN-WAIT-2 STATE CLOSE-WAIT STATE. Send a reset segment: <SEQ=SND.NXT><CTL=RST> All queued SENDs and RECEIVEs should be given "connection reset" notification; all segments queued for transmission (except for the RST form) or retransmission should be flushed, delete the TCB, enter CLOSED state, and return.

- CLOSING STATE LAST-ACK STATE TIME-WAIT STATE. Respond with "ok" and delete the TCB, enter CLOSED state, and return.

INTERNET PROTOCOL

The Internet protocol is designed for use in interconnected systems of packet-switched computer communication networks. The Internet protocol provides for transmitting blocks of data called datagrams from sources to destinations, where sources and destinations are hosts identified by fixed-length addresses. The Internet protocol also provides for fragmentation and reassembly of long datagrams.

The Internet protocol is specifically limited in scope to provide the functions necessary to deliver a package of bits (an Internet datagram) from a source to a destination over an interconnected system of networks. There are no mechanisms to augment end-to-end data reliability, flow control, sequencing, or other services commonly found in host-to-host protocols. The Internet protocol can capitalize on the services of its supporting networks to provide various types and qualities of service.

This protocol is called on by host-to-host protocols in an Internet environment. This protocol calls on local network protocols to carry the Internet datagram to the next gateway or destination host. For example, a TCP module would call on the Internet module to take a TCP segment (including the TCP header and user data) as the data portion of an Internet datagram. The TCP module would provide the addresses and other parameters in the Internet header to the Internet module as arguments of the call. The Internet module would then create an Internet datagram and call on the local network interface to transmit the datagram.

The Internet protocol implements two basic functions: addressing and fragmentation. The Internet modules use the addresses carried in the Internet header to transmit Internet datagrams toward their destinations. The selection of a path for transmission is called routing. The Internet modules use fields in the Internet header to fragment and reassemble Internet datagrams when necessary.

The model of operation is that an Internet module resides in each host engaged in Internet communication and in each gateway that interconnects networks. These modules share common rules for interpreting address fields and for fragmenting and assembling Internet datagrams. In addition, these modules (especially in gateways) have procedures for making routing decisions and other functions.

The Internet protocol treats each Internet datagram as an independent entity unrelated to any other Internet datagram. There are no connections or logical circuits (virtual or otherwise).

The Internet protocol uses four key mechanisms in providing its service: type of service, time to live, options, and header checksum. The type of service is used to indicate the quality of the service desired. The type of service is an abstract or generalized set of parameters that characterize the service choices provided in the networks that make up the Internet. This type of service indication is to be used by gateways to select the actual transmission parameters for a particular network, the network to be used for the next hop, or the next gateway when routing an Internet datagram. The time-to-live is an indication of an upper bound on the lifetime of an Internet datagram. It is set by the sender of the datagram and reduced at the points along the route where it is processed. If the time-to-live reaches zero before the Internet datagram reaches its destination, the Internet datagram is destroyed. The time-to-live can be thought of as a self-destruct time limit.

The options provide for control functions needed or useful in some situations but unnecessary for the most common communications. The options include provisions for timestamps, security, and special routing. The header checksum provides a verification that the information used in processing Internet datagrams has been transmitted correctly. The data may contain errors. If the header checksum fails, the Internet datagram is discarded at once by the entity that detects the error. The Internet protocol does not provide a reliable communication facility. There are no acknowledgments either end-to-end or hop-by-hop. There is no error control for data, only a header checksum. There are no retransmissions. There is no flow control. Errors detected may be reported via the Internet control message protocol (ICMP), which is implemented in the Internet protocol module.

Internet protocol interfaces on one side to the higher-level host-to-host protocols and on the other side to the local network protocol. This is illustrated in Figure 2–4.

The model of operation for transmitting a datagram from one application program to another is illustrated by the following scenario: We suppose that this transmission will involve one intermediate gateway. The sending application program prepares its data and calls on its local Internet module to send that data as a datagram and passes the destination address and other parameters as arguments of the call. The Internet module prepares a data-

Fig. 2–4 The Internet protocol talks to the higher-level TCP protocol and the lower network protocols as well.

gram header and attaches the data to it. The module determines a local network address for this Internet address; in this case, it is the address of a gateway. It sends this datagram and the local network address to the local network interface. The local network interface creates a local network header and attaches the datagram to it, and then sends the result via the local network. The datagram arrives at a gateway host wrapped in the local network header; the local network interface strips off this header, and turns the datagram over to the Internet module. The module determines from the Internet address that the datagram is to be forwarded to another host in a second network. The module determines a local net address for the destination host. It calls on the local network interface for that network to send the datagram. This local network interface creates a local network header and attaches the datagram, sending the result to the destination host. At this destination host, the datagram is stripped of the local net header by the local network interface and handed to the Internet module.

The Internet module determines that the datagram is for an application program in this host. It passes the data to the application program in response to a system call, passing the source address and other parameters as results of the call.

The function or purpose of Internet protocol is to move datagrams through an interconnected set of networks. This is done by passing the datagrams from one Internet module to another until the destination is reached. The Internet modules reside in hosts and gateways in the Internet system. The datagrams are routed from one Internet module to another through individual networks based on the interpretation of an Internet address. Thus, one important mechanism of the Internet protocol is the Internet address.

In the routing of messages from one Internet module to another, datagrams may need to traverse a network whose maximum packet size is smaller than the size of the datagram. To overcome this difficulty, a fragmentation mechanism is provided in the Internet protocol.

A distinction is made between names, addresses, and routes. A name indicates what we seek. An address indicates where it is. A route indicates how to get there. The Internet protocol deals primarily with addresses. It is the task of higher-level (i.e., host-to-host or application) protocols to make the mapping from names to addresses. The Internet module maps Internet addresses to local net addresses. It is the task of lower-level (i.e., local net or gateways) procedures to make the mapping from local net addresses or routes.

Addresses are fixed lengths of four octets (32 bits). An address begins with a network number, followed by local address (called the "rest" field). There are three formats or classes of Internet addresses: In class (a), the high-order bit is zero, the next seven bits are the network, and the last 24 bits are the local address; in class (b), the high-order two bits are one-zero, the next 14 bits are the network, and the last 16 bits are the local address; in class (c), the high-order three bits are one-one-zero, the next 21 bits are the network, and the last eight bits are the local address.

Care must be taken in mapping Internet addresses to local net addresses; a single physical host must be able to act as if it were several distinct hosts to the extent of using several distinct Internet addresses. Some hosts will also have several physical interfaces (multi-homing). That is, provision must be made for a host to have several physical interfaces to the network with each having several logical Internet addresses.

Fragmentation of an Internet datagram is necessary when it originates in a local net that allows a large packet size and must traverse a local net that limits packets to a smaller size to reach its destination.

An Internet datagram can be marked "don't fragment." Any Internet datagram so marked is not to be Internet-fragmented under any circumstances. If an Internet datagram marked "don't fragment" cannot be delivered to its destination without fragmenting it, it is to be discarded instead. Fragmentation, transmission, and reassembly across a local network that is invisible to the Internet protocol module are called Intranet fragmentation and may be used.

The IP fragmentation and reassembly procedure needs to be able to break a datagram into an almost arbitrary number of pieces that can be later reassembled. The receiver of the fragments uses the identification field to ensure that fragments of different datagrams are not mixed. The fragment offset field tells the receiver the position of a fragment in the original datagram. The fragment offset and length determine the portion of the original datagram covered by this fragment. The more-fragments flag indicates (by being reset) the last fragment. These fields provide sufficient information to reassemble datagrams.

The identification field is used to distinguish the fragments of one datagram from those of another. The originating protocol module of an Internet datagram sets the identification field to a value that must be unique for that source-destination pair and protocol for the time the datagram will be active in the Internet system. The originating protocol module of a complete datagram sets the more-fragments flag to zero and the fragment offset to zero.

To fragment a long Internet datagram, an Internet protocol module (for example, in a gateway), creates two new Internet datagrams and copies the contents of the Internet header fields from the long datagram into both new Internet headers. The data of the long datagram is divided into two portions on an eight-octet (64 bit) boundary (the second portion might not be an integral multiple of eight octets, but the first must be). Call the number of eight-octet blocks in the first portion NFB (for number of fragment blocks). The first portion of the data is placed in the first new Internet datagram, and the total length field is set to the length of the first datagram. The more-fragments flag is set to one. The second portion of the data is placed in the second new Internet datagram, and the total length field is set to the length of the second datagram. The more-fragments flag carries the same value as the long datagram. The fragment offset field of the second new Internet datagram is set to the value of that field in the long datagram plus NFB.

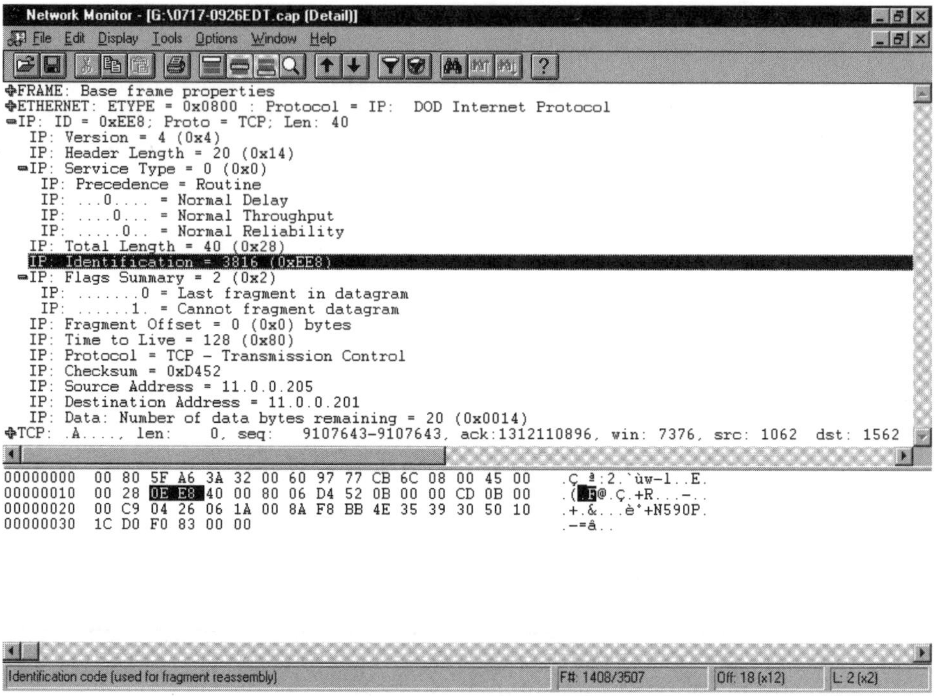

```
Network Monitor - [G:\0717-0926EDT.cap (Detail)]                                    _ 8 X
File  Edit  Display  Tools  Options  Window  Help                                   _ 8 X

[toolbar icons]

+FRAME: Base frame properties
+ETHERNET: ETYPE = 0x0800 ; Protocol = IP:  DOD Internet Protocol
-IP: ID = 0xEE8; Proto = TCP; Len: 40
  IP: Version = 4 (0x4)
  IP: Header Length = 20 (0x14)
 -IP: Service Type = 0 (0x0)
    IP: Precedence = Routine
    IP: ...0.... = Normal Delay
    IP: ....0... = Normal Throughput
    IP: .....0.. = Normal Reliability
  IP: Total Length = 40 (0x28)
  IP: Identification = 3816 (0xEE8)
 -IP: Flags Summary = 2 (0x2)
    IP: .......0 = Last fragment in datagram
    IP: ......1. = Cannot fragment datagram
  IP: Fragment Offset = 0 (0x0) bytes
  IP: Time to Live = 128 (0x80)
  IP: Protocol = TCP - Transmission Control
  IP: Checksum = 0xD452
  IP: Source Address = 11.0.0.205
  IP: Destination Address = 11.0.0.201
  IP: Data: Number of data bytes remaining = 20 (0x0014)
+TCP: .A...., len:    0, seq:   9107643-9107643, ack:1312110896, win: 7376, src: 1062  dst: 1562

00000000  00 80 5F A6 3A 32 00 60 97 77 CB 6C 08 00 45 00    .Ç ª:2.`ùw-l..E.
00000010  00 28 0E E8 40 00 80 06 D4 52 0B 00 00 CD 0B 00    .( F@.Ç.+R...-..
00000020  00 C9 04 26 06 1A 00 8A F8 BB 4E 35 39 30 50 10    .+.&...è'+N590P.
00000030  1C D0 F0 83 00 00                                   .-=â..

Identification code (used for fragment reassembly)    F#: 1408/3507    Off: 18 (x12)    L: 2 (x2)
```

Fig. 2–5   An IP header parsed.

This procedure can be generalized for an n-way split, rather than the two-way split described. To assemble the fragments of an Internet datagram, an Internet protocol module (for example, at a destination host) combines Internet datagrams that all have the same value for the four fields: identification, source, destination, and protocol. The combination is done by placing the data portion of each fragment in the relative position indicated by the fragment offset in that fragment's Internet header. The first fragment will have the fragment offset zero, and the last fragment will have the more-fragments flag reset to zero.

The IP Header

In Figure 2–5, we see a sample IP header as it exists on a Windows NT network. The first field in the IP header is for the version that is four bits long. The version field indicates the format of the Internet header and therefore tells other machines how to interpret the data. We are looking at version 4. The next field is the Internet header length. Four bits are allowed for this information. This number is the length of the Internet header in 32-bit words, and thus points to the beginning of the data. Note that the minimum value for a correct header is five, which is 20 bytes. In the hex pane at the bottom of Figure 2–5, the area highlighted is the IP header. The first number is 45, which tells us that we are looking at an IP version 4 header and that it is 5 x 32 bits long.

The next field uses eight bits for the type of service to provide an indication of the abstract parameters of the quality of service desired. These parameters are to be used to guide the selection of the actual service parameters when transmitting a datagram through a particular network. Several networks offer service precedence, which somehow treats high-precedence traffic as more important than other traffic (generally by accepting only traffic above a certain precedence at time of high load). The major choice is a three-way tradeoff between low-delay, high-reliability, and high-throughput. Table 2–1 illustrates how these bits are used.

- Bit 3: 0 = normal delay, 1 = low delay.
- Bit 4: 0 = normal throughput, 1 = high throughput.
- Bit 5: 0 = normal reliability, 1 = high reliability.
- Bit 6–7: reserved for future use.

The use of the delay, throughput, and reliability indications may increase the cost (in some sense) of the service. In many networks, better performance for one of these parameters is coupled with worse performance on another. Except for very unusual cases, at most two of these three indications should be set. The type of service is used to specify the treatment of the datagram during its transmission through the Internet system. Let's look at each of these choices in a little more depth.

Table 2–1   Type of service bits

Binary	Decimal	Meaning
11100000	224	Network Control
11000000	192	Internetwork Control
10100000	160	Critic/ECP
10000000	128	Flash Override
01100000	96	Flash
01000000	64	Immediate
00100000	32	Priority
00000000	0	Routine
00100000	32	Priority
00010000	16	Low delay
00001000	8	High throughput
00000100	4	High reliability
000000[00]		Reserved for future use

Delay   If you set the delay field to 1, then an IP router will select the route to the destination that has the least delay. For example, an IP router would select a lower-speed terrestrial line over a higher-delay satellite link, even if the satellite link had a higher bandwidth. Interactive sessions such as telnet could request this type of service.

Throughput   When you set throughput to 1, an IP router will select the route with the highest throughput. In the case of the satellite link, it would be selected over the lower-speed terrestrial line from our previous example because it had a higher throughput. If you were using an application such as FTP to download a large file, it would benefit from such service.

Reliability   Again we are granted two choices, normal and high. If we set this field to 1, then when an IP router has to make a decision as to which datagram to discard during periods of congestion, the normal reliability datagrams are discarded first.

Total length field   The next field (16-bits long) is used to indicate the total length of the datagram. This is measured in octets and includes both the Internet header and the data. The size of the field allows the length of a datagram to be up to 65,535 octets. Such long datagrams are impractical for most hosts and networks. All hosts must be prepared to accept datagrams of up to 576 bytes (whether they arrive whole or in fragments). It is recommended that hosts only send datagrams larger than 576 bytes if they have assurance that the destination is prepared to accept the larger datagrams.

The number 576 is selected to allow a reasonable-sized data block to be transmitted in addition to the required header information. For example, this size allows a data block of 512 octets plus 64 header octets to fit in a datagram. The maximum Internet header is 60 bytes, and a typical Internet header is 20 bytes, not counting options, allowing a margin for headers of higher level protocols.

Fragmentation and reassembly   If an IP packet of particular maximum transmission unit (MTU) size is forwarded to a network with a MTU size that is smaller than the current IP datagram size, the datagram must be fragmented. Fragmentation will not occur unless the size of the datagram is equal to or less than the MTU of the network onto which the packet is being forwarded.

Fragmentation can occur at the sending host or at a router. If fragmentation occurs, each fragment is sent with its own IP header with enough information to perform the reassembly at the final destination. The reassembly instructions are contained in the identification, fragmentation flags, and fragment offset fields of the IP header. We look at each of those now.

In Figure 2–5, we can see that the next field is the identification field, which takes up two bytes. This is an identifying value assigned by the sender to aid in assembling the fragments of a datagram. It is used at the final destination to recombine all the fragments of the original IP datagram. The identification field is used for the fragment grouping. The identification field is chosen by the sending node and placed in the original IP datagram without regard as to whether or not fragmentation will occur.

The next field is the flags field, which has three bits allocated to it. The first bit is reserved and must be zero. The next two bits tell us about the fragmentation of the datagram. If Bit 1 is set to 0 then it means the datagram may be fragmented if required to make it over the router. If it is set to 1, it means don't fragment, in which case the datagram would be dropped if a router needed to be able to fragment the datagram and could not because "don't fragment" has been set. In this case, the IP router would drop the datagram and send an ICMP destination unreachable message back to the source. This mechanism is used to aid in Path MTU discovery. We do this with PING as seen in Figure 2–6.

Bit 2 is the more fragments flag, which tells us whether there are more fragments left to transmit. If it is set to 0, it means it is the last fragment; if it is set to 1, then there are more fragments left to come. The more fragments flag is always set to 1 on the first fragment, and on all the middle fragments. It is set to 0 only on the last fragment.

The fragment offset field is 13 bits long and indicates where in the datagram this fragment belongs. The fragment offset is measured in units of eight bytes (64 bits). The first fragment has offset zero. This is used in order to properly reassemble the original IP payload. The payload is fragmented along

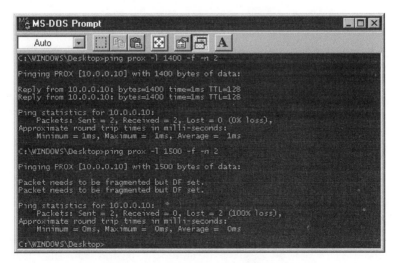

Fig. 2–6 The don't fragment flag set in PING.

eight byte boundaries called fragment blocks, and the value of the fragment offset is the fragment block where the fragment begins. With 13 bits in the fragment offset field, and each number in the count representing eight octets, then a total of 65,536 octet payload can be fragmented into 8,192 fragments. In practice, an IP payload can only be a maximum size of 65,515 (the IP MTU of 65,535 bytes less the minimum size IP header of 20 bytes).

1. Suppose that we have a 1,500-byte IP packet with a 20-byte IP header and a 1,480-byte payload. When fragmented to fit onto a 576-byte network, each fragment will have its own 20-byte IP header, and an IP maximum payload of 552 bytes (which is 69 fragment blocks). When creating fragments, the original IP header is copied (although not all options will necessarily be copied), and then the following fields are changed: header length, TTL, total length, MF, fragment offset, and the header checksum.

2. In the above example, a 1480-byte payload is fragmented into three fragments. The first fragment consists of 69 fragment blocks, the second consists of 69 fragment blocks, and the last segment has 47 fragment blocks.

3. The IP headers for the three fragments will have the following information: fragment 1 will have a total length of 572, the MF flag is set to 1, and the fragment offset is set to 0. Fragment 2 will have a total length of 572, the MF flag is set to 1, and the fragment offset is set to 69. Fragment 3 will have a total length of 396, the MF flag is set to 0, and the fragment offset is set to 138.

Reassembly   The fragments are forwarded by the intermediate IP router to the destination IP address. The fragments may take different paths to the destination and arrive in a different order than the one in which they were sent. The fragments themselves can be fragmented as they travel to their ultimate destination. To reassemble the fragments back into the original payload, IP uses the identification and source IP address fields to group the fragments together.

When the destination node receives the fragments, it allocates reassembly resources. The reassembly resources consist of a data buffer, a header buffer, a fragment block bit table, a total data length field and a timer. If this is the first fragment (the one with the fragment offset set to 0), then its header is placed into the header buffer. If it is the last fragment (the one with the MF flag set to 0), then the total data length is calculated.

The IP standards set the default reassembly timer to 15 seconds. If all the fragments have not been received in this time period, then the fragments will be discarded and an ICMP time exceeded message may be sent back to the source. As the fragments are received, the timer is set to the maximum of the current timer value and the value of the time-to-live field from the received fragment.

As additional fragments arrive, they are placed in the data buffer in order according to the fragment offset and length, and the appropriate bits are set in the fragment block bit table. When the final fragment arrives (when all the fragments in block bit table have been set to 1 for the total length of the original payload), the reassembly is complete and the resulting reconstructed payload is delivered to the appropriate upper-layer protocol.

Fragmentation issues with translational bridging   Translational bridging is used to connect mixed-media networks such as a token ring network and an Ethernet network. A problem could arise in that the MTUs of the two networks are vastly different. On the token ring segment an MTU of between 4,464 and 17,914 is acceptable, while on the Ethernet segment, the MTU is limited to 1,500. If the two segments are connected by a bridge, then we may have a situation where packets are dropped because the bridge cannot fragment the data as a router would be able to do. One solution would be to set the MTU on the NT servers connected to the token ring network to 1,500 to ensure that packets were not dropped due to excessive size. Of course, before doing this, a network monitoring would need to be done to see whether packets were being dropped. If so, then the registry entry below would help.

IN THE REGISTRY:

```
HKEY LOCAL
MACHINE\SYSTEM\CurrentControlSet\Services\adapter\Tcipip\
   parameters
Add a REG DWORD of MTU
This takes a value of from 68 - MTU of the network.
```

The time-to-live field is eight bits long and follows the fragment offset field. This field indicates the maximum time the datagram is allowed to remain in the Internet system. If this field contains the value zero, then the datagram must be destroyed. This field is modified in Internet header processing. The time is measured in units of seconds, but since every module that processes a datagram must decrease the TTL by at least one even if it process the datagram in less than a second, the TTL must be thought of only as an upper bound on the time a datagram may exist. The intention is to cause undeliverable datagrams to be discarded, and to bind the maximum datagram lifetime. The default TTL in Windows NT version 3.5X is 32 seconds; in Windows NT 4.0, it was raised to 128 seconds. This setting essentially is a limit on how many routers an IP datagram can pass through before being discarded. This setting can be changed in the registry as seen on the next page:

> **IN THE REGISTRY:**
>
> ```
> HKEY LOCAL
> MACHINE\SYSTEM\CurrentControlSet\Services\Tcipip\parameters
> Add a REG DWORD of DefaultTTL
> This takes a value of from 1 to 255
> ```

The protocol field is next and indicates the next level protocol used in the data portion of the Internet datagram. Eight bits are used to carry this information. The values for various protocols are specified in "Assigned Numbers."

The header checksum field is next with 16 bits being allocated for a checksum on the header only. Since some header fields change (e.g., time-to-live), this is recomputed and verified at each point that the Internet header is processed. The checksum algorithm is the 16-bit ones complement of the ones complement sum of all 16-bit words in the header. For purposes of computing the checksum, the value of the checksum field is zero.

The next two fields are the source IP address, and the destination IP address. These are four octets each. This is where we find the IP addresses involved in the data exchange. Although this is an important field, we are not going to spend a lot of time on this as it could easily lead us into discussions of routing, broadcasting, and the like. We will look at those issues later when we visit the issue of network traffic.

The options field is the next one, and it may or may not appear in datagrams. They must be implemented by all IP modules (host and gateways). What is optional is their transmission in any particular datagram, not their implementation. In some environments, the security option may be required in all datagrams. The option field is variable in length. The IP options will vary in size from a single octet to 40 octets. This would give a maximum IP header size of 60 bytes. There may be zero or more options. Each option begins with the option type code. This code is divided into three fields, the first of which is the copy field. If this field is set to 1, then the option must be copied to all fragments. If it is set to 0, then it is used only in the first fragment. The next two bits in the option code octet are used to indicate the class of option being used. If this is 0, then it is a datagram or network control; if 2, then it is used for debugging or measurement. The others are reserved. The next five bits are used to indicate the option number within the option class.

The second octet is the option length, which includes the option type code and the length octet, the pointer octet, and length of three bytes of route data. The third octet is the pointer into the route data indicating the octet that begins the next source address to be processed. The pointer is relative to this option, and the smallest legal value for the pointer is 4. Let's look at a few of these options and see what they look like. These options are listed in Table 2–2.

Table 2-2 Option classes and numbers

Option Class	Option Number	Option meaning
Class 0	Option 0	A one-octet option used to indicate the end of an option list. It is copied to each fragment
Class 0	Option 1	A one-octet option used to align octets in a list of options. It is copied to each fragment
Class 0	Option 3	Loose source routing. Variable length option used to route a datagram through a specified path where alternate routes can be taken. It is copied to each fragment.
Class 0	Option 7	Record route. Variable length option used to trace a route through an IP network. It is not copied to each fragment.
Class 0	Option 9	Strict source routing. Variable length option used to route a datagram through a specified path where alternate routes cannot be taken. (Contrast with Option 3 above). It is copied to each fragment.
Class 2	Option 4	Internet timestamp. Variable length option used to record a series of timestamps at each hop. It is not copied to each fragment.

Record route option   The record route option allows a sending note to create an IP header with a series of blank IP addresses as IP options. As the IP datagram travels through the network, each router encountered adds its IP address to the list, thereby recording the route taken to the destination. There has to be enough room allocated in the IP record route option to hold the IP addresses. The size of these fields is determined by the sending computer. As we see in the listing below, the sending computer sets the option field to 0x7, which indicates that it is using the record route option. The next field is the option length field, which is a variable length field in octets set by the sending machine. The next slot pointer field is next, and it is used to specify the octet offset in the record route option field, where the next available slot begins for the recording the IP addresses of the route.

```
IP: ID = 0x1F3D; Proto = ICMP; Len: 92
    IP: Version = 4 (0x4)
    IP: Header Length = 52 (0x34)
  + IP: Service Type = 0 (0x0)
    IP: Total Length = 92 (0x5C)
    IP: Identification = 7997 (0x1F3D)
  + IP: Flags Summary = 0 (0x0)
    IP: Fragment Offset = 0 (0x0) bytes
```

```
          IP: Time to Live = 32 (0x20)
          IP: Protocol = ICMP - Internet Control Message
          IP: Checksum = 0x3639
          IP: Source Address = 206.112.203.201
          IP: Destination Address = 206.112.201.97
          IP: Option Fields = 7 (0x7)
             IP: Record Route Option = 7 (0x7)
          IP: Option Length = 31 (0x1F)
          IP: Next Slot Pointer = 4 (0x4)
          IP: Route Traveled = 0 (0x0)
       IP: End of Options = 0 (0x0)
    IP: Data: Number of data bytes remaining = 40 (0x0028)
```

Now we want to look at the response we get back from our destination. As we see in the printout below, much of the information looks the same; however, now we have filled out some additional information. We are most interested in the route taken to our destination. We see the IP addresses that were used to fill in the router information as the IP datagram passed along to its destination. There are a maximum of nine slots available that can be allocated by the sending computer. In this example, we used three of them.

```
   IP: ID = 0xFC5; Proto = ICMP; Len: 92
       IP: Version = 4 (0x4)
       IP: Header Length = 52 (0x34)
     + IP: Service Type = 0 (0x0)
       IP: Total Length = 92 (0x5C)
       IP: Identification = 4037 (0xFC5)
     + IP: Flags Summary = 0 (0x0)
       IP: Fragment Offset = 0 (0x0) bytes
       IP: Time to Live = 125 (0x7D)
       IP: Protocol = ICMP - Internet Control Message
       IP: Checksum = 0x56EE
       IP: Source Address = 206.112.201.97
       IP: Destination Address = 206.112.203.201
       IP: Option Fields = 7 (0x7)
          IP: Record Route Option = 7 (0x7)
          IP: Option Length = 31 (0x1F)
          IP: Next Slot Pointer = 16 (0x10)
          IP: Route Traveled = 206 (0xCE)
             IP: Gateway = 206.112.201.126
             IP: Gateway = 206.112.201.97
             IP: Gateway = 206.112.196.82
          IP: End of Options = 0 (0x0)
       IP: Data: Number of data bytes remaining = 40 (0x0028)
```

The above listings were done by using the Windows NT PING command and using the –r option. This sends an ICMP Echo request message that records the route taken.

Loose source routing   Normally we allow our routers and Windows NT to make routing decisions based upon the routing tables. However, there are times—when we are troubleshooting, testing, or debugging our network—when we need the ability to specify a route to a destination, without the bother of modifying our routing tables. When we override the path that would normally be taken, we are engaging in IP source routing. IP supports two kinds of source routing: loose source routing and strict source routing. We will look at loose source routing first.

In loose source routing, the IP datagram is addressed to the next router using the destination IP address from the IP header. The good thing about a loose source route is that you can specify a router that is several hops away. Let us look at the option field when we use loose source routing. In the printout below, we see the option code field is set to 131. This tells us that we are using the loose source routing option. This is seen in Figure 2–7.

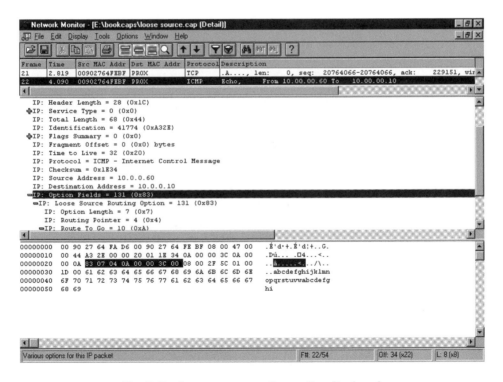

Fig. 2–7   Loose source routing option displayed.

```
IP: ID = 0xA32E; Proto = ICMP; Len: 68
       IP: Version = 4 (0x4)
       IP: Header Length = 28 (0x1C)
   +   IP: Service Type = 0 (0x0)
       IP: Total Length = 68 (0x44)
       IP: Identification = 41774 (0xA32E)
   +   IP: Flags Summary = 0 (0x0)
       IP: Fragment Offset = 0 (0x0) bytes
       IP: Time to Live = 32 (0x20)
       IP: Protocol = ICMP - Internet Control Message
       IP: Checksum = 0x1E34
       IP: Source Address = 10.0.0.60
       IP: Destination Address = 10.0.0.10
       IP: Option Fields = 131 (0x83)
           IP: Loose Source Routing Option = 131 (0x83)
               IP: Option Length = 7 (0x7)
               IP: Routing Pointer = 4 (0x4)
               IP: Route To Go = 10 (0xA)
                   IP: Gateway = 10.0.0.60
           IP: End of Options = 0 (0x0)
   IP: Data: Number of data bytes remaining = 40 (0x0028)
```

The option length field above is the length in bytes taken by the 131 option. This field is set by the sending machine. In this instance, we are using seven bytes for our loose source routing option. The routing pointer is used to specify the octet offset in the 131 option fields to indicate where the router data begins. In this instance, we count over four bytes from the beginning of the option field and we see the first router IP address in hex. We can see this highlighted in Figure 2–7. If we look in the hex pane (at the bottom of the screen), we see that the option field begins with an 83 (the hex value of 131 the loose source routing option code). Now, our offset is specified by the 04, which tells where the first router IP address is located at in our data. By counting over four numbers from the 83, we come to 0A (10 in hex), which is the first octet of our router's IP address.

We can force ping to do a loose source route by using the –j option. The command would look like PING –j 10.0.0.10 10.0.0.60. The first address specified is the destination, and the second and following addresses are the routers to use towards the destination. This is illustrated in Figure 2–8.

Strict source routing option   The strict source routing option looks very much like the loose source route. As we can see in the printout on the next page, the fields look nearly identical to the loose source option. We have the option code field, which in this instance displays 137. This is the code for the strict source routing option. It is 0x89 in hex and what we see in the printouts. The next field is the option length, which is also seven in this in-

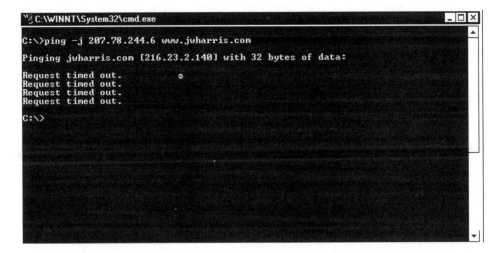

Fig. 2–8 The loose source routing option specifies the route to a destination.

stance. This would vary according to the number of hops you specified for the destination. It is set by the sending machine just as before. The routing pointer is used to mark the beginning of the data for the first router, as was the case in the loose source routing option.

You can perform strict source routing for testing purposes by using the PING command with the –k option. For instance, you could type PING –k 10.0.0.10 10.0.0.60. The first address specified is the destination, and the second and following addresses are the routers to use towards the destination. You cannot do something like this using the TRACERT command.

```
IP: ID = 0xA32E; Proto = ICMP; Len: 68
    IP: Version = 4 (0x4)
    IP: Header Length = 28 (0x1C)
  + IP: Service Type = 0 (0x0)
    IP: Total Length = 68 (0x44)
    IP: Identification = 41774 (0xA32E)
  + IP: Flags Summary = 0 (0x0)
    IP: Fragment Offset = 0 (0x0) bytes
    IP: Time to Live = 32 (0x20)
    IP: Protocol = ICMP - Internet Control Message
    IP: Checksum = 0x1E34
    IP: Source Address = 10.0.0.60
    IP: Destination Address = 10.0.0.10
    IP: Option Fields = 131 (0x83)
```

```
        IP: Loose Source Routing Option = 131 (0x83)
            IP: Option Length = 7 (0x7)
            IP: Routing Pointer = 4 (0x4)
            IP: Route To Go = 10 (0xA)
                IP: Gateway = 10.0.0.60
        IP: End of Options = 0 (0x0)
    IP: Data: Number of data bytes remaining = 40 (0x0028)
```

Internet timestamp option   The Internet timestamp option works in a similar manner as the record route option in that the sending node creates a series of blank spaces that are filled in by the routers in the path to the destination. The entries are the IP address of the router and the time stamp. The time stamp is a 32-bit integer that is the number of milliseconds since midnight universal time (also known as Greenwich Mean Time). If universal time is not available to the router, then it can use something else, but it must indicate that it is using nonuniversal time by setting the high order bit in the timestamp field to 1. The option code is 68 (0x44), which tells us that we are using the Internet timestamp option. The option length field is set by the sender machine, but it has a maximum length of 40 octets including the option type, length, pointer, and overflow flag fields. As we see in our listing, the time pointer field tells us where the timestamp begins. It is an offset from the beginning of the option 68 field. The smallest legal value for this field is five, which is what we have in our printout below.

The next field is the flag field, and it will use 0 to record time stamps only, without the IP addresses, 1 to precede the timestamp with the IP address, and 3 to specify the sending node and a time stamp if it matches the next router IP address. In our printout below, we have the 1 flag set, which is the most common use of this flag.

The size of this option does not change with the number of timestamps collected. If the allocated area for timestamps is exceeded, then the missed stations field will be incremented. The gateway and time point fields are used to hold the IP address and the timestamp. These are filled in by the router when replying to the datagram.

```
    IP: ID = 0xC4BA; Proto = ICMP; Len: 72
        IP: Version = 4 (0x4)
        IP: Header Length = 32 (0x20)
      + IP: Service Type = 0 (0x0)
        IP: Total Length = 72 (0x48)
        IP: Identification = 50362 (0xC4BA)
      + IP: Flags Summary = 0 (0x0)
        IP: Fragment Offset = 0 (0x0) bytes
        IP: Time to Live = 32 (0x20)
        IP: Protocol = ICMP - Internet Control Message
        IP: Checksum = 0x57E1
```

```
IP: Source Address = 206.112.203.201
IP: Destination Address = 206.112.201.97
IP: Option Fields = 68 (0x44)
    IP: Internet Timestamp Option = 68 (0x44)
        IP: Option Length = 12 (0xC)
        IP: Time pointer = 5 (0x5)
        IP: ..0001 = Both time stamps and IP addresses
        IP: Missed stations = 0 (0x0)
        IP: Time Route = 0 (0x0)
            IP: Gateway = 0.0.0.0
            IP: Time Point = 0 (0x0)
            IP: Gateway = 8.0.88.91
            IP: Time Point = 50393600 (0x300F200)
IP: Data: Number of data bytes remaining = 40 (0x0028)
```

CHAPTER REVIEW

In this chapter we have covered a ton of material, much of it very detailed, some of it obscure, but none esoteric. The time we spend here will pay great dividends when we are trying to troubleshoot a vexatious problem, or attempting to get our arms around a noisy network. Knowing the protocols, identifying the parts of a frame, packet, or datagram are crucial skills for any would-be network-sniffer maestro.

We really only looked at two things: TCP and IP. But wow, what a lot to chew on that was!

IN THE NEXT CHAPTER

In the next chapter we look at the SPX/IPX protocol. We will take a good look at the header structure of both protocols. We look at the function of network numbers, and reserved network numbers. We will talk about socket numbers and IPX routing. Then, we will conclude with looking at the message header structures.

The SPX/IPX Protocol

$\mathbf{T}$he SPX/IPX protocol is a still a common occurrence on many corporate networks. It is a fast, small protocol associated with Novell NetWare. A relatively efficient protocol, it is able to route. We are now going to look at it and see some of the things associated with this protocol. We will first examine the sequenced packet exchange (SPX) part of the SPX/IPX protocol.

SPX PROTOCOL

The SPX protocol is a connection-oriented protocol that typically rides on top of the IPX (internetwork packet exchange). It is similar in functionality to the TCP portion of the TCP/IP protocol suite. SPX provides connection control to enable two-way communication, thereby ensuring a steady flow of data. It has the intelligence to establish a connection with its peer on another machine, negotiate buffer size, and ensure proper delivery and receipt of data. It uses sequence numbers and a combination of acknowledgements (ACKS) and non-acknowledgements (NAKS) to make this happen. It does not, however, perform packet-size negotiation as TCP does (although SPX II is able to do packet-size negotiation).

SPX Header

Let us now take a look at the 12-byte SPX header. The network monitor trace in Figure 3–1 shows where SPX is found. Essentially, we have the Ethernet header, the IPX header, and then the SPX header.

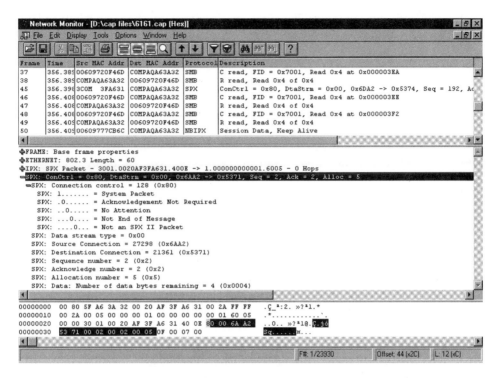

Fig. 3–1 The SPX header follows the Ethernet and IPX headers.

SPX header is made up of the following seven fields.

- Connection Control—1 Byte
- DataStream Type—1 Byte
- Source Connection ID—2 Bytes
- Destination Connection ID—2 Bytes
- Sequence Number—2 Bytes
- Acknowledgment Number—2 Bytes
- Allocation Number—2 Bytes

Connection control   Let us now look at some of the functions provided by the connection-control field. Equivalent to the TCP flags we looked at in Chapter 2, connection control provides the mechanism for bi-directional flow of data, congestion control, and other related capabilities. The connection-control field indicates essentially three types of connection-control packets. These values either can be logical or they can be set together with multiple flags. The first one we want to look at is the end-of-message flag.

- End-of-message flag. The end-of-message flag is set when 0x10 appears in the connection control field. It is used to indicate the end of a message to the transmission partner. Because SPX is a message-based transport protocol, the sending side sets this flag to indicate that the message is complete. After the receiving side gets this packet, it will pass the data in the message buffer to the application above. This is not an end-of-connection request, but rather it indicates that the current message exchange has ended.

- Acknowledgment-Required flag. The acknowledgment-required flag is set when 0x40 appears in the connection-control field. This is used to indicate that data has been sent to a transmission partner and that an acknowledgment is required. The acknowledgment for this packet must be received before more data will be sent.

- SPX needs an acknowledgment of the data sent and, once it is received, sets the flag to signal an "end-of-message" to the partner. The number is the combination of 0x40 and 0x10, which equals 0x50.

- System-Packet flag. The system-packet flag is set when 0x80 appears in the connection-control field. This is an acknowledgment packet used internally by the SPX protocol to confirm that the session partner is up and the connection is still in place. It is an "I am here" type of message.

- System-Packet combination flag. The system-packet combination flag is set when 0xC0 appears in the connection-control field. 0xC0 is 0x80 and 0x40 added together. It is used internally by SPX to ensure that the connection is still in place by requiring an acknowledgement (ACK) from the communications partner. This is the "Are you still there?" packet.

DataStream type   The DataStream field tells us what type of data is carried inside the packet. It can be set to a specific number defined by the application through Winsock. The most important function of this field is to provide a graceful method to disconnect a session. By default, it will be one of the following two values:

- End-of-Connection. If the DataStream type is set to 0xFE, then a session partner wants to terminate the session.

- End-of-Connection. If the DataStream type is set to 0xFF, then the packet is being transmitted because an end-of-connection request has been received.

Some of the other entries found in this field include the numbers listed in Table 3–1.

Table 3–1   Common DataStream field types

Field number	Meaning
0	Data portion of packet has information that needs to be printed.
1	Stop printing and clear the buffers.
2	Stop printing, but keep the current data and wait for more instructions.
3	Restart the print job using the data buffers.
4	Stop printing from the data buffers, and use the data registered in the sideband. The sideband data field has three activities: (a) count, (b) character to print, and (c) the end character.
5	Start a new print job packet.
6	Hands control to a process rather than to a print server.
7	Brings back the printer from the process and returns it to the print server.
8	End of job.
254	End of connection.
255	End of connection ACK.

Source and destination connection ID   We are now at the third and fourth fields of the seven fields in the SPX header. The source and destination connection ID fields occupy two bytes and are used to demultiplex SPX sessions over a single socket at the IPX level. If we are looking at traces and we see the destination connection ID set to 0XFFFF, then we know that this is an initial-connection packet.

Sequence number   The fifth field in the SPX header is the sequence number field. This is a two-byte field containing the data packets transmitted counter. This number will increase after a data-packet transmitted acknowledgment is received.

Acknowledge number   The sixth field is the acknowledge number field, which tells us the next SPX packet sequence number that is expected from the SPX partner.

Allocation number   The last field in the SPX header is the allocation number field. This field tells us the number of receive buffers that are available at a workstation. This number is almost always larger than the acknowledge number. The availability of free buffers is calculated as a Window size that is equal to the allocation number minus the acknowledge number plus one. This field is used as a flow control mechanism. It works like this: When the receiving side sends an allocation number lower than the acknowledgment number, the sender will not send any more data until the receiving side sends a packet with an allocation number greater than the acknowledge number.

Example of establishing a connection   The network monitor trace shown below shows the sequence for a successful session initialization. Notice that the destination connection ID is set to 0xFFFF, and the allocation number is 0xFFFF. This sequence of packets is called an SPX handshake.

```
SPX: ConCtrl = 0xC0, DtaStrm = 0x00, 0xE8A2 -> 0xFFFF, Seq = 0, Ack = 0,
Alloc
= 65535
SPX: ConCtrl = 0x80, DtaStrm = 0x00, 0x9774 -> 0xE8A2, Seq = 0, Ack = 0,
Alloc
= 3
```

Example of normal data flow   The network monitor trace below shows a successful data transmission. Notice how the Seq and ACK relate, and notice that the allocation number (Alloc) is always more than the ACK.

```
SPX: ConCtrl = 0x80, DtaStrm = 0x00, 0xE8A2 -> 0x9774, Seq = 7, Ack = 8,
Alloc = 9
SPX: ConCtrl = 0x50, DtaStrm = 0x00, 0x9774 -> 0xE8A2, Seq = 8, Ack = 7,
Alloc = 10
SPX: ConCtrl = 0x80, DtaStrm = 0x00, 0xE8A2 -> 0x9774, Seq = 7, Ack = 9,
Alloc = 10
SPX: ConCtrl = 0xC0, DtaStrm = 0x00, 0x9774 -> 0xE8A2, Seq = 9, Ack = 7,
Alloc = 10
```

Example of a graceful session closed   The network monitor trace below shows a successful session termination sequence. Notice that the DtaStrm field is set to indicate the end of connection request and response.

```
SPX: ConCtrl = 0x50, DtaStrm = End of Connection Req., 0xE8A2 -> 0x9774,
Seq = 10, Ack = 10, Alloc = 12
SPX: ConCtrl = 0x00, DtaStrm = End of Connection Resp., 0x9774 -> 0xE8A2,
Seq = 10, Ack = 11, Alloc = 14
```

General tips for reading SPX traces   The following tips can be helpful to narrow down problems.

- You may see multiple session IDs coming from the same computer. Try to isolate the trace for a particular session ID to verify that it is normal.

- Look for the number of hops and the physical layer Ethernet vs. Token Ring. The problem may be related to routers in between or the packet size. Remember that SPX does not do packet negotiation.
- Look for the allocation number and verify that it is larger than the acknowledge number. This to verify that we are not running any of the buffer overflow problem. This mostly happens with 16-bit real-mode clients.
- Check for any retransmission of data packets. Normally, a retransmission problem will show up as a performance issue. Check for the time delta in between the data and ACK packet to check whether there is time latency.

Limitations of the SPX protocol   Although SPX provides a connection-oriented transport, SPX does have several limitations.

- Only one packet can be outstanding at any time.
- SPX-based communication does not do any packet negotiation.

NOTE: The above limitations apply only to the SPX protocol. SPX II is an advanced version of SPX with the following improvements:

- SPX II uses the maximum packet size allowable on the network. Example: 1518 bytes on Ethernet (SPX has a 576-byte maximum).
- SPX II Windowing allows multiple outstanding packets and is able to transmit a negative acknowledgment (NAK) to indicate some packets were not received.
- SPX II allows packet size negotiation. A negotiate-size-request packet can be sent at any time in the communications process if packets are not getting through to the destination.

Source-connection ID This field contains a two-byte SPX connection number that is assigned by the source SPX station and is used to keep track of the different virtual SPX connections that a socket can support. This number will appear in the destination-connection ID when packets are coming in from the connection partner to this station.

Destination-connection ID This field contains a two-byte SPX connection number that is assigned to the destination SPX station. This is used to keep track of the different virtual SPX connections that a socket can support. This number will appear in the source-connection ID when packets are sent out to the connection partner.

Sequence number SPX assigns a sequence number to each data packet sent to the connection partner. This number is incremented when the data packet is acknowledged. This ensures a sequenced packet transmission from the source-connection partner to the destination-connection partner. This field is not incremented for packets that do not contain data (system packets).

Acknowledgment number   This is the expected sequence number for the next data packet from the destination-connection partner. This field is not incremented for packets that do not contain data (system packets).

Allocation number   This number is used to calculate how many buffers are available to receive packets sent from the destination connection. This number corresponds to the sequence number of the packet that is being prepared to be sent but has not yet been sent. The source connection cannot exceed the allocation number. As the source connection generates a listen ECB (event control block), SPX increments the allocation number. This field is not incremented for packets that do not contain data (system packets).

Data   The data entry (if there is any) contains any data or codes that are being sent to and from the server.

The socket field indicates an SPX packet being sent from the client to the server. The server's client socket is 8060. The packet also contains some pertinent SPX data for connection purposes. The connection-control entry under the SPX header shows code C0h, meaning that the packet is a system packet that requires an acknowledgment from the server as it is received.

IPX PROTOCOL

The IPX protocol is a connectionless-layer three-datagram protocol. Novell adapted it from the old Xerox Network Systems (XNS) Internet Datagram Protocol (IDP protocol).

Connectionless Protocol

Since it is connectionless, when a process running on a particular node uses IPX to communicate with a process on another node, no connection between the two nodes is established. Thus, IPX packets are addressed and sent to their destinations, but there is no guarantee or verification of successful delivery. Any packet acknowledgment or connection control is provided by protocols above IPX, such as SPX. The term **datagram** means that each packet is treated as an individual entity, having no logical or sequential relation to any other packet.

Operates at the OSI Network Layer

As a network-layer protocol, IPX addresses and routes packets from one location to another on an IPX internetwork. IPX makes its routing decisions by looking at the address fields of the header and on the information it receives from RIP or NLSP. IPX uses this information to forward packets to their destination node or to the next router providing a path to the destination node.

Packet Structure

Because the IPX protocol was adapted from the old XNS IDP protocol, it comes as no surprise that the two packet structures are similar. The IPX packet is made up of two parts. The first part is a 30-byte header which has the network, node, and socket addresses for both the destination and the source machines. The second part is the **data** section, which sometimes has the header of a higher-level protocol, such as SPX. The minimum IPX packet is 30 bytes (not counting the MAC header). The maximum size of routed IPX packets used to be only 576 bytes including both the IPX header and the data payload. Under IPX II, however, that number grows to 1,500 bytes.

As we noted with TCP in Chapter 2, the network layer follows the MAC header, so IPX is placed after the MAC header and before the payload. Figure 3–2 shows that the IPX header is wrapped by the MAC protocol in a similar manner as that shown in Chapter 2.

Let us now look at the structure of the IPX header. It is comprised of the following fields:

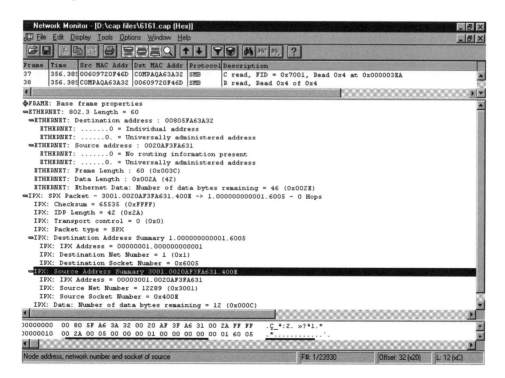

Fig. 3–2 The IPX header is wrapped by the MAC protocol.

- checksum
- packet length
- transport control
- packet type
- destination network
- destination node
- destination socket
- source network
- source node
- source socket

Checksum.   The checksum field is used to ensure packet integrity. The checksum is used by the newer versions of Netware because the 3.x and earlier versions set the field to 0xFFFF and did not use the checksum.

Packet length   The packet length field is the length of the IPX header plus the length of the data in bytes. The packet length must be at least 30 bytes to allow enough room for the IPX header.

Transport control   Transport control is the number of routers a packet has traversed on the way to its destination. This field is always set to zero by the sending nodes when they are building the IPX packet. When the router receives the packet, if it needs further routing to reach the final destination, then it will increment the field by one, and forward the packet.

Packet type   The packet type field indicates the kind of service that is either offered by or required by the packet. Table 3–2 below lists some of the common packet types you are likely to come across in your network traces.

Table 3–2   IPX/SPX packet types

Packet Type	Field value (hex)	Purpose
NLSP	0x00	NLSP packets
Routing information	0x01	RIP packets
Service advertising	0x04	SAP packets
Sequenced	0x05	SPX packets
NCP	0x11	NCP packets
Propagated	0x14	NetBIOS and other propagated packets

Destination network   The destination network is the network number to which the destination node is attached. When a sending computer sets this field to 0x0 the destination node is assumed to be on the same network segment as the sending node.

A special case exists when a workstation sends SAP Get Nearest Server and RIP Get Local Target (or Route Request) broadcast requests at initialization time. Because the workstation does not yet know to which network it belongs, it sets both the source-network and destination-network fields to 0 for these requests. When a router receives one of these requests, it sends a reply directly to the sending workstation, filling in the source-network and destination-network fields with the appropriate network numbers.

NOTE: IPX does not have a broadcast network number (such as 0xFFFFFFFF).

In addition to network number 0, the numbers 0xFFFFFFFF and 0xFFFFFFFE are reserved for specific purposes. For this reason, they should not be assigned to any IPX network. For more information about reserved network numbers, refer to the section on reserved numbers below.

Destination node   The destination-node field contains the physical address of the destination node. A node on an Ethernet network will use all six bytes of this field to define its address. Some other network access methods may use fewer than all six bytes here. A node address of 0xFFFFFFFFFFFF (that is, six bytes of 0xFF) broadcasts the packet to all nodes on the destination network.

Destination socket   The destination-socket field is the socket address of the packet destination process. These sockets will route the packets to different processes inside a single machine.

NOTE: IPX does not have a broadcast socket number (such as 0xFFFF).

Source metwork   The source-network field is the network number to which the source node is attached. If a sending node sets this field to zero, that means that the local network of the source machine is unknown. For routers, the rules that apply to the destination-network field also apply to the source-network field, except that routers can propagate packets that were received with this field set to zero.

Source node   The source-node field is the MAC address of the source node. Broadcast addresses are not allowed.

Source socket   The source socket is the address of the process that transmitted the packet. Processes communicating in a peer-to-peer fashion do not need to send and receive on the same socket number. On a network of workstations and servers, the server usually "listens" on a specific socket for service requests. In such a case, the source socket is not necessarily the same or even significant. All that matters is that the server reply to the source socket. For example, all NetWare file servers have the same socket address, but requests to them can originate from any socket number.

Source-socket numbers follow the same conventions as those for destination sockets.

Higher-level protocol headers   The higher-level protocol headers are protocols, such as NCP or SPX. These headers are often found in the data portion of the IPX packet.

IPX Addressing

Let us now look at IPX addressing. As shown in Table 3–3, IPX has its own node (intranetwork) and intranode addressing. For node addressing, IPX uses the MAC address that was assigned to the network interface card by the manufacturer of the card itself.

The IPX network address uniquely identifies an IPX server on an IPX network and individual processes within the server. An IPX address is a 12-byte hexadecimal number that can be divided into three parts. The first part of the IPX address is a 4-byte network number that is used for routing operations. The next component of the IPX address is the longest part which is the six-byte hardware address of the network adapter. The last part is the two-byte socket number which is used to refer to an actual process running on the machine. Table 3–3 shows what the address looks like.

Each number in an IPX address is contained in a field in the IPX header and represents a source or destination network, node, or socket. The network number is used only for network-layer operations, namely, routing. The node number is used for local, or same-segment, packet transmission. The socket number directs a packet to a process operating within a node.

Each address component is described in the following sections.

Network Number

The IPX four-byte hexadecimal address network number is used for IPX packet routing. Each segment is assigned a unique network number used by routers to forward packets to their final destination on the network.

Table 3–3   IPX address parsed

Network number	Mac address	Process socket number
00000001	006008A1D4B4	435

An IPX network number can contain up to eight digits, including zeros, although leading zeros are usually not displayed. For example, 0x00003001, 0x12345678, and 0xB9 are all valid network numbers.

Reserved Network Numbers

The destination network of an IPX packet is typically an IPX network to which a unique network number has been assigned. However, three network numbers 0x0, 0xFFFFFFFF, and 0xFFFFFFFE are reserved because they have special meanings. Table 3–4 illustrates these numbers.

Both RIP and NLSP recognize 0xFFFFFFFE as the default route. On a RIP network, a RIP router that connects the LAN to a larger network infrastructure, such as a corporate backbone, typically advertises the default route.

Internal Network Number

Microsoft's Services for NetWare, as well as the NetWare 3.x and 4.x servers use an internal network number. This hexadecimal number must be between one and eight digits long. This number is typically assigned at installation. The internal network number is used for services and routing of IPX packets to physical networks.

Node Number

The node number is a six-byte hexadecimal number used to uniquely identify a device in an IPX environment. This number is identical to the physical address of the network interface card that connects the device to the network.

The IPX header contains both a destination-node and a source-node field. Since the node numbers are the same as those in the network interface card addresses, these fields contain the same destination and source ad-

Table 3–4   Reserved network numbers

Number	Meaning
0x00000000	The local network segment. When a router receives a packet with the destination network ID of 0, both the source and destination are considered to be on the same segment.
0xFFFFFFFF	This is the all-routes-request packet. When a router receives a packet with the destination network ID of FFFFFFFF it responds with all the routes it knows about.
0xFFFFFFFE	This is the default route that is the destination for all IPX packets that have an unknown destination network.

dresses we find in the MAC header. A workstation running IPX/SPX, for example, uses the destination-node address to locate and forward packets to another workstation on the same network segment.

The IPX node number only has to be unique on the same network segment. For example, a node on network 3001 can use the number 006008A1D4B4, and a node on network 3002 can also use the number 006008A1D4B4. This works the same as the IP protocol since the host address can be the same on different IP networks. Because each node has a different network number, IPX recognizes each node as having a legitimate, unique address.

Socket Number

A two-byte hexadecimal socket number identifies the destination of process within the node. This can be something like routing (RIP) or advertising (SAP operating within the device). Since several processes typically operate at any given time, the socket number provides a type of "mail slot" used by each process to identify itself to IPX.

When a process needs to communicate on the network it requests a socket number. Any packets received by IPX addressed to the socket are then forwarded to the process. Socket numbers provide a quick method of routing packets within a node. These work in a similar fashion as Windows Sockets or TCP/IP port numbers. They are essentially logical destinations on a remote machine for interprocess communication. Table 3–5 below lists some common socket numbers and processes typically found in a fairly active network.

Socket numbers between 0x4000 and 0x7FFF are dynamic sockets; these are created on the fly when a workstation needs to communicate with a file server or other network devices. Socket numbers between 0x8000 and 0xFFFF are well-known sockets; Novell assigns these to specific processes. For example, 0x9001 is the socket number that identifies NLSP. Software de-

Table 3–5　Common IPX/SPX socket numbers and processes

Socket Number	Process
0x451	NCP
0x452	SAP
0x453	RIP
0x455	Novell NetBIOS
0x456	Diagnostics
0x9001	NLSP
0x9004	IPXWAN™ protocol

velopers writing NetWare applications can contact Novell to reserve well-known sockets.

How IPX Routing Works

When different IPX network segments are interconnected, the instructions for routing the packets between these segments come from the IPX protocol. IPX performs these layer-three functions with the help of RIP, SAP, and NLSP.

If two workstations are on the same network segment, the sending workstation sends packets directly to the destination workstation's physical address (i.e., the MAC address). If the two workstations are on two different network segments, then the first workstation must find a router on its own segment that knows how to forward the packets to the foreign segment.

In order to find this all-important router, our workstation will send out a RIP broadcast packet requesting the fastest route to the destination segment. The same segment router with the shortest path to the destination segment will respond to the request. In the response packet, the router will include its own network and node address in the IPX header.

Obviously, if the sending node is a router instead of a workstation, then it will not need to send out a RIP broadcast to obtain this information. Instead, the router looks up the information from its internal routing table.

Once the sending workstation has the router's address, it sends the packets to the destination workstation by placing the complete destination IPX address (i.e., network, node, and socket number) in the destination field of the IPX header as we saw earlier in the chapter.

Then the sending workstation places its own complete IPX address in the corresponding source field of the IPX header. The sending workstation will also fill out all other fields in the header as well. For instance it will place the node address of the router that responded to the RIP request in the destination-address field of the MAC header. It will place its own address in the source-address field of the MAC header.

The sending workstation finally sends the packet to the router, which now has several tasks to perform. First, the router looks at the Transport Control field of the IPX packet header. The RIP router will discard the packet if this field is greater than 16. If a NLSP router received the packet it will discard it if the number is greater than the hop count limit.

The router now examines the IPX header Packet Type field. If the router sees 20 (0x14) in this field, it indicates that it is a NetBIOS packet and it must also look at the transport-control field. If this value is eight or greater, the router discards the packet because a NetBIOS packet is limited to eight hops (or networks).

The router now compares the network number in the packet to the network number of the segment in which the packet came. If the router finds a match, then it discards the packet to prevent looping. If the network number does not match, then it places the network address in the next available network-number field. It increments the transport-control field and broadcasts the packet to all directly connected network segments that are not in the network-number fields.

The router will now check the destination-address fields to determine how to route the packet. If the packet is addressed to the router, the appropriate socket process will handle it internally; otherwise, the router forwards the packet. In addition to packets directly addressed to the router, it must also deal with 0xFFFFFFFFFFFF, which are usually only RIP, SAP, or diagnostic packets.

If the packet needs to be forwarded, the router places the destination-node address from the IPX header into the destination-address field of the MAC header. The router then places its own address into the source-address field of the MAC header, increments the transport-control field of the IPX header, and forwards the packet to the destination segment. If however, the transport-control field equals the maximum allowable hop count before the field is incremented, the router discards the packet. For RIP routers, this is 16; for NLSP routers, this limit is configurable between 8 and 127.

Broadcast packets are never rebroadcast onto the network segment from which they are received. If the router is not directly connected to the segment on which the final destination node resides, it sends the packet to the next router in the path to the destination node, by putting the node address of the next router in the destination-address field of the MAC header. The router gets this information from its routing information table and then places its own node address in the source-address field of the MAC header, increments the transport-control field in the IPX header and forwards the packet to the next router.

NCP   Each NCP is known primarily by its number, which is made up of three fields. For example, the number for change bindery object password is 0x2222 23 64.

- The first one-word field, "0x2222," is a service category field.
- The second number, "23," is the function number which identifies where in the switch table a generic function exists.
- The third field, "64," identifies the specific NCP function that is executed.

The NCP numbers are divided into loose functional categories. For example, most number 23 functions are accounting, bindery, connection, or file server NCPs. Table 3–6 lists some common NCP service categories.

Table 3–6   NCP service categories

NCP number	Service category
0x1111	Create a service connection
0x2222	Service request
0x3333	Service response
0x5555	Destroy a service connection
0x7777	Packet burst request
0x9999	Previous request still being processed (busy)

It may be rather intuitive that the service request category NCPs (0x2222) and the service response category NCPs (0x3333) are the most commonly used. There are two service categories that do not need a service-response (0x3333) packet generated. These are the destroy service connection (0x5555) and packet burst request (0x7777) NCPs.

If the term previous request still being processed (0x9999) is sent back to the client, it means that the client made another request or resent the same request while the server is still processing the last request made by the same client. This is the NCP way of saying, "hold your horses for few milliseconds."

A client sends a message across a connection to a server that contains all the NCP parameters by using a network protocol such as IPX. The server executes the procedure and returns the results to the client. Each additional message increments the identification numbers in the packet. Once a NCP request from a client is received, it garners a NCP response. It is a one-for-one protocol—one command, one response.

Session and Datagram Interfaces

NCPs allow a client to talk to a server using a message delivery system such as IPX or SPX. SPX has the benefit of supporting sequencing and guaranteed message delivery. IPX can be requested if needed due to performance reasons. It offers the advantage of using a lower-level unreliable datagram interface such as IPX. In addition, datagrams offer porting of NCPs to networks where standard session interfaces do not exist.

Currently, most clients are limited to no more than one outstanding NCP request per connection. However, multiple connections can exist between two computers. If a client is being used on a multi-user system, each user can have a separate connection to a server and each connection is allowed to have an outstanding NCP request.

Because server access security is determined on a per-connection basis, it is normal for multiple tasks to share a single connection. If required, new connections can be established for each task in a multi-tasking environment. Each new connection is treated as a distinct entity, regardless of the physical machine that made the connection. In this way, a client can maintain as many connections to different servers as required.

Message Header Structures

Let us now look at the NCP message. A NCP message contains a seven-byte request header followed by an eight-byte reply header. The request header contains general status information about the current state of the connection and indicates the service required as shown in Table 3–7.

The reply header contains the required parameters for remotely executing procedures. It is structured as outlined in Table 3–8.

Check the ConnectionStatusFlags each time a service response is received. If bit 4 is set, the service connection has probably been terminated on the server's end.

Table 3–7   NCP message request header

Offset	Type	Content	Description
0	Word	Requesttype (0x2222)	Service category field
2	Byte	Sequencenumber (last sequence + 1)	A wraparound message sequence number. When a create service connection request issues, the field is set to zero. Follow-on requests increment it.
3	Byte	ConnectionNumber-Low (serviceConnection)	The service connection returned by the server when responding to a create a service connection request. This field is zero on the first request.
4	Byte	TaskNumber (current taskNumber	This is the client task that is requesting the service. The server keeps track of which tasks open files, and locks data in order to release those resources when the task completes. 255 tasks can share a single connection. Task 0 is reserved for end of task.
5	Byte	ConnectionNumber-High (serviceConnection)	Returned by the server in response to a create a service connection request. Is 0 on first request.

Table 3–8   Required parameters for remotely executing procedures

Offset	Type	Content	Description
0	Word	ReplyType (0x3333)	Service category field
2	Byte	Sequencenumber (RequestSe-quenceNumber)	A wraparound message sequence number. When a create service connection request issues, the field is set to zero. Follow-on requests increment it.
3	Byte	ConnectionNumber-Low (serviceConnec-tion)	The service connection returned by the server when responding to a create a service connection request. This field is zero on the first request.
4	Byte	TaskNumber (current taskNumber	This is the client task that is requesting the service. The server keeps track of which tasks open files, and locks data in order to release those resources when the task completes. 255 tasks can share a single connection. Task 0 is reserved for end of task.
5	Byte	ConnectionNumber-High (serviceCon-nection)	Returned by the server in response to a create a service connection request. Is 0 on first request.
6	Byte	CompletionCode (code)	Completion code returned by the server. It is part of the response to the client machines service request. Any number other than 0 indicates an error occurred during the servicing of the request. When this happens, the rest of the server's response is not returned.
7	Byte	ConnectionStatus-Flags (StatusFlags)	A bit field returned by the server as part of its header response to a client's service request as follows: 0 Bad service connection 2 No connections available 4 Server is down 6 Server is holding a broadcast message

CHAPTER REVIEW

In this chapter we discussed the IPX/SPX protocol suite and saw where it operates in the OSI model. We looked at the packet structure and at IPX addressing and we compared it to both the structure of the TCP/IP and

Ethernet. We looked at the role of the network number and at reserved network numbers. We investigated node numbers and socket numbers, and we looked at how IPX routing takes place. Finally, we ended the chapter with a look at the message header structures.

IN THE NEXT CHAPTER

In the next chapter we look at server message blocks. We will see how they operate, how server names are determined, and how they are resolved. We will analyze dialect negotiation, connection establishment and investigate how they work with down-level clients. We take an in-depth look at session set-up, connection management and, we look at locks as well.

Server Message Blocks

The server message block (SMB) protocol is the dump truck of the Windows NT and Windows 2000 world. It is used for sharing files, printers, serial ports, and communications abstractions such as named pipes and mail slots between computers. SMB is a client server, request-response protocol. If we can take the time to really learn and understand the SMB protocol, we will be miles ahead as we begin our network troubleshooting section of the book.

The SMB protocol has expanded into the common internet file system (CIFS). CIFS provides a cross-platform mechanism for client systems to request file and print services from server systems. It supports file and print using access open, close, read, write, and seek commands. Additionally, it supports file and record access in both a locked and unlocked mode. Once an application locks a file, it cannot be interfered with by other applications. A file or record that is locked is denied to the nonlocking applications.

SMB provides read-ahead and write-behind caching. These are secure operations as long as only one client accesses the file. Read caching and read-ahead optimizations are safe when accessing the file or in read only mode. If many clients attempt to write to the file at the same time, none are safe; therefore, all file operations must be managed at the server. SMB notifies the client accessing a file of changes in the access mode so that the client can use the optimum access method.

Applications register to be notified by the server when file or directory contents are modified. This allows the application to know when to refresh the display without the burden of having constantly to poll the server.

There are nearly as many different versions of SMB protocol as there are software vendors. Each version provides additional functions, features, and capabilities. To deal with this wealth of capacity, SMB performs what is called dialect negotiation. When two computers come into contact, they negotiate the dialect or version of SMB to be used in their conversation. This is a critical step in terms of both performance and in error-free communication because each dialect may provide different messages as well as changes to the fields and semantics of existing messages in other dialects. In addition to the normal file attributes, such as creation and modification times, other items can be added by applications like Word to include such things as the author's name or content description.

The protocol can support virtual volumes by using a file system that can span multiple volumes and servers but looks as if it is on a single server to the client machine. The files and directories of the subtree can be moved to different servers, and the names do not need to change. In this way, you do not need to make modifications to the desktop when you make a change on the server. These subtrees can also be replicated for load balancing and fault tolerance. When the client requests a file, SMB uses referrals to redirect a client to the server housing the data. This all happens behind the scenes without client knowledge.

SMB allows a client to resolve server names using DNS, WINS, LMHOSTS, or any other name resolution mechanism. This moves us from a flat server name space to a hierarchical organization allowing greater interoperability. To conserve bandwidth SMB can batch requests into a single message to minimize round-trip latencies; even when a later request depends on the results of an earlier one, it also supports Unicode file names.

SMB Operation Overview

In order to access a file on a server, a client application must be able to parse the full file name to determine the server name and the relative name within that server, resolve the server name to a transport address, make a connection to the server, and then exchange messages. If the server name has been previously resolved, it may still be cached and therefore name resolution will not be necessary. Additionally, if a previous connection is still available, then a new one will not be required. This process is repeated many times during a normal workday. Once the connection has been idle for a while, it will be torn down.

Server Name Determination

SMB is smart enough to resolve a server name from many different methods. For instance, in the URL file://prox/users/teresa/movies.xls, the client will take the part between the double forward slashes and the next forward slash as the server name, and the rest will be interpreted as a relative name. In our example, the server name is PROX and the relative name is USERS/TERESA/MOVIES.XLS.

In the path name, \\prox\users\ed\booksbymred.ppt, the client will take the part between the leading double backslashes (whack whack), the next whack as the server name, and the remainder as the relative name. In our example, the server name is PROX and the relative name is USERS\ED\BOOKSBYMRED.PPT.

In the path name, h:\booksbymred.ppt, the client will use "h" as an index into a table that contains a server name and a file name prefix. If the contents of the table for h is PROX and users\ed, then the server name and relative name would be the same as in the previous example.

Server Name Resolution

Once the server name has been determined, the next step is to resolve the name. There must be some means to resolve the name of an SMB server to a transport address. Also, a server must register its name with a name resolution service known by its clients. This is typically either WINS or DNS.

The server name can also be specified as the string form of an IP address in the usual dotted decimal notation, such as 10.0.0.10. In this case, "resolution" consists of converting to the 32-bit IP address.

The type of name resolution used may place limits on the form of the server name. For instance, with NETBIOS, the server name must be fewer than 15 uppercase characters.

Message Transport

When SMB uses a reliable connection-oriented transport, it does not need to ensure sequenced delivery of messages between the client and server. Instead, it relies on layer four (the transport layer) to do this. However, the transport must be able to detect failures at either the client or server node, and report them to the software so that corrections can be made. When a reliable transport connection from a client ends, work in progress and all resources open by the client on the server are closed. Message transport is done by using the NETBIOS session service.

Sample Message Flow

A typical message exchange sequence for a client connecting to a user-level server includes opening a file, reading its data, closing the file, and disconnecting from the server (Table 4–1). The CIFS request batching mechanism (called the "AndX" mechanism) allows the second to sixth messages in this sequence to be combined into one, so there are really only three round

Table 4–1   SMB message flow

Client command	Server response
SMB_COM_NEGOTIATE	This is the first message sent by the client machine to the server. It will include a list of SMB dialects supported by the client machine. When the server responds, it will indicate which SMB dialect should be used.
SMB_COM_SESSION_SETUP_ANDX	Transmits the user's name and credentials to the server for verification. A successful response from the server will include the UID to be used in subsequent SMB's from the user.
SMB_COM_TREE_CONNECT	This is the name of the disk share the client wants to access. The server response will include the TID field to be used in subsequent requests.
SMB_COM_OPEN	This frame will transmit the name of the file relative to the TID that the client wants to open. Success from this command will include the FID the client should use for subsequent operations on the file.
SMB_COM_READ	Here, the client supplies the TID, the FID, the file offset, and the number of bytes to read. When this command is successful, the server obviously returns the data requested.
SMB_COM_CLOSE	The client closes the file represented by the TID and the FID in the frame. The server responds with a success code.
SMB_COM_TREE_DISCONNECT	The client disconnects from the resource represented by the TID.

trips in the sequence, and the last one can be done asynchronously by the client.

The redirector on the client machine has the primary function of formatting remote requests in a manner that can be understood by the destination machine and sending them across the network. The redirector uses the SMB structure as the standard vehicle for sending and responding to redirector requests.

Each SMB header contains a command code (which specifies the task that the redirector wants the remote station to perform) and several environment and parameter fields (which specify how the command is to be carried out). In addition to the SMB header, the last field in the SMB may contain up to 64K of data to be sent to the remote station.

Read SMB (request) The read SMB (sometimes called read byte range) tells the server to read a specific range of bytes from a disk file. It also includes a file handle, the number of bytes to read, and so on. The file offset is based on a "seek pointer" that is kept by the redirector locally for the file. The server's seek pointer for this file handle is not valid in this case because many remote workstation processes may be accessing the same server operating the system file handle.

The "est'd total" parameter (estimated total bytes to be read, including those read by this request) is optional. The server can use this information for read-ahead or to optimize buffer allocation.

Read SMB (response) The response to the read SMB carries with it the data requested. The multiplex identifier (MID) keeps the SMB response labeled for the corresponding SMB request.

Here is how the process works:

- Program submits an I/O request to operating system through an application programmer interface (API) call.
- The operating system (or the redirector by way of the "int 21" hook) determines that the request is for a remote resource and passes it to the redirector.
- The redirector formats the I/O request as an SMB request and sends it to the server across the network.
- The server receives the SMB and submits the I/O request to the server's local operating system.
- The server formats the SMB response data. The data is returned if read or returns code if (write, etc.) and sends it back to the requesting workstation across the network.
- The redirector passes the response back to the operating system.
- The operating system passes the response to the calling application.

DIALECT NEGOTIATION

Connection Establishment

After the server name has been resolved to an IP address, a connection to the server needs to be established. Connection establishment is done using the *call* primitive of the NETBIOS session service, which requires the client to provide both a "calling name" and a "called name." The calling name is not significant in CIFS, except that an identical name from the same transport address is assumed to represent the same client; the called name is always

"*SMBSERVER". Over TCP, the call primitive results in a "session request" packet to port 139.

Backwards Compatibility

If a CIFS client wishes to interoperate with older SMB servers, then it can retry with a new called name if call is rejected by the server. The choice of the new name depends on the type of name resolution being used. For instance, if DNS is used, the called name would be constructed from the first component of the server's DNS name and then truncated to 15 characters if required. Next, it would be padded to 16 characters with blank (20 hex) characters. If NETBIOS was used, then the called name is the NETBIOS name. If these fail, then a NETBIOS "Adapter Status" request may be made to obtain the server's NET-BIOS name, and the connection establishment retried.

Session Setup

A CIFS server MUST register a NETBIOS Listen that accepts any calling name on the name "*SMBSERVER". In addition, if it wishes to support older SMB clients, it may have a NETBIOS name and register port 139 to listen on that name as well.

Connection Management

Once a connection is established, the rules for reliable transport connection dissolution are listed below:

- If a server receives a transport establishment request from a client with which it is already conversing, the server may terminate all other transport connections to that client. This allows the server to recover from the situation where the client was suddenly rebooted and was unable to cleanly terminate its resource sharing activities with the server.
- A server may drop the transport connection to a client at any time if the client generates malformed or illogical requests. However, wherever possible, the server will first return an error code to the client indicating the cause of the abort.
- If a server gets a hard error on the transport (such as a send failure), the transport connection to that client may be aborted.
- A server may terminate the transport connection if the client has no open resources on the server.

SMB Signing

Windows NT 4 with Service Pack 3 includes an updated version of the SMB authentication protocol, also known as the common internet file system (CIFS) file sharing protocol. The updated protocol has two main improvements:

It supports mutual authentication, which closes a "man-in-the-middle" attack, and it supports message authentication, which prevents active message attacks. SMB signing provides this authentication by placing a digital security signature into each SMB, which is then verified by both the client and the server.

In order to use SMB signing, you have two choices. You can enable it or you can require it on both the client and the server. If SMB signing is enabled on a server, then enabled clients will use CIFS during all subsequent sessions. The advantage is that clients not enabled for SMB signing will be able to use the older SMB protocol. If SMB signing is required on a server, then a client will not be able to establish a session unless it has been specifically enabled for SMB signing. SMB signing is disabled by default on a server system when you install the service pack. It is, however, enabled by default when you apply the service pack on a workstation system.

Note: SMB signing will not work with the direct host IPX protocol. This is because the direct-host IPX protocol modifies SMB's in a way that is incompatible with signature-enabled SMB's. This incompatibility will be most obvious when you have direct-host IPX clients and you require SMB signing on the server. Requiring SMB signatures on the server will cause the server to not bind to the direct-host IPX interface, which will then force all connections to the server to be signed. If you disable the NWLink binding on the server, then you will be able to use SMB signing.

In addition, SMB signing will impose a performance penalty on your system. Although it does not consume any more network bandwidth, it does use more CPU cycles on the client and server sides.

Opportunistic Locks

Network performance is increased if the client can locally buffer file data. This is because the client does not have to write information into a file on the server if the client knows that no other process is accessing the data. In the same manner, the client can buffer read-ahead data from the file if the client knows that no other process is writing the data.

Opportunistic locks, or oplocks, allow clients to dynamically alter their buffering strategy in a consistent manner. All SMB versions from LAN-MAN 1.0 forward support oplocks.

There are actually three different kinds of opportunistic locks. These are listed below.

1. An exclusive oplock allows a client to open a file for its own personal use in order to perform arbitrary buffering.
2. A batch oplock allows a client to keep a file open on the server, even though the local accessor on the client machine has closed the file.

3. A Level II oplock allows several machines to read a file if there are no writers among them. Level II oplocks are supported if the negotiated dialect is LM 0.12 or greater.

When a client opens a file, it requests the server to set a particular oplock on the file. The response from the server indicates the type of oplock granted to the client, allowing the client to adjust its buffering policy accordingly.

The SMB_COM_LOCKING_ANDX SMB is used to convey oplock break and response information. Let us now look at each of these locking mechanisms in more detail.

Exclusive Oplocks

When a client is granted an exclusive oplock, it can buffer lock information, read-ahead data, and write data on the client side of the conversation because the client knows that there will be no other accessor to the file. The way it works is thus: The redirector on the client opens the file requesting that an oplock be given to the client. If the file is open by anyone else, then the client is refused the oplock and no local buffering may be performed on the local client. This also means that no read-ahead may be performed to the file, unless the redirector knows that it has the read-ahead range locked. If the server grants the exclusive oplock, the client can perform certain optimizations for the file such as buffering lock, read, and write data.

The exclusive oplock protocol is illustrated in Table 4–2.

Table 4–2   Exclusive oplock operation

Client A	Client B	Server
Open \\coolfile ->		
		<- open ok. Exclusive oplock granted
	Open \\coolfile ->	
		<- oplock break to client A
Locks ->		
		<- locks response
Writes ->		
		<- writes response
Close or done ->		
		<- open response to client B

As can be seen, when client A opens the file, it can request an exclusive oplock. If no one else has the file open on the server, then the oplock is granted to client A. If, at some point in the future, another client, such as client B, requests an open to the same file, then the server must have client A break its oplock. Breaking the oplock involves client A sending the server any lock or write data that it has buffered, and then letting the server know that it has acknowledged that the oplock has been broken. This synchronization message informs the server that it is now permissible to allow client B to complete its open.

Client A must also purge any read-ahead buffers that it has for the file.

Batch Oplocks

Batch oplocks are used where common programs on a client behave in such a way that causes the amount of network traffic on a wire to go beyond an acceptable level for the functionality provided by the program.

For example, the command processor executes commands from within a command procedure by performing the following steps:

- Opening the command procedure.
- Seeking to the "next" line in the file.
- Reading the line from the file.
- Closing the file.
- Executing the command.

This process is repeated for each command executed from the command procedure file. Obviously, this causes many files processing, thereby creating lots of network traffic that could otherwise be curtailed if the program simply left the file open, read a line, executed the command, and then read the next line.

Batch oplocking does this very thing, thereby allowing clients to skip extraneous open and close requests (Table 4–3). When the command processor asks for the next line in the file, the client either asks the server, or it may already have the data as read-ahead cache. Either way, the amount of network traffic from the client is greatly reduced.

If the server receives a rename or delete request for a file that has a batch oplock, it informs the client that the oplock needs to be broken. The client then changes to the open and close mode discussed earlier.

Client A opens the file and requests an oplock. If no one has the file open on the server, the oplock is granted to client A. In the case above, client A keeps the file open for its caller across multiple open/close operations. Data may be read ahead for the caller, and other optimizations, such as buffering locks, can also be performed.

Table 4–3   Batch oplock protocol operation

Client A	Client B	Server
Open \\coolfile ->		
		<- open ok. Batch oplock granted
Read ->		
		<- data
Close		
Open		
Seek		
->		Read
		<- data
Close		
	Open \\coolfile ->	
		<- oplock break to client A
Close ->		
		<- close ok to client A
		<- open ok to client B

When another client requests an open, rename, or delete operation to the server for the file, however, client A must clean up its buffered data and synchronize with the server. Most of the time, this involves actually closing the file, provided that client A's caller believes that it has closed the file. Once the file is closed, client B's open request can be completed.

Level II Oplocks

Level II oplocks allow multiple clients to have the same file open, provided that no client is performing write operations to the file. This is important for environments with older machines. Most compatibility mode opens from these clients map to an open request for shared read/write access to the file. While it makes sense to do this, it also tends to break oplocks for other clients even though neither client actually intends to write to the file.

This sequence looks like an exclusive oplock (Table 4–4). The basic difference is that the server informs the client that it should break to a level II lock when no one has been writing the file. That is, client A, for example, may have opened the file for a desired access of READ and a share access of READ/WRITE. This means, by definition, that client A will not perform any writes to the file.

When client B opens the file, the server must synchronize with client A in case client A has any buffered locks. Once it is synchronized, client B's

Table 4–4 Level II oplock protocol

Client A	Client B	Server
Open \ \coolfile ->		
		<- open ok. Exclusive oplock granted
Read ->		
		<- data
	Open \ \coolfile ->	
		<- break to level II oplock to client A
Locks ->		
		<- locks response
Done ->		
		<- open ok. Oplock II granted to client B

open request may be completed. Client B, however, is informed that it has a level II oplock, rather than an exclusive oplock to the file.

In this case, no client with a level II oplock on the file may buffer any lock information on the local client machine. This enables the server to guarantee that if any write operation is performed, it need only notify the level II clients that the lock should be broken without having to synchronize all of the accessors of the file.

The level II oplock may be BROKEN TO NONE, meaning that some client that had the file opened has now performed a write operation to the file. Because no level II client can create a buffer locked situation, information on the server remains in a consistent state. The writing client, for example, could not have written to a locked range, by definition. Read-ahead data may be buffered in the client machines, however, thereby cutting down on the amount of network traffic required to the file. Once the level II oplock is broken, however, the buffering client must flush its buffers and degrade to performing all operations on the file across the network. No oplock break response is expected from a client when the server breaks a client from LEVEL II to NONE.

Security Model

Each server makes a set of resources available to clients on a network. The resource may be a directory tree, named pipe, printer, etc. Client machines view the server as the sole provider of the file or other resource being accessed, and therefore, they are unaware of any storage or service dependencies.

The CIFS protocol requires server authentication of users before file accesses are allowed, and each server authenticates its own users. A client system must send authentication information to the server before the server will allow access to its resources.

The CIFS protocol defines two methods that can be selected by the server for security: share level and user level.

A share-level server makes some directory on a disk device (or other resource) available. An optional password may be required to gain access. Thus, any user on the network who knows the name of the server, the name of the resource, and the password has access to the resource. Share-level security servers may use different passwords for the same shared resource with different passwords allowing different levels of access.

A user-level server makes some directory on a disk device (or other resource) available but in addition requires the client to provide a user name and corresponding user password to gain access. User-level servers are preferred over share-level servers for any new server implementation, since organizations generally find user-level servers easier to administer as employees come and go. User-level servers may use the account name to check access control lists on individual files or have one access control list that applies to all files in the directory.

When a user-level server validates the account name and password presented by the client, an identifier representing that authenticated instance of the user is returned to the client in the User ID (UID) field of the response SMB. This UID must be included in all further requests made on behalf of the user from that client. A share-level server returns no useful information in the UID field.

The user-level security model was added after the original dialect of the CIFS protocol was issued, and subsequently, some clients may not be capable of sending account names and passwords to the server. A server in user-level security mode communicating with one of these clients will allow a client to connect to resources even if the client has not sent account name and password information:

1. If the client's computer name is identical to an account name known on the server, and if the password supplied to connect to the shared resource matches that account's password, an implicit "user logon" will be performed using those values. If this fails, the server may fail the request or assign a default account name of its choice.
2. The value of UID in subsequent requests by the client will be ignored, and all access will be validated assuming the account name selected above.

Resource Share/Access Example

The following examples illustrate a command line interface for a server to offer a disk resource, and for a client to connect to and use that resource.

a) NET SHARE
The NET SHARE command, when executed on the server, specifies a directory name to be made available to clients on the network. A share

name must be given, and this name is presented by clients wishing to access the directory.

Examples:

NET Share docs=c:\dir1\
Shares all files within the directory C:\DIR1 and its subdirectories with the share name *docs* as the name used to connect to this resource.

b) NET USE
Clients can gain access to one or more offered directories via the NET USE command. Once the NET USE command is issued, the user can access the files freely without further special requirements.

Examples:

NET USE d: \\SERVER1\DOCS maps the drive d: to the DOCS share on Server1. The user may now address files on SERVER1 C:\DIR1 by referencing d:. For example, dir d:*.* will give a listing of all the files on SERVER1 c:\dir1.
NET USE * \\SERVER1\DOCS mycoolpwd maps the next available drive the DOCS share on server1 that has been password protected with mycoolpwd.

For user-level servers, the client does not normally need to provide a password with the NET USE command. If the user is prompted for a password, it is usually indicative of a network problem (for example, it cannot contact a domain controller to verify credentials). This scenario provides a great chance to try out our network monitoring tools, which we will do in Part Four. For now, you may want to try something like the following to verify whether it is a security problem:

NET USE * \\SERVER1\DOCS /USER:domainname\username password

The client software must remember the drive identifier supplied with the NET USE request and associate it with the Tree ID (TID) value returned by the server in the SMB header. Subsequent requests using this TID must include only the pathname relative to the connected subtree because the server treats the subtree as the root directory (virtual root). When the user references one of the remote drives, the client software looks through its list of drives for that node and includes the tree ID associated with this drive in the TID field of each request.

Note that one shares a directory, and all files underneath that directory are then affected. If a particular file is within the range of multiple shares, connecting to any of the share ranges gains access to the file with the permissions specified for the offer named in the NET USE. The server will not check for nested directories with more restrictive permissions.

Authentication

A CIFS server keeps an encrypted form of a client's password. To gain authenticated access to server resources, the server sends a challenge to the client, to which the client responds in a way that proves it knows the client's password.

Authentication makes use of DES encryption in block mode. The DES encryption function is denoted as E(K,D), which accepts a seven-byte key (K) and an eight-byte data block (D) and produces an eight-byte encrypted data block as its value. If the data to be encrypted is longer than eight bytes, the encryption function is applied to each block of eight bytes in sequence, and the results are appended together. If the key is longer than seven bytes, the data is first completely encrypted using the first seven bytes of the key, then the second seven bytes, etc., appending the results each time. In other words, to encrypt the 16-byte quantity D0D1 with the 14-byte key K0K1,

```
E(K0K1,D0D1) = E(K0,D0)E(K0,D1)E(K1,D0)E(K1,D1)
```

The *EncryptionKey* field in the SMB_COM_NEGPROT response contains an eight-byte challenge denoted below as "C8", chosen to be unique to prevent replay attacks; the client responds with a 24-byte response denoted "P24" and computed as described below. (*Note:* The name *"EncryptionKey"* is historical—it does not actually hold an encryption key.)

Clients send the response to the challenge in the SMB_COM_TREE_CONNECT, SMB_COM_TREE_CONNECT_ANDX, and/or SMB_COM_SESSION_SETUP_ANDX request, which follows the SMB_COM_NEGPROT message exchange. The server must validate the response by performing the same computations the client performed to create it and ensuring that the strings match.

If the comparisons fail, the client system may be incapable of encryption; if so, the string may be the user password in clear text. The server should try to validate the string as though it were the unencrypted password.

The SMB field used to store the response depends upon the request:
Password in SMB_COM_TREE_CONNECT
Password in SMB_COM_TREE_CONNECT_ANDX
Account Password in SMB_COM_SESSION_SETUP_ANDX
(*Note:* Again, the names are historical and do not reflect this usage.)

The contents of the response to the challenge depend on the CIFS dialect, as outlined in the following sections.

Distributed File System (DFS) Support

Protocol dialects of NT LM 0.12 and later versions support distributed file system operations. The DFS provides a way for this protocol to use a single consistent file-naming scheme, which may span a collection of different servers and shares. The DFS model employed is a referral-based model. This protocol specifies the manner in which clients receive referrals.

The client can set a flag in the request SMB header indicating that the client wants the server to resolve this SMB's paths within the DFS known to the server. The server attempts to resolve the requested name to a file contained within the local directory tree indicated by the TID of the request and then proceeds normally. If the request pathname resolves to a file on a different system, the server returns the following error:

STATUS_DFS_PATH_NOT_COVERED—the server does not support the part of the DFS namespace needed to resolve the pathname in the request. The client should request a referral from this server for further information.

A client asks for a referral with the TRANS2_DFS_GET_REFERRAL request containing the DFS pathname of interest. The response from the server indicates how the client should proceed.

The method by which the topological knowledge of the DFS is stored and maintained by the servers is not specified by this protocol.

SMB Header

While each SMB command has specific encoding, there are some fields in the SMB header that have meaning to all SMBs. As we see in the printout below, the SMB protocol is carried on top of NetBIOS, which is carried on top to TCP, which is on top of IP, which is on top of the Ethernet media access method. These fields and considerations are described in the following sections.

```
+ ETHERNET: ETYPE = 0x0800 : Protocol = IP:  DOD Internet Protocol
+ IP: ID = 0x414; Proto = TCP; Len: 82
+ TCP: .AP..., len:   42, seq:    365595-365636, ack:  13582702, win: 8760,
src: 1032  dst:  139 (NBT Session)
+ NBT: SS: Session Message, Len: 38
  SMB: C get attributes, File =
     SMB: SMB Status = Error Success
        SMB: Error class = No Error
        SMB: Error code = No Error
     SMB: Header: PID = 0x2011 TID = 0x1002 MID = 0xC502 UID = 0x1003
        SMB: Tree ID     (TID) = 4098 (0x1002)
        SMB: Process ID  (PID) = 8209 (0x2011)
        SMB: User ID     (UID) = 4099 (0x1003)
        SMB: Multiplex ID (MID) = 50434 (0xC502)
        SMB: Flags Summary = 0 (0x0)
```

```
          SMB: .......0 = Lock & Read and Write & Unlock not supported
          SMB: ......0. = Send No Ack not supported
          SMB: ....0... = Using case sensitive pathnames
          SMB: ...0.... = No canonicalized pathnames
          SMB: ..0..... = No Opportunistic lock
          SMB: .0...... = No Change Notify
          SMB: 0....... = Client command
     SMB: flags2 Summary = 32768 (0x8000)
          SMB: ..............0 = Understands only DOS 8.3 filenames
          SMB: ..............0. = Does not understand extended
attributes
          SMB: ...0............ = No DFS capabilities
          SMB: ..0............ = No paging of IO
          SMB: .0............. = Using SMB status codes
          SMB: 1.............. = Using UNICODE strings
  SMB: Command = C get attributes
     SMB: Word count = 0
     SMB: Byte count = 3
     SMB: Byte parameters
     SMB: File name =
```

TID Field

The TID represents an instance of an authenticated connection to a server resource. TID is returned by the server to the client when the client successfully connects to a resource, and the client uses TID in subsequent requests referring to the resource.

If the server is executing in share-level security mode, TID is the only thing used to allow access to the shared resource. Thus, if the user is able to perform a successful connection to the server specifying the appropriate netname and password (if any), the resource may be accessed according to the access rights associated with the shared resource (same for all who gained access this way).

UID Field

If, however, the server is executing in user-level security mode, access to the resource is based on the UID (validated on the SMB_COM_SESSION_SETUP_ANDX request), and the TID is NOT associated with access control but rather merely defines the resource (such as the shared-directory tree).

In most SMB requests, TID must contain a valid value. Exceptions prior to getting a TID established include SMB_COM_NEGOTIATE, SMB_COM_TREE_CONNECT, SMB_COM_ECHO, and the SMB_COM_SESSION_SETUP_ANDX 0xFFFF should be used for TID for these situations. The server is always responsible for enforcing the use of a valid TID where appropriate.

PID Field

The Process ID (PID) uniquely identifies a client process. Clients inform servers of the creation of a new process by simply introducing a new PID value into the dialogue for new processes.

In the core protocol, the SMB_COM_PROCESS_EXIT SMB was used to indicate the catastrophic termination of a process on the client. In the single-tasking DOS system, it was possible for hard errors to occur causing the destruction of the process with files remaining open. Thus, an SMB_COM_PROCESS_EXIT SMB was sent for this occurrence to allow the server to close all files opened by that process.

In the LANMAN 1.0 and newer dialects, no SMB_COM_PROCESS_EXIT SMB is sent. The client operating system must ensure that the appropriate close and cleanup SMB's will be sent when the last process referencing the file closes it. From the server's point of view, there is no concept of a File ID (FID) belonging to a process. A FID returned by the server to one process may be used by any other process using the same transport connection and TID. There is no process creation SMB sent to the server; it is up to the client to ensure only valid client processes gain access to FID's (and TID's). On SMB_COM_TREE_DISCONNECT (or when the client and server session is terminated), the server will invalidate any files opened by any process on that client.

MID Field

Clients using the LANMAN 1.0 and newer dialects will typically be multitasked and allow multiple asynchronous input/output requests per task. Therefore, a Multiplex ID (MID) is used along with PID to allow multiplexing the single client and server connection among the client's multiple processes, threads, and requests per thread.

Regardless of negotiated dialect, the server is responsible for ensuring that every response contains the same MID and PID values they request. The client may then use the MID and PID values for associating requests and responses and may have up to the negotiated number of requests outstanding at any time to a particular server.

Flags Field

Let us now take a closer look at the first of the two flag fields as detailed in Table 4–5. This field contains eight individual flags (only seven are used), which are numbered from least significant to most significant and have the following meanings:

```
SMB: Flags Summary = 0 (0x0)
            SMB: .......0 = Lock & Read and Write & Unlock not supported
            SMB: ......0. = Send No Ack not supported
            SMB: ....0... = Using case sensitive pathnames
            SMB: ...0.... = No canonicalized pathnames
            SMB: ..0..... = No Opportunistic lock
            SMB: .0...... = No Change Notify
            SMB: 0....... = Client command
```

Table 4–5   SMB flag1 summary

Bit number	Meaning	Earliest dialect
0	When set from the server in the SMB_COM_ NEGOTIATE response, this bit indicates that the server supports Lock and Read; Write and Unlock.	LANMAN 1.0
1	When this flag is set, the client guarantees that there is a receive buffer posted that will support a Send without Acknowledgement.	
2	Reserved. Must be zero.	
3	When this flag is set, pathnames must be treated as case sensitive. When not set, pathnames are not case sensitive.	LANMAN 1.0
4	No canonicalized pathnames are used when zero. When the flag is set, file/directory names are in uppercase, are valid characters, and have been removed, and single backslashes are used as separators.	LANMAN 1.0
5	Opportunistic lock—when set, the client requests that the file be opportunistically locked if this process is the only process that has the file open at the time of the open request. If the server "grants" this oplock request, then this bit should remain set in the corresponding response SMB to indicate to the client that the oplock request was granted.	LANMAN 1.0
6	Change Notify indicates that the server should notify the client on any action that can modify the file (delete, setattrib, rename, etc.) by another client. If not set, the server need only notify the client about another open request by a different client.	LANMAN 1.0
7	Client Command—when on, this SMB is being sent from the server in response to a client request. The command field usually contains the same value in a protocol request from the client to the server as in the matching response from the server to the client. This bit unambiguously distinguishes the command request from the command response.	PC Network program 1.0

Flags2 Field

This field contains six individual flags, which are numbered from least significant bit to most significant bit and defined in Table 4–6. Flags that are not defined must be set to zero.

```
SMB: flags2 Summary = 32768 (0x8000)
SMB: ..............0 = Understands only DOS 8.3 filenames
SMB: .............0. = Does not understand extended
attributes
SMB: ...0............ = No DFS capabilities
SMB: ..0............. = No paging of IO
SMB: .0.............. = Using SMB status codes
SMB: 1............... = Using UNICODE strings
```

Status Field

An SMB returns error information to the client in the status field, as seen below. Protocol dialects prior to NT LM 0.12 return status to the client using the combination of Status.DosError.ErrorClass and Status.DosError .Error. Beginning with NT LM 0.12 CIFS, servers can return 32-bit error information to clients using Status.Status if the incoming client SMB has bit 14 set in the Flags2 field of the SMB header. The contents of response parameters is not guaranteed in the case of an error return and must be ignored. For write-behind activity, a subsequent write or close of the file may return the

Table 4–6 SMB flags2 section

Bits	Meaning	Earliest dialect
0	If set in a request, the server may return long components in path names in the response.	
1	If set, the client is aware of extended attributes.	
12	If set, any request pathnames should be resolved in the distributed file system.	NT LM 0.12
13	If set, this flag indicates that a read will be permitted if the client does not have read permission but has execute permission. Only useful on a read request.	
14	If set, this flag specifies that the returned error code is a 32-bit error code in status.status. Otherwise, the status doserror class is used. This flag should be set when using NT status codes.	NT LM 0.12
15	When this flag is set, STRING fields are encoded as UNICODE. When not set, then STRING fields are encoded as ASCII.	NT LM 0.12

fact that a previous write failed. Normally, write-behind failures are limited to hard-disk errors and device out of space.

```
SMB: SMB Status = Error Success
        SMB: Error class = No Error
        SMB: Error code = No Error
```

Timeouts

In general, SMB's are not expected to block at the server; they should return "immediately." But some SMB requests do indicate timeout periods for the completion of the request on the server. If a server implementation cannot support timeouts, then an error can be returned just as if a timeout had occurred if the resource was not available immediately upon request.

Data Buffer (*BUFFER*) and String Formats

The data portion of SMB's typically contains the data to be read or written, file paths, or directory paths. The format of the data portion depends on the message. All fields in the data portion have the same format. In every case, it consists of an identifier byte followed by the data. (Table 4–7).

When the identifier indicates a data block or variable block, then the format is a word indicating the length followed by the data.

In all dialects prior to NT LM 0.12, all strings are encoded in ASCII. If the agreed dialect is NT LM 0.12 or later, Unicode strings may be exchanged. Unicode strings include file names, resource names, and user names. This applies to null-terminated strings, length-specified strings, and the type-prefixed strings. In all cases where a string is passed in Unicode format, the Unicode string must be word-aligned with respect to the beginning of the SMB. Should the string not naturally fall on a two-byte boundary, a null byte of padding will be inserted, and the Unicode string will begin at the next address. In the description of the SMB's, items that may be encoded in Unicode or ASCII are labeled as STRING. If the encoding is

Table 4–7   Data buffer and string formats

Identifier	Description	Value
Data block		1
Dialect	Null terminated string	2
Pathname	Null terminated string	3
ASCII	Null terminated string	4
Variable block		5

ASCII, even if the negotiated string is Unicode, the quantity is labeled as UCHAR.

For type-prefixed Unicode strings, the padding byte is found after the type byte. The type byte is four (indicating SMB_FORMAT_ASCII), independent of whether the string is ASCII or Unicode. For strings whose start addresses are found using offsets within the fixed part of the SMB (as opposed to simply being found at the byte following the preceding field), it is guaranteed that the offset will be properly aligned.

Strings that are never passed in Unicode are:

The protocol strings in the Negotiate SMB request.

The service name string in the Tree Connect And X SMB.

When Unicode is negotiated, bit 15 should be set in the FLAGS2 field of every SMB header.

Despite the flexible encoding scheme, no field of a data portion may be omitted or included out of order. In addition, neither a WORDCOUNT nor BYTECOUNT of value 0 at the end of a message may be omitted.

Access Mode Encoding

Various client requests and server responses, such as SMB_COM_OPEN, pass file access modes encoded into a USHORT. The encoding of these is as follows:

```
1111 11
5432 1098 7654 3210
rWrC rLLL rSSS rAAA
```

where:

- W—Write through mode. No read-ahead or write-behind allowed on this file or device. When the response is returned, data is expected to be on the disk or device.
- S—Sharing mode:
  0—Compatibility mode
  1—Deny read/write/execute (exclusive)
  2—Deny write
  3—Deny read/execute
  4—Deny none
- A—Access mode
  0—Open for reading
  1—Open for writing
  2—Open for reading and writing
  3—Open for execute
    rSSSrAAA = 11111111 (hex FF) indicates FCB open (???)
    C—Cache mode

0—Normal file
1—Do not cache this file
* L—Locality of reference
0—Locality of reference is unknown
1—Mainly sequential access
2—Mainly random access
3—Random access with some locality
4 to 7—Currently undefined

Open Function Encoding

Open Function specifies the action to be taken depending on whether or not the file exists. This word has the following format:
bits:
1111 11
5432 1098 7654 3210
rrrr rrrr rrrC rrOO
where:

* C—Create (action to be taken if file does not exist)
0—Fail
1—Create file
    r—Reserved (must be zero)
* O—Open (action to be taken if file exists)
0—Fail
1—Open file
2—Truncate file

Open Action Encoding

Action in the response to an open or create request describes the action taken as a result of the request. It has the following format:
bits:
1111 11
5432 1098 7654 3210
Lrrr rrrr rrrr rrOO
where:

* L—Lock (single user total file lock status)
0—File opened by another user (or mode not supported by server)
1— File is opened only by this user at the present time
    r—Reserved (must be zero)
* O—Open (action taken on Open)
1—The file existed and was opened

2—The file did not exist but was created

3—The file existed and was truncated

File Attribute Encoding

When SMB messages exchange file attribute information, it is encoded in 16 bits as seen in Table 4–8.

Table 4–8   File attributes

Value	Description
0x01	Read only file
0x02	Hidden file
0x04	System file
0x08	Volume
0x10	Directory
0x20	Archive file
Others	Reserved. Must be set to 0

Extended File Attribute Encoding

The extended file attributes is a 32-bit value composed of attributes and flags.

Any combination of the attributes listed in Table 4–9 is acceptable, except that all other file attributes override FILE_ATTRIBUTE_NORMAL.

Any combination of the flags listed in Table 4–10 is acceptable.

Batching Requests ("AndX" Messages)

LANMAN1.0 and later dialects of the CIFS protocol allow multiple SMB requests to be sent in one message to the server. Messages of this type are called AndX SMBs, and they obey the following rules:

- The embedded command does not repeat the SMB header information. Rather, the next SMB starts at the *WordCount* field.
- All multiple (chained) requests must fit within the negotiated transmit size. For example, if SMB_COM_TREE_CONNECT_ANDX included SMB_COM_OPEN_ANDX which included SMB_COM_WRITE were sent, they would all have to fit within the negotiated buffer size. This would limit the size of the write.

Table 4–9   Extended file attributes

Attribute	Designation	Description
FILE_ATTRIBUTE_ ARCHIVE	0x020	The file has not been archived since last modified. Used primarily for backup purposes.
FILE_ATTRIBUTE_ COMPRESSED	0x800	The file or directory is compressed. For a file means that data in file is compressed. For a directory means that this is default for directory. New files will be compressed.
FILE_ATTRIBUTE_ NORMAL	0x080	No special attributes. Only valid if used alone.
FILE_ATTRIBUTE_ HIDDEN	0x002	File is hidden and is not included in normal directory listing.
FILE_ATTRIBUTE_ READONLY	0x001	File is read only. Apps can read but not write to or delete the file.
FILE_ATTRIBUTE_ TEMPORARY	0x100	The file is a temporary file.
FILE_ATTRIBUTE_ DIRECTORY	0x010	Identifies a directory. Not a file as such.
FILE_ATTRIBUTE_ SYSTEM	0x004	The file is part of or used exclusively by the operating system.

- There is one message sent containing the chained requests, and there is one response message to the chained requests. The server may NOT elect to send separate responses to each of the chained requests.
- All chained responses must fit within the negotiated transmit size. This limits the maximum value on an embedded SMB_COM_READ, for example. It is the client's responsibility to not request more bytes than will fit within the multiple response.
- The server will implicitly use the result of the first command in the "X" command. For example, the TID obtained via SMB_COM_TREE_CON-NECT_ANDX would be used in the embedded SMB_COM_OPEN_ANDX, and the FID obtained in the SMB_COM_OPEN_ANDX would be used in the embedded SMB_COM_READ.
- Each chained request can only reference the same FID and TID as the other commands in the combined request. The chained requests can be thought of as performing a single (multi-part) operation on the same resource.
- The first *COMMAND* to encounter an error will stop all further processing of embedded commands. The server will not back out commands that succeeded. Thus, if a chained request contained SMB_COM_OPEN_

Table 4–10   Additional flags

Attribute	Designation	Description
FILE_FLAG_WRITE_ THROUGH	0x80000000	Tells the OS to write through any intermediate cache and go instead directly to file. Does not allow lazy writes.
FILE_FLAG_NO_ BUFFERING	0x20000000	Requests the server to open file with no intermediate buffering. This is a request and the server does not have to accept it.
FILE_FLAG_RANDOM_ ACCESS	0x10000000	Indicates that the application will use the file in a random access fashion. The server can use this information to optimize file caching.
FILE_FLAG_SEQUENTIAL_ SCAN	0x08000000	Indicates that the application will access the file in a sequential fashion. The server can use this flag to optimize caching.
FILE_FLAG_DELETE_ON_ CLOSE	0x04000000	Tells the server to delete the file immediately after all the handles have been closed.
FILE_FLAG_BACKUP_ SEMANTICS	0x02000000	The file is being opened for a backup or restore operation. The server should allow file security to override if appropriate permissions have been granted.
FILE_FLAG_POSIX_ SEMANTICS	0x01000000	Use Posix rules (allows case sensitive names).

ANDX and SMB_COM_READ, and the server was able to open the file successfully but the read encountered an error, the file would remain open. This is exactly the same as if the requests had been sent separately.

If an error occurs while processing chained requests, the last response (of the chained responses in the buffer) will be the one that encountered the error. Other unprocessed chained requests will have been ignored when the server encountered the error and will not be represented in the chained response. Actually, the last valid ANDXCOMMAND (if any) will represent the SMB on which the error occurred. If no valid ANDXCOMMAND is present, then the error that occurred on the first request/response and *COMMAND* contains the command that failed. In all cases, the error information is returned in the SMB header at the start of the response buffer.

Each chained request and response contains the offset (from the start of the SMB header) to the next chained request/response (in the *AndXOffset* field in the various "and X" protocols for example, SMB_COM_OPEN_ ANDX). This allows building the requests unpacked. There may be space between the end of the previous request (as defined by *WordCount* and *ByteCount*) and the start of the next chained request. This simplifies the building of chained protocol requests. Note that because the client must know the size of the data being returned in order to post the correct number of receives (e.g., SMB_COM_TRANSACTION, SMB_COM_READ_MPX), the data in each response SMB is expected to be truncated to the maximum number of 512-byte blocks (sectors) that will fit (starting at a 32-bit boundary) in the negotiated buffer size with the odd bytes remaining (if any) in the final buffer.

CHAPTER REVIEW

In this chapter we looked at the SMB protocol. We began with an overview of the way it operates, and we looked at server name determination. We followed with a discussion of server name resolution and looked at the message transport function. We took an in-depth look at dialect negotiation, connection establishment, and the ways that SMB uses to be backwardly compatible.

After we talked about the more academic items, we dove into a down and dirty look at session set-up, connection management, and SMB signing. We looked at all kinds of locks, including opportunistic locks, exclusive oplocks, batch locks, and level II oplocks. We did not stop there; we next moved into looking at the security model and looked at an example using resource access and share access.

After we had worked with that for a while, we got into the actual structure of the SMB header. Here we looked at the MID, the TID, the PID, the UID, and the FID. We looked at timeouts, data buffers, and access mode encoding. Finally, when we thought we had looked at all we could, we talked about how the SMB protocol permits batching of requests.

IN THE NEXT CHAPTER

In the next chapter we move into Part Two and begin our investigation of network traffic. We will begin on the client side and then move into the server side of traffic.

PART 2

NETWORK TRAFFIC ANALYSIS AND OPTIMIZATION: A LOOK AT THE ISSUES

There are many things involved in performing network traffic analysis and optimization. We need to look at the conversations between machines as well as the general flow of information. In this section we eavesdrop on the conversations between the computers. First, we look at the chatter between clients and their servers. Next, we listen to the servers themselves. We find out what they are talking about, and then we come up with methods to reduce as much of the clutter as possible.

5

A Look at Client Traffic

We begin this section of the book by first looking at client traffic. In this chapter we will look at many of the sources of client traffic. We will discuss traffic related to protocols, traffic related to finding things on the network, and the like. In this section we will find suggestions for reducing the traffic so common on many of our networks. We will begin by looking at where client traffic begins, that is, when the machine is first turned on.

CLIENT INITIALIZATION

Client machines begin generating traffic from the moment they are turned on, and they do not stop causing traffic until they are physically turned off. For this reason, as we seek to optimize our network, we must come to grips with just how much traffic these machines generate, and to some extent, we want to be able to reduce this traffic if at all possible. So where does all this traffic come from when a machine is turned on? Well, it depends on what protocols are running on the machine. For our initial look at this traffic, we want to look at a "typical Windows 98 machine" that is using DHCP for IP address assignment, WINS for NetBIOS name resolution, and DNS for Internet browsing. The machine itself is not doing any file or print sharing. It is configured to log on to a Windows NT domain, and it does not use any policies or profiles. In short, this could be any PC at work. Then what kind of traffic is this modest, tame computer going to generate when it logs onto the network? There will be at least four different kinds of traffic created when this machine boots up and the user gets logged onto the network. Let us now look at each of these types of traffic as listed in Table 5–1.

Table 5–1   Client initialization traffic summary

Type of traffic	Description of traffic	Number of frames	Number of bytes
DHCP	Obtain an IP address from a DHCP server	4 frames	At least 1368 bytes
WINS	NetBIOS name registration	At least 4 frames	At least 428 bytes
Logon validation	Logon validation by domain controller	At least 24 frames	At least 3105 bytes
Total initialization traffic		At least 32 frames	At least 4901 bytes

DHCP Traffic

If you are using TCP/IP on your network, then chances are that you are also using DHCP to hand out IP addresses to your client machines, and maybe to some of the printers as well. It goes without saying, if TCP/IP is the only protocol on the network, then a client machine must have a valid IP address in order to communicate with other devices on the network such as computers, routers, printers, and servers. This IP address must have a proper network address, host address, and subnet mask or else communication simply will not take place. If you have multiple segments, then a default gateway is also required.

DHCP can handle these simple tasks, and do more as well. In reality, it is a clean and efficient protocol requiring just four frames to hand out an address, and only two frames to renew the address later on. OK, let's take a look now at how all this works.

Lease acquisition process   When a DHCP client boots up, the first thing it needs to do is to find a DHCP server that is handing out IP addresses for the subnet to which it is attached. In order to do this, the device will send out a DHCP discover message indicating that it would like to lease an IP address. This is similar to sending out a solicitation for bids. A DCHP server, upon hearing the discover message, will respond with a DHCP offer. It is saying, "I have received your solicitation, and here is the address I have for you." The client machine may in fact receive several DHCP offers from multiple servers that are able to hear the DHCP discover message. The client will select the first DHCP offer it receives and respond to the DHCP server saying that it wants to accept the IP address contained in the DHCP offer. This is called a DHCP request. The DHCP server, upon receiving the request, will respond with an acknowledgment (ACK) saying, "go ahead and use the IP address." Table 5–2 summarizes this process.

As we see in Table 5–2, the DHCP process uses broadcasts throughout the entire process. This allows other machines on the network to be aware of what is happening. Let us look at this process in a little more detail. In the printout below of the Ethernet header, we see that the destination address is FFFFFFFFFFFF. This is the broadcast address for the media access layer. All devices on the Ethernet segment will have to process this frame until they get to the UDP (user datagram port) section and discover that they do not have the indicated UDP port. We also see in the printout the Ethernet frame size of 342 bytes. This is the size of this Ethernet frame including the header. The number of bytes remaining is 328 bytes, which is the payload minus the 14-byte Ethernet header.

```
ETHERNET: ETYPE = 0x0800 : Protocol = IP:  DOD Internet Protocol
    ETHERNET: Destination address : FFFFFFFFFFFF
        ETHERNET: .......1 = Group address
        ETHERNET: ......1. = Locally administered address
    ETHERNET: Source address : 00104BEC8DB2
        ETHERNET: .......0 = No routing information present
        ETHERNET: ......0. = Universally administered address
    ETHERNET: Frame Length : 342 (0x0156)
    ETHERNET: Ethernet Type : 0x0800 (IP:  DOD Internet Protocol)
  ETHERNET: Ethernet Data: Number of data bytes remaining = 328
(0x0148)
```

The IP header portion is parsed in the printout that follows this paragraph. First, note that the payload uses a user datagram protocol (UDP). This is a small, efficient "best effort" protocol that is ideally suited for the DHCP

Table 5–2   DHCP lease acquisition process

Type	Destination	Description
DHCP Discover	Broadcast	Client is looking for a DHCP server.
DHCP Offer	Broadcast	DHCP server upon hearing a DHCP Discover message responds with an IP address.
DHCP Request	Broadcast	DHCP Client responds agreeing to accept your IP address offer.
DHCP ACK	Broadcast	DHCP server acknowledges the lease.

process. Next, we notice the IP source address of 0.0.0.0. This actually makes sense since the machine has not yet acquired an IP address; therefore, the 0.0.0.0 values are simply placeholders. The destination address 255.255. 255.255 indicates a broadcast message. This means that it goes to every device on the particular subnetwork. If the routers are configured to forward DHCP broadcasts, then they would go to other subnetworks as well. After the IP header is completed, there are another 308 bytes remaining. These bytes subtracted from the original 328 bytes give us an IP header length of 20 bytes.

```
IP: ID = 0x0; Proto = UDP; Len: 328
        IP: Version = 4 (0x4)
        IP: Header Length = 20 (0x14)
        IP: Service Type = 0 (0x0)
            IP: Precedence = Routine
            IP: ...0.... = Normal Delay
            IP: ....0... = Normal Throughput
            IP: .....0.. = Normal Reliability
        IP: Total Length = 328 (0x148)
        IP: Identification = 0 (0x0)
        IP: Flags Summary = 0 (0x0)
            IP: .......0 = Last fragment in datagram
            IP: ......0. = May fragment datagram if necessary
        IP: Fragment Offset = 0 (0x0) bytes
        IP: Time to Live = 128 (0x80)
        IP: Protocol = UDP—User Datagram
        IP: Checksum = 0x39A6
        IP: Source Address = 0.0.0.0
        IP: Destination Address = 255.255.255.255
        IP: Data: Number of data bytes remaining = 308 (0x0134)
```

Now we come to the UDP section of the DHCP discover message. We notice in the printout below that we are using an IP Multicast and that the source UDP port is 68. This port is used for BOOTP client requests, while the destination UDP port is 67, the BOOTP server port. If a router does not allow these two UDP ports to be forwarded, and the DHCP server is on another subnet, then these requests will not be answered unless a separate BOOTP relay agent is configured.

```
UDP: IP Multicast: Src Port: BOOTP Client, (68); Dst Port:
BOOTP Server (67); Length = 308 (0x134)
        UDP: Source Port = BOOTP Client
        UDP: Destination Port = BOOTP Server
        UDP: Total length = 308 (0x134) bytes
        UDP: UDP Checksum = 0x78C3
        UDP: Data: Number of data bytes remaining = 300 (0x012C)
```

The last section of the DHCP discover message is the actual bread and butter section of the frame. Note that this frame is a discover frame and is identified as such. Next, we see some parameters that tell the receiving computers how to read the message. For instance, the hardware address length is six bytes. It has come over 0 hops and there are no flags set. The flag setting allows receiving machines to process the message in a more efficient manner without having to read the flags section. Now we come to the address section. We see that all are set to "0.0.0.0". Then, we have the actual MAC address of the client machine. In this instance, it is 00104BEC8DB2. In the requested address field, we see that the "Kenny" machine (a Windows 98 DHCP client machine) has had an IP address on this network before and is requesting the same address. This information is kept in the registry and pulled out whenever formulating a DHCP discover message. If the requested address is not available on the network, then a NAK would be issued to the requesting machine.

```
DHCP: Discover            (xid=05D105D1)
        DHCP: Op Code          (op)     = 1 (0x1)
        DHCP: Hardware Type    (htype)  = 1 (0x1) 10Mb
Ethernet
        DHCP: Hardware Address Length (hlen) = 6 (0x6)
        DHCP: Hops             (hops)   = 0 (0x0)
        DHCP: Transaction ID   (xid)    = 97584593
(0x5D105D1)
        DHCP: Seconds          (secs)   = 0 (0x0)
        DHCP: Flags            (flags)  = 0 (0x0)
                    DHCP: 0.............. = No Broadcast
        DHCP: Client IP Address (ciaddr) = 0.0.0.0
        DHCP: Your   IP Address (yiaddr) = 0.0.0.0
        DHCP: Server IP Address (siaddr) = 0.0.0.0
        DHCP: Relay  IP Address (giaddr) = 0.0.0.0
        DHCP: Client Ethernet Address (chaddr) = 00104BEC8DB2
        DHCP: Server Host Name  (sname)  = <Blank>
        DHCP: Boot File Name    (file)   = <Blank>
        DHCP: Magic Cookie = [OK]
        DHCP: Option Field      (options)
            DHCP: DHCP Message Type     = DHCP Discover
            DHCP: Client-identifier     = (Type: 1) 00 10
4b ec 8d b2
            DHCP: Requested Address     = 10.0.0.76
            DHCP: Host Name             = kenny
            DHCP: Parameter Request List = (Length: 8) 01
03 06 0f 2c 2e 2f 39
            DHCP: End of this option field
```

Now we come to the DHCP Offer from the server. This Ethernet header has the same features as the one from the DHCP Discover frame, so there is no need to repeat that here. The interesting thing about the IP header is seen in the printout below. The source address is the IP address of the DHCP server, and we see that it is still using a broadcast. Remember, at this point in the process, the client machine does not have an IP address. The data remaining is 308 bytes, which is identical to the DHCP offer packet at the end of the IP header.

```
IP: Protocol = UDP — User Datagram
    IP: Checksum = 0x787B
    IP: Source Address = 10.0.0.11
    IP: Destination Address = 255.255.255.255
    IP: Data: Number of data bytes remaining = 308 (0x0134)
```

The UDP section looks just like the UDP header of the DHCP Discover message, except that the source and destination ports are switched as seen below.

```
UDP: IP Multicast:  Src Port: BOOTP Server, (67); Dst Port:
BOOTP Client (68); Length = 308 (0x134)
    UDP: Source Port = BOOTP Server
    UDP: Destination Port = BOOTP Client
    UDP: Total length = 308 (0x134) bytes
    UDP: UDP Checksum = 0x6D2F
    UDP: Data: Number of data bytes remaining = 300
(0x012C)
```

Now we come to the DHCP section of the DHCP offer packet. Notice that the offer, Ethernet, and flags sections look similar to the DHCP request packet. However, your IP address has now been filled in using the exact IP address that was submitted in the DHCP request. This is obviously not always the case, but it is relatively common on smaller networks with large address pools at their disposal.

The DHCP Options section has now been filled out. The client machine has everything it needs to properly evaluate the offer from the server. In this instance, the subnet mask is 255.0.0.0, the lease is good for three days, the DHCP server making this offer is 10.0.0.11, and the router is 10.0.0.15. In addition, the DNS server is 10.0.0.10. The same server is also providing NetBIOS name resolution services with a default method of 0x08.

```
DHCP: Offer                    (xid=05D105D1)
    DHCP: Op Code             (op)     = 2 (0x2)
    DHCP: Hardware Type       (htype)  = 1 (0x1) 10Mb
Ethernet
DHCP: Hardware Address Length (hlen) = 6 (0x6)
```

```
DHCP: Hops                  (hops)    = 0 (0x0)
DHCP: Transaction ID        (xid)     = 97584593
(0x5D105D1)
DHCP: Seconds               (secs)    = 0 (0x0)
DHCP: Flags                 (flags)   = 0 (0x0)
     DHCP: 0.............. = No Broadcast
DHCP: Client IP Address (ciaddr) = 0.0.0.0
DHCP: Your   IP Address (yiaddr) = 10.0.0.76
DHCP: Server IP Address (siaddr) = 0.0.0.0
DHCP: Relay  IP Address (giaddr) = 0.0.0.0
DHCP: Client Ethernet Address (chaddr) = 00104BEC8DB2
DHCP: Server Host Name  (sname)   = <Blank>
DHCP: Boot File Name    (file)    = <Blank>
DHCP: Magic Cookie = [OK]
DHCP: Option Field      (options)
     DHCP: DHCP Message Type      = DHCP Offer
     DHCP: Subnet Mask            = 255.0.0.0
     DHCP: Renewal Time Value (T1) = 1 Days, 12:00:00
     DHCP: Rebinding Time Value (T2) = 2 Days, 15:00:00
     DHCP: IP Address Lease Time  = 3 Days,  0:00:00
     DHCP: Server Identifier      = 10.0.0.11
     DHCP: Router                 = 10.0.0.15
     DHCP: Domain Name Server     = 10.0.0.10
     DHCP: NetBIOS Name Service   = 10.0.0.10
     DHCP: NetBIOS Node Type      = (Length: 1) 08
     DHCP: End of this option field
```

If all of the above looks good to the client machine (and I am sure it will), then the machine will send out a DHCP request message as seen in the printout below. We have omitted the Ethernet header, the IP header, and the UDP header as they look similar to the other ones. Something interesting we see near the bottom is a DHCP request frame, and we see the requested address, and the host name fields filled in by the client machine.

```
DHCP: Request               (xid=05D105D1)
     DHCP: Op Code           (op)     = 1 (0x1)
     DHCP: Hardware Type     (htype)  = 1 (0x1) 10Mb
Ethernet
     DHCP: Hardware Address Length (hlen) = 6 (0x6)
     DHCP: Hops              (hops)   = 0 (0x0)
     DHCP: Transaction ID    (xid)    = 97584593
(0x5D105D1)
     DHCP: Seconds           (secs)   = 0 (0x0)
     DHCP: Flags             (flags)  = 0 (0x0)
         DHCP: 0.............. = No Broadcast
     DHCP: Client IP Address (ciaddr) = 0.0.0.0
     DHCP: Your   IP Address (yiaddr) = 0.0.0.0
     DHCP: Server IP Address (siaddr) = 0.0.0.0
```

```
DHCP: Relay  IP Address (giaddr) = 0.0.0.0
DHCP: Client Ethernet Address (chaddr) = 00104BEC8DB2
DHCP: Server Host Name  (sname)  = <Blank>
DHCP: Boot File Name    (file)   = <Blank>
DHCP: Magic Cookie = [OK]
DHCP: Option Field       (options)
     DHCP: DHCP Message Type      = DHCP Request
     DHCP: Client-identifier      = (Type: 1) 00 10 4b
ec 8d b2
     DHCP: Requested Address      = 10.0.0.76
     DHCP: Server Identifier      = 10.0.0.11
     DHCP: Host Name              = kenny
     DHCP: Parameter Request List = (Length: 8) 01 03
06 0f 2c 2e 2f 39
     DHCP: End of this option field
```

Now we come to the final frame in this conversation, which is the DHCP ACK frame from the server. Again, we will omit all headers but the DHCP portion of the frame. In this frame, we see it looks very similar to the DHCP offer that was tendered by the DHCP server in the second frame. We see that the client is indeed allowed to use the IP address the machine had requested, and all the options have remained the same. Once again, it is a broadcast sent out to all machines on the subnet. Once the client machine receives this packet, it will begin using the address.

```
DHCP: ACK                (xid=05D105D1)
     DHCP: Op Code         (op)     = 2 (0x2)
     DHCP: Hardware Type   (htype)  = 1 (0x1) 10Mb
Ethernet
     DHCP: Hardware Address Length (hlen) = 6 (0x6)
     DHCP: Hops            (hops)   = 0 (0x0)
     DHCP: Transaction ID  (xid)    = 97584593
(0x5D105D1)
     DHCP: Seconds         (secs)   = 0 (0x0)
     DHCP: Flags           (flags)  = 0 (0x0)
        DHCP: 0.............. = No Broadcast
     DHCP: Client IP Address (ciaddr) = 0.0.0.0
     DHCP: Your   IP Address (yiaddr) = 10.0.0.76
     DHCP: Server IP Address (siaddr) = 0.0.0.0
     DHCP: Relay  IP Address (giaddr) = 0.0.0.0
     DHCP: Client Ethernet Address (chaddr) = 00104BEC8DB2
     DHCP: Server Host Name  (sname)  = <Blank>
     DHCP: Boot File Name    (file)   = <Blank>
     DHCP: Magic Cookie = [OK]
     DHCP: Option Field       (options)
        DHCP: DHCP Message Type      = DHCP ACK
        DHCP: Renewal Time Value (T1) = 1 Days, 12:00:00
```

```
DHCP: Rebinding Time Value (T2) = 2 Days, 15:00:00
DHCP: IP Address Lease Time  = 3 Days,  0:00:00
DHCP: Server Identifier      = 10.0.0.11
DHCP: Subnet Mask            = 255.0.0.0
DHCP: Router                 = 10.0.0.15
DHCP: Domain Name Server     = 10.0.0.10
DHCP: NetBIOS Name Service   = 10.0.0.10
DHCP: NetBIOS Node Type      = (Length: 1) 08
DHCP: End of this option field
```

DHCP lease renewal   A leased IP address must be renewed prior to expiration. As we can see in the printout above, when the lease is acknowledged, it is also assigned a renewal time. This renewal process requires only two frames: a DHCP request and a subsequent ACK.

There are basically two times when a DHCP client will request a renewal—at startup and at half the lease time. On each of these occasions, if the request is successful, it takes only two frames. These two frames look just like the request and ACK frames we saw in the previous section. The only difference is that at the half-time request, it is a directed datagram, not a broadcast as is the case for the startup renewal.

These two frames total 684 bytes in size and take only 100 milliseconds to complete. If the DHCP client machine is unsuccessful after two renewal attempts, then it will wait until the next renewal period. If the lease expires, then the machine reverts to the previously described four-frame process, as if it were attempting to acquire an address for the first time.

DHCP traffic optimization   In reality, DHCP traffic has only a minimal impact on the amount of network traffic that is generated. There are only six occasions in which the traffic would be present at all. These are listed below.

- DHCP client needs an address for the first time—four frames.
- Automatic renewal at half lease expiration—two frames.
- DHCP client machine restarts—two frames.
- Machine is moved to a new subnet. This will generate two renewal frames, which will be nacked (a negative acknowledgement), then the four lease acquisition frames—six frames total.
- Nic is replaced on the machine—four frames.
- IP address is manually released or renewed with either ipconfig or winipcfg.

One of the main ways to reduce the amount of DHCP traffic is to adjust the lease duration. This is done in DHCP manager, as seen in Figure 5–1. If the lease duration is changed from the default of three days to thirty days,

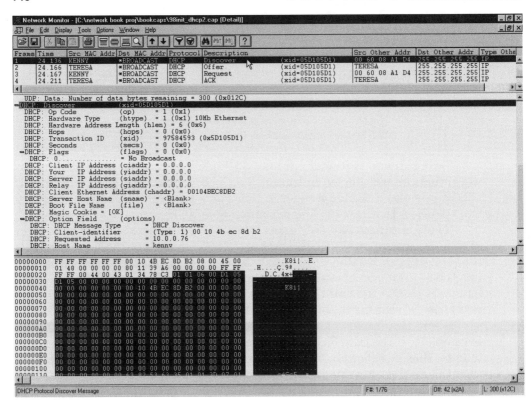

Fig. 5–1 DHCP traffic can be reduced by adjusting the default lease duration.

then the amount of traffic reduced can be significant—13,684 bytes per machine. Making this change makes sense when the scope of addresses is much larger than the number of hosts that need addresses. If this is not the case, then you will need to use either the default lease duration, or make the duration even shorter. Another scenario when adjusting the lease duration can occur when there is a large laptop pool that joins the network on a regular basis. Unless you can train the users to release their IP addresses when leaving the network, they can hold a number of addresses, thereby requiring a larger scope of addresses than would otherwise be needed.

WINS Client Traffic

The next thing a client computer needs to do, after obtaining a proper IP address, is to register its NetBIOS name on the network. In most instances, this registration is going to involve WINS. Most of the resources accessed on a network involve some sort of computer name. Computers on a network must register at least one name. In fact, in most instances, they will register more than one name, to enable communication by name across the network. In the Windows NT world, the host name and the NetBIOS name are usually the same (they are not the same thing, but they are the same word or character combination). In the Unix world, the host name and the NetBIOS name can be, and often are, different.

As we recall from Chapter One, NetBIOS (network basic input output system) is not the same as NetBEUI. NetBIOS is a protocol used by different applications. It can be carried over TCP/IP, IPX/SPX, and of course NetBEUI. We will be looking at NetBIOS because it is used over TCP/IP.

In order for applications to communicate, the NetBIOS name must be resolved to an IP address. The way that it is usually done is by using either a b-node broadcast or a NetBIOS name server such as WINS. There are several advantages to using a WINS server, rather than just relying on broadcasts. The first is that broadcasts are a very expensive proposition when we are talking about network performance. Every single device on a segment must stop and examine every single broadcast frame to determine whether it is able to service the request. In a large network, NetBIOS broadcasts could literally bring the network to its knees, gasping for dear life. This is not a career-enhancing move, so we wish to do something about it. Luckily, Microsoft developed WINS for us to utilize. WINS is a fully compliant RFC-based NetBIOS name-server implementation. With WINS, hosts are able to discard the frame as soon as they look at the destination MAC address. All NetBIOS over TCP/IP name service functions use UDP port 137. Let us now take a look at the name registration and renewal process.

Name Registration and Renewal

NetBIOS names must be registered for every service or application that wants to use its communication mechanism. Examples of these services that get registered include the workstation service and the server service. Other names indicate special roles that are performed on the network such as the primary domain controller (PDC), or the backup domain controller (BDC). The domain name itself gets registered, as well as the names of users logging into the domain. These names are needed for certain messaging and communication functions. For instance, if I want to send a message using the net send command to my buddy Jason, then Jason needs a user name registered or else it will not happen. The total number of names that get registered is obviously dependent on how many services are started. Typically, we will see at least two or three names registered. Each name registered will generate a total of 214 bytes—110 bytes for the name registration request, and 104 bytes for the response. We will now look at such a transaction in the listing below.

```
+ FRAME: Base frame properties
  ETHERNET: ETYPE = 0x0800 : Protocol = IP:  DOD Internet
Protocol
    + ETHERNET: Destination address : 00805FA63A32
    + ETHERNET: Source address : 00609788CF96
      ETHERNET: Frame Length : 110 (0x006E)
```

```
        ETHERNET: Ethernet Type : 0x0800 (IP:  DOD Internet
Protocol)
        ETHERNET: Ethernet Data: Number of data bytes remain-
ing = 96 (0x0060)
+ IP: ID = 0x1501; Proto = UDP; Len: 96
  UDP: Src Port: NETBIOS Name Service, (137); Dst Port: NET-
BIOS Name Service (137); Length = 76 (0x4C)
        UDP: Source Port = NETBIOS Name Service
        UDP: Destination Port = NETBIOS Name Service
        UDP: Total length = 76 (0x4C) bytes
        UDP: UDP Checksum = 0x3D0F
        UDP: Data: Number of data bytes remaining = 68
(0x0044)
```

In the listing above we see that the frame size is 110 bytes. The UDP destination port is the NetBIOS name service port of 137. From this information, we know that it is probably a request frame. Let's take a look at the next section below.

```
    NBT: NS: Registration req. for ED            <03>
        NBT: Transaction ID = 32894 (0x807E)
        NBT: Flags Summary = 0x2900 — Req.; Registration;
Success
            NBT: 0.............. = Request
            NBT: .0101.......... = Registration
            NBT: .....0......... = Non-authoritative Answer
            NBT: ......0........ = Datagram not truncated
            NBT: .......1....... = Recursion desired
            NBT: ........0...... = Recursion not available
            NBT: .........0..... = Reserved
            NBT: ..........0.... = Reserved
            NBT: ...........0... = Not a broadcast packet
            NBT: ............0000 = Success
        NBT: Question Count = 1 (0x1)
        NBT: Answer Count = 0 (0x0)
        NBT: Name Service Count = 0 (0x0)
        NBT: Additional Record Count = 1 (0x1)
        NBT: Question Name = ED            <03>
        NBT: Question Type = General Name Service
        NBT: Question Class = Internet Class
        NBT: Resource Record Name = ED            <03>
        NBT: Resource Record Type = NetBIOS General Name
Service
        NBT: Resource Record Class = Internet Class
        NBT: Time To Live = 300000 (0x493E0)
        NBT: RDATA Length = 6 (0x6)
        NBT: Resource Record Flags = 24576 (0x6000)
```

```
         NBT: 0............... = Unique NetBIOS Name
         NBT: .11............. = Reserved
         NBT: ...0000000000000 = Reserved
NBT: Owner IP Address = 11.0.0.190
```

In some respects, the NetBIOS name service packet looks like a DNS type of structure. In the printout above, the header consists of the transaction ID, the flags section, the question count, the answer count, the name service count, and the additional record count. Each of these is summarized below.

Transaction ID   The transaction ID field uses 16 bits (2 bytes) to keep track of the messages. The originator picks out a unique number for each active transaction. The machine that responds to the message will use the same transaction ID.

Flags   The flags field also uses 16 bits. These are parsed in the printout above. The list below explains what these flags mean.

- Request/response. The request/response is a one bit flag. It is set to "0" to indicate a request or to "1" to indicate a response.
- Opcode. The Opcode flag uses four bits to indicate the particular NetBIOS operation. The Opcodes commonly found in this flag are listed in Table 5–3.

```
NBT: Flags Summary = 0xAD80—Resp.; Registration; Success
         NBT: 1............... = Response
         NBT: .0101.......... = Registration
         NBT: .....1.......... = Authoritative Answer
         NBT: ......0........ = Datagram not truncated
         NBT: .......1........ = Recursion desired
         NBT: ........1....... = Recursion available
```

Table 5–3   NetBIOS opcode flags

Opcode in hex	Meaning
0x0	Name query.
0x5	Name registration.
0x6	Name release.
0x7	WACK (wait for acknowledgment). Sent when WINS is too busy to answer. But at least lets the sending machine know the packet was received (thereby preventing retransmissions).
0x8	Name refresh.
F	Multihomed name registration.

```
NBT: .........0...... = Reserved
NBT: ..........0..... = Reserved
NBT: ...........0.... = Not a broadcast packet
NBT: ...........0000 = Success
```

- Authoritative answer. This flag uses one bit and is set to 1 if the responding machine is authoritative for that domain. It is always set to 0 in a request. In the printout above, we see part of a response packet, and the flag is set to 1.
- Truncation. This one-bit flag is set to 1 if the message had to be cut short due to packet size.
- Recursion desired. The recursion desired flag is set to 1 if the client machine wants WINS to iterate on the query, registration, or release. WINS will also set this flag in a response packet.
- Recursion available. This one-bit flag is set to 1 only in WINS responses to indicate that it supports recursive query, registration, and release.
- Broadcast. Another one-bit flag set to 1 if the packet is broadcasted or multicasted. It is set to 0 if the packet is unicasted. The packet in the printout above was not broadcasted.
- Return code. This is the last flag with four bits allocated for its use. The return code is 0x0 for all requests, and it is also 0x0 for a positive response. Other values indicate error conditions.

Question count   After the flag section, we come to the question count, which has 16 bits allocated for its use. The question count is always 0 for responses. For a properly formatted request, however, this field must have a number such as the 0x1 we saw in the printout earlier. In the printout below, we have a response packet, and the question count has been reset to 0x0.

```
NBT: Question Count = 0 (0x0)
    NBT: Answer Count = 1 (0x1)
    NBT: Name Service Count = 0 (0x0)
```

Answer count   The answer count section is allocated 16 bits, and it is used to indicate the number of resource records contained in the answer section of the packet. The answer listed above has only one record in the answer section.

Name service count   The name service count section also has 16 bits, and it indicates the number of resource records contained in the authority section of the packet.

```
NBT: Additional Record Count = 0 (0x0)
```

Additional record count The additional record count field is the last field in the name service header, and it also uses 16 bits. The additional record count is used to indicate the number of resource records in the additional resource records section of the packet. There are no additional records in the listing above.

After the header information, we come to the question entry. This section is made up of three fields. The first field is the **question name**, which is the NetBIOS resource name. For a NetBIOS name without a scope ID, this field is 34 bytes long. The second field is the **question type**. This is set to 0x00–20 to indicate that it is a NetBIOS name (it is underlined in the trace below). The third field is the **question class**, which is set to 0x00–01 to indicate that it is an internet (IN) question class (it has been underlined below for clarity). These numbers do not show up in the parse section of Network Monitor; rather, they are in the hex data below.

```
NBT: Question Name = SERVERPDC      <00>
     NBT: Question Type = General Name Service
     NBT: Question Class = Internet Class
00000:  00 08 C7 33 F3 E2 08 00 02 1B 35 B0 08 00 45 00
...3......5...E.
00010:  00 4E 04 06 00 00 1E 11 1F 1C 0A 03 01 02 0A 01
.N..............
00020:  64 78 00 89 00 89 00 3A 30 AD 00 D2 01 00 00 01
dx.....:0.......
00030:  00 00 00 00 00 00 20 46 44 45 46 46 43 46 47 45
...... FDEFFCFGE
00040:  46 46 43 46 41 45 45 45 44 43 41 43 41 43 41 43
FFCFAEEEDCACACA
00050:  41 43 41 43 41 41 41 00 00 20 00 01
ACACAAA.. ..
```

Resource record name The resource record name is the next field of the NetBIOS packet.

```
NBT: Resource Record Name = ORCO          <1D>
     NBT: Resource Record Type = NetBIOS General Name Service
     NBT: Resource Record Class = Internet Class
```

Resource record type The next field is the record type. As we see in the printout above, it is a NetBIOS name. This shows up as 0x00–20 in the hex trace.

Resource record class The resource record class is set to 0x00–01, which indicates the internet class (IN) of name.

```
NBT: Time To Live = 518400 (0x7E900)
```

Time to live   The time to live field is a 32-bit field that is used to indicate how long the name is good. In a name registration, refresh, or release request packet, this value is not relevant. This field is set to 0x04–93-E0 (300,000 seconds).

RDATA length   This field is allocated 16 bits and is used to indicate the number of bytes of resource data for this record. It is set to 0x00–06 as seen below.

```
NBT: RDATA Length = 6 (0x6)
```

Resource record flags   The resource record flags are given 16 bits to be used for two specific flags. The high-order bit is used to determine whether the name being registered, or refreshed, or renewed is a unique NetBIOS name, or if it is a group NetBIOS name. If this flag is set to 1, then it is a group name. If the flag is set to 0, then it is a unique NetBIOS name. In the printout below a group name is being registered. The next two bits indicate the node type of the owner. It is set to 00 for B node, 01 for P node, 10 for M node, and 11 for H node. As we can see below, we have an H node owner.

```
NBT: Resource Record Name = ORCO            <1D>
      NBT: Resource Record Type = NetBIOS General Name Service
      NBT: Resource Record Class = Internet Class
      NBT: Time To Live = 518400 (0x7E900)
      NBT: RDATA Length = 6 (0x6)
      NBT: Resource Record Flags = 24576 (0x6000)
          NBT: 0.............. = Unique NetBIOS Name
          NBT: .11............ = Reserved
          NBT: ...0000000000000 = Reserved
      NBT: Owner IP Address = 192.168.2.2
```

Owner IP address   The last field is the owner IP address, which corresponds to the name being registered, refreshed, or released. In this instance, it is the famous 192.168.2.2 machine.

Logon Traffic

After the client computer is up and has been granted an IP address, the next step is to log on to the domain. This occurs once the user types in the user name and password, and then presses OK. The domain controller (either the primary or one of the backup domain controllers) will validate the request.

A client machine has to find a logon server, initiate the conversation to authenticate the user, and do other things such as running logon scripts, copying profiles, and the like. As we see in Table 5–4, there is a decent amount of traffic generated during the logon process.

Finding a Logon Server

Before the client machine can log on to the domain, the first step is to find the logon server. There are commonly two. The first is to simply issue a broadcast request to the netlogon mailslot, and the second method is to ask WINS for a list of domain controllers that have registered with the name resolution service. This second method is a direct query if the client is the default H-node name resolution type. Let us look at each of these methods in more detail. First the broadcast method.

Broadcast method

```
ETHERNET: ETYPE = 0x0800 : Protocol = IP:  DOD Internet
Protocol
    + ETHERNET: Destination address : FFFFFFFFFFFF
    + ETHERNET: Source address : 00104BEC8DB2
      ETHERNET: Frame Length : 260 (0x0104)
      ETHERNET: Ethernet Type : 0x0800 (IP:  DOD Internet
Protocol)
      ETHERNET: Ethernet Data: Number of data bytes remain-
ing = 246 (0x00F6)
```

The broadcast frame is addressed to FFFFFFFFFFFF, is 260 bytes in length (including the 14 byte Ethernet header), and uses ethertype 0x0800,

Table 5–4 Logon traffic

Step	Type of traffic	Amount of traffic
Find the logon server	Broadcast or WINS	4+ frames
		700+ bytes
Session preparation	TCP, NBT, SMB	11 frames
		1,280 bytes for win95
		1,370 bytes for winnt
Validation	SMB	4–20 frames
		765–3725 bytes
Session termination	SMB	5 frames
		360 bytes
	Total frames	24+ frames
	Total bytes	3,105+ bytes

which is IP. Next, we see the source address (10.0.0.76) and the destination is 10.255.255.255, which is the broadcast address for the 10 network. We also see that the transport protocol is the user datagram protocol. In the UDP section, we see that both the source and destination ports are 138, which is the NetBIOS datagram service.

```
IP: ID = 0x2800; Proto = UDP; Len: 246
      IP: Version = 4 (0x4)
      IP: Header Length = 20 (0x14)
    + IP: Service Type = 0 (0x0)
      IP: Total Length = 246 (0xF6)
      IP: Identification = 10240 (0x2800)
    + IP: Flags Summary = 0 (0x0)
      IP: Fragment Offset = 0 (0x0) bytes
      IP: Time to Live = 128 (0x80)
      IP: Protocol = UDP — User Datagram
      IP: Checksum = 0xFCAC
      IP: Source Address = 10.0.0.76
      IP: Destination Address = 10.255.255.255
      IP: Data: Number of data bytes remaining = 226
 (0x00E2)
   UDP: Src Port: NETBIOS Datagram Service, (138); Dst Port:
 NETBIOS Datagram Service (138); Length = 226 (0xE2)
      UDP: Source Port = NETBIOS Datagram Service
      UDP: Destination Port = NETBIOS Datagram Service
      UDP: Total length = 226 (0xE2) bytes
      UDP: UDP Checksum = 0x1702
      UDP: Data: Number of data bytes remaining = 218
 (0x00DA)
```

Let's look at the NetBIOS section next. In the printout below, this datagram is directed to a group. Again, we see the source IP address and the UDP port listed. This time, however, we see the NetBIOS name of the machine being used. This machine is named KENNY, and the destination name is NETMON, which is the desired logon domain. It is important to note that both of these NetBIOS names have a type of <00> associated with them. This means that they are unique names.

```
NBT: DS: Type = 17 (DIRECT GROUP)
      NBT: Datagram Packet Type = DIRECT GROUP
    + NBT: Datagram Flags = 2 (0x2)
      NBT: Datagram ID = 20 (0x14)
      NBT: Source IP Address = 10.0.0.76
      NBT: Source Port = 138 (0x8A)
      NBT: Datagram Length = 204 (0xCC)
      NBT: Packet Offset = 0 (0x0)
```

```
NBT: Source Name = KENNY              <00>
NBT: Destination Name = NETMON           <00>
NBT: DS Data: Number of data bytes remaining = 136
(0x0088)
```

Now we come to the SMB section of the frame. The cool thing about this section is that we see it is using an SMB C Transact. The header is not expanded in this view, but it has the TID, PID, UID, and the MID that we would expect for any SMB communication. Since this is a rather long printout, I have underlined the most important sections. Note that it is a write to the mailslot, using an unreliable class. The filename it wants to be able to use is the \mailslot\net\netlogon. Pretty neat stuff.

```
SMB: C transact, File = \MAILSLOT\NET\NETLOGON
   + SMB: SMB Status = Error Success
   + SMB: Header: PID = 0x152F TID = 0xFFFF MID = 0x0081
UID = 0xFFFF
       SMB: Command = C transact
           SMB: Word count = 17
           SMB: Word parameters
           SMB: Total parm bytes = 0
           SMB: Total data bytes = 44
           SMB: Max parm bytes = 0
           SMB: Max data bytes = 0
           SMB: Max setup words = 0 (0x0)
         + SMB: Transact Flags Summary = 2 (0x2)
           SMB: Transact timeout = 0 (0x0)
           SMB: Parameter bytes = 0 (0x0)
           SMB: Parameter offset = 92 (0x5C)
           SMB: Data bytes = 44 (0x2C)
           SMB: Data offset = 92 (0x5C)
           SMB: Max setup words = 3
           SMB: Setup words
           SMB: Mailslot opcode = Write mailslot
           SMB: Transaction priority = 0
           SMB: Mailslot class = Unreliable (broadcast)
           SMB: Byte count = 67
           SMB: Byte parameters
           SMB: File name = \MAILSLOT\NET\NETLOGON
           SMB: Transaction data
       SMB: Data: Number of data bytes remaining = 44
   (0x002C)
```

Now we get to the netlogon section of the trace. What we see here is the request from user MGROCE on machine KENNY. The frame indicates that it can use either a LM1.0 or a LM2.0 type of logon. Notice too that there is a request count of 1, which means that this is the first time the client has tried to log on in this session.

```
NETLOGON: LM1.0/2.0 LOGON Request from client
      NETLOGON: Opcode = LM1.0/2.0 LOGON Request from client
      NETLOGON: Computer Name = KENNY
      NETLOGON: User Name = MGROCE
      NETLOGON: Mailslot Name = \MAILSLOT\TEMP\NETLOGON
      NETLOGON: Request Count = 1 (0x1)
      NETLOGON: LM20 Token = OS/2 LAN Manager 2.0 (or later)
Networking
```

The funny thing in this particular trace (98_login.cap on the CD) is that it is followed immediately by an ARP_RARP from Teresa (the domain controller). One would think that it could have pulled the MAC address from the frame we just looked at. The information was there. Oh well. Once the Kenny machine responds to the Teresa ARP, we get the netlogon response frame, which looks very much like the previous frame we went over in so much detail. The significant portion, however, is below. In this section, we see opcode is a response to a LOGON request, and the name of the logon server is \\teresa. The Teresa domain controller will accept an LM2.0 type of logon.

```
NETLOGON: LM2.0 Response to LOGON Request
    NETLOGON: Opcode = LM2.0 Response to LOGON Request
    NETLOGON: Logon Server Name = \\TERESA
    NETLOGON: LM20 Token = OS/2 LAN Manager 2.0 (or later) Networking
```

Using WINS   An H-node client will use WINS to find a domain controller to service the logon request. This is a standard WINS 92 byte request directed to UDP port 137. As we see in the printout below, the NBT query (the question name) is for <1C>, which technically is a WINS request for the first 25 domain controllers that have the domain name registered. Locally registered domain controllers are given priority in the response message. The first entry in the response is always the PDC. In the printout below, notice that the authoritative answer is 0, the question count is 1, and the answer count is 0. This tells us that this is a request packet.

```
NBT: NS: Query req. for NETMON          <1C>
      NBT: Transaction ID = 32774 (0x8006)
      NBT: Flags Summary = 0x0110 — Req.; Query; Success
          NBT: 0.............. = Request
          NBT: .0000.......... = Query
          NBT: .....0......... = Non-authoritative Answer
          NBT: ......0........ = Datagram not truncated
```

```
NBT: .......1........ = Recursion desired
NBT: ........0....... = Recursion not available
NBT: .........0...... = Reserved
NBT: ..........0..... = Reserved
NBT: ...........1.... = Broadcast packet
NBT: ...........0000 = Success
NBT: Question Count = 1 (0x1)
NBT: Answer Count = 0 (0x0)
NBT: Name Service Count = 0 (0x0)
NBT: Additional Record Count = 0 (0x0)
NBT: Question Name = NETMON          <1C>
NBT: Question Type = General Name Service
NBT: Question Class = Internet Class
```

The response comes back stating that it is an authoritative answer. Notice that the question count this time is 0, and the answer count is 1. Once the logon server has been identified, the process described above continues by sending a broadcast to the netlogon mailslot on the logon server. This, in return, should get a response from the logon server stating the type of logon supported.

```
NBT: NS: Query (Node Status) resp. for NETMON          <1C>,
Success
     NBT: Transaction ID = 32774 (0x8006)
     NBT: Flags Summary = 0x8500 — Resp.; Query; Success
          NBT: 1............... = Response
          NBT: .0000.......... = Query
          NBT: .....1.......... = Authoritative Answer
          NBT: ......0......... = Datagram not truncated
          NBT: .......1........ = Recursion desired
          NBT: ........0....... = Recursion not available
          NBT: .........0...... = Reserved
          NBT: ..........0..... = Reserved
          NBT: ...........0.... = Not a broadcast packet
          NBT: ...........0000 = Success
     NBT: Question Count = 0 (0x0)
     NBT: Answer Count = 1 (0x1)
     NBT: Name Service Count = 0 (0x0)
     NBT: Additional Record Count = 0 (0x0)
     NBT: Resource Record Name = NETMON          <1C>
     NBT: Resource Record Type = NetBIOS General Name
Service
     NBT: Resource Record Class = Internet Class
     NBT: Time To Live = 300000 (0x493E0)
     NBT: RDATA Length = 6 (0x6)
   + NBT: Resource Record Flags = 32768 (0x8000)
     NBT: Owner IP Address = 10.0.0.11
```

Session establishment and logon validation   After the logon server has been found and the logon request has been answered, the next step is to establish a session. Let's look at that now.

TCP session establishment   The first step in establishing the session is to perform the three-way handshake. This process takes three frames and 180 bytes. In the first frame below, we see the S, which is the synchronize flag, and we see the sequence range of 45091–45098. Notice also that the destination is port 139, which is the NBT session port. The next frame comes from the Teresa server; in this frame we see that both the A and the S flags are set. The A flag ACKs the previous frame from the Kenny machine. The S flag, the synchronize number flag from the Teresa machine, offers up a range of 7972459–7972462. Notice here that the source port is 139, and the destination port is 1025, which was the source port of the previous frame from the Kenny machine. It is also interesting to notice that the ACK number of 45092 is in the sequence range from the Kenny machine. The last part of the three-way handshake is the Kenny machine ACKing the previous frame from the Teresa machine. Notice once again that the destination is port 139, and the ACK is in the range from the Teresa machine. In this instance, the ACK is sequence number 792460.

```
FRAME: Base frame properties
+ ETHERNET: ETYPE = 0x0800 : Protocol = IP:  DOD Internet
Protocol
+ IP: ID = 0x3100; Proto = TCP; Len: 48
+ TCP: ....S., len:    8, seq:     45091-45098, ack:
0, win: 8192, src: 1025  dst:  139 (NBT Session)

+ FRAME: Base frame properties
+ ETHERNET: ETYPE = 0x0800 : Protocol = IP:  DOD Internet
Protocol
+ IP: ID = 0xB106; Proto = TCP; Len: 44
+ TCP: .A..S., len:    4, seq:     7972459-7972462, ack:
45092, win: 8760, src:  139 (NBT Session)  dst: 1025

+ FRAME: Base frame properties
+ ETHERNET: ETYPE = 0x0800 : Protocol = IP:  DOD Internet
Protocol
+ IP: ID = 0x3200; Proto = TCP; Len: 40
+ TCP: .A...., len:    0, seq:     45092-45092, ack:
7972460, win: 8760, src: 1025  dst:  139 (NBT Session)
```

Once the TCP session has been established, the next step is to establish a NetBIOS session with the logon server.

NetBIOS session establishment   The NetBIOS session establishment is a relatively straightforward process only requiring two frames and 182 bytes. The request frame is 126 bytes, while the response is only 56 bytes. Notice that the called name is Teresa, and the calling name is Kenny. Because these two names have been previously resolved, this session should work.

```
NBT: SS: Session Request, Dest: TERESA, Source: KENNY
<00>, Len: 68
    NBT: Packet Type = Session Request
    NBT: Packet Flags = 0 (0x0)
       NBT: .......0 = Add 0 to Length
    NBT: Packet Length = 68 (0x44)
    NBT: Called Name = TERESA
    NBT: Calling Name = KENNY            <00>
```

Below is a positive response to the Kenny request to establish a NetBIOS session with the logon server Teresa. We omitted the TCP section of these printouts here, but if we were to look at that section, we would notice the above from the Kenny machine coming from port 1025 with a destination to port 139 as we saw above in the three-way handshake. Obviously, the response frame below comes from port 139 to port 1025.

```
NBT: SS: Positive Session Response, Len: 0
    NBT: Packet Type = Positive Session Response
    NBT: Packet Flags = 0 (0x0)
       NBT: .......0 = Add 0 to Length
    NBT: Packet Length = 0 (0x0)
```

After getting the NetBIOS session established, it is time to do the SMB protocol negotiation, and then to establish a SMB session.

SMB dialect negotiation and session set-up   Now we must decide which dialect of SMB we are going to use. Therefore, this must be negotiated prior to setting up the session. This takes two frames of 212 bytes and 149 bytes respectively. The Kenny machine sends an SMB frame with a C negotiate command listing the dialect strings understood. This is still originating from the Kenny port 1025 and is still going to port 139 on the Teresa machine.

```
SMB: C negotiate, Dialect = NT LM 0.12
   + SMB: SMB Status = Error Success
     SMB: Header: PID = 0x152F TID = 0x0000 MID = 0x0101
UID = 0x0000
         SMB: Tree ID     (TID) = 0 (0x0)
```

```
        SMB: Process ID    (PID) = 5423 (0x152F)
        SMB: User ID       (UID) = 0 (0x0)
        SMB: Multiplex ID (MID) = 257 (0x101)
      + SMB: Flags Summary = 0 (0x0)
      + SMB: flags2 Summary = 0 (0x0)
     SMB: Command = C negotiate
        SMB: Word count = 0
        SMB: Byte count = 119
        SMB: Byte parameters
        SMB: Dialect Strings Understood
            SMB: Dialect String = PC NETWORK PROGRAM 1.0
            SMB: Dialect String = MICROSOFT NETWORKS 3.0
            SMB: Dialect String = DOS LM1.2X002
            SMB: Dialect String = DOS LANMAN2.1
            SMB: Dialect String = Windows for Workgroups
    3.1a
            SMB: Dialect String = NT LM 0.12
```

We see the response from the Teresa machine below. It sends a response choosing protocol index 5 which is the NT LM 0.12 dialect.

```
    SMB: R negotiate, Dialect # = 5
      + SMB: SMB Status = Error Success
        SMB: Header: PID = 0x152F TID = 0x0000 MID = 0x0101
UID = 0x0000
            SMB: Tree ID      (TID) = 0 (0x0)
            SMB: Process ID    (PID) = 5423 (0x152F)
            SMB: User ID       (UID) = 0 (0x0)
            SMB: Multiplex ID (MID) = 257 (0x101)
          + SMB: Flags Summary = 128 (0x80)
          + SMB: flags2 Summary = 0 (0x0)
        SMB: Command = C negotiate
            SMB: Word count = 17
            SMB: Word parameters
            SMB: Protocol Index = 5
```

Now we come to the SMB session set-up, which will also take two frames of 207 bytes and 154 bytes respectively. In the first frame below, we see two commands: a C session set-up & X command passing the user name MGROCE. The second command is the C tree connect & X command, which tells us that the Kenny machine is attempting to connect to the IPC$ hidden share on the Teresa machine. This is used for interprocess communication. The second listing is from the Teresa machine to the Kenny machine, and it is a response to both commands that were passed in the previous packet. Note that there are no errors here, so the SMB session was established successfully.

```
SMB: C session setup & X, Username = MGROCE, and C tree con-
nect & X, Share = \\TERESA\IPC$
   + SMB: SMB Status = Error Success
   + SMB: Header: PID = 0x152F TID = 0x0000 MID = 0x0101
UID = 0x0001
   + SMB: Command = C session setup & X
   + SMB: Command = C tree connect & X
     SMB: Command = No secondary command


 SMB: R session setup & X, and R tree connect & X, Type =
 IPC
   + SMB: SMB Status = Error Success
   + SMB: Header: PID = 0x152F TID = 0x0801 MID = 0x0101
UID = 0x0801
   + SMB: Command = C session setup & X
   + SMB: Command = C tree connect & X
     SMB: Command = No secondary command
```

The Windows 98 machine (Kenny) now initiates a conversation with the logon server (Teresa) by using two remote API calls to validate the logon. These API's are called using the SMB C transact, remote API command. The first API called is the NetWkstaUserLogon, which requests logon validation. The Teresa machine responds with a success message in the second printout below.

```
SMB: C transact, Remote API
   + SMB: SMB Status = Error Success
   + SMB: Header: PID = 0x152F TID = 0x0801 MID = 0x0201
UID = 0x0801
   + SMB: Command = C transact
     SMB: Data: Number of data bytes remaining = 94
(0x005E)


SMB: R transact
   + SMB: SMB Status = Error Success
   + SMB: Header: PID = 0x152F TID = 0x0801 MID = 0x0201
UID = 0x0801
   + SMB: Command = C transact
     SMB: Data: Number of data bytes remaining = 103
(0x0067)
```

The second API called is the NetRemoteTOD. This API retrieves the server's time information to determine the time zone offset for calculating the time file date and time stamping. The server responds with the time as kept at the domain controller.

```
SMB: C transact, Remote API
   + SMB: SMB Status = Error Success
```

```
    + SMB: Header: PID = 0x152F TID = 0x0801 MID = 0x0281
UID = 0x0801
  + SMB: Command = C transact
    SMB: Data: Number of data bytes remaining = 20
(0x0014)


SMB: R transact, Remote API (response to frame 25)
  + SMB: SMB Status = Error Success
  + SMB: Header: PID = 0x152F TID = 0x0801 MID = 0x0281
UID = 0x0801
  + SMB: Command = C transact
    SMB: Data: Number of data bytes remaining = 25
(0x0019)
```

The remaining steps at this point include connecting to the \\teresa\ netlogon share and run login scripts, user profiles, or system policies. This will generate additional traffic. Once all this is done, all that remains is to gracefully terminate the sessions that were built during the logon process. This of course will entail closing the IPC$ session, the NetBIOS session, and the TCP session. This will generate another five frames and 360 bytes of traffic. You can refer to the 98_logon1.cap file on the CD-ROM to look at some of these steps.

Netlogon Optimization

Use LMHOSTS   We began this section by talking about two ways a workstation finds the logon machine—one by broadcast, and two by WINS. There is a third way: using a lmhosts file. Let's look at one now.

```
10.0.0.25 NTS1        #PRE #DOM:DOMAIN          #DOMAIN PDC
10.0.0.26 NTS2        #PRE #DOM:DOMAIN          #DOMAIN BDC
10.0.0.10 EXCHANGE    #PRE                      #EXCHANGE SERVER
```

By using the #PRE entry, we are telling the machine to preload the entry into the NetBIOS name cache. This is found when we type a nbtstat – c, as illustrated in Figure 5–2. When we also put the #DOM with the domain name, we are telling the machine that it is a domain controller, and therefore we get the additional entries such as the <1C>, also seen in Figure 5–2.

If we use the LMHOSTS file, then we speed up the logon process by not performing either the broadcast or the WINS query, and additionally, we save network traffic. The standard problem with implementing LMHOSTS is getting it onto all the client machines. The answer here is simple: Put it in the logon script and allow it to copy it to the client machines. On a WIN NT machine, it goes into the \\system32\drivers\etc directory. On a Windows 9.x machine, it goes into the \\windows directory.

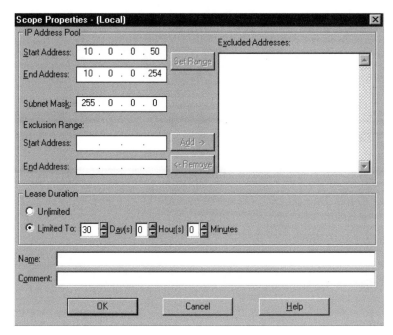

Fig. 5–2   The nbtstat –c command provides a way to view the NetBIOS name cache.

Need more domain controllers?   Typically, the logon process takes place between 8:00 and 9:00 in the morning. How many logon servers do you really need? Remember, adding additional backup domain controllers will increase network traffic, as we will see in the next chapter. That means it is not a good idea to make every server on your network a backup domain controller (which I have seen in more than one location).

Using a very conservative estimate, one domain controller can easily handle 2,000 users. If we go back to our logon window of one hour, that is 3600 seconds, which would mean that we would be averaging fewer than two logons per second (if the logon requests were spaced out evenly). What do we do in this instance? The first thing we will do is use performance monitor to create a log in the morning of logon activity. As we see in Figure 5–3, the best way to do this is to create a performance monitor log and log the memory, processor, and the server object. To do this, you go to view\log and then select options. From the options menu, you select log and then type a name for the log. I simply used logon.log, although I normally use some fashion of a date. Select a good location for the log (off of the root), select the update interval, and then press save. Now you need to add some counters by pressing the plus button, as seen in Figure 5–3.

Once the counters are added, you need to go back into the options menu, select log, and then start the log, as seen in Figure 5–4. This will be a fairly large log, as we want to have our logging set for every second.

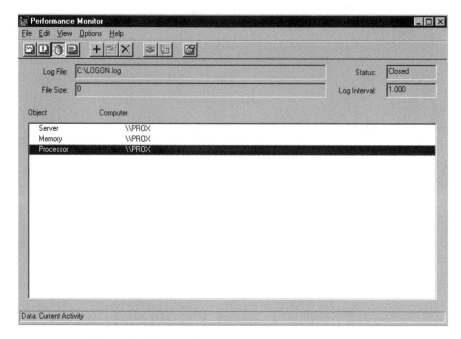

Fig. 5–3 Create a log view to monitor logon traffic.

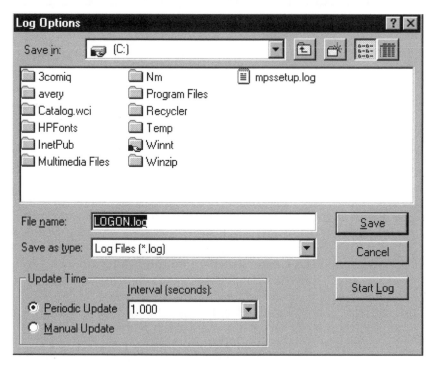

Fig. 5–4 Once the log is created, it still must be started.

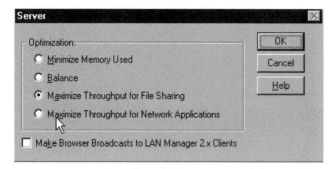

Fig. 5–5 By properly configuring the server service, logon validation is improved.

If after logging you notice periods of time where there are multiple logon attempts per second, you need to make some more changes.

Increase concurrent logon validations When a domain controller is built, the server service is optimized for file and print sharing. This is great for a file and print server, but provides suboptimal performance for a logon server. To change this, go into the network applet in control panel (or right-click on the network icon on the desktop) and select server from the services tab and click on properties. As we see in Figure 5–5, we want to select maximize throughput for network applications and click on OK. *Note:* This will require a reboot to take effect! By making this change, a domain controller can triple the number of simultaneous logons—from six per second to nearly 20 logons per second.

Logon server placement In general, the closer the users are to the domain controller, the better when it comes to logging on. When you have a remote site, it is not necessarily a no-brainer to place a BDC on the other side of a slow link and hope for the best. There are other considerations as well. The impact on WAN traffic due to directory services synchronization must be considered. In addition to that, what will happen if the WAN link goes down and the directory services become out of date? These are some of the things that must be considered prior to implementation. Additionally, you will probably want to implement WINS and DHCP, and configure some sort of replication for these as well to reduce that sort of traffic. We will talk about those things in the next chapter, but for now, it is probably best to place a BDC on the other side of a slow wan link, but it must be a well-thought-out implementation.

BROWSING

I hate browsing. It is commonly a slow process, and if there is anything I hate worse than misbehaving computers, it is a slow computer. They are never fast enough for me, but when I sit for hours and hours over the period of a week looking at a flashlight waving back and forth, it is enough to make me want to do something about it. And we are going to do just that very thing in this section.

If you were looking at some of the logon capture files on the disk, then you no doubt saw some browsing junk on the nt4wslogon.cap file. I skipped over it in the last section, because we will look at it here. Yep, that is right! If you have not gotten your browsing optimized, then you generate browser traffic while you are trying to log on in the morning.

While I assume that you are familiar with the concept of browsing, let's go over a few of the terms to make sure we are on the same page, so to speak. There are essentially five browser roles present in the browser system. While looking at the list below, remember that more than one role can be played by the same computer.

1. **Domain master browser**. This is always the primary domain controller. It is responsible for collecting announcements for the entire domain, including all TCP network subnets, and network segments. Once this list is collected, the domain master browser provides the list of resources to all master browsers on the network. The domain master browser can also be a master browser for its segment.

2. **Master browser**. The master browser is responsible for collecting information to create and maintain the browse list, which includes all servers in the master browser domain or workgroup, as well as all the domains on the network. A server will make a server announcement to the domain or workgroup master browser by sending a directed datagram. This server announcement lists the services available on the computer, and therefore, in addition to being made by NT servers, this server will also be made by NT workstations, Windows 9.x machines, and Windows for Workgroup computers that are performing any kind of file and print sharing. The master browser receives this announcement and adds the computer to the browse list. If the domain includes more than one TCP subnet, then the master browser is responsible only for its segment, but it will also maintain a list of backup browsers on the local subnet.

3. **Backup browser**. The backup browser obtains a copy of the browse list from the master browser and hands out the list upon request to computers in the domain. All domain controllers are automatically configured as either a master browser or as a backup browser. Windows NT workstations, Windows 9.x computers, and Windows for workgroups can all be backup browsers if there are fewer than three NT servers performing backup browser functions in the domain. Backup browsers call the master browser every 15 minutes to get the latest and greatest copy of the browse list as well as the current list of domains on the network. If the master browser is unavailable, then the backup browser will force an election.

4. **Potential browser**. The potential browser is a computer capable of maintaining the network resource browse list, but it does not have the list yet. It will only maintain the browse list if instructed to do so by the master browser. In this case, the potential browser becomes a backup browser.

5. **Non-browser**. A non-browser has been specifically configured to not maintain the browse list. Unless it has been configured to be a non-browser, a computer will be a potential browser when it has server components that are active.

Browser Host Announcements

A computer that provides resources on the network makes host announcements every 12 minutes, although this frequency is higher during client initialization to ensure that it is properly added to the browse list. This announcement is 243 bytes, as seen in the printout below. Notice the Ethernet destination of FFFFFFFFFFFF indicating that it is a broadcast. In the section on IP, we see that the transport protocol is UDP. The IP destination is also a broadcast destination here, it is 10.255.255.255. Once we subtract the 14 bytes for the Ethernet header, we are left with 209 bytes in the IP payload.

```
ETHERNET: ETYPE = 0x0800 : Protocol = IP:  DOD Internet Proto-
col
  + ETHERNET: Destination address : FFFFFFFFFFFF
  + ETHERNET: Source address : 00902764FEBF
  ETHERNET: Frame Length : 243 (0x00F3)
  ETHERNET: Ethernet Type : 0x0800 (IP:  DOD Internet
Protocol)
  ETHERNET: Ethernet Data: Number of data bytes remain-
ing = 229 (0x00E5)
  IP: ID = 0x8004; Proto = UDP; Len: 229
      IP: Version = 4 (0x4)
      IP: Header Length = 20 (0x14)
    + IP: Service Type = 0 (0x0)
      IP: Total Length = 229 (0xE5)
      IP: Identification = 32772 (0x8004)
    + IP: Flags Summary = 0 (0x0)
      IP: Fragment Offset = 0 (0x0) bytes
      IP: Time to Live = 128 (0x80)
      IP: Protocol = UDP — User Datagram
      IP: Checksum = 0xA4C9
      IP: Source Address = 10.0.0.60
      IP: Destination Address = 10.255.255.255
      IP: Data: Number of data bytes remaining = 209
  (0x00D1)
```

The first thing we notice is that the host announcement uses UDP port 138, which is the NetBIOS datagram service port. Although the browser uses a directed datagram, it is still broadcast (10.255.255.255). In this instance, the destination is the MRED domain. Notice also that the browser announcement uses the services of the SMB protocol doing a C transact to \mailslot\browse.

```
+ UDP: Src Port: NETBIOS Datagram Service, (138); Dst Port:
NETBIOS Datagram Service (138); Length = 209 (0xD1)
   NBT: DS: Type = 17 (DIRECT GROUP)
       NBT: Datagram Packet Type = DIRECT GROUP
     + NBT: Datagram Flags = 26 (0x1A)
       NBT: Datagram ID = 32892 (0x807C)
       NBT: Source IP Address = 10.0.0.60
       NBT: Source Port = 138 (0x8A)
       NBT: Datagram Length = 187 (0xBB)
       NBT: Packet Offset = 0 (0x0)
       NBT: Source Name = 2400
       NBT: Destination Name = MRED            <1D>
       NBT: DS Data: Number of data bytes remaining = 119
(0x0077)
     SMB: C transact, File = \MAILSLOT\BROWSE
       + SMB: SMB Status = Error Success
       + SMB: Header: PID = 0x0000 TID = 0x0000 MID = 0x0000
UID = 0x0000
       + SMB: Command = C transact
         SMB: Data: Number of data bytes remaining = 33
(0x0021)
```

Let's now look at the format of the actual host announcement itself. First, we see the announcement interval, which is 12 minutes, and the browser name, which is 2400. The server type summary tells us that the services running on the machine. The 2400 server is running both server and workstation components, and it is a backup controller. The tricky part about reading this section is that some fields use 1 for yes, and others use 1 for no. Notice that the field listed is not NT server. Here we have 0, meaning no it is NOT not an NT server (yes it is). There is a 1 in the field backup browser field, telling us that it is a backup browser.

```
BROWSER: Host Announcement [0x01] 2400
        BROWSER: Command = Host Announcement [0x01]
        BROWSER: Update Count = 0 (0x0)
        BROWSER: Annoucement Interval [minutes] = 12
        BROWSER: Name = 2400
        BROWSER: Major Version = 4 (0x4)
        BROWSER: Minor Version = 0 (0x0)
```

```
BROWSER: Server Type Summary = 135187 (0x21013)
      BROWSER: ........................1 = Workstation
      BROWSER: .......................1. = Server
      BROWSER: .............0.. = Not SQL Server
      BROWSER: ............0... = Not Domain Controller
      BROWSER: ...............1.... = Backup Controller
      BROWSER: ................0..... = Not Time Source
      BROWSER: ..............0...... = Not Apple Server
      BROWSER: .................0....... = Not Novell
      BROWSER: ..............= Not Domain Member Server
      BROWSER: ......0......... = Not Print Queue Server
      BROWSER: .........0.......... = Not Dialin Server
      BROWSER: ........0........... = Not Xenix Server
      BROWSER: ..1........... = Windows NT Workstation
      BROWSER: ........0............. = Not WFW System
      BROWSER: .......0.............. = Not NT Server
      BROWSER: ...0........... = Not Potential Browser
      BROWSER: ......1........ = Backup Browser Server
      BROWSER: ...0.............. = Not Master Browser
      BROWSER: ........0....= Not Domain Master Browser
      BROWSER: ......0................... = Not OSF
      BROWSER: .......0.................... = Not VMS
      BROWSER: 0..............= Not Windows 95 or above
      BROWSER: .0............... = Not Local List Only
      BROWSER: 0.................... = Not Domain Enum
   BROWSER: Browser Election Version = 271 (0x10F)
   BROWSER: Browser Constant = 43605 (0xAA55)
```

Where Are the Backup Browsers?

When a client machine needs to browse the network, the first thing it needs to do is find a backup browser to provide it with a list of network resources. In order to obtain this list of backup browsers, it will need to find the master browser, which as we know is the keeper of the list of backup browsers. Once this is done, it can contact the backup browser and get the browse list.

Theoretically, there would only be two frames required to get the backup browser list. This would involve a simple broadcast with a 216-byte frame containing the following. The browser command is a request to get the backup list 0x09.

```
BROWSER: Get Backup List Request [0x09]
      BROWSER: Command = Get Backup List Request [0x09]
      BROWSER: Get Backup List Requested Count = 4 (0x4)
      BROWSER: Backup Request Token = 1 (0x1)
```

This would be followed with a 226-byte frame in response, depending of course on the number of servers enumerated. As we see below, the browser command is getting backup list response 0x0a, and we see that there are two backup browsers listed, PROX and 2400.

```
BROWSER: Get Backup List Response [0x0a] 2 Servers
        BROWSER: Command = Get Backup List Response [0x0a]
        BROWSER: Backup Server Count = 2 (0x2)
        BROWSER: Backup Response Token = 1 (0x1)
        BROWSER: Backup Servers = PROX
        BROWSER: Backup Servers = 2400
```

Once the client computer has received the list of backup servers, it is time to contact the backup browser directly and retrieve the browse list. In Table 5–5, the sequence of events for a Windows NT workstation took 16 frames. It began by making an SMB connection to the \srvsvc on our Teresa machine. Once that had been successful, edlt next makes a RPC call and calls the remote API NetServerGetInfo. Once again, the SMB's take over, bring down the information, and like a good customer, the edlt machine closes the connection.

Once the above procedure has completed, and the client machine has retrieved the list of backup browsers, it is time for the computer to select a server and obtain the list of shared resources. This can take another 18 or 19 frames and consume about 2,000 bytes of traffic for a server with nine shares enumerated. The total amount of traffic depends of course on the number of shares listed on the server.

Browser Traffic Optimization

While network browsing does make it rather convenient for certain users to be able to explore resources on the LAN/WAN, it comes with a rather steep price tag in terms of traffic utilization. As we have seen in this section, browser traffic with the associated overhead and maintenance can take large bytes out of the available network bandwidth. With this in mind, we need to be able to conserve our resources and deploy them to the best of our ability. Let's look at a few ideas for doing this very thing.

Disable server services on workstations   Disable file and print sharing on your Windows 9.x machines if they are not actually providing file and print services. This will cut down on the announcements and reduce the size of the browse list. Even if not providing any resources, these machines will require an entry in the browse list that takes a minimum of 27 bytes. Additionally server comments take up more space in the browse list and often are not value added. For instance, a server with the name of exchange really does not need a comment of exchange server. On a Windows NT workstation or server, all that is needed to disable the server service is to go into the services applet in control panel, select the server service, and set it to manual.

Table 5–5   Procedure for obtaining the browse list

Source	Destination	Protocol	Description
EDLT	TERESA	SMB	C NT create & X, File = \srvsvc
TERESA	EDLT	SMB	R NT create & X, FID = 0x1007
EDLT	TERESA	MSRPC	c/o RPC Bind: UUID 4B324FC8–1670–01D3–1278–5A47BF6EE188 ca
TERESA	EDLT	MSRPC	c/o RPC Bind Ack: call 0x3 assoc grp 0x7931 xmit 0x1630 recv
EDLT	TERESA	R_SRVSVC	RPC Client call srvsvc:NetrServerGetInfo(..)
TERESA	EDLT	R_SRVSVC	RPC Server response srvsvc:NetrServerGetInfo(..)
EDLT	TERESA	SMB	C close file, FID = 0x1007
TERESA	EDLT	SMB	R close file
EDLT	TERESA	SMB	C NT create & X, File = \wkssvc
TERESA	EDLT	SMB	R NT create & X, FID = 0x1008
EDLT	TERESA	MSRPC	c/o RPC Bind: UUID 6BFFD098–A112–3610–9833–46C3F87E345A ca
TERESA	EDLT	MSRPC	c/o RPC Bind Ack: call 0x1 assoc grp 0x7932 xmit 0x1630 recv
EDLT	TERESA	MSRPC	c/o RPC Request: call 0x1 opnum 0x0 contex 0x0 hint 0x28
TERESA	EDLT	MSRPC	c/o RPC Response: call 0x1 context 0x0 hint 0x58 cancels 0x0
EDLT	TERESA	SMB	C close file, FID = 0x1008
TERESA	EDLT	SMB	R close file

Limit the number of potential browsers   To control the number of browser elections, backup browsers coming and going, and all the traffic we have seen associated with this, we can limit which machines participate in the browsing hierarchy. This requires a modification to be made to each machine, as listed below.

- On a Windows NT machine, there is a registry setting that needs to be changed: HKEY_LOCAL_MACHINE\SYSTEM\CurrentControlSet\Services\Browser\Parameters\MaintainServerList should be set to no.
- On a Windows 9.x machine, use the network applet in control panel, select the file and print sharing service. Select the properties and set the browse master parameter to disabled.
- On a Windows for Workgroups computer, you need to edit the system.ini file. In the network section, add MaintainServerList = no.

Reduce unnecessary protocols   Browsing occurs on each protocol. If a computer has four protocols installed, the browser announcements and elections will be repeated for each protocol. If you eliminate two of the protocols, then you have made a huge dent in the amount of browser traffic.

Use shortcuts to network resources   Instead of double-clicking on the network neighborhood icon, and looking at a silly flashlight, why not create shortcuts to frequently used network resources? It is a whole lot faster, and it reduces a ton of network traffic. In fact, if you use policy editor and turn off the network neighborhood for most of the users, you can really reduce network traffic. Create a folder with shortcuts to the resources they need, and make this a shared desktop icon group.

CHAPTER REVIEW

In this chapter we looked at client traffic. We began with an investigation of the sources of client traffic when the machine is first turned on. We looked at DHCP as the machine requests the IP address. Next, we looked at the WINS client traffic as the computer tries to register its name on the network, and as it looks for other computers to communicate with.

We took a good look at logon traffic and the process involved in finding a logon server. This was followed with some suggestions for reducing some of this traffic. Next, we moved into browsing and we investigated the browsing process. We saw how hosts announcements work and how backup browsers are selected, identified, and utilized. This section concluded with a look at some ways to reduce that traffic.

IN THE NEXT CHAPTER

In the next chapter, we look at server-based traffic. We will begin with an investigation into DNS. We will see how DNS resolves a name and uses recursive looks. We will see how DNS integrates with WINS and talk about ways to optimize DNS traffic.

Following our discussion of WINS, we will look at BDC initialization traffic. We will see how it locates the PDC and how it updates its database, and we will look at ways to optimize both the account synchronization traffic and the NetLogon service.

6

A Look at Server Traffic

The amount of traffic that servers generate may surprise you. I know it surprised me. We are not talking about normal traffic associated with file transfer, print services, and the like. We are talking about the cost of having a server on the network. A total cost of ownership, if you will, for putting the big new server on the network. What is it going to do to my network? You will find out in this chapter.

DNS

The domain name system (DNS) is a relatively efficient protocol designed to assist computers to resolve a host name into an IP address. It is the big brother to WINS, which as we know from the last chapter resolves a NetBIOS name into an IP address. In this strange world of networks, different applications communicate in different ways. For instance, when we type a net use command, we are using a command that talks NetBIOS. When we type a ping command, we are using a command that uses a host name. Another way to look at it is: DNS is to hosts file as WINS is to lmhosts file.

As DNS is designed to be an efficient protocol, most of the traffic is generated when a client machine queries the DNS server and gets its reply. Determining how often this happens will aid in measuring the DNS impact on your network. All networks are different, and all users are different (although at times they seem to share rather annoying characteristics).

One factor that does have considerable influence on the network is DNS recursive lookups. A recursive lookup occurs when a DNS server cannot resolve a name on its own, and therefore asks another DNS server or even a WINS server for the answer. The obtained answer is then handed back to the client in response to the request. This has the potential of doubling the amount of traffic related to DNS.

Resolving an Address

When it works, it is a dream. A DNS lookup is a simple conversation between a client machine and a DNS server. The request is approximately 81 bytes, and the response will be approximately 97 bytes, depending on how many name servers are listed. Notice that DNS is a directed protocol, and the destination MAC address is an actual DNS server, not a broadcast, as we have seen with other protocols. Additionally, we see in the IP section that the destination is an actual IP address of the DNS server on this network.

```
+ ETHERNET: Destination address : 0008C733F3E2
    ETHERNET: Source address : 00805F36CA55
        ETHERNET: .....0 = No routing information present
        ETHERNET: ...0. = Universally administered address
    ETHERNET: Frame Length : 81 (0x0051)
    ETHERNET: Ethernet Type : 0x0800 (IP:  DOD Internet
Protocol)
    ETHERNET: Ethernet Data: Number of data bytes remain-
ing = 67 (0x0043)
  IP: ID = 0xB0EE; Proto = UDP; Len: 67
    IP: Version = 4 (0x4)
    IP: Header Length = 20 (0x14)
  + IP: Service Type = 0 (0x0)
    IP: Total Length = 67 (0x43)
    IP: Identification = 45294 (0xB0EE)
  + IP: Flags Summary = 0 (0x0)
    IP: Fragment Offset = 0 (0x0) bytes
    IP: Time to Live = 128 (0x80)
    IP: Protocol = UDP - User Datagram
    IP: Checksum = 0x101E
    IP: Source Address = 10.1.1.36
    IP: Destination Address = 10.1.100.120
    IP: Data: Number of data bytes remaining = 47 (0x002F)
```

DNS uses the UDP protocol for improved speed and efficiency. In the printout below, note that the source port is the one chosen by the client machine. In this instance, it is port 1185. The client machine, however, does not choose the destination port; rather, it is well-known port 53.

```
UDP: Src Port: Unknown, (1185); Dst Port: DNS (53); Length =
47 (0x2F)
        UDP: Source Port = 0x04A1
        UDP: Destination Port = DNS
        UDP: Total length = 47 (0x2F) bytes
        UDP: UDP Checksum = 0x4FF1
        UDP: Data: Number of data bytes remaining = 39
(0x0027)
```

In the printout below, note that the question count is 1 (0x1) and the answer count is 0 (0x0). This lets us know that it is a question frame. In the question section we see "where is Donnald.Duck.Com?" It is a host address question of the internet address class. This is a typical DNS client request.

```
DNS: 0x1:Std Qry for Donnald.Duck.Com. of type Host Addr on
class INET addr.
        DNS: Query Identifier = 1 (0x1)
      + DNS: DNS Flags = Query, OpCode - Std Qry, RD Bits Set,
RCode - No error
        DNS: Question Entry Count = 1 (0x1)
        DNS: Answer Entry Count = 0 (0x0)
        DNS: Name Server Count = 0 (0x0)
        DNS: Additional Records Count = 0 (0x0)
        DNS: Question Section: Donnald.Duck.Com. of type Host
Addr on class INET addr.
            DNS: Question Name: Donnald.Duck.Com.
            DNS: Question Type = Host Address
            DNS: Question Class = Internet address class
```

The response comes back from the DNS server in the following format. Notice that now the answer entry count is set to 1 (0x1) and, in addition to the question section (which was carried over from the previous frame), there is now an answer section added. In the answer section, we have a time-to-live field that is set to the default 3600 seconds, a data length of four bytes, and the IP address of Donnald.Duck.Com.

```
DNS: 0x1:Std Qry Resp. for Donnald.Duck.Com. of type Host
Addr on class INET addr.
        DNS: Query Identifier = 1 (0x1)
      + DNS: DNS Flags = Response, OpCode - Std Qry, AA RD RA
Bits Set, RCode - No error
        DNS: Question Entry Count = 1 (0x1)
        DNS: Answer Entry Count = 1 (0x1)
```

```
DNS: Name Server Count = 0 (0x0)
DNS: Additional Records Count = 0 (0x0)
DNS: Question Section: Donnald.Duck.Com. of type Host
Addr on class INET addr.
    DNS: Question Name: Donnald.Duck.Com.
    DNS: Question Type = Host Address
    DNS: Question Class = Internet address class
DNS: Answer section: Donnald.Duck.Com. of type Host
Addr on class INET addr.
    DNS: Resource Name: Donnald.Duck.Com.
    DNS: Resource Type = Host Address
    DNS: Resource Class = Internet address class
    DNS: Time To Live = 3600 (0xE10)
    DNS: Resource Data Length = 4 (0x4)
    DNS: IP address = 10.1.100.3
```

Recursive Look-ups

If the queried DNS server does not have the information to satisfy the client request, then there are basically two choices: tell the client the name does not exist, or ask another DNS server for the record if recursive look-ups are permitted.

The client makes a request to the DNS server in the same way as in the previous example. When the server checks its database and does not have the record, it forwards the request to its recursive partner. This is essentially the same frame, except that the first DNS server changes the destination address from itself to the recursive partner. The second DNS server receives the request as it would any other DNS request, looks up the information in its database, and sends the response back to the first server. This response looks like the response frame in the printout above. The first DNS server now takes the response from the second DNS server, changes the destination from itself to the original asking client machine, and sends the response back to the client. In this manner, the client does not know that the look-up was recursed.

Integration with WINS

Just as a DNS server can ask for recursive look-ups from another DNS server, it can also query a WINS server for information if the record is not contained in the DNS system. This allows DNS to contain the static DNS records and get the benefit of dynamic WINS name registrations. This works in a similar fashion as the DNS recursive look-up. The DNS server gets a request from a client machine. If the DNS server does not have the information, it will ask the WINS server for the information. When the record is obtained from the WINS server, the destination address is changed to the client's address and the frame is forwarded to the client machine as if the information had come from the DNS server.

DNS Optimization

A DNS look-up only takes two relatively small frames if the information is on the server. There are essentially three methods for reducing DNS traffic. These methods are listed below.

- Do not configure recursion. Of course, this might limit the functionality of DNS. One thing that would help here is to make sure that all the hosts were put into DNS, but this of course would be a problem when using DHCP, which hands out IP addresses dynamically.
- Configure recursion, but make sure that the most frequently used servers are put into the DNS server. This will reduce the need for recursive look-ups.
- Increase the TTL (time to live) of cached entries. When the DNS server makes a recursive look-up, it will cache the record for 60 minutes. It will cache a NetBIOS name recursed to WINS for 10 minutes. Using the DNS manager can increase these defaults by selecting DNS properties for the zone as seen in Figure 6–1.

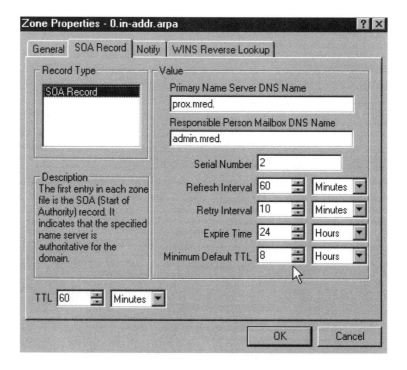

Fig. 6–1   Change the cache TTL in DNS manager to reduce traffic.

BDC INITIALIZATION

When a BDC comes online after a reboot, it can generate a sizable amount of traffic and requires quite a bit of attention from the PDC as a result. A BDC must do several things upon initialization. It needs to find the PDC and synchronize both the user accounts database and the LSA secrets database. It needs to make various announcements such as name registration and browser elections. In the capture file BDC startup on the CD-ROM, the initialization took 123 frames. What are some of these things the BDC is doing? Let us now look at the BDC activity in this process.

Administrative changes take place on the PDC. They can be made anywhere, but the PDC keeps the actual user accounts database. The BDC's only have copies that they work with. It is therefore important that the copy the BDC actually has is up to date. The process that ensures this is known as user accounts database synchronization. There are actually three separate databases that need to be synchronized: the SAM (security accounts manager), the built-in SAM database (the one that contains the built-in local groups such as administrators and users), and the LSA (local security authority) secrets database, which contains the domain controller computer account passwords and trust relationship information.

Where Is the PDC?

The first thing the BDC does after making the normal browser broadcasts, ARP requests, name registrations, and host registrations is try to find the primary domain controller. In order to do this, it will send out an NBT broadcast using UDP port 137 (NetBIOS name service) as both the source and destination port, and it will query for <1B> associated with the domain name. The question frame takes 92 bytes and the response takes 104 bytes, as noted in the printout below. In our example, notice that the query is for MRED, which is the domain name. The <1B> is registered only by the primary domain controller. Notice that the question count in this frame is set to 1, and the answer count is 0, indicating that this is a question frame.

```
NBT: NS: Query req. for MRED           <1B>
    NBT: Transaction ID = 32782 (0x800E)
    NBT: Flags Summary = 0x0110 - Req.; Query; Success
        NBT: 0............... = Request
        NBT: .0000.......... = Query
        NBT: .....0......... = Non-authoritative Answer
        NBT: ......0........ = Datagram not truncated
        NBT: .......1....... = Recursion desired
        NBT: ........0...... = Recursion not available
        NBT: .........0..... = Reserved
        NBT: ..........0.... = Reserved
        NBT: ...........1... = Broadcast packet
```

```
        NBT: ............0000 = Success
   NBT: Question Count = 1 (0x1)
   NBT: Answer Count = 0 (0x0)
   NBT: Name Service Count = 0 (0x0)
   NBT: Additional Record Count = 0 (0x0)
   NBT: Question Name = MRED            <1B>
   NBT: Question Type = General Name Service
   NBT: Question Class = Internet Class
```

The response comes back immediately with the frame below. Notice that the flags have changed between the two frames with the response, and the authoritative answer flags both flipped. The answer count section is now set to 1, and the question count is 0. At the very end of the frame, it associates an owner with the name MRED <1B>, giving us the owner IP address of 10.0.0.10.

```
   NBT: NS: Query (Node Status) resp. for MRED          <1B>,
   Success
        NBT: Transaction ID = 32782 (0x800E)
        NBT: Flags Summary = 0x8500 - Resp.; Query; Success
            NBT: 1............... = Response
            NBT: .0000.......... = Query
            NBT: .....1......... = Authoritative Answer
            NBT: ......0........ = Datagram not truncated
            NBT: .......1....... = Recursion desired
            NBT: ........0...... = Recursion not available
            NBT: .........0..... = Reserved
            NBT: ..........0.... = Reserved
            NBT: ...........0... = Not a broadcast packet
            NBT: ............0000 = Success
        NBT: Question Count = 0 (0x0)
        NBT: Answer Count = 1 (0x1)
        NBT: Name Service Count = 0 (0x0)
        NBT: Additional Record Count = 0 (0x0)
        NBT: Resource Record Name = MRED            <1B>
        NBT: Resource Record Type = NetBIOS General Name Ser-
   vice
        NBT: Resource Record Class = Internet Class
        NBT: Time To Live = 300000 (0x493E0)
        NBT: RDATA Length = 6 (0x6)
        NBT: Resource Record Flags = 24576 (0x6000)
            NBT: 0.............. = Unique NetBIOS Name
            NBT: .00............ = B Node
            NBT: ...0000000000000 = Reserved
        NBT: Owner IP Address = 10.0.0.10
```

After these two frames have passed back and forth, the BDC will now send a UDP datagram to port 138, the NetBIOS datagram service. It is sent as an unreliable mailslot to the \mailslot\net\netlogon on the machine whose IP address was returned from the previous query. This is done in order to retrieve the name of the primary domain controller. Notice in the NetLogon section of the frame that the computer name of the inquiring PC is listed and that the mailslot name is listed as well as the different versions of Lanman supported. This section does not have to repeat the information listed above because the frame is sent directly to the specific machine.

```
NETLOGON: Query for Primary DC
     NETLOGON: Opcode = Query for Primary DC
     NETLOGON: Computer Name = 2400
     NETLOGON: Mailslot Name = \MAILSLOT\NET\GETDC116
     NETLOGON: Unicode Computer Name = 2400
     NETLOGON: NT Version = 1 (0x1)
     NETLOGON: LMNT Token = WindowsNT Networking
     NETLOGON: LM20 Token = OS/2 LAN Manager 2.0 (or later)
  Networking
```

The response comes back from the PDC. Notice that the format of this section has changed just a little. Under the opcode, which tells us that it is a response to a primary query, we see the PDC name, in this instance, PROX. The unicode PDC name is also PROX, and the domain name is MRED.

```
NETLOGON: Response to Primary Query
     NETLOGON: Opcode = Response to Primary Query
     NETLOGON: Primary DC Name = PROX
     NETLOGON: Pad = 0 (0x0)
     NETLOGON: Unicode Primary DC Name = PROX
     NETLOGON: Unicode Domain Name = MRED
     NETLOGON: NT Version = 1 (0x1)
     NETLOGON: LMNT Token = WindowsNT Networking
     NETLOGON: LM20 Token = OS/2 LAN Manager 2.0 (or later)
  Networking
```

Now that the primary domain controller has been located, a session needs to be established. In order to do this, a three-way handshake is first performed. After the three-way handshake (for more information on the three-way handshake, refer to Chapter Two), we have NetBIOS session establishment as seen in the printout below. This is the NBT session request frame (listed as packet type = session request) 0x81 from the BDC. The calling name 2400 is the name of the BDC; in this instance it is directed to the

PDC (called name PROX is the name of the PDC in this case). This is a small frame, only 126 bytes in length counting the Ethernet header. The source port in this instance is port 1025 and can be seen in the trace on the CD-ROM (BDC initialize.cap). The destination port is the well-known port of 139 (NBT session 0x8B).

```
NBT: SS: Session Request, Dest: PROX         , Source:
2400             <00>, Len: 68
     NBT: Packet Type = Session Request
     NBT: Packet Flags = 0 (0x0)
         NBT: .......0 = Add 0 to Length
     NBT: Packet Length = 68 (0x44)
     NBT: Called Name = PROX
     NBT: Calling Name = 2400           <00>
```

Now, let's take a look at the response frame. Network monitor parses the frame extremely well for us, and in the NBT section of the frame we see that it is a packet type = positive session response (0x82). This frame, which is even smaller than the NetBIOS request frame (only 58 bytes counting the Ethernet header), is returned from the PDC (PROX) to the BDC (2400). In this instance, the source port is 139 and the destination is port 1025 on the BDC.

```
NBT: SS: Positive Session Response, Len: 0
     NBT: Packet Type = Positive Session Response
     NBT: Packet Flags = 0 (0x0)
         NBT: .......0 = Add 0 to Length
     NBT: Packet Length = 0 (0x0)
```

It took just two frames and 184 bytes to establish a NetBIOS session between the BDC and the PDC. Now we have to do the SMB protocol negotiation. This will take just two frames and add 373 bytes of traffic to the network. These frames are still using the same ports that were utilized in the previous exchange; that is, on the BDC they are coming from port 1025 and on the PDC they are directed to port 139. Let us look at these frames in the printout below. (For more information on SMB dialect negotiation, refer to Chapter Four.) Below, we see the SMB section of the frame from the BDC as it attempts to negotiate a dialect to be used in conversations with the PDC. We see that the TID, UID, and MID are all 0x0; however, we do have a PID of 0xCAFE. The flags and flags2 sections are similar to the respective sections we covered in detail in Chapter Four and therefore are not exploded here. We see the SMB command of C negotiate, and the dialect strings understood by the BDC listed. If we start counting at 0 (a common computer tactic), then notice that dialect #7 is NT LM 0.12.

```
        SMB: C negotiate, Dialect = NT LM 0.12
           SMB: SMB Status = Error Success
              SMB: Error class = No Error
              SMB: Error code = No Error
           SMB: Header: PID = 0xCAFE TID = 0x0000 MID = 0x0000
   UID = 0x0000
              SMB: Tree ID      (TID) = 0 (0x0)
              SMB: Process ID   (PID) = 51966 (0xCAFE)
              SMB: User ID      (UID) = 0 (0x0)
              SMB: Multiplex ID (MID) = 0 (0x0)
              SMB: Flags Summary = 24 (0x18)
              SMB: flags2 Summary = 3 (0x3)
              SMB: Command = C negotiate
              SMB: Word count = 0
              SMB: Byte count = 135
              SMB: Byte parameters
              SMB: Dialect Strings Understood
                 SMB: Dialect String = PC NETWORK PROGRAM 1.0
                 SMB: Dialect String = XENIX CORE
                 SMB: Dialect String = MICROSOFT NETWORKS 1.03
                 SMB: Dialect String = LANMAN1.0
                 SMB: Dialect String = Windows for Workgroups
   3.1a
                 SMB: Dialect String = LM1.2X002
                 SMB: Dialect String = LANMAN2.1
                 SMB: Dialect String = NT LM 0.12
```

Now let's look at the response from the PDC to the BDC and see how they resolve their communication issues. This is a 145-byte frame (including the 14-byte Ethernet header) that comes from port 139 on the PDC side and goes to port 1025 on the BDC side. Notice in the printout below that the SMB status is error success, which means there were no errors in this section. Once again, we still do not have a TID, UID, or an MID, but we do have a PID (0xCAFE), which is the same as the PID in the previous frame. The SMB command is C negotiate. Notice that the Protocol Index has been selected as 7, which corresponds to the NT LM 0.12 dialect from the previous frame. Other things of interest are agreed upon here as well. These are such things as NT Max Buffer size (4356) and Max Raw Size (65536), which are discussed in Chapter Four. One more thing of interest here is the domain name is listed as ???. This is because, as yet, the IPC$ channel has not been established. This is the next thing that needs to be accomplished.

```
        SMB: R negotiate, Dialect # = 7
           SMB: SMB Status = Error Success
              SMB: Error class = No Error
              SMB: Error code = No Error
```

```
        SMB: Header: PID = 0xCAFE TID = 0x0000 MID = 0x0000
UID = 0x0000
            SMB: Tree ID      (TID) = 0 (0x0)
            SMB: Process ID   (PID) = 51966 (0xCAFE)
            SMB: User ID      (UID) = 0 (0x0)
            SMB: Multiplex ID (MID) = 0 (0x0)
            SMB: Flags Summary = 152 (0x98)
            SMB: flags2 Summary = 3 (0x3)
        SMB: Command = C negotiate
            SMB: Word count = 17
            SMB: Word parameters
            SMB: Protocol Index = 7
          + SMB: Security Mode Summary (NT) = 3 (0x3)
            SMB: Max MPX requests = 50
            SMB: Max VCs = 1 (0x1)
            SMB: NT Max Buffer Size = 4356 (0x1104)
            SMB: Max Raw Size = 65536 (0x10000)
            SMB: Session Key = 0
          + SMB: Capabilities = 17405 (0x43FD)
            SMB: Server Time = Aug 21, 1999 19:6:3.84
            SMB: Server time zone = 240 (0xF0)
            SMB: Encryption key length = 8 (0x8)
            SMB: Byte count = 18
            SMB: Byte parameters
            SMB: Domain name = ???
```

Now we need to establish a connection to the IPC$ share. This is a default share created by Windows NT (sometimes referred to as one of the administrative shares) used for interprocess communication. It uses NetBIOS, and in this instance NetBIOS is riding on top of TCP, which of course is riding on top of IP, which of course is on top of Ethernet. This frame is a 230-byte frame, still going to port 139 for the NetBIOS session service. This frame contains two SMB commands. The first is C session setup & X, which is used to set up the session. The next command is the C tree connect & X, which tells us that the BDC desires to connect to the IPC$ share. This section always says file name, but there are other flags that tell us it is not really a file but merely the way SMB refers to objects in this area.

```
        SMB: C session setup & X, Username = , and C tree connect &
        X, Share = \\PROX\IPC$
          + SMB: SMB Status = Error Success
          + SMB: Header: PID = 0xCAFE TID = 0x0000 MID = 0x0000
        UID = 0x0000
            SMB: Command = C session setup & X
                SMB: Word count = 13
                SMB: Word parameters
```

```
                    SMB: Next offset = 0x0084
                    SMB: Max Buffer Size = 4356 (0x1104)
                    SMB: Max MPX requests = 50
                    SMB: VC number = 0
                    SMB: Session Key = 0
                    SMB: Password length = 1 (0x1)
                    SMB: Unicode Password length = 0 (0x0)
                  + SMB: Capabilities = 212 (0xD4)
                    SMB: Byte count = 71
                    SMB: Byte parameters
                    SMB: Account name =
                    SMB: Domain name =
                    SMB: Native OS = Windows NT 1381
                    SMB: Native Lanman = Windows NT 4.0
             SMB: Command = C tree connect & X
                    SMB: Word count = 4
                    SMB: Word parameters
                    SMB: Next offset = 0x0000
                    SMB: Disconnect flag = 0x0000
                    SMB: Password length = 1 (0x1)
                    SMB: Byte count = 29
                    SMB: Byte parameters
                    SMB: Password =
                    SMB: File name = \\PROX\IPC$
                    SMB: Service Name = IPC
             SMB: Command = No secondary command
```

Now we come to the response from the PDC to the BDC. This response, listed in the printout below, will tell us that we have now connected to the IPC$ share. We see that we have an error success, and the first SMB command is a C session setup & X with a domain name of MRED, which is our domain. The next command is the C tree connect & X to the IPC service name. This is a smaller frame with a size of 194 bytes. Thus, this conversation took just two frames and 424 bytes to establish the connection to the IPC$ share.

```
     + SMB: SMB Status = Error Success
         + SMB: Header: PID = 0xCAFE TID = 0x7807 MID = 0x0000
     UID = 0xC803
             SMB: Command = C session setup & X
                    SMB: Word count = 3
                    SMB: Word parameters
                    SMB: Next offset = 0x0078
                  + SMB: Setup action = 0x0000
                    SMB: Byte count = 79
                    SMB: Byte parameters
                    SMB: Native OS = Windows NT 4.0
```

```
        SMB: Native Lanman = NT LAN Manager 4.0
        SMB: Domain name = MRED
    SMB: Command = C tree connect & X
        SMB: Word count = 3
        SMB: Word parameters
        SMB: Next offset = 0x0088
      + SMB: Optional Support = 1 (0x1)
        SMB: Byte count = 7
        SMB: Byte parameters
        SMB: Service Name = IPC
        SMB: Native FS = Ł?ï??
    SMB: Command = No secondary command
```

The process of establishing a session with the PDC has taken nine frames and used about 1200 bytes of traffic. The final step in order to synchronize the SAM database is to establish a secure channel with the primary domain controller. This traffic will occur only during system initialization because the secure channel is always present unless one of the machines is shut down. This allows new sessions to be created when they time out and permits immediate verification and update without having to create a new secure channel. In this way, it conserves network bandwidth and speeds up access times.

The first step in establishing a secure channel to the PDC is to create a named pipe open request to NetLogon in order to make some API (application programming interface) calls to the NetLogon service. Look at the printout below. In this frame, we see only one SMB command—the C NT create & X command directed to the file \NetLogon. The flags tell us the type of access required, and if this file does not exist, then the command will fail. The Create Flags DWord 0x00000006 tells us that it is requesting both an Oplock and an OpBatch.

```
    SMB: C NT create & X, File = \NETLOGON
      + SMB: SMB Status = Error Success
        SMB: Header: PID = 0x5020 TID = 0x7807 MID = 0x0040
UID = 0xC803
            SMB: Tree ID      (TID) = 30727 (0x7807)
            SMB: Process ID   (PID) = 20512 (0x5020)
            SMB: User ID      (UID) = 51203 (0xC803)
            SMB: Multiplex ID (MID) = 64 (0x40)
          + SMB: Flags Summary = 24 (0x18)
          + SMB: flags2 Summary = 32771 (0x8003)
        SMB: Command = R NT create & X
            SMB: Word count = 24
            SMB: Word parameters
            SMB: Next offset = 0x0000
            SMB: Word count = 24
            SMB: Word parameters
```

```
SMB: Name Length (NT) = 18 (0x12)
SMB: Create Flags DWord = 0x00000006
SMB: Root Dir FID = 0x00000000
SMB: Desired Access = 0x0002019F
SMB: File Allocation Size = 0x0000000000000000
+ SMB: NT File Attributes = 0x00000000
SMB: File Share Access = 0x00000003
SMB: Create Disposition = Open:If exist,Open,else
fail
+ SMB: Create Options = 0 (0x0)
SMB: Impersonation Level = 0x00000002
SMB: Security Flags = 0x01
    SMB: .......1 = dynamic tracking
    SMB: ......0. = effective only bit not set
SMB: Byte count = 21
SMB: File name = \NETLOGON
```

Now let's look at the response from the PDC to the previous frame. The first thing we see is that the SMB status is error success. The command is R NT create & X, which tells us the response. Notice that the TID, PID, UID, and MID match the previous frame. One thing that is interesting here is that in the previous frame, even though it requested Oplocks, the current Oplock level is none. We also see that create action is the file that was opened. Notice also that the file type is a message mode named pipe, which we would have expected to see.

```
SMB: R NT create & X, FID = 0x802
   + SMB: SMB Status = Error Success
     SMB: Header: PID = 0x5020 TID = 0x7807 MID = 0x0040
UID = 0xC803
         SMB: Tree ID     (TID) = 30727 (0x7807)
         SMB: Process ID  (PID) = 20512 (0x5020)
         SMB: User ID     (UID) = 51203 (0xC803)
         SMB: Multiplex ID (MID) = 64 (0x40)
       + SMB: Flags Summary = 152 (0x98)
       + SMB: flags2 Summary = 32771 (0x8003)
         SMB: Command = R NT create & X
         SMB: Word count = 34
         SMB: Word parameters
         SMB: Next offset = 0x0067
         SMB: Word count = 34
         SMB: Word parameters
         SMB: Oplock Level = NONE
         SMB: File ID (FID) = 2050 (0x802)
         SMB: File name = \NETLOGON
         SMB: Create Action = File Opened
         SMB: Creation Time = Jan 1, 1601 0:0:0.0
```

```
        SMB: NT Last Access Time = Jan 1, 1601 0:0:0.0
        SMB: Last Write Time = Jan 1, 1601 0:0:0.0
        SMB: Change Time = Jan 1, 1601 0:0:0.0
      + SMB: NT File Attributes = 0x00000080
        SMB: File Allocation Size = 0x0000000000001000
        SMB: End of File = 0x0000000000000000
        SMB: File type = Message mode named pipe
        SMB: Device state = 0x05FF
        SMB: Boolean Is Directory = 0 (0x0)
```

In the two previous frames, we successfully established a named pipe to the NetLogon service to enable us to make RPC (remote procedure call) API calls. It took two frames and 323 bytes to accomplish this. Now we need to create a RPC connection between the PDC and the BDC. This will happen using the RPC bind and bind-acknowledgment frames. Let us look at the first of these two frames in the printout below. The first frame will use an SMB C transact TransactNmPipe command to the NetLogon file. Thus, in this frame we now have the MSRPC (Microsoft Remote Procedure Call), SMB, TCP, IP, and Ethernet protocols. The printout below comes from a 214-byte frame. This is a bind RPC packet type, and no flags have been set. The flag options are expanded below, but notice that each field has 0, indicating that the flag is not in effect. The abstract interface uses UUID (universally unique identifier), which is a unique identification string associated with a remote procedure call interface. It is also sometimes called a GUID (globally unique identifier). In the frame below, we see that 12345678-1234-ABCD-EF00-01234567CFFB is the UUID.

```
MSRPC: c/o RPC Bind:          UUID 12345678-1234-ABCD-EF00-
01234567CFFB  call 0x1  assoc grp 0x0  xmit 0x1630  recv
0x1630
      MSRPC: Version = 5 (0x5)
      MSRPC: Version (Minor) = 0 (0x0)
      MSRPC: Packet Type = Bind
      MSRPC: Flags 1 = 0 (0x0)
          MSRPC: .......0 = Reserved -or- Not the first
fragment (AES/DC)
          MSRPC: ......0. = Not a last fragment -or- No can-
cel pending
          MSRPC: .....0.. = Not a fragment -or- No cancel
pending (AES/DC)
          MSRPC: ....0... = Receiver to respond with a fack
PDU -or- Reserved (AES/DC)
          MSRPC: ...0.... = Not used -or- Does not support
concurrent multiplexing (AES/DC)
          MSRPC: ..0..... = Not for an idempotent request
-or- Did not execute guaranteed call (Fault PDU only)
(AES/DC)
```

```
            MSRPC: .0...... = Not for a broadcast request -or-
'Maybe' call semantics not requested (AES/DC)
            MSRPC: 0....... = Reserved -or- No object UUID
specified in the optional object field (AES/DC)
        MSRPC: Packed Data Representation
        MSRPC: Fragment Length = 72 (0x48)
        MSRPC: Authentication Length = 0 (0x0)
        MSRPC: Call Identifier = 1 (0x1)
        MSRPC: Max Trans Frag Size = 5680 (0x1630)
        MSRPC: Max Recv Frag Size = 5680 (0x1630)
        MSRPC: Assoc Group Identifier = 0 (0x0)
        MSRPC: Presentation Context List
            MSRPC: Number of Context Elements = 1 (0x1)
            MSRPC: Presentation Context Identifier = 0 (0x0)
            MSRPC: Number of Transfer Syntaxs = 1 (0x1)
            MSRPC: Abstract Interface UUID = 12345678-1234-
ABCD-EF00-01234567CFFB
            MSRPC: Abstract Interface Version = 1 (0x1)
            MSRPC: Transfer Interface UUID = 8A885D04-1CEB-
11C9-9FE8-08002B104860
            MSRPC: Transfer Interface Version = 2 (0x2)
```

The response comes back from the PDC. This is an RPC bind-acknowledgement frame, as seen in the printout below. There are two flags (0x3) that are set. These are the same flag fields as we see in the frame above, and the 1's position tells us that it is the first fragment, the 2's position the last fragment (this gives us 0x3). The associated group identifier is 106023 (0x19E27) and is used for tracking. Notice that the transfer interface UUID is the same in the previous frame and in the frame below. This RPC interface is used for transferring commands back and forth.

```
        MSRPC: c/o RPC Bind Ack:      call 0x1  assoc grp 0x19E27
    xmit 0x1630  recv 0x1630
        MSRPC: Version = 5 (0x5)
        MSRPC: Version (Minor) = 0 (0x0)
        MSRPC: Packet Type = Bind Ack
        MSRPC: Flags 1 = 3 (0x3)
        MSRPC: Packed Data Representation
        MSRPC: Fragment Length = 68 (0x44)
        MSRPC: Authentication Length = 0 (0x0)
        MSRPC: Call Identifier = 1 (0x1)
        MSRPC: Max Trans Frag Size = 5680 (0x1630)
        MSRPC: Max Recv Frag Size = 5680 (0x1630)
        MSRPC: Assoc Group Identifier = 106023 (0x19E27)
        MSRPC: Secondary Address
            MSRPC: Secondary Address Length = 12 (0xC)
            MSRPC: Secondary Address Port
```

```
MSRPC: Padding Byte(s)
MSRPC: Result List
    MSRPC: Number of Results = 1 (0x1)
    MSRPC: Reserved = 0 (0x0)
    MSRPC: Reserved 2
    MSRPC: Presentation Context Results
        MSRPC: Result = Acceptance
        MSRPC: Reason = Reason not specified
        MSRPC: Transfer Syntax
            MSRPC: Transfer Interface UUID = 8A885D04-
1CEB-11C9-9FE8-08002B104860
            MSRPC: Transfer Interface Version = 2 (0x2)
```

Now that the RPC connection has been established between the two domain controllers (using two frames and 396 bytes), the BDC needs to establish a secure channel. This will be done by verifying the credentials of the BDC. It will take four frames to do this. In the printout below, we see the backup domain controller issue a NetrServerReqChallenge to request verification of the account name for the BDC that exists on the primary domain controller. This NetrServerReqChallenge call is made to the NetLogon service using RPC's. Notice also that in the credential section it says Client-Challenge. This indicates that it is coming from the client machine in this conversation.

```
R_LOGON: RPC Client call logon:NetrServerReqChallenge(..)
    R_LOGON: LOGONSRV_HANDLE PrimaryName = \\PROX
    R_LOGON: wchar_t ComputerName = 2400
    R_LOGON: PNETLOGON_CREDENTIAL ClientChallenge {..}
        R_LOGON: CHAR data [..] = 9A 53 AC F4 00 FF B2 01
```

The response comes back from the PDC, as seen below. We are still using the NetrServerReqChallenge call at this point. This frame comes from port 139 on the PDC and goes to port 1025 on the BDC, as all the other frames we have looked at so far in this section have done. Notice that the credential section says ServerChallenge, which indicates the server machine in the conversation.

```
R_LOGON: RPC Server response logon:NetrServerReqChallenge(..)
  + R_LOGON: PNETLOGON_CREDENTIAL ServerChallenge {..}
    R_LOGON: Return Value = 0 (0x0)
```

Now we come to the third frame in this exchange. The BDC verifies the account password at the PDC by using the NetrServerAuthenticate2 API. In the printout below, we see logon server name \\prox and the account name, which is 2400$. The $ at the end of the account name indicates that it is a "hidden" account name used primarily for administrative purposes. In this instance, it is the account being used to establish the secure channel. We also see the computer name, which is 2400, and the ClientCredential, which indicates that this is from the client machine.

```
R_LOGON: RPC Client call logon:NetrServerAuthenticate2(..)
      R_LOGON: LOGONSRV_HANDLE PrimaryName = \\PROX
      R_LOGON: wchar_t AccountName = 2400$
      R_LOGON: NETLOGON_SECURE_CHANNEL_TYPE AccountType = 6 (0x6)
      R_LOGON: wchar_t ComputerName = 2400
    + R_LOGON: PNETLOGON_CREDENTIAL ClientCredential {..}
      R_LOGON: PULONG NegotiateFlags = 1073742335 (0x400001FF)
```

We have come to the last frame in this section, and all the sessions and the secure channel are finally established. Now we have the RPC server response. Again, it uses the NetrServerAuthenticate2 API. Notice the credential section states that this is ServerCredential, indicating that it comes from the server machine in this conversation.

```
R_LOGON: RPC Server response logon:NetrServerAuthenticate2(..)
    + R_LOGON: PNETLOGON_CREDENTIAL ServerCredential {..}
      R_LOGON: PULONG NegotiateFlags = 1073742335 (0x400001FF)
      R_LOGON: Return Value = 0 (0x0)
```

It took four frames and 794 bytes to establish the secure channel. We are now ready to verify the user accounts database. As we indicated earlier, there are really three databases that need to be checked. These are the SAM accounts database, which contains the user and group accounts created by the administrator; the SAM built-in database, which has the NT standard groups and accounts; and the LSA secrets database, which contains the computer account passwords as well as the passwords for trust relationships. There will be an RPC client call made for each of these databases as we begin the process of verifying the user accounts database. Each of these client calls will elicit an appropriate response from the PDC. We know that there will be six frames associated with this process. What we do not know is how much traffic will actually be generated, as it is dependent to an extent on the number of changes required. If you want to look at these frames in more detail, look at frames 59–64 in the BDC initizize.cap file on the CD-ROM.

The first frame contains a single command: NetrDatabaseDeltas. Of course, this command is directed to the IP address of the PDC and is going to port 139, the well-known port associated with the NetBIOS session service. We are still originating from port 1025 on the BDC.

```
R_LOGON: RPC Client call logon:NetrDatabaseDeltas(..)
```

The second frame contains the response to the NetrDatabaseDeltas that was issued by the BDC. This frame is the PDC response to the BDC, and it contains any changes that need to be made to the first database. These changes are enumerated in the last section of the frame.

```
R_LOGON: RPC Server response logon:NetrDatabaseDeltas(..)
    + R_LOGON: PNETLOGON_AUTHENTICATOR ret_auth {..}
    + R_LOGON: PNLPR_MODIFIED_COUNT DomainModifiedCount {..}
      R_LOGON: PNETLOGON_DELTA_ENUM_ARRAY DeltaArray {..}
          R_LOGON: DWORD CountReturned = 1352648495
(0x509FC72F)
          R_LOGON: PNETLOGON_DELTA_ENUM Deltas = 3072610600
(0xB7245128)
          R_LOGON: PNETLOGON_DELTA_ENUM Deltas [..]
            + R_LOGON: PNETLOGON_DELTA_ENUM Deltas {..}
            + R_LOGON: PNETLOGON_DELTA_ENUM Deltas {..}
            + R_LOGON: PNETLOGON_DELTA_ENUM Deltas {..}
            + R_LOGON: PNETLOGON_DELTA_ENUM Deltas {..}
            + R_LOGON: PNETLOGON_DELTA_ENUM Deltas {..}
            + R_LOGON: PNETLOGON_DELTA_ENUM Deltas {..}
```

The BDC once again issues the NetrDatabaseDeltas command to begin the verification process for the second database.

```
R_LOGON: RPC Client call logon:NetrDatabaseDeltas(..)
```

The response comes back from the PDC with the changes enumerated below.

```
R_LOGON: RPC Server response logon:NetrDatabaseDeltas(..)
    + R_LOGON: PNETLOGON_AUTHENTICATOR ret_auth {..}
    + R_LOGON: PNLPR_MODIFIED_COUNT DomainModifiedCount {..}
      R_LOGON: PNETLOGON_DELTA_ENUM_ARRAY DeltaArray {..}
          R_LOGON: DWORD CountReturned = 1607628464
(0x5FD276B0)
          R_LOGON: PNETLOGON_DELTA_ENUM Deltas = 3144190501
(0xBB688A25)
          R_LOGON: PNETLOGON_DELTA_ENUM Deltas [..]
            + R_LOGON: PNETLOGON_DELTA_ENUM Deltas {..}
            + R_LOGON: PNETLOGON_DELTA_ENUM Deltas {..}
            + R_LOGON: PNETLOGON_DELTA_ENUM Deltas {..}
            + R_LOGON: PNETLOGON_DELTA_ENUM Deltas {..}
            + R_LOGON: PNETLOGON_DELTA_ENUM Deltas {..}
            + R_LOGON: PNETLOGON_DELTA_ENUM Deltas {..}
```

The BDC issues the command NetrDatabaseDeltas for a third time.

```
R_LOGON: RPC Client call logon:NetrDatabaseDeltas(..)
```

The last frame in this conversation comes back from the PDC in response to the NetrDatabaseDeltas command. Each of the R_Logon sections has a + beside it indicating that there is more information contained below the heading. These are on the CD-ROM for your perusal.

```
R_LOGON: RPC Server response logon:NetrDatabaseDeltas(..)
   + R_LOGON: PNETLOGON_AUTHENTICATOR ret_auth {..}
   + R_LOGON: PNLPR_MODIFIED_COUNT DomainModifiedCount {..}
     R_LOGON: PNETLOGON_DELTA_ENUM_ARRAY DeltaArray {..}
         R_LOGON: DWORD CountReturned = 69777434
(0x428B81A)
         R_LOGON: PNETLOGON_DELTA_ENUM Deltas = 3587951417
(0xD5DBCB39)
         R_LOGON: PNETLOGON_DELTA_ENUM Deltas [..]
           + R_LOGON: PNETLOGON_DELTA_ENUM Deltas {..}
           + R_LOGON: PNETLOGON_DELTA_ENUM Deltas {..}
           + R_LOGON: PNETLOGON_DELTA_ENUM Deltas {..}
           + R_LOGON: PNETLOGON_DELTA_ENUM Deltas {..}
           + R_LOGON: PNETLOGON_DELTA_ENUM Deltas {..}
           + R_LOGON: PNETLOGON_DELTA_ENUM Deltas {..}
```

It has taken six frames and 1584 bytes (including Ethernet headers) here to verify the user accounts database. These frames included very few changes and resulted in very little account synchronization. If there had been many changes, it may have taken more than six frames and would have generated more than 1584 bytes of traffic.

UPDATES TO THE DATABASE

The PDC will verify its database every five minutes by default. If it spots changes in any of the three databases, then it will send out a message to all the backup domain controllers indicating a change to the SAM. The PDC has a table of each BDC that contains the version ID of each of their database. If the BDC has an up-to-date database and no changes are required, then it is not notified.

Windows NT 4.0 will send an update announcement to a maximum of ten BDC's at a time in order to conserve network bandwidth. This amount is of course configurable for situations where bandwidth is not a concern. The advantage of controlling the updates is to reduce network bandwidth consumption. The other side to this is that it takes longer for changes to be made to all the BDC's.

As we see in the printout below, the PDC makes the announce change to UAS or SAM. Notice that it includes the PDC name, as well as the domain name in the frame. It also includes the serial numbers used for comparing database versions. This frame is sent from the PDC directly to the BDC. It is not a broadcast; rather, it goes to UDP port 138, which is the NetBIOS datagram service port. It is a directed datagram to \mailslot\net\NetLogon.

```
NETLOGON: Announce Change to UAS or SAM
        NETLOGON: Opcode = Announce Change to UAS or SAM
        NETLOGON: Low Serial Number = 210 (0xD2)
        NETLOGON: Date and Time = 909938475 (0x363C8F2B)
        NETLOGON: Pulse = 7200 (0x1C20)
        NETLOGON: Random = 1 (0x1)
        NETLOGON: Primary DC Name = PROX
        NETLOGON: Domain Name = MRED
        NETLOGON: Unicode Primary DC Name = PROX
        NETLOGON: Unicode Domain Name = MRED
        NETLOGON: DB Count = 3 (0x3)
      + NETLOGON: DBChange Info Structure, DB Info = 0x0000
      + NETLOGON: DBChange Info Structure, DB Info = 0x0001
      + NETLOGON: DBChange Info Structure, DB Info = 0x0002
        NETLOGON: Domain SID Size = 24 (0x18)
        NETLOGON: Domain SID = 01 04 00 00 00 00 00 05 15 00
 00 00 5D 5B 3F 41 E1 24 3C 3A C7...
        NETLOGON: NT Version = 1 (0x1)
```

Table 6–1 lists the remainder of the conversation required to update the database. Notice that following the PDC announcement frame we see the same types of things as we looked at in detail earlier in this chapter. The BDC makes a named pipe connection to NetLogon, establishes an RPC session, and then updates the database by using RPC to call the NetrDatabaseDeltas API. After the database is updated, it uses SMB to disconnect and log off.

OPTIMIZING ACCOUNT SYNC TRAFFIC

Several things can be done to optimize user database account synchronization traffic. These optimizations involve editing the registry and adjusting parameters associated with the NetLogon service. In a normal registry, these keys are not even there—they have to be manually added. Figure 6–2 shows a domain controller that has had these additional parameters added to the NetLogon key. As we can see in the bottom of the figure, these parameters are located at HKEY_LOCAL_MACHINE\SYSTEM\CurrentControlSet\Services\

Table 6–1 Domain controller periodic update sequence

Origin	Destination	Protocol	Description
Prox	2400	NETLOGON	Announce Change to UAS or SAM
2400	Prox	SMB	C NT create & X, File = \NETLOGON
Prox	2400	SMB	R NT create & X, FID = 0x100a
2400	Prox	MSRPC	c/o RPC Bind: UUID 12345678–1234-ABCD-EF00–01234567CFFB call 0x1 assoc grp 0x0 xm
Prox	2400	MSRPC	c/o RPC Bind Ack: call 0x1 assoc grp 0x2A0A2 xmit 0x1630 recv 0x1630
2400	Prox	R_LOGON	RPC Client call logon:NetrDatabaseDeltas(..)
Prox	2400	R_LOGON	RPC Server response logon: NetrDatabaseDeltas(..)
2400	Prox	TCP	.A...., len: 0, seq: 15861295–15861295, ack: 235568, win: 8760, src: 1072 dst: 139
2400	Prox	SMB	C tree disconnect
Prox	2400	SMB	R tree disconnect
2400	Prox	SMB	C logoff & X
Prox	2400	SMB	R logoff & X

NetLogon\parameters. The CD-ROM has these entries saved as a .REG file, and double-clicking on it will add them to the registry of your machine; however, **DO NOT make such an addition to a production machine**. Also, make sure that you have backed up the registry before making any change! At the very least, save the key prior to making a change. Each of these values must be weighed with the pros and cons before they are implemented. Additionally, you MUST know what the effect of each will be before these values are added. Once they are added, a reboot of the machine is required.

NetLogon Service

The NetLogon service is used to synchronize the user accounts database between the BDC and the PDC. In addition to this function, the NetLogon does other things as well. These are listed below.

1. NetLogon provides logon validation for users.
2. NetLogon provides support for trust relationships between domains.
3. NetLogon provides for membership of computers in the domain.

Obviously, if the NetLogon service fails, none of the above will happen. Let's look at some registry entries that can be made to optimize the NetLogon

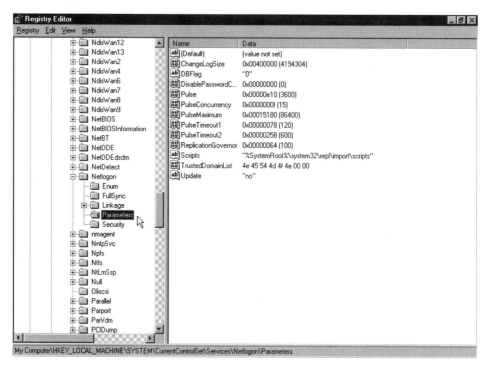

Fig. 6–2   The NetLogon service is controlled by making additions to the registry.

service and reduce some of the traffic we have looked at in this chapter. Each of these entries can be seen in Figure 6.2 and are located at the \NetLogon\parameters key.

ChangeLogSize is used to define the size of the change log in bytes. Since the change log is found both in memory and on the hard drive (\\winnt\netlogon.chg), if we increase the size, we will use more memory and drive space. However, if resources are that scarce on the PDC, it needs an upgrade anyway. The default for this value is 64 KB, which is also the minimum setting. This would hold roughly 2000 changes (a change takes about 32 bytes), which may sound like a lot until you consider all the passwords, machine account passwords, rights, permissions, group memberships, new members, and the like. In a large organization this can quickly be exceeded, causing new entries to overwrite changes that have not yet been synchronized. When this happens, a full synchronization starts up, producing unnecessary traffic.

This is one of the safest changes we can make to the NetLogon service. The maximum setting is 4194304 (4 meg), which will support 131,072 changes to the log. It does not degrade domain controller performance. This should be increased to reduce the number of full synchronizations with BDC's. The other reason to increase this number is if you expect that a BDC will not synchronize with the PDC within the allocated 2000 changes.

DisablePasswordChange defaults to 0, which means that the machine account password must be changed every three days and must be synchronized with the one on the PDC. If the Windows NT machine does not access the PDC after changing the password, then the PDC will cache the existing password for another three days. After six days, when the Windows NT computer tries to authenticate the machine account, the password will not match the one in the security database. This should not be changed unless you completely evaluate the need to do so. The machine account password is used to protect against computer account impersonation and is therefore an integral part of NT security.

Pulse is used to control how often the PDC will look for changes in the directory services database and send announce change to UAS or SAM messages to the BDC's that need updating. The default pulse value is 300 seconds (5 minutes); it can, however, take a maximum value of 17,200 seconds (48 hours). The NetLogon service collects SAM and LSA changes made during the pulse period and sends announce change to UAS or SAM to the BDC's that need the changes. When the NetLogon service first starts up, the PDC will send out a pulse to every BDC with a machine account. In addition, when the PulseMaximum value is reached, the PDC will send out a pulse to all the BDC's regardless of whether they need any changes or not.

In an environment where we are concerned about network traffic, having a pulse of every five minutes is a little over the top! However, changing it to every two days is just as excessive except for very stable environments. If you increase this value to 172,800 seconds, you risk the BDC's machine account password expiring. Of course, you can set the DisablePasswordChange key, but this is a security risk with which most people are not comfortable. If you set this value too high, then it can also result in a situation in which you cause a full synchronization to occur and therefore you get the traffic you were trying to avoid. Setting pulse to something like 3,600 (one hour) or even 7,200 (two hours) results in adequate reduction of traffic in a relatively safe manner. A remote office BDC can even be increased to 86,400 seconds (one day) with few problems.

PulseConcurrency is used to control how many pulses will be sent out to BDC's at once. That is, it governs how many BDC's will contact at the same time to the PDC for database verification. If the PDC sends out 10 pulses at one time (the default for Windows NT 4.0), then 10 BDC's could connect at the same time to update their directory database. The concern here is with network bandwidth and with the power of the PDC to handle numerous simultaneous RPC's without causing an adverse load on the machine.

This can normally be increased from the default without too much trouble. Of course if you have only three or four BDC's, then you can reduce this number and free up some resources on the server. If you increase PulseConcurrency, it will increase the load on the PDC, but normally modern servers can handle this load with ease. If you decrease PulseConcurrency, then it will increase the amount of time it takes for a domain to propagate all the SAM and LSA changes to the BDC's. In a large domain, you can reduce this to the point that the domain never gets synchronized!

PulseMaximum is used to control how often a PDC will send out a pulse message to its BDC's even if the databases are up to date. The default is 7,200 seconds (two hours) and the maximum PulseMaximum is 172,800 seconds (two days). This can be set up to ensure that the PDC is not always contacting the BDC's with changes. If PulseMaximum is set to the maximum of two days, you run the risk of the machine account password expiring. Setting to one day seems to be a relatively safe move for a network with a large number of BDC's in remote WAN locations.

PulseTimeout1 controls how long the PDC will wait for a response from the BDC when the announce change to UAS or SAM message has been sent out. If the BDC does not respond within this period, then it is considered unresponsive. An unresponsive BDC does not count against the PulseConcurrency number, and therefore would allow an additional BDC to connect. It can then update the changes to the database if one exceeded the PulseTimeout1 limit. If, however, the PulseConcurrency had been increased to include all the BDC's, then it would not make any difference anyway. The default is 10 seconds to respond to the pulse before being considered unresponsive.

In a WAN with slow links, PulseTimeout1 may cause a problem if left at the default, and therefore should be increased to the maximum of 120 seconds. The issues to consider before doing this are, of course, if you have a large number of BDC's that need to synchronize, and the PDC has to wait two minutes for each one before declaring it as unresponsive. Then it can take a very long time to complete a partial synchronization. If the number is set too low (the minimum is one second), then the PDC may consider a BDC unresponsive when in fact it is not. This will cause an increased load on the PDC when the BDC finally responds and begins the partial synchronization process.

PulseTimeout2 defines how long the PDC will wait for a BDC to complete partial replication after responding to an announce change to UAS or SAM message from the PDC. If the number of changes increases (such as by making s changes to the ChangeLogSize), then if the BDC does not continue to contact the PDC for additional changes, it is considered unresponsive. The default is 300 seconds, which means that when the BDC contacts the PDC, it is given an additional five minutes to contact it again or else it is considered unresponsive.

If PulseTimeout2 is set too large (the maximum is 3,600 seconds), a slow BDC will consume one of the PulseConcurrency slots for a long time (two hours), thereby extending the time to perform a partial synchronization. If it is too low (the minimum is 60 seconds), then the load on the PDC will increase due to the large number of BDC's performing partial synchronizations.

ReplicationGovernor is used to control the percent of network bandwidth the NetLogon service can use while doing a database validation. The default value is 100 percent of the network bandwidth while using a buffer of 128 KB of data at a time. This can easily eat up the entire pipe on a slow link between remote WAN sites. By setting this key to 50 percent you are changing two things. You now say the NetLogon service will buffer 64 KB of data and only have synchronization messages on the network 50 percent of the time.

This value should never be set below 25 or synchronization may never complete! One thing that can be done, however, is to use the command scheduler the AT command to change this parameter to different values during the day. For instance, you may want to set the ReplicationGovernor to 25 during the day and set it to 100 at night. Of course, this would need to be done on each BDC, but that is not that big a deal!

CHAPTER REVIEW

In this chapter we looked at server traffic. We began with an in-depth look at DNS traffic. We saw how DNS resolves an address, performs recursive lookups, and integrates with WINS.

Following the discussion of DNS, we looked at BDC initialization. In this section we investigated how the BDC locates the PDC and how it updates its database. We looked at some registry settings for optimizing the account synchronization traffic, as well as ways to optimize the NetLogon service.

IN THE NEXT CHAPTER

In the next chapter we look at application traffic. We look at file and print traffic, the TCP handshake, and Internet browsing traffic. We look at Internet mail as well.

A Look at Application Traffic

$\mathbf{T}$he traffic associated with applications is the subject of our inquiry in this chapter. Although this is going to be somewhat of an overview, there are so many different kinds of applications that it would be impossible to look at them all. We want to give you some seminal suggestions, which when fully blossomed will aid you in becoming a real sniffer hound. You will have a real nose for it, if you pardon the pun.

FILE AND PRINT

When you open a file on the server, or send a document to a network printer, a session is established between the client machine and the server. The traffic associated with establishing this session is not huge, and there is little that can be done to optimize it. As in most transactions, the first thing that needs to be done is to find the machine. This can involve WINS, broadcasts, and ARP. Let's take a look at this traffic in the printout below.

WINS Request

This is a standard WINS request. It is directed to UDP port 137, which is the NetBIOS name service port. The question name is where is ED1750. Notice the question count is set to 1, indicating that it is a request frame.

```
       + UDP: Src Port: NETBIOS Name Service, (137); Dst Port:
       NETBIOS Name Service (137); Length = 58 (0x3A)
         NBT: NS: Query req. for ED1750
             NBT: Transaction ID = 33696 (0x83A0)
           + NBT: Flags Summary = 0x0100 - Req.; Query; Success
             NBT: Question Count = 1 (0x1)
             NBT: Answer Count = 0 (0x0)
             NBT: Name Service Count = 0 (0x0)
             NBT: Additional Record Count = 0 (0x0)
             NBT: Question Name = ED1750
             NBT: Question Type = General Name Service
             NBT: Question Class = Internet Class
```

The request above is repeated three times before the client machine gives up asking WINS and resorts to a broadcast.

Broadcast

In the broadcast below, we see that it is addressed to 10.255.255.255, which is the network broadcast address for this subnet. The remainder of the packet looks like the WINS request. It is still addressed to NetBIOS name service port 137, and it contains the same request for the target machine of ED1750.

```
        IP: ID = 0x602C; Proto = UDP; Len: 78
            IP: Version = 4 (0x4)
            IP: Header Length = 20 (0x14)
          + IP: Service Type = 0 (0x0)
            IP: Total Length = 78 (0x4E)
            IP: Identification = 24620 (0x602C)
          + IP: Flags Summary = 0 (0x0)
            IP: Fragment Offset = 0 (0x0) bytes
            IP: Time to Live = 128 (0x80)
            IP: Protocol = UDP - User Datagram
            IP: Checksum = 0xC538
            IP: Source Address = 10.0.0.60
            IP: Destination Address = 10.255.255.255
            IP: Data: Number of data bytes remaining = 58 (0x003A)
       + UDP: Src Port: NETBIOS Name Service, (137); Dst Port:
       NETBIOS Name Service (137); Length = 58 (0x3A)
         NBT: NS: Query req. for ED1750
             NBT: Transaction ID = 33696 (0x83A0)
           + NBT: Flags Summary = 0x0110 - Req.; Query; Success
             NBT: Question Count = 1 (0x1)
             NBT: Answer Count = 0 (0x0)
             NBT: Name Service Count = 0 (0x0)
             NBT: Additional Record Count = 0 (0x0)
```

```
NBT: Question Name = ED1750
NBT: Question Type = General Name Service
NBT: Question Class = Internet Class
```

Once the request has been broadcast, the target machine hears the NBT request for ED1750 and responds to the client machine with the answer. This is a directed UDP datagram and is not broadcast. It goes directly to the inquiring machine to port 137 with the IP address of the machine in the answer field.

```
IP: ID = 0x7530; Proto = UDP; Len: 90
    IP: Version = 4 (0x4)
    IP: Header Length = 20 (0x14)
  + IP: Service Type = 0 (0x0)
    IP: Total Length = 90 (0x5A)
    IP: Identification = 30000 (0x7530)
  + IP: Flags Summary = 0 (0x0)
    IP: Fragment Offset = 0 (0x0) bytes
    IP: Time to Live = 128 (0x80)
    IP: Protocol = UDP - User Datagram
    IP: Checksum = 0xB0C3
    IP: Source Address = 10.0.0.100
    IP: Destination Address = 10.0.0.60
    IP: Data: Number of data bytes remaining = 70 (0x0046)
 + UDP: Src Port: NETBIOS Name Service, (137); Dst Port:
NETBIOS Name Service (137); Length = 70 (0x46)
  NBT: NS: Query (Node Status) resp. for ED1750, Success
      NBT: Transaction ID = 33696 (0x83A0)
    + NBT: Flags Summary = 0x8500 - Resp.; Query; Success
      NBT: Question Count = 0 (0x0)
      NBT: Answer Count = 1 (0x1)
      NBT: Name Service Count = 0 (0x0)
      NBT: Additional Record Count = 0 (0x0)
      NBT: Resource Record Name = ED1750
      NBT: Resource Record Type = NetBIOS General Name Serv-
ice
      NBT: Resource Record Class = Internet Class
      NBT: Time To Live = 300000 (0x493E0)
      NBT: RDATA Length = 6 (0x6)
    + NBT: Resource Record Flags = 24576 (0x6000)
      NBT: Owner IP Address = 10.0.0.100
```

Once the client machine has obtained the IP address from the target computer, the next step is to resolve the IP address to a hardware address.

ARP

In order to resolve the IP address to a hardware address, the ARP protocol will be used as seen in the printout below. Notice that the target hardware address is listed as all zeros because right now the client machine does not know what the MAC address is. The Opcode of 1 indicates that it is an ARP request.

```
ARP_RARP: ARP: Request, Target IP: 10.0.0.100
       ARP_RARP: Hardware Address Space = 1 (0x1)
       ARP_RARP: Protocol Address Space = 2048 (0x800)
       ARP_RARP: Hardware Address Length = 6 (0x6)
       ARP_RARP: Protocol Address Length = 4 (0x4)
       ARP_RARP: Opcode = 1 (0x1)
       ARP_RARP: Sender's Hardware Address = 00902764FEBF
       ARP_RARP: Sender's Protocol Address = 10.0.0.60
       ARP_RARP: Target's Hardware Address = 000000000000
       ARP_RARP: Target's Protocol Address = 10.0.0.100
```

The answer comes back from the target machine, as seen below. Upon hearing the ARP request, the target machine replies with the hardware address filled in. This is not a broadcast frame; rather, it is directed specifically to the requesting machine's MAC address.

```
ARP_RARP: ARP: Reply, Target IP: 10.0.0.60 Target Hdwr Addr:
00902764FEBF
       ARP_RARP: Hardware Address Space = 1 (0x1)
       ARP_RARP: Protocol Address Space = 2048 (0x800)
       ARP_RARP: Hardware Address Length = 6 (0x6)
       ARP_RARP: Protocol Address Length = 4 (0x4)
       ARP_RARP: Opcode = 2 (0x2)
       ARP_RARP: Sender's Hardware Address = 00609788CF96
       ARP_RARP: Sender's Protocol Address = 10.0.0.100
       ARP_RARP: Target's Hardware Address = 00902764FEBF
       ARP_RARP: Target's Protocol Address = 10.0.0.60
       ARP_RARP: Frame Padding
```

It has taken seven frames and 574 bytes to find the IP address and the MAC address of the target machine. If WINS had worked, we could have reduced this traffic by a few frames. If LMHOSTS files had been deployed, the traffic could have been reduced even further.

Three-Way Handshake

The next step is to establish a TCP session. This entails the three-way handshake that will generate another 172 bytes of traffic. The first of these frames comes from the client machine. Notice that the flags are set to S (0x02) to synchronize the numbers.

```
TCP: ....S., len:    4, seq:  42718986-42718989, ack:
0, win: 8192, src: 1164  dst:  139 (NBT Session)
     TCP: Source Port = 0x048C
     TCP: Destination Port = NETBIOS Session Service
     TCP: Sequence Number = 42718986 (0x28BD70A)
     TCP: Acknowledgement Number = 0 (0x0)
     TCP: Data Offset = 24 (0x18)
     TCP: Reserved = 0 (0x0000)
   + TCP: Flags = 0x02 : ....S.
     TCP: Window = 8192 (0x2000)
     TCP: Checksum = 0x84DA
     TCP: Urgent Pointer = 0 (0x0)
   + TCP: Options
```

The response to this frame comes from the target machine. It has two flags (0x12): the A and the S. The A says that the acknowledgement field is significant and I am acknowledging your last transmission. In addition, the S says that I want to give you my sequence number.

```
TCP: .A..S., len:    4, seq: 141140299-141140302, ack:
42718987, win: 8760, src:  139 (NBT Session)  dst: 1164
     TCP: Source Port = NETBIOS Session Service
     TCP: Destination Port = 0x048C
     TCP: Sequence Number = 141140299 (0x869A14B)
     TCP: Acknowledgement Number = 42718987 (0x28BD70B)
     TCP: Data Offset = 24 (0x18)
     TCP: Reserved = 0 (0x0000)
   + TCP: Flags = 0x12 : .A..S.
     TCP: Window = 8760 (0x2238)
     TCP: Checksum = 0xD8DC
     TCP: Urgent Pointer = 0 (0x0)
   + TCP: Options
     TCP: Frame Padding
```

The third frame in the three-way handshake contains the A flag (0x10), stating that the acknowledgement field is significant. This states I acknowledge your sequence number. At this point, a TCP session has been established.

```
TCP: .A...., len:   0, seq:  42718987-42718987, ack:
141140300, win: 8760, src: 1164  dst:  139 (NBT Session)
     TCP: Source Port = 0x048C
     TCP: Destination Port = NETBIOS Session Service
     TCP: Sequence Number = 42718987 (0x28BD70B)
     TCP: Acknowledgement Number = 141140300 (0x869A14C)
     TCP: Data Offset = 20 (0x14)
     TCP: Reserved = 0 (0x0000)
   + TCP: Flags = 0x10 : .A....
```

```
TCP: Window = 8760 (0x2238)
TCP: Checksum = 0xF099
TCP: Urgent Pointer = 0 (0x0)
```

NetBIOS Session

Once the TCP session has been established, the next step is to establish a NetBIOS session. This has to take place between the two machines before any further communication can occur. This will take two frames and 186 bytes. The important thing here is that the called name and the calling name are correct.

```
NBT: SS: Session Request, Dest: ED1750            , Source:
2400            <00>, Len: 68
    NBT: Packet Type = Session Request
  + NBT: Packet Flags = 0 (0x0)
    NBT: Packet Length = 68 (0x44)
    NBT: Called Name = ED1750
    NBT: Calling Name = 2400            <00>
```

The second frame is the smaller of the two frames and comes directly to the client machine. In order for an NetBIOS session to be established, the packet type has to state that it is a positive session response.

```
NBT: SS: Positive Session Response, Len: 0
    NBT: Packet Type = Positive Session Response
  + NBT: Packet Flags = 0 (0x0)
    NBT: Packet Length = 0 (0x0)
    NBT: Frame Padding
```

SMB Dialect Negotiation

Now that the TCP session has been established and a NetBIOS session is established, the next task is to negotiate an SMB dialect. The two computers will choose the highest level of dialect that is understood between the two machines. In the example below, the highest dialect is NT LM 0.12, and we see the SMB command of C negotiate.

```
SMB: C negotiate, Dialect = NT LM 0.12
    SMB: SMB Status = Error Success
        SMB: Error class = No Error
        SMB: Error code = No Error
    + SMB: Header: PID = 0xCAFE TID = 0x0000 MID = 0x0000
UID = 0x0000
    + SMB: Command = C negotiate
```

The response from the server machine tells us that it is a successful status, and we have the SMB response to the negotiate command. In addition, the server supports the NT LM 0.12 SMB protocol, indicated by the position in the first message of #7. These two frames take up 371 bytes on the network.

```
SMB: R negotiate, Dialect # = 7
     SMB: SMB Status = Error Success
         SMB: Error class = No Error
         SMB: Error code = No Error
    + SMB: Header: PID = 0xCAFE TID = 0x0000 MID = 0x0000
UID = 0x0000
    + SMB: Command = C negotiate
```

After the SMB dialect negotiation, we have the actual connection to the network directory share. When the connection occurs, a directory of the share or drive will be copied across the network to the client machine. However, before this can happen, we have to negotiate the connection to the actual resource. At this point the two computers will check security. Let us see how this happens. The client machine uses an SMB C session setup & X command to set up the SMB session. In this frame, we see the account name and domain name listed as credentials, which are being passed to the server machine. In this instance, it is the cool user named ed from the MRED domain. We also see that it is a native Lanman Windows NT 4.0 machine. Since this is an advanced version of the SMB dialect, it can handle multiple commands in the same frame. Therefore, the second command is the SMB C tree connect & X. It is used to make a connection to the share, which in this instance is the IPC$ share on the BIGGUY machine (a Windows 98 workstation).

```
SMB: C session setup & X, Username = ed, and C tree connect
& X, Share = \\BIGGUY\IPC$
    + SMB: SMB Status = Error Success
    + SMB: Header: PID = 0xCAFE TID = 0x0000 MID = 0x0000
UID = 0x0000
      SMB: Command = C session setup & X
          SMB: Word count = 13
          SMB: Word parameters
          SMB: Next offset = 0x0096
          SMB: Max Buffer Size = 2920 (0xB68)
          SMB: Max MPX requests = 2
          SMB: VC number = 0
          SMB: Session Key = -2147483587
          SMB: Password length = 24 (0x18)
          SMB: Unicode Password length = 24 (0x18)
        + SMB: Capabilities = 212 (0xD4)
```

```
                    SMB: Byte count = 89
                    SMB: Byte parameters
                    SMB: Account name = ed
                    SMB: Domain name = MRED
                    SMB: Native OS = Windows NT 1381
                    SMB: Native Lanman = Windows NT 4.0
              SMB: Command = C tree connect & X
                    SMB: Word count = 4
                    SMB: Word parameters
                    SMB: Next offset = 0x0000
                    SMB: Disconnect flag = 0x0000
                    SMB: Password length = 1 (0x1)
                    SMB: Byte count = 19
                    SMB: Byte parameters
                    SMB: Password =
                    SMB: File name = \\BIGGUY\IPC$
                    SMB: Service Name = IPC
              SMB: Command = No secondary command
```

Now let's look at the response to the C session setup & X command. In this frame, we are looking primarily for the SMB status of error success. We also want to double check the credentials that are used to establish this session as well as the capabilities the session carries.

```
  SMB: C session setup & X, Username = ed
    + SMB: SMB Status = Error Success
    + SMB: Header: PID = 0x0000 TID = 0x0800 MID = 0xAA82
UID = 0x0002
        SMB: Command = C session setup & X
              SMB: Word count = 13
              SMB: Word parameters
              SMB: Next offset = 0x0075
              SMB: Max Buffer Size = 2920 (0xB68)
              SMB: Max MPX requests = 50
              SMB: VC number = 1
              SMB: Session Key = 0
              SMB: Password length = 24 (0x18)
              SMB: Unicode Password length = 0 (0x0)
            + SMB: Capabilities = 5 (0x5)
              SMB: Byte count = 56
              SMB: Byte parameters
              SMB: Account name = ed
              SMB: Domain name = MRED
              SMB: Native OS = Windows 4.0
              SMB: Native Lanman = Windows 4.0
        SMB: Command = No secondary command
```

After all the negotiations have taken place, the data transfers to the client machine. The first step is to find the file to bring down to the client machine using a transact2 Findfirst command. This command will use the Findfirst function to look for a specific file (in our instance, the Browstat.exe utility). Two flags are set for this operation. It will close the search handle when complete, and it will resume for each entry found. These can be read as binary numbers. The close search handle flag is the one position, and the resume key flag is the four position (0101).

```
SMB: Command = R transact2
        SMB: Word count = 15
        SMB: Word parameters
        SMB: Total parm bytes = 58
        SMB: Total data bytes = 0
        SMB: Max parm bytes = 10
        SMB: Max data bytes = 608
        SMB: Max setup words = 0 (0x0)
      + SMB: Transact Flags Summary = 0 (0x0)
        SMB: Transact timeout = 0 (0x0)
        SMB: Parameter bytes = 58 (0x3A)
        SMB: Parameter offset = 68 (0x44)
        SMB: Data bytes = 0 (0x0)
        SMB: Data offset = 0 (0x0)
        SMB: Max setup words = 1
        SMB: Setup words
        SMB: Transact2 function = Findfirst
        SMB: Byte count = 61
        SMB: Byte parameters
        SMB: Transaction parameters
          + SMB: Search attributes = 0x0016
            SMB: Find count = 6
            SMB: Find Flags = 5 (0x5)
                    SMB: ..............1 = Close search han-
dle upon completing request
                    SMB: ..............0. = Keep search handle
open if end of search reached
                    SMB: ............1.. = Resume key is re-
quired for each entry found
                    SMB: ............0... = Start search from
the beginning
                SMB: Info Level = Both Directory Info (NT)
                SMB: File name = \NTRESKIT\BROWSTAT.EXE
```

After getting the response from the server, the client machine next issues an R NT create & X command. The create flags Dword of 0x00000006 is requesting both an Oplock and an Opbatch. The file share access of 0x00000001 is asking for read access to the file.

```
SMB: Command = R NT create & X
        SMB: Word count = 24
        SMB: Word parameters
        SMB: Next offset = 0x0000
        SMB: Word count = 24
        SMB: Word parameters
        SMB: Name Length (NT) = 44 (0x2C)
    +   SMB: Create Flags DWord = 0x00000006
        SMB: Root Dir FID = 0x00000000
    +   SMB: Desired Access = 0x00020089
        SMB: File Allocation Size = 0x0000000000000000
    +   SMB: NT File Attributes = 0x00000000
    +   SMB: File Share Access = 0x00000001
        SMB: Create Disposition = Open:  If exist, Open,
else fail
    +   SMB: Create Options = 68 (0x44)
        SMB: Impersonation Level = 0x00000002
    +   SMB: Security Flags = 0x03
        SMB: Byte count = 47
        SMB: File name = \NTRESKIT\BROWSTAT.EXE
```

Now the computer begins the process of figuring out how to transfer the file, and what it will do with the file once it gets it. This process again uses an R NT create & X command, and it currently is using a Batch Oplock. In the printout below, we can see all the normal information we would see in a detailed directory listing. The file allocation size is 0x000000000000A800, which is 4,308 bytes in decimal. When this is divided by 1,024 it gives us 42 K, which is the size of browstat.exe. We also have our File ID showing up now. This FID is used to monitor our transaction and keep up with the file.

```
SMB: Command = R NT create & X
        SMB: Word count = 34
        SMB: Word parameters
        SMB: Next offset = 0x0067
        SMB: Word count = 34
        SMB: Word parameters
        SMB: Oplock Level = Batch
        SMB: File ID (FID) = 6157 (0x180D)
        SMB: File name = \NTRESKIT\BROWSTAT.EXE
        SMB: Create Action = File Opened
        SMB: Creation Time = Jul 26, 1996 5:0:0.0
        SMB: NT Last Access Time = Aug 15, 1999 20:59:1.79
        SMB: Last Write Time = Jul 26, 1996 5:0:0.0
        SMB: Change Time = Aug 24, 1999 1:33:11.25
    +   SMB: NT File Attributes = 0x00000020
        SMB: File Allocation Size = 0x000000000000A800
        SMB: End of File = 0x000000000000A510
        SMB: File type = Disk file or directory
```

```
SMB: Device state = 0x0000
SMB: Boolean Is Directory = 0 (0x0)
```

A few frames later, the SMB protocol begins the actual transfer of the data from the server to the client machine. The SMB command C read & X begins copying the data across the wire. This was a full-sized Ethernet frame (1,514 bytes including the Ethernet header), but it is carrying a payload of only 1,397—that is, 117 bytes of overhead from the Ethernet header, the IP header, the TCP header, the NBT header, and finally the SMB commands.

```
SMB: Command = C read & X
        SMB: Word count = 12
        SMB: Word parameters
        SMB: Next offset = 0x0000
        SMB: File name = \NTRESKIT\BROWSTAT.EXE
        SMB: Bytes left = 65535
        SMB: Data length = 32768 (0x8000)
        SMB: Data offset = 59 (0x3B)
        SMB: Byte count = 32768
        SMB: Byte parameters
    SMB: Data: Number of data bytes remaining = 1397
(0x0575)
```

Once the data begins to flow, SMB will drop out of the picture for a little while and allow NBT to carry the load while it uses TCP to ensure the data is delivered safely. Our payload is now up to 1,460 bytes, where it will remain for the transmission.

```
+ FRAME: Base frame properties
+ ETHERNET: ETYPE = 0x0800 : Protocol = IP:  DOD Internet
Protocol
+ IP: ID = 0x191C; Proto = TCP; Len: 1500
+ TCP: .A...., len: 1460, seq:   2012325-2013784, ack:
8796927, win: 7328, src:  139 (NBT Session)  dst: 1073
  NBT: SS: Session Message Cont., 1460 Bytes
      NBT: SS Data: Number of data bytes remaining = 1460
(0x05B4)
```

Once the data has been transferred, it is time to close the session. This will use the SMB C tree disconnect command. The C tree disconnect command does not use the file name (such as what was used when transferring the data); rather, the client uses the tree ID (TID) of the remote drive to be disconnected. The server assigned the TID when the connection was first established.

```
        SMB: C tree disconnect
          + SMB: SMB Status = Error Success
            SMB: Header: PID = 0xCAFE TID = 0xD002 MID = 0xB2C0
  UID = 0x6802
              SMB: Tree ID       (TID) = 53250 (0xD002)
              SMB: Process ID    (PID) = 51966 (0xCAFE)
              SMB: User ID       (UID) = 26626 (0x6802)
              SMB: Multiplex ID (MID) = 45760 (0xB2C0)
            + SMB: Flags Summary = 24 (0x18)
            + SMB: flags2 Summary = 32771 (0x8003)
          SMB: Command = C tree disconnect
              SMB: Word count = 0
              SMB: Byte count = 0
```

The response comes back from the server with an error success and matching TID number. When this command completes, the SMB session has been disconnected. It takes two small frames of 93 bytes each to disconnect the session.

```
        SMB: R tree disconnect
          + SMB: SMB Status = Error Success
            SMB: Header: PID = 0xCAFE TID = 0xD002 MID = 0xB2C0
  UID = 0x6802
              SMB: Tree ID       (TID) = 53250 (0xD002)
              SMB: Process ID    (PID) = 51966 (0xCAFE)
              SMB: User ID       (UID) = 26626 (0x6802)
              SMB: Multiplex ID (MID) = 45760 (0xB2C0)
            + SMB: Flags Summary = 152 (0x98)
            + SMB: flags2 Summary = 32771 (0x8003)
          SMB: Command = C tree disconnect
              SMB: Word count = 0
              SMB: Byte count = 0
```

INTERNET BROWSING

Internet browsing traffic is increasingly having an impact on corporate networks from both an intranet and an Internet perspective. Both types of traffic have similar patterns of behavior; however, intranets often utilize a higher degree of graphics and therefore require greater bandwidth. Let's look at what happens when we load a single Web page.

Web Pages

For our example, we will look at what happens when I fire up Microsoft's Internet Explorer browser and open with the default start page at MSN. The browser begins with a standard DNS query, as we see in the printout below. This is a small UDP datagram directed to port 53 on the DNS server. It uses 78 bytes, including the Ethernet header for this frame. This frame is repeated before the answer comes back in the third frame of the captures (open msn page.cap on the CD-ROM).

```
DNS: 0x1:Std Qry for home.microsoft.com. of type Host Addr
on class INET addr.
      DNS: Query Identifier = 1 (0x1)
    + DNS: DNS Flags = Query, OpCode - Std Qry, RD Bits Set,
RCode - No error
      DNS: Question Entry Count = 1 (0x1)
      DNS: Answer Entry Count = 0 (0x0)
      DNS: Name Server Count = 0 (0x0)
      DNS: Additional Records Count = 0 (0x0)
      DNS: Question Section: home.microsoft.com. of type
Host Addr on class INET addr.
          DNS: Question Name: home.microsoft.com.
          DNS: Question Type = Host Address
          DNS: Question Class = Internet address class
```

The response to the question, where is home.Microsoft.com, comes back as a 380-byte monster. The UDP payload is 264 bytes of DNS data. For clarity, the frame has been trimmed a bit. The question entry count is one indicating that there is one question that is repeated from the previous frame. The answer count is four, which tells us that there are four answers to the question, where is home.Microsoft.com. The first resource record returned gives the client machine an IP address.

```
DNS: 0x1:Std Qry Resp. for home.microsoft.com. of type Host
Addr on class INET addr.
      DNS: Query Identifier = 1 (0x1)
    + DNS: DNS Flags = Response, OpCode - Std Qry, RD RA
Bits Set, RCode - No error
      DNS: Question Entry Count = 1 (0x1)
      DNS: Answer Entry Count = 4 (0x4)
      DNS: Name Server Count = 4 (0x4)
      DNS: Additional Records Count = 4 (0x4)
      DNS: Question Section: home.microsoft.com. of type
Host Addr on class INET addr.
          DNS: Question Name: home.microsoft.com.
          DNS: Question Type = Host Address
          DNS: Question Class = Internet address class
        DNS: Answer section: home.microsoft.com. of type Host
Addr on class INET addr.(4 records present)
          DNS: Resource Record: home.microsoft.com. of type
Host Addr on class INET addr.
```

```
DNS: Resource Name: home.microsoft.com.
DNS: Resource Type = Host Address
DNS: Resource Class = Internet address class
DNS: Time To Live = 95 (0x5F)
DNS: Resource Data Length = 4 (0x4)
DNS: IP address = 207.46.176.13
```

Once the name has been resolved, it is time to initiate contact by using the three-way handshake. This is directed to port 80, which is the port used for the hypertext transfer protocol. The flags 0x02 (there are two flags set here) tell us that it wants to synchronize sequence numbers. The client machine chose the source port as 3488 (0x0DA0 hex).

```
TCP: ....S., len:    4, seq:    241730-241733, ack:
0, win: 8192, src: 3488  dst:   80
      TCP: Source Port = 0x0DA0
      TCP: Destination Port = Hypertext Transfer Protocol
      TCP: Sequence Number = 241730 (0x3B042)
      TCP: Acknowledgement Number = 0 (0x0)
TCP: Data Offset = 24 (0x18)
      TCP: Reserved = 0 (0x0000)
    + TCP: Flags = 0x02 : ....S.
```

The second frame of the handshake comes back with flags set to 0x12, which means that the acknowledgement field is significant and synchronized sequence numbers are set. The source comes from port 80 and goes to the 3488 port on the client machine. The acknowledgement number is one more than the sequence number from the client machine. In addition, the server hands out a sequence number of its own, as seen in the printout below.

```
TCP: .A..S., len:    4, seq: 142002582-142002585, ack:
241731, win: 8760, src:   80  dst: 3488
      TCP: Source Port = Hypertext Transfer Protocol
      TCP: Destination Port = 0x0DA0
      TCP: Sequence Number = 142002582 (0x876C996)
      TCP: Acknowledgement Number = 241731 (0x3B043)
      TCP: Data Offset = 24 (0x18)
      TCP: Reserved = 0 (0x0000)
    + TCP: Flags = 0x12 : .A..S.
```

The third frame, the acknowledgement field, is significant, and we can compare the ACK to the sequence number in the previous frame. Once again, the same destination and source ports are used. The flags 0x10 (010000 binary is 16 decimal and 10 hex) indicates an ACK frame.

```
TCP: .A...., len:    0, seq:    241731-241731, ack:
142002583, win: 8760, src: 3488  dst:    80
        TCP: Source Port = 0x0DA0
        TCP: Destination Port = Hypertext Transfer Protocol
        TCP: Sequence Number = 241731 (0x3B043)
        TCP: Acknowledgement Number = 142002583 (0x876C997)
        TCP: Data Offset = 20 (0x14)
        TCP: Reserved = 0 (0x0000)
      + TCP: Flags = 0x10 : .A....
```

This completes the three-way handshake, and we are ready to download the Web page. Let us look at frame 9 in our "open msn page.cap" file. The TCP portion of the frame looks similar to the other ones we have seen. It is still going to port 80. There are two flags present, but this time they are the ACK and the Push flags. Compare the acknowledgement number with the number from the previous frame, and you see that they are ACKing the same frame. The push flag tells the server to go ahead and send whatever data it has in the buffer.

The HTTP section issues a GET command from home.Microsoft.com using protocol HTTP/1.1. The undocumented header contains cookie data with city, state, and zip code information that can be used to personalize the MSN start page with personalized news.

```
TCP: .AP..., len:  577, seq:    241731-242307, ack:
142002583, win: 8760, src: 3488  dst:    80
        TCP: Source Port = 0x0DA0
        TCP: Destination Port = Hypertext Transfer Protocol
        TCP: Sequence Number = 241731 (0x3B043)
        TCP: Acknowledgement Number = 142002583 (0x876C997)
        TCP: Data Offset = 20 (0x14)
        TCP: Reserved = 0 (0x0000)
        TCP: Flags = 0x18 : .AP...
            TCP: ..0..... = No urgent data
            TCP: ...1.... = Acknowledgement field significant
            TCP: ....1... = Push function
            TCP: .....0.. = No Reset
            TCP: ......0. = No Synchronize
            TCP: .......0 = No Fin
        TCP: Window = 8760 (0x2238)
        TCP: Checksum = 0xF9B5
        TCP: Urgent Pointer = 0 (0x0)
        TCP: Data: Number of data bytes remaining = 577
(0x0241)
      HTTP: GET Request (from client using port 3488)
        HTTP: Request Method = GET
        HTTP: Uniform Resource Identifier = /
```

```
        HTTP: Protocol Version = HTTP/1.1
        HTTP: Accept = image/gif, image/x-xbitmap, image/jpeg,
image/pjpeg, */*
        HTTP: Accept-Language = en-us
        HTTP: Accept-Encoding = gzip, deflate
        HTTP: User-Agent = Mozilla/4.0 (compatible; MSIE 4.01;
Windows NT)
        HTTP: Host = home.microsoft.com
        HTTP: Connection = Keep-Alive
        HTTP: Undocumented Header = Cookie:
HMCMISC=FCDEG=F&CITYCODE=OH%5FHamilton&LN=RTCI&CITYGUIDE=gCI
NC&VCARD%5FPOSTALCODE=45011&MINDIF=11&P=t;
CATEGORIES=MAIL%2CNEWS%2C
            HTTP: Undocumented Header Fieldname = Cookie
            HTTP: Undocumented Header Value =
HMCMISC=FCDEG=F&CITYCODE=OH%5FHamilton&LN=RTCI&CIT
```

In the printout above, the browser says I want to GET the page from home.Microsoft.com, and here is my cookie. The frame below is the response from the server. The page is spelled out in the undocumented header location and would actually be displayed in the address window of the browser. We see the HTML tags that tell the browser how to format the text. This particular page was never displayed in the browser, but it is a redirection page that generated a rather interesting response, as we will see in the next frame.

```
    HTTP: Response (to client using port 3488)
        HTTP: Protocol Version = HTTP/1.1
        HTTP: Status Code = Found
        HTTP: Reason = Object moved
        HTTP: Server = Microsoft-IIS/4.0
        HTTP: Date = Tue, 24 Aug 1999 03:02:35 GMT
        HTTP: Undocumented Header = Location:
http://www.msn.com/default.asp?HMC2MSN=1
            HTTP: Undocumented Header Fieldname = Location
            HTTP: Undocumented Header Value =
http://www.msn.com/default.asp?HMC2MSN=1
        HTTP: Content-Type = text/html
        HTTP: Undocumented Header = <head><title>Object
moved</title></head>
            HTTP: Undocumented Header Fieldname =
<head><title>Object
            HTTP: Undocumented Header Value =
moved</title></head>
        HTTP: Undocumented Header = <body><h1>Object
Moved</h1>This object may be found <a
HREF="http://www.msn.com/default.asp?HMC2MSN=1">here</a>.</
body>
```

```
        HTTP: Undocumented Header Fieldname =
<body><h1>Object
        HTTP: Undocumented Header Value = Moved</h1>This
object may be found <a HREF="http:/
```

The server throws two flags: an ACK, which we would expect, but also an FIN (no more data from sender 0x01). The msn.com server is closing the connection.

```
TCP: .A...F, len:    0, seq: 142002909-142002909, ack:
242308, win: 8183, src:   80  dst: 3488
        TCP: Source Port = Hypertext Transfer Protocol
        TCP: Destination Port = 0x0DA0
        TCP: Sequence Number = 142002909 (0x876CADD)
        TCP: Acknowledgement Number = 242308 (0x3B284)
        TCP: Data Offset = 20 (0x14)
        TCP: Reserved = 0 (0x0000)
        TCP: Flags = 0x11 : .A...F
            TCP: ..0..... = No urgent data
            TCP: ...1.... = Acknowledgement field significant
            TCP: ....0... = No Push function
            TCP: .....0.. = No Reset
            TCP: ......0. = No Synchronize
            TCP: .......1 = No more data from sender
```

As the client computer receives the FIN flag from the MSN server, it has no choice but to reset the connection. This is indicated in the flags section (0x04).

```
TCP: ...R.., len:    0, seq:    242308-242308, ack:
142002583, win:    0, src: 3488  dst:   80
        TCP: Source Port = 0x0DA0
        TCP: Destination Port = Hypertext Transfer Protocol
        TCP: Sequence Number = 242308 (0x3B284)
        TCP: Acknowledgement Number = 142002583 (0x876C997)
        TCP: Data Offset = 20 (0x14)
        TCP: Reserved = 0 (0x0000)
        TCP: Flags = 0x04 : ...R..
            TCP: ..0..... = No urgent data
            TCP: ...0.... = Acknowledgement field not signifi-
cant
            TCP: ....0... = No Push function
            TCP: .....1.. = Reset the connection
            TCP: ......0. = No Synchronize
            TCP: .......0 = No Fin
```

At this point, the client machine concludes that the previous response from DNS was not completely accurate, so it tries again with another DNS query, as we see in the printout below.

```
UDP: Src Port: Unknown, (3489); Dst Port: DNS (53); Length =
37 (0x25)
  DNS: 0x1:Std Qry for www.msn.com. of type Host Addr on
class INET addr.
       DNS: Query Identifier = 1 (0x1)
     + DNS: DNS Flags = Query, OpCode - Std Qry, RD Bits Set,
RCode - No error
       DNS: Question Entry Count = 1 (0x1)
       DNS: Answer Entry Count = 0 (0x0)
       DNS: Name Server Count = 0 (0x0)
       DNS: Additional Records Count = 0 (0x0)
       DNS: Question Section: www.msn.com. of type Host Addr
on class INET addr.
            DNS: Question Name: www.msn.com.
            DNS: Question Type = Host Address
            DNS: Question Class = Internet address class
```

After another DNS query, we get lucky with a good address, and we go through the three-way handshake process as well. The GET request is submitted, and finally our Web page begins to download, as seen in the printout below. The first frame that begins transporting the data has additional HTTP header information and is therefore limited to a 1263 payload. Subsequent frames will not be required to duplicate as much of the header information and will be able to carry up to 1,460 bytes of data, as seen in the next frame.

```
HTTP: Response (to client using port 3491)
       HTTP: Protocol Version = HTTP/1.1
       HTTP: Status Code = OK
       HTTP: Reason = OK
       HTTP: Server = Microsoft-IIS/4.0
       HTTP: Date = Tue, 24 Aug 1999 03:02:37 GMT
       HTTP: Content-Length = 35376
       HTTP: Content-Type = text/html
       HTTP: Expires = Tue, 24 Aug 1999 03:02:37 GMT
       HTTP: Undocumented Header = Cache-control: private
           HTTP: Undocumented Header Fieldname = Cache-
control
           HTTP: Undocumented Header Value = private
       HTTP: Data: Number of data bytes remaining = 1263
(0x04EF)
```

As we can see in the HTTP header below, the packet is maximized just to transport the data, relying on TCP to perform the error handling and sequencing of data.

```
HTTP: Response (to client using port 3491)
        HTTP: Data: Number of data bytes remaining = 1460 (0x05B4)
```

Once the data begins to flow through the pipe, it is like any other data transfer using TCP/IP. In the trace, we see a couple of HTTP frames followed by a couple of TCP ACK frames. When the drive finally stops spinning, it has taken 28 seconds, 113 frames, and 53,219 bytes to load the home.Microsoft.com Web page, which is on a dedicated 128K ISDN line.

Secure Sockets

Secure sockets layer (SSL) implementation is integral to the success of e-commerce and business on the Internet. It normally begins with a connection to port 80 as seen in other traces. When the client machine clicks on a page requiring SSL, the server will return an FIN from port 80 to the destination port on the client machine.

```
CP: .A...F, len:    0, seq:   2958296-2958296, ack:
256976, win: 8092, src:   80  dst: 4346
     TCP: Source Port = Hypertext Transfer Protocol
     TCP: Destination Port = 0x10FA
     TCP: Sequence Number = 2958296 (0x2D23D8)
     TCP: Acknowledgement Number = 256976 (0x3EBD0)
     TCP: Data Offset = 20 (0x14)
     TCP: Reserved = 0 (0x0000)
     TCP: Flags = 0x11 : .A...F
          TCP: ..0..... = No urgent data
          TCP: ...1.... = Acknowledgement field significant
          TCP: ....0... = No Push function
          TCP: .....0.. = No Reset
          TCP: ......0. = No Synchronize
          TCP: .......1 = No more data from sender
```

The client machine ACKs the FIN still using the same source port and still going to the HTTP port 80 on the server.

```
TCP: .A...., len:    0, seq:    256976-256976, ack:
2958297, win: 7885, src: 4346  dst:   80
     TCP: Source Port = 0x10FA
     TCP: Destination Port = Hypertext Transfer Protocol
     TCP: Sequence Number = 256976 (0x3EBD0)
     TCP: Acknowledgement Number = 2958297 (0x2D23D9)
```

```
TCP: Data Offset = 20 (0x14)
TCP: Reserved = 0 (0x0000)
TCP: Flags = 0x10 : .A....
     TCP: ..0..... = No urgent data
     TCP: ...1.... = Acknowledgement field significant
     TCP: ....0... = No Push function
     TCP: .....0.. = No Reset
     TCP: ......0. = No Synchronize
     TCP: .......0 = No Fin
```

Now, an interesting thing happens on the server: It switches ports on the client machine. The source port on the server is changed to 443—the well known port for secure sockets layer communication, and the destination port on the client machine is changed as well. In this instance, the destination port is changed to 4347, one more than used in the last conversation. The server also ACKs the previous frame from the client machine and sends a request to synchronize sequence numbers to the requesting machine. Once this arrangement has taken place, the data begins to flow between the two machines.

```
TCP: .A..S., len:    4, seq:   2913904-2913907, ack:
252920, win: 8760, src:   443  dst: 4347
     TCP: Source Port = 0x01BB
     TCP: Destination Port = 0x10FB
     TCP: Sequence Number = 2913904 (0x2C7670)
     TCP: Acknowledgement Number = 252920 (0x3DBF8)
     TCP: Data Offset = 24 (0x18)
     TCP: Reserved = 0 (0x0000)
     TCP: Flags = 0x12 : .A..S.
          TCP: ..0..... = No urgent data
          TCP: ...1.... = Acknowledgement field significant
          TCP: ....0... = No Push function
          TCP: .....0.. = No Reset
          TCP: ......1. = Synchronize sequence numbers
          TCP: .......0 = No Fin
```

OPTIMIZING INTRANET BROWSER TRAFFIC

The best thing that can be done to optimize intranet browser traffic is to create small, effective Web pages, where the majority of traffic is created. Several things can be done to help with this optimization.

1. Reduce the number of graphics used in the Web page because this is a great source of network traffic. When graphics are used, make sure you

use a graphics format that is optimized for the Web (i.e., do not use .bmp files or .tiff files because they have a lot of associated overhead).

2. Limit the use of frames because using many frames can cause multiple downloads for each page.

3. Reduce the need for scrolling on a page. To do so, break the page into smaller chunks. In this way, if a client is not interested in the entire page, you do not waste time downloading meaningless information.

4. Deploy proxy servers in remote locations and enable active caching. Increasing the cache time to live will further eliminate repetitive downloads of identical information. This will reduce the need to go upstream to pull in live data.

5. Increase the cache size on the local machine. Caching data on the local data will speed up the browsing process for the user, reduce the network traffic, and act as a good use of hard drive space on the PC. All of this will reduce the need for the computer to download the same information when revisiting Web sites.

6. Carefully evaluate the need for security (both on password-protected sites and SSL) because too little security causes additional network traffic.

CHAPTER REVIEW

In this chapter we looked at various types of application traffic. We began by looking at file and print traffic. In addition to the traffic involved in transferring the data, we also saw the overhead associated with name resolution methods, connection establishment and SMB dialect negotiation. After looking at file and print traffic, we turned the network monitor loose on Internet traffic and looked at the conversations involved with Web browsing. Here again, we saw name resolution traffic and connection establishment traffic. The overhead was less than file and print traffic as the protocols are optimized for low-bandwidth environments.

IN THE NEXT CHAPTER

In the next chapter we will look at Microsoft Exchange server traffic and compare it with Internet POP3. We will look at the sequence of operations when Exchange opens and closes a connection and at name resolution issues as well.

Exchange and Internet Mail

These services—Exchange and Internet Mail—are killing my server and me. Why do I need them all in the first place? Well, there is a good possibility that you do not need all these services. When applications are installed, they will load and auto-start services. If it is a well-behaved service, then it will be merely one or two services. However, many applications nowadays load tons of services, all of which are advertising their existence.

EXCHANGE

SMTP (simple mail transport protocol) is used to receive mail from the Internet. Once the address of the server has been resolved (using DNS), then a port 25 connection is made. The SMTP commands are used to control the flow of mail from one machine to another. Each of these commands is ended with the enter or return key. The SMTP commands are not case sensitive, although SMTP will preserve case in addressing as some implementations may have case-sensitive user names. As seen in Figure 8–1, Telnet can be used to make the connection as well as another SMTP server. This is often done to test Internet mail connectivity with exchange. This will begin with a mail command issued by the sender with a **from:** in the form of username@ domainname. The **from:** is a field that tells the SMTP server the name of the user. The username@domainname will become a reply to address as well.

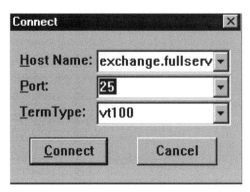

Fig. 8–1   Telnet can be used to test Exchange connectivity.

The HELO command (HELLO in some implementations) lets you know whether the two machines are talking. While the connection greeting identifies the receiver server, HELO is used to identify the sender to the SMTP server. HELO and the accompanying 250 OK let us know that the sender and receiver are in the initial connection state with no transaction in progress and buffers cleared. The mail command tells the SMTP server that a new transaction is beginning. If everything is correct, a reply of 250 OK will be returned. The from: is also called the reverse-path address, and it can hold more than one mailbox. It can hold a list of hosts for reverse-source routing.

The next command is the MAIL command, which is used to begin a mail transaction. This line will also contain the from:, which is also known as the reverse-path and is used for nondelivery notices. This information is stored by the receiver SMTP server in a reverse-path buffer, which will be processed after all the data has been entered.

RCPT identifies the recipient of the message and is the command entered after the mail command. If this mail command is received correctly by the SMTP server, then a 250-OK reply will be returned. If the recipient is unknown, then a 550 failure will come back from the server. If the recipient is entered incorrectly, it will generate a 553 malformed-address error. The protocol will allow multiple recipients to be inputted at this point in the process. Pressing the return key at the end of the RCPT line and typing another RCPT command enters additional recipients. In addition to holding a mailbox in the RCPT field, you can also put in a source-route list of hosts. The RCPT data is stored in a forward-path buffer until needed by the server.

The third step is the DATA command, which is followed by pressing enter or issuing a carriage return line feed (<CRLF>), a somewhat anachronistic term. Once the server has accepted this command, the SMTP protocol considers all subsequent traffic as data for this field until it receives a line containing only a period. In other words, the data section ends when the receiver server receives the character sequence return-period-return (<CRLF>.<CRLF>). The end-of-data indicator confirms the transaction and tells the SMTP server to process the data in both the reverse-path buffer, the forward-path buffer, and the mail data. Once this processing is complete, the server will return an OK. When the server accepts the message, it inserts a time stamp at the beginning of the mail data line that indicates the identity of both the sending and receiving hosts. On final delivery of the message, it also inserts a return-path line that contains the information from the reverse path entered with the mail command. The mail-data field can also include such items as the data subject, to, cc, and from lines if desired. Figure 8–2 illustrates the usage of these commands from a Telnet session established with an Exchange server. This is in fact a good way to test Exchange Internet e-mail connectivity.

The DATA command will fail only if the transaction is incomplete or if there are no available resources to process the request. The Microsoft Exchange implementation of SMTP will not allow you to have an incomplete message. As can be seen in Figure 8–3, Exchange requires the commands to be input in the proper order before it will process the data.

The SMTP protocol includes additional features to assist with finding recipients and distribution lists. These commands are the VRFY command, which is used to provide mailbox information of users, and the EXPN command, which is used for distribution lists. However, as we see in Figure 8–4, these commands are not implemented on Microsoft Exchange for security reasons. Instead, Exchange uses LDAP to provide this information.

The NOOP command is used to specify a no operation. It does not affect any previously entered commands or parameters. It simply means do nothing and will elicit an OK reply from the server.

The RSET command is the reset command, which aborts the current transaction. All information in the buffers will be flushed, and the state

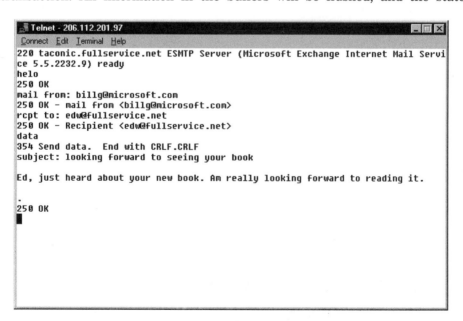

Fig. 8–2 SMTP commands issued during a test session.

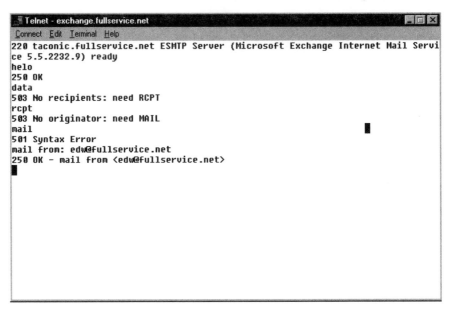

Fig. 8–3   Microsoft Exchange requires SMTP commands to be in the proper order.

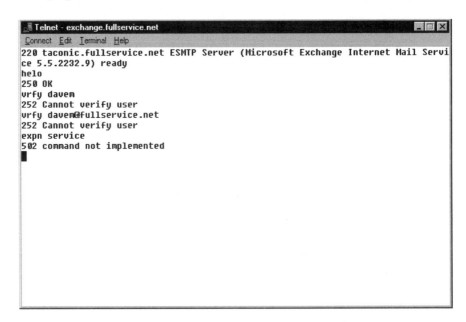

Fig. 8–4   Additional SMTP features such as VRFY and EXPN are not implemented on Exchange.

tables are cleared. This will also receive an OK reply from the server. It can be issued at any time during the conversation.

Opening and Closing the Session

When the session is first established between the two computers, there is a chance to make sure that the servers are talking to whom they think they are. The HELO command is used for this purpose. This command can be issued only one time and takes the form of HELO mred.com. The HELO identifies the sending computer to the SMTP server. If no errors occur in processing the command, the response will be 250 OK. This command can be interpreted as "Hello, I am mred.com." If the HELO command is issued a second time, the response will be a 503 bad sequence. No checking is done on the domain listed, and in fact, the domain name can be left blank as it was in Figure 8–2.

When the session is over, a QUIT command is issued to close the channel.

Exchange Server in Action

Let us now look at some traces showing how SMTP e-mail works in real life. It takes five frames and 420 bytes to establish an SMTP connection with Exchange. This involves the famous three-way handshake, the SMTP service ready frame, and one more ACK frame. Look at the service-ready frame in the printout below. The 220 response code we know from Table 8–1 means that the service is ready. This frame comes from port 25, which is used for the SMTP service. This 220 was sent as standard ASCII (American Standard Code for Information Interchange) and shows up in the hex pane as 32 32 30. The ASCII character for 20 is 50, which when translated into hex is 32. The ASCII character for 0 is 48, which translates into 30 hex.

```
SMTP: Rsp: Service ready, 102 bytes
      SMTP: Response = 220 taconic.fullservice.net ESMTP
Server (Microsoft Exchange Internet Mail
         SMTP: Data = Service 5.5.2232.9) ready
```

Although the TCP is a full duplex protocol, SMTP only operates in half-duplex mode, which means that a character is sent and must be acknowledged prior to sending another character. This requirement generates a lot of ACK traffic. For instance, just sending the HELO command took 11 frames and 695 bytes. Once HELO is sent and ACKed, the next frame from the client machine sends 0D 0A (ASCII 13, the carriage return, and ASCII 10, the line feed) as seen in the printout below.

```
TCP: .AP..., len:    2, seq:    123557-123558, ack:
1430817, win: 8658, src: 1667  dst:   25 (SMTP)
      TCP: Source Port = 0x0683
```

Table 8–1   SMTP reply codes

Code	Meaning
211	Status or help ready.
214	Help message.
220	Domain service ready.
221	Domain service closing transmission channel.
250	Action completed OK.
251	User not local. Forwarding to destination.
354	Start mail input.
421	Service not available. Closing channel.
450	Action not taken. Mailbox unavailable (mailbox busy).
451	Action aborted. Local error in processing.
452	Action not taken. Insufficient system storage.
500	Syntax error. Command not recognized.
501	Syntax error in parameters or arguments.
502	Command not implemented on system.
503	Bad sequence of commands. The commands are in the wrong order.
504	Command parameter not implemented. The command is valid, but the parameter is not.
550	Action not taken. Mailbox unavailable (not found or no access).
551	User not local. Message needs to be forwarded.
552	Action aborted. Exceeded storage allocation.
553	Action not taken. Mailbox name not allowed (wrong syntax for mailbox).
554	Transaction failed.

```
          TCP: Destination Port = SMTP
          TCP: Sequence Number = 123557 (0x1E2A5)
          TCP: Acknowledgement Number = 1430817 (0x15D521)
          TCP: Data Offset = 20 (0x14)
          TCP: Reserved = 0 (0x0000)
        + TCP: Flags = 0x18 : .AP...
          TCP: Window = 8658 (0x21D2)
          TCP: Checksum = 0x997F
          TCP: Urgent Pointer = 0 (0x0)
          TCP: Data: Number of data bytes remaining = 2 (0x0002)
       SMTP: Cmd: completed, 2 bytes

00000:   F8 E0 07 00 01 01 00 01 B0 81 66 80 08 00 45 10
.........f...E.
00010:   00 2A C2 B3 40 00 80 06 0F 15 CE 70 C2 B2 CE 70
.*..@......p...p
```

```
00020:   C9 61 06 83 00 19 00 01 E2 A5 00 15 D5 21 50 18
.a.........!P.
00030:   21 D2 99 7F 00 00 0D 0A
!.. ....
```

Once the sending machine transmits the command-completed frame, the receiving SMTP server acknowledges with a response of 250 OK (250 ASCII in hex is 32 35 30; the 20 hex is the space character; and ASCII 79 4F in hex ASCII 75 4B in hex. Notice the 0D 0A as the last two bytes in the hex pane).

```
TCP: .AP..., len:    8, seq:   1430817-1430824, ack:
123559, win: 8754, src:   25 (SMTP)  dst: 1667
     TCP: Source Port = SMTP
     TCP: Destination Port = 0x0683
     TCP: Sequence Number = 1430817 (0x15D521)
     TCP: Acknowledgement Number = 123559 (0x1E2A7)
     TCP: Data Offset = 20 (0x14)
     TCP: Reserved = 0 (0x0000)
   + TCP: Flags = 0x18 : .AP...
     TCP: Window = 8754 (0x2232)
     TCP: Checksum = 0xE776
     TCP: Urgent Pointer = 0 (0x0)
     TCP: Data: Number of data bytes remaining = 8 (0x0008)
  SMTP: Rsp: Requested mail action okay, completed, 8 bytes
     SMTP: Response = 250 OK

00000:   00 01 B0 81 66 80 F8 E0 07 00 01 01 08 00 45 00
....f.........E.
00010:   00 30 15 00 40 00 7D 06 BF D2 CE 70 C9 61 CE 70
.0..@.}....p.a.p
00020:   C2 B2 00 19 06 83 00 15 D5 21 00 01 E2 A7 50 18
.........!....P.
00030:   22 32 E7 76 00 00 32 35 30 20 4F 4B 0D 0A
"2.v..250 OK..
```

POP3 Protocol

The POP3 protocol is used as a lightweight e-mail protocol that stores messages on a server until the client machine connects and downloads them on request. It does not do a great deal of message processing on the server; rather, the POP3 service simply listens on TCP port 110 until the mail is retrieved and deleted out of the mail drop. It is not a very advanced protocol, but it is relatively efficient.

When a POP3 client wants to make a connection, it follows a pattern of single work commands. Like the SMTP protocol we looked at earlier, the commands are all ASCII characters separated by a space. These commands are all three to four characters long. The modifiers to the POP3 commands can be up to 40 characters long.

There are two responses the POP3 server will give. The first one is the positive responsive, which will be a +OK, as seen in Figure 8–5. The negative response is –ERR. Both of these responses must be in all caps and include either the + or the – as appropriate.

Some commands will generate a multiple-line response from the server (such as the list command), and each line will end with a carriage return line feed combination (the same ASCII 13 and ASCII 10 we used in the SMTP protocol). When all the lines have been sent, the server will send the . (ASCII 46) and an additional line feed. This is the same <CRLF>.[period]<CRLF> combination we saw in the SMTP protocol.

The four POP3 states   POP3 progresses through four states during the process of a client connecting and receiving the mail. After the initial TCP connection and subsequent greeting, the server enters into the authorization state in which the client identifies itself. Following the authorization state, POP3 enters into the transaction state and receives commands from the client machine to process the mail. After the mail is successfully processed and the client issues the quit command, the session enters the update phase and releases resources used during the transaction state. The TCP connection is then closed. This sequence of events for a successful session is detailed in the following list.

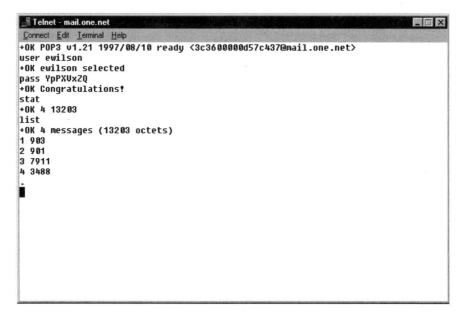

Fig. 8–5   POP3 commands issued during a telnet session.

1. The client machine will typically query DNS for the address.
2. Once the address is given, the machine will initiate a three-way handshake to port 110.
3. Following the three-way handshake, the server sends a greeting.
4. The client responds with a user name.
5. The server checks to see whether the user exists on the system and responds with a +OK.
6. The client responds with the password.
7. The server responds with +OK congratulations.
8. The client asks for a status on the mailbox.
9. The server responds by sending the number and size of the messages in the mailbox.
10. The client asks for a list of the messages.
11. The server responds.
12. The client downloads the messages.
13. The client clears the messages off the server.
14. When done, it issues the quit command.
15. The server responds with +OK clean.

Table 8–2 summarizes the POP3 commands normally found in network monitoring traces.

Let us look at an actual POP3 session. This frame occurs immediately after the three-way handshake to port 110 and signals the entry into the greeting phase. POP3 uses TCP to carry the data commands as ASCII text. In the printout below, we see the +OK POP3 greeting.

```
TCP: .AP..., len:   66, seq: 836990619-836990684, ack:
124982, win:32736, src:   110  dst: 1844
      TCP: Source Port = Post Office Protocol - Version 3
      TCP: Destination Port = 0x0734
      TCP: Sequence Number = 836990619 (0x31E3769B)
      TCP: Acknowledgement Number = 124982 (0x1E836)
      TCP: Data Offset = 20 (0x14)
      TCP: Reserved = 0 (0x0000)
   +  TCP: Flags = 0x18 : .AP...
      TCP: Window = 32736 (0x7FE0)
      TCP: Checksum = 0x5437
      TCP: Urgent Pointer = 0 (0x0)
      TCP: Data: Number of data bytes remaining = 66
(0x0042)

00000:   00 01 B0 81 66 80 F8 E0 07 00 01 01 08 00 45 10
....f.........E.
```

Table 8–2   Common POP3 commands

Command	Arguments	Description
QUIT	None	Used in a graceful close to a POP3 session. Allows the server to enter the update state, where it releases resources.
STAT	None	Asks the server for the number and size of messages in the mailbox. The answer will be +OK nn mm, where nn is the number of messages and mm is the number of bytes used.
LIST	The message number (optional)	Lists the messages by number and size.
RETR	The message number (required)	Retrieves the message by number from the POP3 server. The server responds with +OK the number of bytes and the text of the message.
DELE	The message number (required)	Deletes the message by number from the server.
NOOP	None	No Operation. Elicits +OK message from the server.
RSET	None	Resets the session. Unmarks any messages that have been marked for deletion (by using the DELE command).
QUIT	None	The server removes messages marked by the DELE command, releases resources, and closes the TCP connection.
TOP	Message number and number of lines to retrieve (required)	Used to retrieve a number of lines from a particular message. If the number of lines requested is greater than the amount in the message, retrieves the entire message.
USER	User name on the server (required)	During the greeting state prior to the transaction state, tells the server which mailbox to open.
PASS	The password (required)	Used during the authorization state immediately after a successful USER command. When successful, the server responds +OK.

```
00010:   00 6A EE 25 40 00 3D 06 1F 69 CE 70 C0 64 CE 70
.j.%@.=..i.p.d.p
00020:   D2 A9 00 6E 07 34 31 E3 76 9B 00 01 E8 36 50 18
...n.41.v....6P.
00030:   7F E0 54 37 00 00 2B 4F 4B 20 50 4F 50 33 20 76
.T7..+OK POP3 v
00040:   31 2E 32 31 20 31 39 39 37 2F 30 38 2F 31 30 20
1.21 1997/08/10
```

We now enter the authorization phase, which proceeds from the client machine to TCP port 110 on the server. Notice that the A- and P-flags are set in the frame telling us that the acknowledgement field is significant as well as telling the server to push the data. In the HEX field, we see the USER command and the edwilso argument. The frame ends with the 0D 0A hex we have seen in other frames. Notice that this traffic is sent as plain ASCII text.

```
TCP: .AP..., len:   14, seq:    124982-124995, ack:
836990685, win: 8694, src: 1844  dst:  110
      TCP: Source Port = 0x0734
      TCP: Destination Port = Post Office Protocol - Version
3
      TCP: Sequence Number = 124982 (0x1E836)
      TCP: Acknowledgement Number = 836990685 (0x31E376DD)
      TCP: Data Offset = 20 (0x14)
      TCP: Reserved = 0 (0x0000)
    + TCP: Flags = 0x18 : .AP...
      TCP: Window = 8694 (0x21F6)
      TCP: Checksum = 0xA9DE
      TCP: Urgent Pointer = 0 (0x0)
      TCP: Data: Number of data bytes remaining = 14
(0x000E)

00000:  F8 E0 07 00 01 01 00 01 B0 81 66 80 08 00 45 10
.........f...E.
00010:  00 36 06 D0 40 00 80 06 C3 F2 CE 70 D2 A9 CE 70
.6..@......p...p
00020:  C0 64 07 34 00 6E 00 01 E8 36 31 E3 76 DD 50 18
.d.4.n...61.v.P.
00030:  21 F6 A9 DE 00 00 55 53 45 52 20 65 64 77 69 6C
!.....USER edwil
00040:  73 6F 0D 0A
so..
```

The server responds by indicating that there is a user with a mailbox named ewilso. The ASCII ensures that case is preserved whether or not the particular implementation uses it. The PASS command is case sensitive. This response comes from port 110 to the destination computer with the A-and-P flags set. We will see this often as the POP3 server moves through the various states. Notice that the acknowledgement number matches the sequence number in the next frame.

```
TCP: .AP..., len:   22, seq: 836990685-836990706, ack:
124996, win:32736, src:  110  dst: 1844
      TCP: Source Port = Post Office Protocol - Version 3
      TCP: Destination Port = 0x0734
      TCP: Sequence Number = 836990685 (0x31E376DD)
      TCP: Acknowledgement Number = 124996 (0x1E844)
```

```
        TCP: Data Offset = 20 (0x14)
        TCP: Reserved = 0 (0x0000)
      + TCP: Flags = 0x18 : .AP...
        TCP: Window = 32736 (0x7FE0)
        TCP: Checksum = 0x8AAD
        TCP: Urgent Pointer = 0 (0x0)
        TCP: Data: Number of data bytes remaining = 22
(0x0016)

00000:  00 01 B0 81 66 80 F8 E0 07 00 01 01 08 00 45 10
....f.........E.
00010:  00 3E EE 30 40 00 3D 06 1F 8A CE 70 C0 64 CE 70
.>.0@.=....p.d.p
00020:  D2 A9 00 6E 07 34 31 E3 76 DD 00 01 E8 44 50 18
...n.41.v....DP.
00030:  7F E0 8A AD 00 00 2B 4F 4B 20 65 64 77 69 6C 73
.....+OK edwils
00040:  6F 20 73 65 6C 65 63 74 65 64 0D 0A                          o
selected..
```

Now comes a concern with POP3 e-mail. The password is sent in clear text across the Internet. The PASS command carries the password argument clearly discernible in the hex trace. Of course, you would have to be in the right place at the right time to catch it, but the password is there. It goes from the client machine to port 110 on the server. Once again, the A-and-P flags are set and the frame ends with 0D 0A hex. Compare the sequence number in the frame below with the acknowledgement number from the previous frame—they are identical.

```
    TCP: .AP..., len:   15, seq:    124996-125010, ack:
836990707, win: 8672, src: 1844  dst:  110
        TCP: Source Port = 0x0734
        TCP: Destination Port = Post Office Protocol - Version
3
        TCP: Sequence Number = 124996 (0x1E844)
        TCP: Acknowledgement Number = 836990707 (0x31E376F3)
        TCP: Data Offset = 20 (0x14)
        TCP: Reserved = 0 (0x0000)
      + TCP: Flags = 0x18 : .AP...
        TCP: Window = 8672 (0x21E0)
        TCP: Checksum = 0x6533
        TCP: Urgent Pointer = 0 (0x0)
        TCP: Data: Number of data bytes remaining = 15
(0x000F)

00000:  F8 E0 07 00 01 01 00 01 B0 81 66 80 08 00 45 10
..........f...E.
```

```
00010:    00 37 07 D0 40 00 80 06 C2 F1 CE 70 D2 A9 CE 70
.7..@......p...p
00020:    C0 64 07 34 00 6E 00 01 E8 44 31 E3 76 F3 50 18
.d.4.n...D1.v.P.
00030:    21 E0 65 33 00 00 50 41 53 53 20 5A 31 61 2A 30
!.e3..PASS Z1a*0
00040:    6D 38 69 0D 0A
m8i..
```

The server responds from port 110 with +OK congratulations and the 0D 0A. This signals an end to the authorization state. We see the A- and P-flags set pushing the data back to the client machine.

```
TCP: .AP..., len:    22, seq: 836990707-836990728, ack:
125011, win:32736, src:   110  dst: 1844
     TCP: Source Port = Post Office Protocol - Version 3
     TCP: Destination Port = 0x0734
     TCP: Sequence Number = 836990707 (0x31E376F3)
     TCP: Acknowledgement Number = 125011 (0x1E853)
     TCP: Data Offset = 20 (0x14)
     TCP: Reserved = 0 (0x0000)
   + TCP: Flags = 0x18 : .AP...
     TCP: Window = 32736 (0x7FE0)
     TCP: Checksum = 0x8797
     TCP: Urgent Pointer = 0 (0x0)
     TCP: Data: Number of data bytes remaining = 22
(0x0016)


00000:    00 01 B0 81 66 80 F8 E0 07 00 01 01 08 00 45 10
....f.........E.
00010:    00 3E F2 24 40 00 3D 06 1B 96 CE 70 C0 64 CE 70
.>.$@.=....p.d.p
00020:    D2 A9 00 6E 07 34 31 E3 76 F3 00 01 E8 53 50 18
...n.41.v....SP.
00030:    7F E0 87 97 00 00 2B 4F 4B 20 43 6F 6E 67 72 61
.....+OK Congra
00040:    74 75 6C 61 74 69 6F 6E 73 21 0D 0A
tulations!..
```

The first frame in the transaction phase issues the STAT command to see how many messages are waiting in the mail drop.

```
TCP: .AP..., len:    6, seq:    125011-125016, ack:
836990729, win: 8650, src: 1844  dst:   110
     TCP: Source Port = 0x0734
     TCP: Destination Port = Post Office Protocol - Version 3
     TCP: Sequence Number = 125011 (0x1E853)
```

```
        TCP: Acknowledgement Number = 836990729 (0x31E37709)
        TCP: Data Offset = 20 (0x14)
        TCP: Reserved = 0 (0x0000)
      + TCP: Flags = 0x18 : .AP...
        TCP: Window = 8650 (0x21CA)
        TCP: Checksum = 0x2377
        TCP: Urgent Pointer = 0 (0x0)
        TCP: Data: Number of data bytes remaining = 6 (0x0006)


00000:   F8 E0 07 00 01 01 00 01 B0 81 66 80 08 00 45 10
.........f...E.
00010:   00 2E 08 D0 40 00 80 06 C1 FA CE 70 D2 A9 CE 70
....@......p...p
00020:   C0 64 07 34 00 6E 00 01 E8 53 31 E3 77 09 50 18
.d.4.n...S1.w.P.
00030:   21 CA 23 77 00 00 53 54 41 54 0D 0A
!.#w..STAT..
```

The server responds with the number of messages and bytes in the mail-box for the user. The +OK indicates a successful command. In this instance, there are nine messages totaling 48564 bytes on the server, as shown in the hex pane in the printout below.

```
TCP: .AP..., len:   13, seq: 836990729-836990741, ack:
125017, win:32736, src:   110  dst: 1844
      TCP: Source Port = Post Office Protocol - Version 3
      TCP: Destination Port = 0x0734
      TCP: Sequence Number = 836990729 (0x31E37709)
      TCP: Acknowledgement Number = 125017 (0x1E859)
      TCP: Data Offset = 20 (0x14)
      TCP: Reserved = 0 (0x0000)
    + TCP: Flags = 0x18 : .AP...
      TCP: Window = 32736 (0x7FE0)
      TCP: Checksum = 0x0FFB
      TCP: Urgent Pointer = 0 (0x0)
      TCP: Data: Number of data bytes remaining = 13
(0x000D)


00000:   00 01 B0 81 66 80 F8 E0 07 00 01 01 08 00 45 10
....f.........E.
00010:   00 35 F2 32 40 00 3D 06 1B 91 CE 70 C0 64 CE 70
.5.2@.=....p.d.p
00020:   D2 A9 00 6E 07 34 31 E3 77 09 00 01 E8 59 50 18
...n.41.w....YP.
00030:   7F E0 0F FB 00 00 2B 4F 4B 20 39 20 34 38 35 36
.....+OK 9 4856
00040:   34 0D 0A
4..
```

The next command in the interactive phase is the LIST command followed by the 0D 0A to tell the server that the command is finished. We see this in the hex pane below.

```
TCP: .AP..., len:    6, seq:    125017-125022, ack:
836990742, win: 8637, src: 1844  dst:   110
        TCP: Source Port = 0x0734
        TCP: Destination Port = Post Office Protocol - Version
3
        TCP: Sequence Number = 125017 (0x1E859)
        TCP: Acknowledgement Number = 836990742 (0x31E37716)
        TCP: Data Offset = 20 (0x14)
        TCP: Reserved = 0 (0x0000)
      + TCP: Flags = 0x18 : .AP...
        TCP: Window = 8637 (0x21BD)
        TCP: Checksum = 0x187C
        TCP: Urgent Pointer = 0 (0x0)
        TCP: Data: Number of data bytes remaining = 6 (0x0006)

00000:  F8 E0 07 00 01 01 00 01 B0 81 66 80 08 00 45 10
.........f...E.
00010:  00 2E 09 D0 40 00 80 06 C0 FA CE 70 D2 A9 CE 70
....@......p...p
00020:  C0 64 07 34 00 6E 00 01 E8 59 31 E3 77 16 50 18
.d.4.n...Y1.w.P.
00030:  21 BD 18 7C 00 00 4C 49 53 54 0D 0A
!..|..LIST..
```

The POP3 server responds with +OK and nine messages (48,564 octets). This is all spelled out in the hex pane—even the left and right parentheses. This frame is actually longer than printed out below (it has been truncated for clarity). Following the number of octets, each message is numbered and sized. The software will use this information to request the messages individually from the POP3 server.

```
TCP: .AP..., len:  107, seq: 836990742-836990848, ack:
125023, win:32736, src:  110  dst: 1844
        TCP: Source Port = Post Office Protocol - Version 3
        TCP: Destination Port = 0x0734
        TCP: Sequence Number = 836990742 (0x31E37716)
        TCP: Acknowledgement Number = 125023 (0x1E85F)
        TCP: Data Offset = 20 (0x14)
        TCP: Reserved = 0 (0x0000)
      + TCP: Flags = 0x18 : .AP...
        TCP: Window = 32736 (0x7FE0)
        TCP: Checksum = 0xF276
        TCP: Urgent Pointer = 0 (0x0)
```

```
         TCP: Data: Number of data bytes remaining = 107
    (0x006B)


    00000:  00 01 B0 81 66 80 F8 E0 07 00 01 01 08 00 45 10
    ....f........E.
    00010:  00 93 F2 3D 40 00 3D 06 1B 28 CE 70 C0 64 CE 70
    ...=@.=..(.p.d.p
    00020:  D2 A9 00 6E 07 34 31 E3 77 16 00 01 E8 5F 50 18
    ...n.41.w....._P.
    00030:  7F E0 F2 76 00 00 2B 4F 4B 20 39 20 6D 65 73 73
    ..v..+OK 9 mess
    00040:  61 67 65 73 20 28 34 38 35 36 34 20 6F 63 74 65
    ages (48564 octe
```

The client now begins downloading the messages on an individual basis. The first command is the TOP command requesting the first message as we see in the hex pane in the printout below.

```
    TCP: .AP..., len:     9, seq:     125023-125031, ack:
    836990849, win: 8530, src: 1844  dst:  110
         TCP: Source Port = 0x0734
         TCP: Destination Port = Post Office Protocol - Version
    3
         TCP: Sequence Number = 125023 (0x1E85F)
         TCP: Acknowledgement Number = 836990849 (0x31E37781)
         TCP: Data Offset = 20 (0x14)
         TCP: Reserved = 0 (0x0000)
       + TCP: Flags = 0x18 : .AP...
         TCP: Window = 8530 (0x2152)
         TCP: Checksum = 0xB57D
         TCP: Urgent Pointer = 0 (0x0)
         TCP: Data: Number of data bytes remaining = 9 (0x0009)

    00000:  F8 E0 07 00 01 01 00 01 B0 81 66 80 08 00 45 10
    ..........f...E.
    00010:  00 31 0A D0 40 00 80 06 BF F7 CE 70 D2 A9 CE 70
    .1..@......p...p
    00020:  C0 64 07 34 00 6E 00 01 E8 5F 31 E3 77 81 50 18
    .d.4.n..._1.w.P.
    00030:  21 52 B5 7D 00 00 54 4F 50 20 31 20 30 0D 0A
    !R.}..TOP 1 0..
```

The server responds +OK to the TOP command, and the text of the first message begins to flow down. This message is 4,292 octets long, and this frame contains the first of the message headers received: . . . Much of the hex pane is left out, but this frame carries a payload of 1,024 bytes, most of which are taken up by various types of mail headers. Once again we see the A-and-P flags set. This frame is coming from the server to the client because the source is port 110.

```
TCP: .AP..., len: 1024, seq: 836990849-836991872, ack:
125032, win:32736, src:  110  dst: 1844
        TCP: Source Port = Post Office Protocol - Version 3
        TCP: Destination Port = 0x0734
        TCP: Sequence Number = 836990849 (0x31E37781)
        TCP: Acknowledgement Number = 125032 (0x1E868)
        TCP: Data Offset = 20 (0x14)
        TCP: Reserved = 0 (0x0000)
      + TCP: Flags = 0x18 : .AP...
        TCP: Window = 32736 (0x7FE0)
        TCP: Checksum = 0x1D4E
        TCP: Urgent Pointer = 0 (0x0)
        TCP: Data: Number of data bytes remaining = 1024
(0x0400)


00000:   00 01 B0 81 66 80 F8 E0 07 00 01 01 08 00 45 10
....f.........E.
00010:   04 28 F2 7B 40 00 3D 06 17 55 CE 70 C0 64 CE 70
.(.{@.=..U.p.d.p
00020:   D2 A9 00 6E 07 34 31 E3 77 81 00 01 E8 68 50 18
...n.41.w....hP.
00030:   7F E0 1D 4E 00 00 2B 4F 4B 20 34 32 39 32 20 6 F
..N..+OK 4292 o
00040:   63 74 65 74 73 0D 0A 52 65 63 65 69 76 65 64 3A
ctets..Received:
```

The client and the server continue to download the messages with a combination of ACK frames and ACK/PUSH frames. The session is finally terminated by the QUIT command and one last ACK. It took two minutes, 29 seconds, 154 frames, and 75,704 bytes to complete the transaction. The number of frames is dependent on the size of the messages, but the essential conversation remains the same.

Exchange Server to Server

When Exchange talks to another server, it does not use POP3 or SMTP, but rather remote procedure calls (RPC's), which are a much more secure and robust form of communication. In order to understand more fully how this communication works, we need to look at a few things unique to RPC's. The remote procedure call service (also called the end point mapper) runs on the Windows NT server and performs a variety of tasks, such as identifying the port number on which a particular service is listening. The end point mapper aids Exchange as it looks for the UUID (universally unique identification) numbers associated with a particular service. These UUID's are categorized by the first two characters of the number, and although other services besides Exchange use these numbers, a few of them are unique to the product. Three of the more important numbers are listed below.

- A4—the exchange store
- F5—the exchange directory
- E1—the endpoint mapper service

If the remote procedure call service fails, then exchange servers cannot talk to one another, nor can they talk to their client machines. For this reason, a good understanding of the function of RPC's will greatly aid us in our troubleshooting skills.

If two exchange servers want to communicate with one another, the first thing that must be done is to query the end point mapper service on the other exchange server to find out where the MTA (message transport agent) is listing. The reason for this is that the MTA will move around and listen on different ports on subsequent reboots. The end point mapper is tasked with keeping up with each of the various services and maintaining a listing of what port each is listening on. When the Microsoft Exchange server starts up, it will register with the end point mapper and ask for an assigned port number. The end point mapper listens on port 135 for TCP/IP requests. The end point mapper has a fixed UUID of E1AF8308-5D1F-11C9-91A4-08002B14A0FA.

The conversation between servers will begin with a name resolution mechanism (WINS, DNS, Broadcast, LMHOST's lookup) followed by the three-way handshake. Exchange then sends the frame to TCP port 135, which is the location service on the other server, and binds RPC to the other exchange server's end point mapper. We know this by looking at the abstract interface UUID E1AF8308-5D1F-11C9-91A4-08002B14A0FA. The E1 tells us that it is the end point mapper service.

```
+ TCP: .AP..., len:   72, seq:  22639100-22639171, ack:
1469213, win: 8760, src: 1238  dst:  135
  MSRPC: c/o RPC Bind:        UUID E1AF8308-5D1F-11C9-91A4-
08002B14A0FA  call 0x0  assoc grp 0x0  xmit 0x16D0   recv
0x16D0
      MSRPC: Version = 5 (0x5)
      MSRPC: Version (Minor) = 0 (0x0)
      MSRPC: Packet Type = Bind
      MSRPC: Flags 1 = 0 (0x0)
          MSRPC: .......0 = Reserved -or- Not the first
fragment (AES/DC)
```

```
        MSRPC: ......0. = Not a last fragment -or- No can-
cel pending
        MSRPC: .....0.. = Not a fragment -or- No cancel
pending (AES/DC)
        MSRPC: ....0... = Receiver to respond with a fack
PDU -or- Reserved (AES/DC)
        MSRPC: ...0.... = Not used -or- Does not support
concurrent multiplexing (AES/DC)
        MSRPC: ..0..... = Not for an idempotent request -
or- Did not execute guaranteed call (Fault PDU only) (AES/DC)
        MSRPC: .0...... = Not for a broadcast request -or-
'Maybe' call semantics not requested (AES/DC)
        MSRPC: 0....... = Reserved -or- No object UUID
specified in the optional object field (AES/DC)
      MSRPC: Packed Data Representation
      MSRPC: Fragment Length = 72 (0x48)
      MSRPC: Authentication Length = 0 (0x0)
      MSRPC: Call Identifier = 0 (0x0)
      MSRPC: Max Trans Frag Size = 5840 (0x16D0)
      MSRPC: Max Recv Frag Size = 5840 (0x16D0)
      MSRPC: Assoc Group Identifier = 0 (0x0)
      MSRPC: Presentation Context List
        MSRPC: Number of Context Elements = 1 (0x1)
        MSRPC: Presentation Context Identifier = 0 (0x0)
        MSRPC: Number of Transfer Syntaxs = 1 (0x1)
        MSRPC: Abstract Interface UUID = E1AF8308-5D1F-
11C9-91A4-08002B14A0FA
        MSRPC: Abstract Interface Version = 3 (0x3)
        MSRPC: Transfer Interface UUID = 8A885D04-1CEB-
11C9-9FE8-08002B104860
        MSRPC: Transfer Interface Version = 2 (0x2)
```

The other exchange server acknowledges the bind with a BindAck in the packet type field, as we see in the printout below. In the results section, we see acceptance. We have successfully created an RPC connection between the two exchange servers' end point mappers.

```
    TCP: .AP..., len:   60, seq:   1469213-1469272, ack:
22639172, win: 8688, src:  135  dst: 1238
  MSRPC: c/o RPC Bind Ack:      call 0x0  assoc grp 0x7622B
xmit 0x16D0  recv 0x16D0
      MSRPC: Version = 5 (0x5)
      MSRPC: Version (Minor) = 0 (0x0)
      MSRPC: Packet Type = Bind Ack
      MSRPC: Flags 1 = 3 (0x3)
          MSRPC: .......1 = Reserved -or- First fragment
  (AES/DC)
```

```
          MSRPC: ......1. = Last fragment -or- Cancel pend-
ing
          MSRPC: .....0.. = Not a fragment -or- No cancel
pending (AES/DC)
          MSRPC: ....0... = Receiver to respond with a fack
PDU -or- Reserved (AES/DC)
          MSRPC: ...0.... = Not used -or- Does not support
concurrent multiplexing (AES/DC)
          MSRPC: ..0..... = Not for an idempotent request
-or- Did not execute guaranteed call (Fault PDU only) (AES/DC)
          MSRPC: .0...... = Not for a broadcast request -or-
'Maybe' call semantics not requested (AES/DC)
          MSRPC: 0....... = Reserved -or- No object UUID
specified in the optional object field (AES/DC)
      MSRPC: Packed Data Representation
      MSRPC: Fragment Length = 60 (0x3C)
      MSRPC: Authentication Length = 0 (0x0)
      MSRPC: Call Identifier = 0 (0x0)
      MSRPC: Max Trans Frag Size = 5840 (0x16D0)
      MSRPC: Max Recv Frag Size = 5840 (0x16D0)
      MSRPC: Assoc Group Identifier = 483883 (0x7622B)
    + MSRPC: Secondary Address
      MSRPC: Padding Byte(s)
      MSRPC: Result List
        MSRPC: Number of Results = 1 (0x1)
        MSRPC: Reserved = 0 (0x0)
        MSRPC: Reserved 2
        MSRPC: Presentation Context Results
          MSRPC: Result = Acceptance
          MSRPC: Reason = Reason not specified
          MSRPC: Transfer Syntax
            MSRPC: Transfer Interface UUID = 8A885D04-
1CEB-11C9-9FE8-08002B104860
            MSRPC: Transfer Interface Version = 2
(0x2)
```

The first exchange server now sends an RPC Request Opnum 0x3 to the other exchange server. Included in this is the UUID of the service it is looking for. This command is used to request the port number of the service associated with the UUID. Once the first server has this port number, it has all the information needed to contact the service on the other machine. The first server will now close the TCP connection between them and establish a connection with the particular service directly.

Once again the servers use the TCP/IP three-way handshake to establish a connection, and then the connection makes a two-way RPC binding, meaning that the first exchange makes an RPC bind, followed by a BindAck from the second exchange server. Then, the second exchange server makes a bind to the first one with a subsequent BindAck from it. There are then two binds and two BindAcks in this conversation.

CHAPTER REVIEW

In this chapter we looked at Exchange and Internet mail traffic. We began by looking at the sequence of operations when Exchange opens and closes a session. We investigated name resolution issues, and we looked at the role of TCP/IP. We then moved on and saw exchange in action. We took an in-depth look at conversations involved in an exchange of messages.

Following that, we shifted tracks a little and looked at the POP3 protocol. We saw how exchange uses POP3 when it needs to communicate with other Internet e-mail systems. We then looked at Exchange-to-Exchange conversations and saw how RPC's are used.

IN THE NEXT CHAPTER

In the next chapter we begin our section on the network monitoring tools. We look at the Microsoft family line of monitors, beginning with the lite versions included in Windows NT 4.0 and Windows 2000. Then, we graduate to the full featured product line included with SMS 1.2 and 2.0. We look at some security concerns and at ways to automate the collection of network monitor traces.

COMMON NETWORK MONITORS: A LOOK AT THE TOOLS

There are many tools out there that provide the kind of low-level detail we need in order to perform network monitoring and analysis. Microsoft has some good programs that ship with the server products, as well as a more robust one that comes with the Systems Management Server product.

Microsoft's Network Monitor Family

There are currently many different network monitors available from Microsoft. All of them are called simply network monitor. In this chapter we will look at these offerings and show you how to install, configure, and get the most from these powerful tools. In the right hands, network monitor can provide a wealth of information. How do you use this tool? Let's find out!

NETWORK MONITOR

Back in the dark ages when you had a problem with your network, you pretty much had to guess as to what might have been causing problems. Later came specialized devices that were expensive, hard to operate, and even more difficult to understand. Now we have network monitor, which is a software-based analysis tool from Microsoft. This program comes in two flavors: a scaled-down version that ships with the server operating systems and a full version that comes with the systems management server. Microsoft Network Monitor Lite is able to capture traffic destined only for the machine running the software. The full version puts the network adapter into "promiscuous mode"—which means that it will capture traffic destined for other devices as well as traffic directed to the computer running Microsoft Network Monitor.

Network Monitor 2.0 comes with Windows 2000 in the Lite version, and the full version comes with SMS 2.0. The Network Monitor 1.2 version comes with Windows NT 4.0 and SMS 1.2. In reality, there is little difference between the 2.0 and the 1.2 versions of the product since they are functionally the same. We will point out the differences that do in fact exist, but most of what we look at applies to any version of the product.

Microsoft Network Monitor copies frames into a capture buffer, which is a resizable area of memory. By default, this capture buffer is one megabyte, but this is easily changed. However, because of this memory-dependant capture buffer, network monitor can capture only as much information as will fit in available memory. Once this buffer is filled, it will begin to drop packets, and you may miss the information you were looking for. In addition, network monitor has a tendency to lock up and tie up lots of CPU time when it is allowed to run for extended periods after the buffer is completely full. Luckily, it is easily killed with task manager, but then you lose all of your capture file. We will talk about some work-arounds for these features when we examine unattended network monitoring. Fortunately, this file loss is not normally a problem because you can select which part of the frame you need to see by designing a capture filter. A capture filter (which is somewhat like doing a query on a database) allows you to capture only certain addresses, or types of frames. We will talk about this in the section on capturing data.

Because Microsoft Network Monitor is readily available, very powerful, and captures data from your network, you will need to address security for this tool. As we have seen in other chapters, if you know what you are doing, you can obtain some very sensitive information from the network. While it is a great tool for troubleshooting, it can also be a significant threat if allowed unabated utilization in the wrong hands. There are several things you can do to help protect your network from unauthorized use of this tool. We will talk about this later in the section on network monitor security.

Microsoft Network Monitor is not installed by default. In order to install it, go to the services tab of the network applet in control panel and choose add network monitor tools and agent. (NOTE: Make sure to choose network monitor tools and agent, and not the network monitor agent, which is in the list just above and does not include the Microsoft Network Monitor program.) The SMS versions install using a separate Setup.exe program found in the NMEXT directory on the CD-ROM.

Making the Capture

When you capture data, the Ethernet card will pass on a portion of the frames it sees on the network to the capture buffer. If the capture buffer overflows, then it will use FIFO (first in first out) to determine what is retained in memory. To prevent the capture buffer from overflowing, you can adjust the buffer settings by selecting buffer settings from the capture menu.

A dialog box appears allowing you to specify your new capture buffer in megabytes. Here you can also specify whether to capture the entire frame or a certain number of bytes of the frame, allowing you to save just the header information.

The other way to reduce the amount of data selected is to design a capture filter to refine what the card passes on to the capture buffer. Begin your capture session by selecting start from the capture menu (or pressing the record button). As shown in Figure 9–1, network monitor displays statistics about the capture session as it is running. These statistics provide a quick look at the network performance at that instance. It is important to remember that this is a snapshot and although it may provide some insight, it cannot be used as a planning tool in and of itself. If, however, you document these recordings, spread them out over time, and compare them with information from managed hubs, switches, and routers, then you begin to have a better picture to measure network performance.

The graph pane (upper left, Figure 9–1) provides a quick representation of the status of your network. These panes are resizable, allowing a better

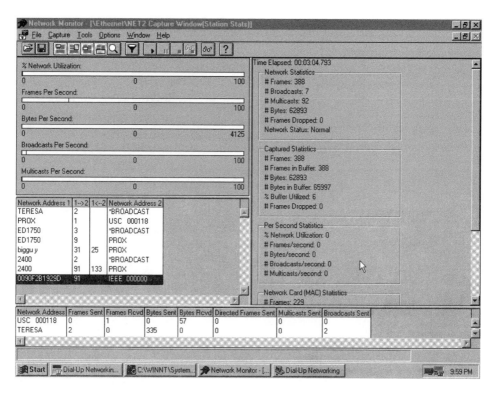

Fig. 9–1 A quick network health check is obtained from the session statistics in the capture window of network monitor.

presentation of the data. This is a particularly useful feature when monitoring the progress of a capture. This high-level overview can assist in troubleshooting by providing the information listed below:

- % Network utilization
- Frames per second
- Bytes per second
- Broadcasts per second
- Multicasts per second

The total statistics pane (upper right pane, Figure 9–1) shows a numerical summary of the information contained in the graph pane. Statistics regarding the captured data appear as well. The pane tells how many frames are in the buffer, how much of the buffer is in use, and whether or not any frames have been dropped because of a full buffer. Additional statistics provide information about the network card.

The session statistics pane (under the graph pane) lists network addresses of the computers talking during the current capture session. It details how many frames are on the network and in which direction they are going. Pay close attention to the arrow because it is used in network monitor to indicate the direction of data flow (also used in designing capture filters.) The arrow always points toward the computer that will receive the information. For instance in Figure 9–1, bigguy in column network address 1 sends 31 frames to PROX in the network address 2 column. PROX sends 25 frames to bigguy.

The station statistics pane (under session statistics) breaks the information from the session statistics down even further by listing the number of bytes sent and received from each station represented in the capture buffer. The information on broadcasts sent and multicasts is particularly helpful in quickly pointing out potential problems on your network. In addition, you might want to investigate the direction of data flow and sizes of the various exchanges taking place. These can all be possible bottlenecks on the network.

Manually Capturing Traffic

Now it is time to run network monitor. To control a manual capture, you use the capture menu (refer to Figure 9–2). However, before you click on start, you probably want to set the buffer size. Selecting buffer settings from the capture menu allows you to configure the buffer. The default maximum capture buffer size is eight MB fewer than the amount of RAM installed on the machine. Although you can use virtual memory for your capture buffer, it is better not to do so in order to ensure that critical frame information is reliably captured. In fact, Microsoft Network Monitor will warn you if you try to enter a capture buffer greater than the physical memory on the machine. The message says, "The buffer size you have requested may cause frames to be dropped due to swapping. Are you sure you want to allocate a buffer of this size?"

In addition to selecting the buffer size, you can also select the frame size you wish to capture. For instance, if you were interested only in header information for a particular protocol, you could set that information here and not waste space by capturing extraneous frame data. How much of the frame you capture is dependent on the particular protocol you are investigating. For instance, since we know that the normal Ethernet header is 14 bytes, we can set a capture buffer of 14 bytes and capture only Ethernet headers. This would allow us to capture 73,142 frames with a one-megabyte capture buffer. We could use a 34-byte frame to capture the IP header (14 bytes for Ethernet header and 20 bytes for the IP header). This is extremely useful with investigation file transfer problems that often contain 1,200 or more bytes of user data, which can quickly fill up your capture buffer.

Updating the capture statistics window shown in Figure 9–1 puts a load on the CPU that may not be needed. By selecting dedicated capture mode from the capture menu, you can avoid the load associated with updating the display and thereby provide additional resources for capturing frames. As shown in Figure 9–3, when in dedicated capture mode, you have the option of switching to normal mode to view real time capture statistics, and from there you can switch back to dedicated mode by selecting it from the capture menu. You can make all these switches while Microsoft Network Monitor is running and never miss a frame. In addition, you can pause Netmon and continue the application while in this mode.

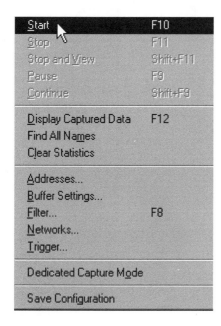

Fig. 9–2 The capture menu allows you to fully manage a capture session. This is also where you set the buffer settings.

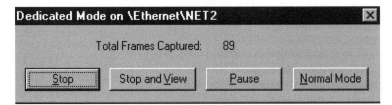

Fig. 9–3 Dedicated capture mode reduces the CPU load, thereby helping to avoid frame loss during a capture session.

Viewing the Capture

Once you are done with the capture session, what do you have? Network monitor simplifies the task of analyzing the data by organizing the captured data into several different views and performing much of the protocol analysis for you. In Figure 9–4, we see the summary view. This view is helpful in gaining an overview of the information contained in the captured data. The large number of BPDU frames in Figure 9–4 are configuration messages from a switch.

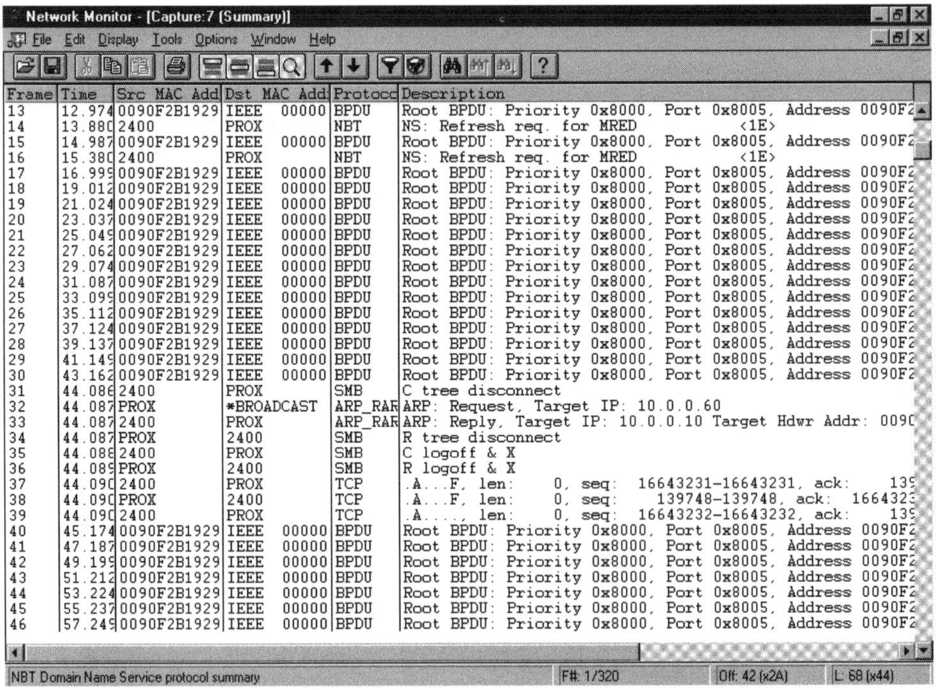

Fig. 9–4 The summary view of network monitor enables you to quickly spot anomalies in your captured data.

By adding the detail and the hex views from the Window menu, you can find information such as the source address and the destination address of the frame. We see the source and destination of the BPDU traffic in Figure 9–5 that are obviously eating up much of the bandwidth on the network. Armed with this information, you can go to the machine and do a little investigative work to find out why the machine is flooding your network with useless information. This view also gives the detail you need about the protocols to change your buffer settings if you are focusing on one particular item.

Saving the Capture

Once you have captured the data from the network, you will want to save it for baseline information while doing some network tuning, or to provide grist for long-term analysis. At any rate, you will save it as a .cap file that you can open in network monitor later. Additionally, make sure to save the data to file before you start another capture session, or you can lose the capture. Saving the capture is as simple as selecting save from the file menu.

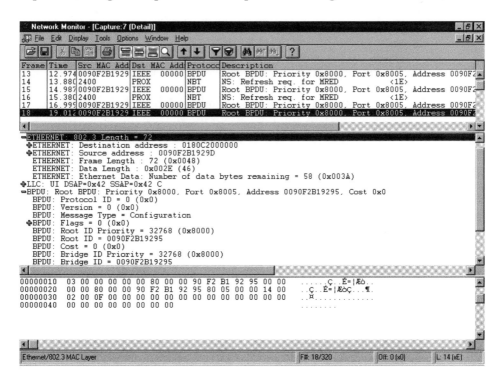

Fig. 9–5 The detail and hex views of network allow you to find the source and destination address of the machine sending the information across the network.

You are given the opportunity to choose the location as well as the range of frames you wish to save. The default is to save all the frames in the capture. You can also choose to save the filtered capture. For instance, if you have configured a display filter (as we discuss in the next section), you can save only the data in the current display. This allows you to customize your .cap file. You can also create several .cap files from one larger capture, allowing you to save only the data of interest.

Filtering the Capture

Two kinds of filters are used with network monitor. The first is a capture filter, and the second is a display filter. They both work in a similar fashion. A filter works somewhat like a query you would use on a database. It allows you to select a portion, or a subset of the available data. For instance, if you have narrowed down a problem to a specific computer, then you can filter out all the other traffic and focus only on that computer. One other feature is that you can save your filters and reuse them later (several useful filters are included on the CD-ROM). This is helpful when you are trying to correct a particular problem. You save a data set, and after you make changes, you run the filter again, thereby enabling you to track your progress.

The capture filter   To design a capture filter, you select filter from the capture menu. As seen in Figure 9–6, you can filter data by protocol, by address, or by data pattern (or by a combination of all three).

If you wanted to filter by protocol, you would select the SAP/ETYPE line and press the edit line button. A menu appears that allows you to select the type of protocol you want to filter. To select one particular protocol, the easiest thing to do is to disable all protocols and then just enable the one protocol you want to examine. Although the dialog boxes get a little cumbersome to use, you can quickly go to a section by clicking on the name header and then typing the first letter of the protocol or address you want. While not perfect, it is a little better than scrolling through a long list of addresses.

If you are interested in just one machine, select the address pairs and again select the edit line button (or just double-click on the expression). This particular filter works the same in both capture mode and display mode and is a great tool to use for analyzing the conversation between servers and workstations, or between printers.

The pattern match capture filter is a little tricky to use because it requires specific knowledge of the location in the frame a particular pattern will appear. The way to find this information is by analyzing existing capture information in the hex pane. Once you find the pattern for a particular manifestation, then create a capture filter and test it to see if it does what you want it to do. It does not have to be perfect, only close—but it does have to

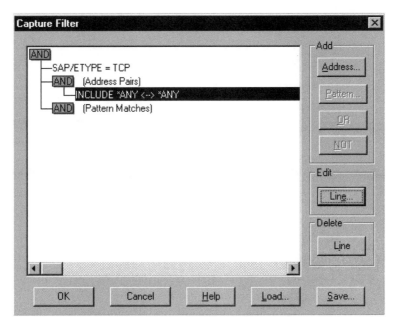

Fig. 9–6 A capture filter functions much like a database query in that it allows you to specify a subset of data for analysis.

be really close to work properly. We will look at this when we explore hex pane analysis.

The display filter A display filter works much like a capture filter, however, because it only works on data already captured. It will not affect the contents of the capture buffer. With the display filter you can choose a particular protocol, address, or data property to help you sort through the data. You make the selections in the same manner as when designing a capture filter. However, there is one important distinction in that you can also apply the logic expressions of AND, OR, and NOT. This ability provides a greater range of selectivity when creating your filter than is available in the capture filter mode. As seen in Figure 9–7, a menu appears that allows you to select the address you want to examine. You are given options to include an address or to exclude an address. In addition, you can pick the direction of information flow. Select the name for station 1 in the left column, choose the direction arrow (remember, the arrowhead points in the direction of data flow), and then select the recipient under the station 2 column. For instance, in Figure 9–7, our filter includes data traffic from ED1750 to any station on the network, as well as traffic from any station on the network to ED1750. This might be a useful filter to use when analyzing server traffic patterns.

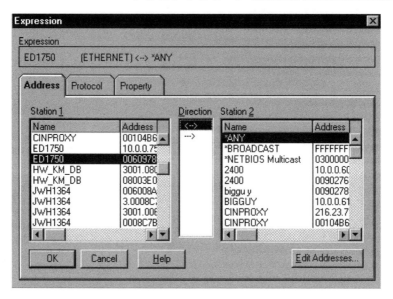

Fig. 9–7   Filtering on addresses simplifies troubleshooting with network monitor.

Analyzing the Capture

Once we have captured the data and applied our display filter, it is time to begin the work of analyzing the frames. The top pane is the summary pane, which contains the information listed below. These columns can be rearranged by holding down the column head and dragging to the new desired position.

- Frame number. Microsoft Network Monitor assigns the frame number to the frame for accounting purposes. It does not actually appear in the frame itself but is added by the program to make it easier to refer to information found in the capture.

- Time. The time, also assigned by Microsoft Network Monitor, allows us to know how much time transpired between frames. This provides useful information when doing network performance analysis. The time that is displayed in this column is configured from the display menu options. There are three choices: time of day, seconds from beginning of capture, and seconds from previous frame. By selecting time of day, you can match information from the windows event log with information captured by Microsoft Network Monitor. Matching in this way allows for powerful troubleshooting of error messages.

- Source MAC address. This is the device that generated the frame in the first place. There are three choices for displaying the MAC address, all of which are made from the options menu. You can choose to display the name you assigned to the MAC address in the Microsoft Network

Monitor address book; you can choose to show just the MAC address (default behavior); or you can choose to display the vendor name associated with the first six bytes of the MAC address. This is sometimes helpful in trying to find an unknown device on the network.

- Destination MAC address. This is the destination hardware address of the packet.

- Protocol. This is the main protocol in the frame.

- Description. This provides summary information about the frame. The description is also configurable from the display menu options. There are two choices: the last protocol in the frame or auto select based on the display filter in use. Often you can gather enough information from the summary to get the flow of what is happening in the capture session. The TCP three-way handshake is easily spotted from the description. TCP flag information often shows up here.

- Source other address. In order to see this field, you often have to move the slide bar at the bottom of the summary pane. The source other address is the other protocol address contained in the frame.

- Destination other address. This is the other protocol address contained in the frame.

- Type other address. This address tells you which protocol the other address fields contain.

The detail pane is the middle one and is where most of the analysis takes place. Microsoft Network Monitor uses .dll files and .ini files to enable it to parse a protocol. There are, for example, TCP.dll and TCP.ini files stored in the Microsoft Network Monitor parser directory. In order to properly analyze protocols that Microsoft Network Monitor does not understand, you need a parser .dll and .ini file. You can write them yourself or obtain them from third-party vendors.

The hex pane is the bottom one and contains very specific information about the frame we are analyzing. For instance, looking at the POP3 protocol traces, we note that all the information is in the hex trace and not in the detail pane. Understanding how to read the hex trace will enable us to create custom capture filters that are very specific. See Figure 9–8.

Figure 9–8 is a NetBIOS transport frame that rides on top of TCP, IP, and the Ethernet protocol. This particular frame is a session keep-alive frame. If we wanted to create a capture filter that captures only NetBIOS session keep-alive frames (perhaps to analyze the impact of NetBIOS keep-alive traffic on the network), we would need to use a pattern offset. We expand the NBT section of the trace by clicking on the plus beside the NBT summary line. Next, we select the NBT: packet type line. Notice that the appropriate section of the hex trace is automatically highlighted as we select different lines in the detail pane. When we select the packet type = session keep alive, the hex number 85 is highlighted in line 30. We can now count

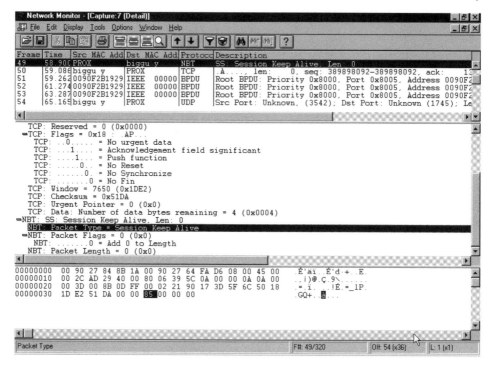

Fig. 9–8 Analyzing the hex trace enables very detailed information about the frame.

over until we see that the hex number 85 is in offset position 36 hex from the beginning of the frame. Instead of counting over, we can look in the lower right corner of the Microsoft Network Monitor screen. There we see that it is offset 54 (decimal) x36 (hexadecimal). This is the information we would enter into our pattern match capture filter, as seen in Figure 9–9. The additional 00 added after the 85 is what follows in the hex trace and reduces the number of bogus hits. Possible filtering on two or three numbers ensures finer control of the capture process.

Customize the display There are a couple of settings that can be used to make the hours looking at Microsoft Network Monitor traces pass somewhat more easily. The first is the size of the display text, which is set by selecting font from the display menu. A more functional change is assigning particular protocols to specific colors. You can, for example, assign red to TCP, green to Browser, and yellow to NetLogon traffic. This makes it much easier to trace particular conversations in a capture with a large number of frames. You can choose between foreground colors that change just the color of the font, or background colors that make the trace similar to the old green-bar paper, or any combination of both.

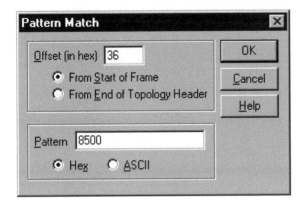

Fig. 9–9 The pattern match capture filter requires both a pattern and offset.

Another feature of Microsoft Network Monitor is the duplicate feature, which is selected from the window menu. This copies the capture into another window and allows you to work on both as if they were different captures. You can use different display filters and compare the two views of the same capture. To assist you in keeping track of this process, you can also add a label to the window from the same menu. This avoids the ambiguity involved in working on two views with the same name. When working with the duplicate, you can close one window without affecting the other one. Once you get the setting configured the way you like it, you can save your settings by selecting save configuration from the display menu.

By selecting insert comment frame from the tools menu, you can add information to the .cap file to aid in interpreting the data at a later date, or for training purposes. You can insert two different kinds of frames: the bookmark frame and the comment frame. The data will show up in the trace as a comment or bookmark frame, and it allows you to type a message that will be stored in the frame (see Figure 9–10). You can also choose comment or bookmark from the list of protocols when creating a display filter. This would be helpful for a heavily documented .cap file, and you could then print the results. When adding comments to a .cap file, it is useful not to include them in the statistics computation because it will corrupt your readings of how many frames transmitted during the period of the capture. If you are not analyzing this aspect of the traffic, then it does not matter if you include the comment frame in your capture statistics.

You can also transmit a comment frame onto a live network to aid in finding particular frames when certain network problems are manifesting themselves. This involves using the full version of Microsoft Network Monitor and running two instances of it in order to both transmit and receive at the same time. When using a bookmark, you can bring together a nice array of information in the trail section of the bookmark frame, as seen in the detail pane of Figure 9–10.

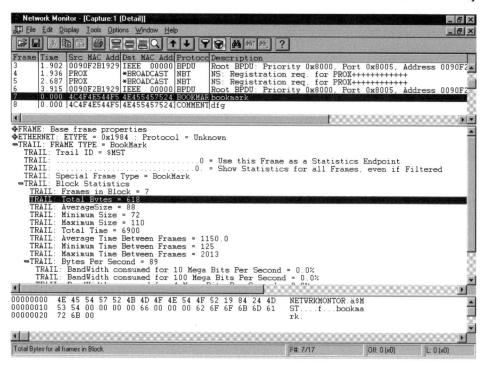

Fig. 9–10   The comment frame provides a place to write notes that stay with the capture file.

NETWORK MONITOR SECURITY

With the power available in network monitor, it is extremely important to take appropriate security measures to safeguard your network from misuse of this tool. Microsoft has already implemented one security feature for you in the server products, and that is that network monitor will monitor traffic only between the server it is running on and the rest of the network. This will safeguard you from a certain amount of misuse. However, the version that ships with Systems Management Server (SMS) is able to capture frames sent to or from any computer on the network, as well as capturing frames over a remote network.

Password Protection

Two passwords can be set for network monitor using the monitoring agent icon in control panel; these are the display password and the capture password, shown in Figure 9–11. The display password allows access to a saved capture (a .cap) file. With this password, you are only allowed to open a

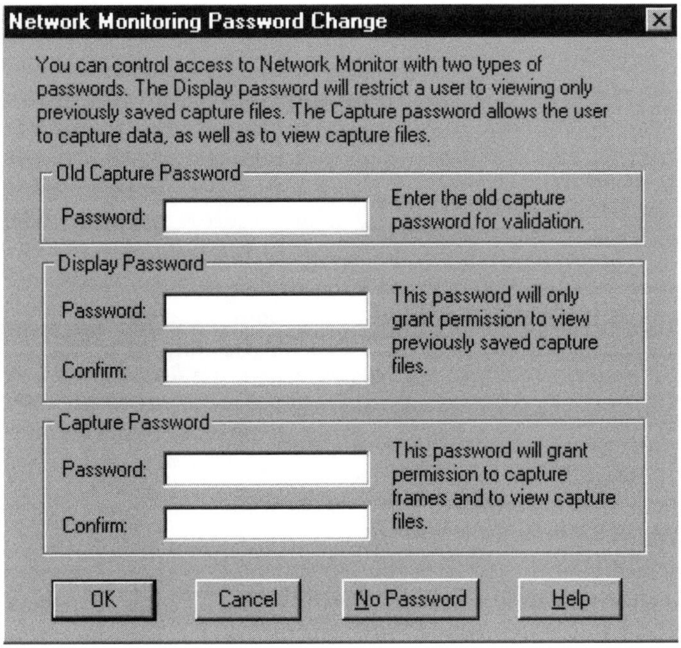

Fig. 9–11 The network monitor agent password applet in control panel provides basic security for network monitor.

previously saved capture file. You are not allowed to capture new data. This applies only to the Microsoft Network Monitor installed on the machine on which the password was set. It also does not protect the .cap file from being viewed across the network with another Microsoft Network Monitor. In other words, it is password-protecting the installation of the program and the associated agent—not the data.

The capture password allows unlimited access to network monitor. With this password you are able to open saved capture files as well as create new captures. The password is prompted for each time Microsoft Network Monitor is launched. If you enter the capture password, then you have full access to all the features; if you enter the display password, then you can display only .cap files.

It is essential to assign these passwords on remote workstations and servers that have the agent installed on them. If the service is running without password protection, then anyone with the SMS version of network monitor can connect to your server and use it to capture data from your network. These passwords should be safeguarded because there is no way to recover them other than to uninstall and reinstall Microsoft Network Monitor and the associated agents. Deleting the security key under the BH service in the registry does not work for recovering from a lost password.

Network Monitor Installations: Detecting Others

In order to protect your network from unauthorized snooping, network monitor can easily detect other instances of the program on your network. It can do this whether or not the program is running. As shown in Figure 9–12, if the driver is installed on a machine, it will tell you the name of the machine, the name of the user logged onto the computer, the Ethernet address of the machine, the version number of the program, and whether the program is capturing data or merely installed. In order to gain this information, you select identify network monitor users from the tools menu. It is important to note that if you have network segments separated by a router that does not forward multicasts, then you will not be able to detect network monitor installations on the other segment without being connected to that segment. This is because Netmon uses a NetBIOS suffix to announce its presence on the network. A BE suffix announces the network monitor agent, and a BF suffix announces the network monitor application itself to the network. If these are not forwarded, then you will need to connect to the specific segment in order to detect rogue installations of these tools.

When you click on identify network monitor users, the Netmon machine sends out a BONE station query request, as seen in the printout on the next page. The BONE protocol (which stands for Bloodhound Oriented Network Entity) is used by network monitor to allow it to communicate. This station query is a very small multicast 802.3 frame that uses only 29 bytes.

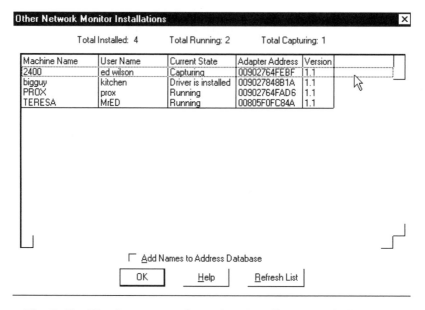

Fig. 9–12   The detect network monitor installations tool allows you to control Microsoft Network Monitor usage.

```
BONE: Station Query Request  C (0x00)
      BONE: Signature = RTSS
      BONE: Command = Station Query Request  C (0x00)
      BONE: Flags = 0x00
      BONE: Bone Data: Number of data bytes remaining = 0
(0x0000)
```

The response is directed to the machine that sent the query and is a small 802.3 frame this time requiring about 125 bytes. The response tells us the status of the driver; 0x00000003 means that the driver is installed and active but not capturing data. It gives us the driver version, machine, MAC address of the machine, and any user name that was configured when the driver was configured.

```
BONE: Station Query Response R (0x01)
      BONE: Signature = RTSS
      BONE: Command = Station Query Response R (0x01)
      BONE: Flags = 0x00
      BONE: Response Data Length = 96 (0x0060)
         BONE: Station Query Flags = 0x00000003
         BONE: Station Query Version = 1.01
         BONE: Station Query License Number = 0x00000000
         BONE: Station Query Machine Name = TERESA
         BONE: Station Query User Name = MrED
         BONE: Station Query Node Address = 00805F0FC84A
      BONE: Bone Data: Number of data bytes remaining = 0
(0x0000)
```

SYSTEMS MANAGEMENT SERVER 1.2 NETWORK MONITOR

The network monitor that comes with SMS 1.2 (v4.00.351) works in much the same way as the NT 4.0 network monitor does. However, there are several additional features that make it a much more useful tool for the busy network administrator.

Additional Features

Perhaps the most powerful additional feature provided by the full version of network monitor is the ability to connect to remote agents running on other machines. By doing this, you can view network traffic not normally seen in a segmented network, or one broken up by switches.

Using the connect to remote network feature, the SMS version of Netmon can connect to another NT server, workstation, or Windows 95 or 98 machine that has the network monitor agent installed and running. The network monitor agent installs as a service under Windows NT, and it can be set to autostart if desired to provide for ease of use for remote troubleshooting. If desired, the service can be left in manual and remotely started by using the NETSVC utility from the NT Resource Kit. This utility allows you to query, list, start, and stop services on remote Windows NT machines.

NETSVC SYNTAX

```
Netsvc \\computername /command
     Netsvc \\computername /list
     Netsvc \\computername /query "network monitor agent"
     Netsvc \\computername /start "network monitor agent"
```

Installation and configuration of the Windows 9.x Network Monitor Agent   The installation and operation of the Windows 9.x network monitor agent is not all straightforward. The agent is found on the CD-ROM in the \admin\nettools\Netmon directory and consists of two parts. There is a protocol driver that provides performance counters to the system monitor tool for NDIS 3.1 adapters. This allows system monitor to look at network traffic statistics. The network monitor agent uses some of the functionality provided by the protocol driver to pass information back to the Netmon application. Here are the steps to install the Windows 9.x network monitor agent.

1. Open the network applet in control panel and click add.
2. Select the network component type and double-click on service.
3. In the service dialog box, click on have disk.
4. The install from directory will be your CD-ROM \admin\nettools\ Netmon directory on the Windows 9.x disk.
5. In the select network service box, click on Microsoft Network Monitor Agent and say OK.

The above steps will install both the protocol driver and the agent. In order to configure the agent, go back into the network applet, select the Microsoft Network Monitor Agent, and click on properties. This brings up the box similar to the one we looked at earlier for the Windows NT machines and enables us to assign both a capture password and a display password. This password must be set when the agent is not running and system monitor is not displaying network performance data.

Once the agent has been installed and configured, it is time to start the agent. This is done from the run command by typing nmagent. The agent is stopped from the run command by typing nmagent –close. The agent can also be run as a service on a Windows 9.x machine by making a change to the registry as seen on the next page.

RUN THE NMAGENT AS A SERVICE

```
Select the following line in the registry on a Windows
9.x machine
    HKEY_LOCAL_MACHINE\Software\Microsoft\CurrentVersion
    \RunServicesOnce
    Add a new string value of nm agent
    Modify the value of the new string and type
nmagent.exe
```

Since the agent is now running as a service on the Windows 9.x machine, it will continue to run whether or not a user is logged onto the computer. To stop the service at any time, use the nmagent –close command from the run box.

Connecting to Remote Agents

In order to connect to a remote agent, select networks from the capture menu. The select capture network box that is revealed lists all network adapters installed in the machine and one additional adapter called remote. The state of it is by default disconnected and is of an unknown type. If you were successful in the network agent query, you can simply double-click on the remote unknown network and the box shown in Figure 9–13 below appears. Type in the machine name of one of the agents returned from that query, and the connection should be established. If the agent is password protected, then a dialog box will be displayed requesting a password. Once connected, the session works in the same way as local capture. You still want to adjust your capture buffer settings and maybe configure a capture filter, but there is no difference in the way the session is operated.

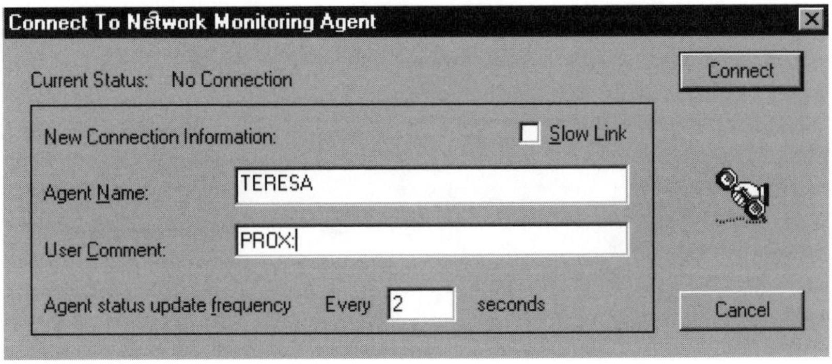

Fig. 9–13 To connect to a remote network, type in the name of the agent-enabled machine.

The Wizards

The SMS 1.2 Network Monitor includes several wizards that will find several important details for you. These reports (they are not really wizards) are a top-user report and a protocol-distribution report. The other functions the wizards perform are: The wizards will find all routers in the capture file, **and the wizards** will find all names in the capture file, and they can resolve addresses from a name. The bad thing about these reports is that there is no way to save the information short of doing a print screen to capture the on-screen report. This is a serious annoyance because often it is very useful to print out the data, particularly the top-user report. Let us begin by looking at the top-user report.

The top-user report is activated when in display mode (when you are displaying the captured data as opposed to looking at the session statistics). You select the report from the tools menu and have the option of showing how many top users to display, and whether the list is based on the link layer address or the MAC address. You can also apply the current display filter or choose to ignore the display filter and base the report on the entire capture file. As we can see in Figure 9–14, the report lists the name, address, number

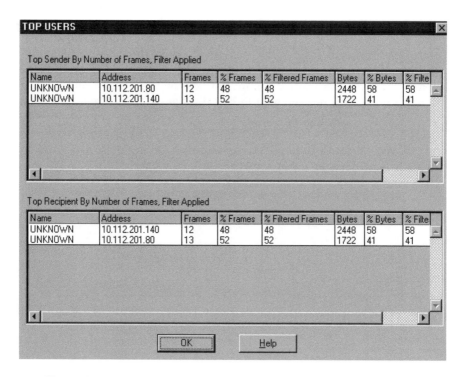

Figure 9–14   The Netmon top-user report can assist with network planning.

of frames, and percentages by both frame number and frame size. This information can assist in network planning and expansion. It can help in spotting network abuses as well.

The protocol-distribution report is accessed in the same way as the top-user report: from the tools menu in display mode. The choices for this report include reporting on all protocols in the frame, reporting on the last protocol in the frame, and reporting on the first effective protocol in the frame. In addition, you can choose to further limit the report by applying the current display filter to the report. This report can be of tremendous assistance when trying to spot anomalies on the network. For this information to be of greatest benefit, however, you need to know what a normal distribution is for the network. If, for example, the network normally has very few ARP_RARP frames, and suddenly it is flooded with these, then you have a good place to begin looking. If, on the other hand, there were a sudden flood of UDP packets, it would have a different meaning. Knowledge of what is normal for your network cannot be overestimated. As we see in Figure 9–15, the report lists each protocol, the number of frames and bytes, and the percentages for the capture.

The find network addresses from name allows inputting a computer name, and it will find the MAC address for you. This is not a very hard trick to perform on a TCP/IP network as you can ping the host name and then pull the information from the ARP cache with an ARP –a command. However, it

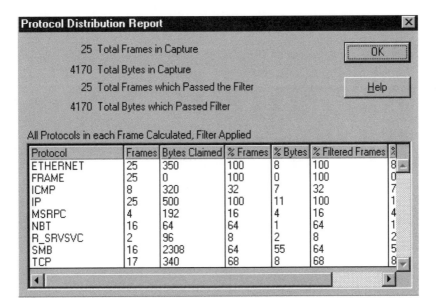

Fig. 9–15 The Netmon protocol distribution report assists in spotting network anomalies.

can also use SAP, DNS, and query the SMS database, so it can be a more powerful solution. If it is just a normal verification of the MAC address, it is often faster to go to the CMD window and do a quick ping and ARP –a. As we see in Figure 9–16, once the name is resolved, it will display all information found about the name. Selecting only the services that are present on the network can optimize this process. In addition, you can speed up the process by making the local ADR database the first source to be queried by using the plus and minus buttons beside the service-selection display box.

Configuring Triggers

A trigger examines frames as they pass. The network monitor collects data to see if the frames meet certain criteria. If they meet the preset condition, then the network monitor will take whatever action you have selected. This is a very powerful tool and opens up nearly unlimited possibility. A very simple trigger that will keep you from losing data during a monitoring session is created by selecting trigger on buffer space, choosing 100% on the buffer space setting, and then setting the trigger action to stop capture. To

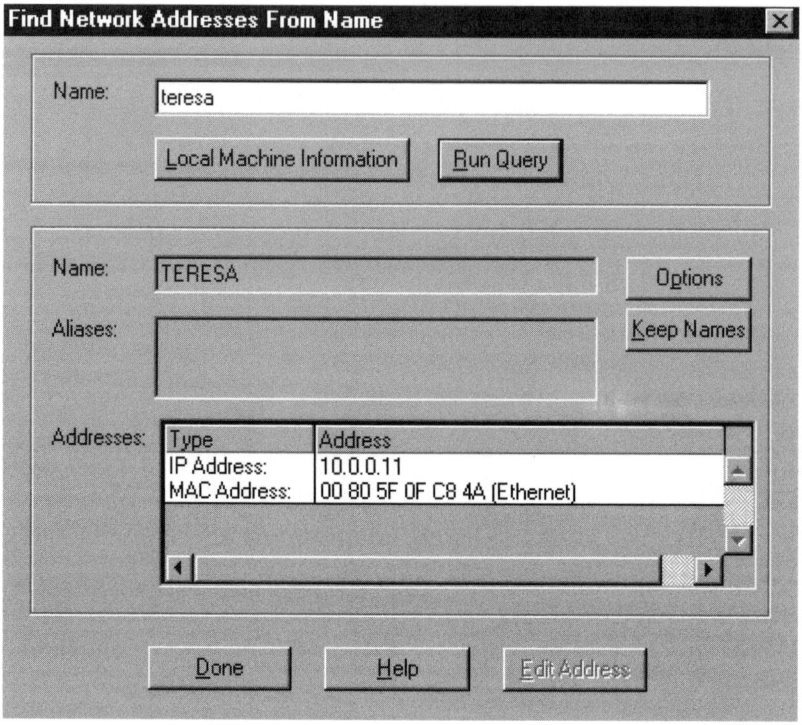

Fig. 9–16 The find network address from name queries multiple sources to resolve the name.

take this trigger one step further, write a simple batch file that will do a net send to let you know the capture has stopped, and then tell the trigger to execute that .bat file when the capture stops. This batch file can be as simple as a single line and look like the one in the box below. You can write this in notepad, and then rename the resulting .txt file with a .bat extension and point the execute command line to the location of the file.

A SIMPLE BATCH FILE NOTIFIES WHEN CAPTURING STOPS

Net send administrator the capture has ceased!
Notes:
    Net send will use the following: user name, machine name, or *, meaning all.
    The message follows the destination and does not require " "

The use of triggers can get very complex when you introduce the elements of the pattern offset. By using pattern offsets, network monitor can identify a wide variety of events and run anything that can be executed from a command line—including another instance of network monitor on another machine! Using the hex pane to identify both the offset and the pattern to specify the event to be triggered upon can identify these pattern offsets. You would do this in the same manner we discussed in the section on developing capture filters earlier in this chapter.

Automatically launching network monitor If you want to automatically launch network monitor either through the use of a batch file with trigger, or by using the Windows NT scheduler service (the AT command), the following command line switches can be used. Each of these switches modifies the command netmon. A sample batch file is included in the batch directory on the CD-ROM. To ease the use of command line Netmon, add the directory to the executable to the path of the computer by modifying your system environment path variable.

- /autostart—causes network monitor to start capturing data immediately upon launch. Ex: netmon /autostart.
- /remote *computer*—*computer* is the name of the remote agent you wish to connect with. Ex: Netmon /remote exchange.
- /net *number*—*number* specifies a connection to the network interface indicated. This information is found when you use the networks command from the capture menu. Ex: Netmon /net 2 (will launch Netmon using the #2 network interface listed in the networks dialog box, but will not start capturing data as we did not specify /autostart).

- /capturefilter *path*—specifies a particular capture filter to be used when network monitor runs. *Path* gives the location of the particular capture filter.
- /displayfilter *path*—specifies a particular display filter to be loaded upon startup of network monitor.
- /buffersize *number*—indicates the buffer size to preset in bytes (one-megabyte capture buffer would be specified as /buffersize 1024000).
- /quickfilter *type, address*—indicates that network monitor will begin capturing as soon as it is started, and it will filter on the address specified.
- /autostop—causes network monitor to stop capturing data when the buffer is full. Ex: Netmon /autostart /buffersize 1024000 /autostop (launches Netmon and immediately begins capturing data with a capture buffer of one megabyte. It will stop when the capture buffer is full).

NETWORK MONITOR 2.0

When you open up the Systems Management Server Network Monitor 2.0 version (V5.00646), you may feel as if you are greeting an old friend. This is the full version of the Windows 2000 Network Monitor. Yes, the interface is really pretty much the same, and most of the tools work the same. However, some things have changed, and there are some cool new features.

The Cool New Features

The experts—there are six experts that come with Network Monitor 2.0—are listed below.

- Average server response time expert calculates the average amount of time it takes for a server to respond to a user's request for data. It can use SMB, specified TCP ports, or specific IPX sockets to arrive at this number expressed in seconds.
- Property distribution calculates frame statistics for a specific property found in the frames of the capture. These properties can be very specific, such as HTTP accept.
- Protocol coalesce tool recombines data for a transaction that was sent across the network in multiple frames. This expert is able to put these fragments back together based upon information contained in the frames.
- Protocol distribution expert examines the captured data and presents statistics on the packets in much the same way as the old protocol distribution wizard did in the 1.2 product.

- TCP retransmit expert finds the TCP frames that have been retransmitted to the same computer. This is helpful in running down problem computers.
- Top users expert finds the top senders and receivers of data in the capture file by examining the source and destination addresses contained in the frames.

The SMS 2.0 Platform Software Development Kit (SDK) enables you to develop your own experts, or you can purchase them from third-party vendors. The experts are launched from the tools expert menu when in display mode. As we see in Figure 9–17, the average server response time expert can quickly highlight a problem with network response times. In the figure, server 11.0.0.206 has an average response time of 2.378751 seconds, while all the other destinations have response times in fractions of a second. To make matters worse, ten clients are using this slow beast. In the old days, this process would have translated into ten phone calls (which makes troubleshooting and fixing the problem rather difficult because you spend all the time on the phone). But now, since we are being proactive in our network

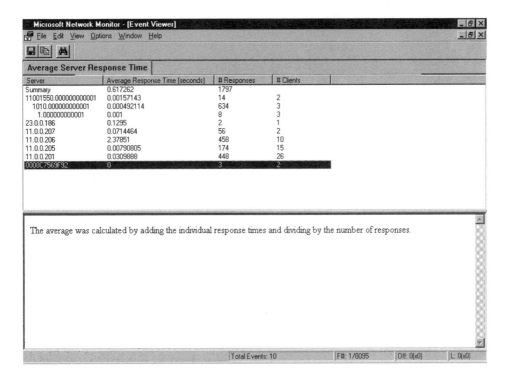

Fig. 9–17 The experts produce reports that quickly point out matters needing attention.

monitoring and analysis, we can solve the problem before we get all those phone calls. The only thing the user will notice is that it seems faster once we are done solving the problem.

The TCP retransmit expert in Figure 9–18 tells us that there are indeed several retransmissions, but none are going to or from the machine with the long response time. Since this is not on a switched backbone, the retransmissions can be due to network congestion, which may indicate a possible reason for some of the delays.

The protocol coalesce tool tells us there are no fragmented packets in the capture, so that possible culprit can be ruled out.

When we look at the top-user expert, we see that five of the 10 top users are connected to server 11.0.0.206, and our protocol expert tells us that there are a large number of RPC connections to the same machine as well. We investigate and find out that the 11.0.0.206 is an older machine, is on a 10-megabit Ethernet segment, and does not even have a PCI Ethernet card in it. Clearly we have found the reason for the slow performance. The users had not complained previously because "it is always slow" and they had "learned to live with it." Changing out the old card with a 100-megabit PCI card solved that problem rather easily.

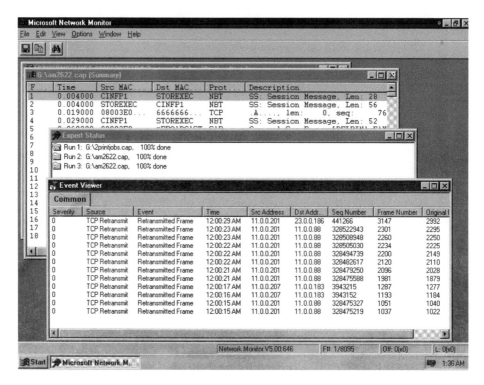

Fig. 9–18 The TCP retransmit expert identifies retransmitted frames, which indicates potential networking problems.

As we can see in Figure 9–18, the experts record their progress in an expert status window. Monitoring this window will keep you from trying to run two experts at the same time (which generates an error message). This is important because running an expert on a large capture file can take a long time on a slow machine, and the expert status window is the only place that will let you know that your computer has not locked up. During these times, you will notice CPU utilization going to 100 percent, so do not run the experts on a production server because the server will most assuredly generate complaints from the user community.

Things That Don't Work

You cannot connect to a Windows 95 or 98 machine and run remote network monitor sessions on it with Network Monitor 2.0 because it requires the Network Monitor version 2 driver, which requires Windows NT 4 with service pack 4 at a minimum. This also precludes running the network monitor application on a Windows 9.x machine. In the old days, you could install the full version of network monitor on a Windows 95 or 98 laptop and enjoy the enhanced portability features of 9.x, such as enhanced power management and plug and play as well as have a portable sniffer. You cannot install Network Monitor 2.0 on that platform. However, Windows 2000 professional runs great on a laptop, and you can run Network Monitor 2.0 on that platform.

Nevertheless, you can keep both versions of network monitor installed on the same machine without any problems. In fact, you can run both versions on the same machine at the same time if you are so inclined.

You cannot open a .cap file created with Network Monitor 2.0 on a Network Monitor 1.2 machine. If you try, you will get an error message that says, "The capture file is not valid." Because there is no way to tell what format the .cap file is in, it is best to create separate directories to avoid confusion when running both versions on a network.

Multiple capture transmissions are no longer permitted with Network Monitor 2.0. This is somewhat unfortunate from a testing perspective; however, in real life it has little bearing. When you go to tools transmit capture, the only choices are to transmit all frames, to transmit selected frames, or to apply the current display filter. This is another reason to keep the 1.2 tools available—at least in a lab environment.

Additional Security Features

The monitor control tool watches the network on a continuous basis for predefined events. These events are listed below.

- ICMP redirect monitor generates an event when a router on the network redirects frames.

- IP router monitor generates an event when a router on the network fails.
- IPRange monitor generates an event when a frame has a source address that is outside the range of addresses set by the administrator as valid for the particular network.
- IPX router monitor generates an event when an IPX router on the network fails.
- Rogue DHCP and WINS monitors generate an event when an invalid or unauthorized DHCP server or WINS server is found on-line on the network.
- SynAttack monitor watches for signs of a SynAttack on the network. This attack will generate a large number of unresponsive connections on a network server, which in turn soaks up a considerable amount of resources. Like leeches, the synattack will suck the life out of a server. This is a denial of service attach, and the SynAttack monitor knows how to watch for characteristics that indicate that this type of attack is in progress.
- Security monitor detects unauthorized instances of network monitor running on the network.

When the monitor control tool is used to configure and activate a particular monitor either locally or remotely, the monitor examines the frames that flow by the machine as it looks for a specific property that is associated with the event it is looking for. When a router stops working, it no longer announces itself on the network. The monitor control tool can spot the absence of these router announcements for the specified period of time. Then it will generate an event and open up the network monitor control tool in the event viewer window.

In order to use the monitor, the monitor control service must be running. It is installed when Network Monitor 2 is installed, but the monitor service is set to manual by default. In addition to the monitors that ship with Network Monitor 2, you can use custom or third-party monitors to further expand the functionality of the product. You cannot run the monitor control tool on any system that does not meet the requirements to run the Network Monitor 2 application. In addition, it requires administrator rights on the computer that will be running the monitor control tool. In order to use the event service, WBEM (windows based enterprise management) is required, and you receive this prompt when you launch the monitor control tool on a computer that does not have WBEM installed. Windows 2000 has WBEM installed by default, and you get WBEM when you install the SMS 2.0 administrator tools on a Windows NT 4.0 machine. You can launch the tool from the MMC by right-clicking on network monitor and selecting start network monitor control tool, or you can create a shortcut to mcsui.exe (which is easier and faster). Additionally, if you add the netmon2 directory to your path, then you can launch both netmon.exe and mcsui.exe from the run box or a CMD prompt. Once the monitor control tool is launched, you can select from the monitors listed earlier in this section, as seen in Figure 9–19.

You do not want to run the monitor control tool from the same machine that is running your SMS primary site; rather, it is better (due to resource requirements) to set up a separate machine to do the monitoring. You can then use this machine to monitor several remote computers as well as to perform unattended network monitor traces and triggers. In effect, this becomes your network management computer.

Let us now look at how we would configure a monitor to alert us when one of our routers goes down. In Figure 9–19, the installed monitors are listed in the left display panel. Enabled monitors are listed in the right display panel. In order to configure a monitor, it must be first enabled by selecting from the list on the left and pressing the enable button. The network monitor control tool will then prompt you to configure the particular monitor you just enabled. You do not have to configure the monitor at this time and can press no to the question. If you do not configure the monitor, then it will be listed as enabled on the right panel. If you choose to go ahead and configure the monitor, you will be presented with a screen similar to the one in Figure 9–20. To monitor a particular router, you type in the IP address in the box on the left of the screen and select the number of seconds before a router is considered down by placing that value in the box in the lower left side of the screen. Once this is done, press the set monitor configuration button in the lower right side on the screen (not shown in Figure 9–20).

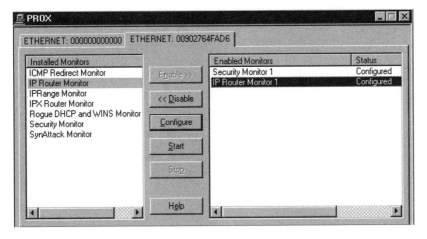

Fig. 9–19 The network monitor control tool automates much of the monitoring activities.

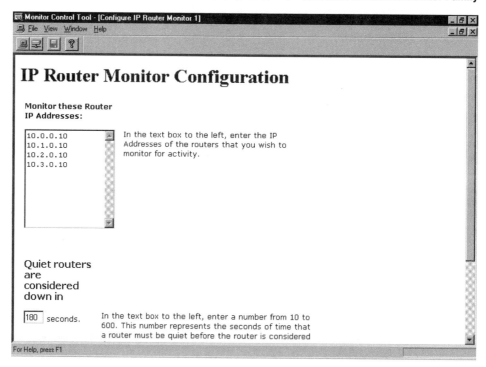

Fig. 9–20   The IP router monitor configuration window lists routers being currently monitored.

The IP router monitor is now configured, but it is not active until you select it on the right panel and press the start button. It is now displayed as running.

If a configured IP router is detected as inactive, then the network monitor control tool will display an event in the monitor event log (see Figure 9–21). Unfortunately, it does not write to the windows event log, and therefore event log tools will not be able to respond to this event.

The cool thing about the network monitor control tool is that you can configure multiple monitors of the same type. This means that you can configure multiple IP router monitors and activate them separately or at the same time. This would enable you to take a particular router off-line for maintenance without having to turn off the IP router monitor altogether. You can do this for the other monitors as well. For example, you can use multiple security monitors that allow a particular administrator to perform sniffing, but he would need permission from the senior administrator. In this scenario, the senior administrator simply starts a previously enabled security monitor to allow the junior administrator to perform his sniffing activities. Once completed, the monitor that includes his MAC address is turned off.

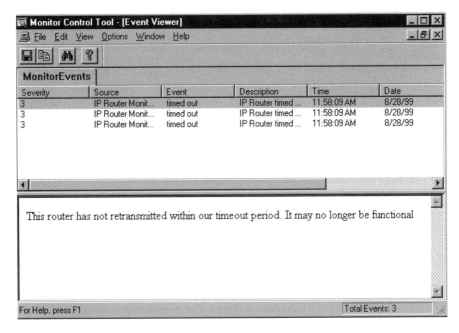

Fig. 9–21   Detected events are displayed in the network control tool event log.

Launching Network Monitor 2 from the command line   The launching network monitor works in the same way as it does with Netmon 1.2; however, the syntax is just a little different: A colon is placed between the switch and the modifier. For example, Netmon /remote:*computername* launches Netmon v.2 and connects to a remote computer. One command has changed, however: the /buffersize now takes the buffer in megabytes, not in bytes. For example, to launch Netmon v.2 and start capturing data with a 3-megabyte capture buffer, type Netmon /autostart /buffersize:3 from the command line or run command. There is one new command line variable, which is the /quickfiltername switch. It is used to specify a filter that is specified by the /quickfilter option. It is ignored if there is no /quickfilter option specified.

CHAPTER REVIEW

In this chapter, we have covered the ins and outs of the Microsoft network monitor family of products. We have looked at the similarities and differences between two generations of products and given ideas for employing their power to aid in monitoring, analysis, troubleshooting, and security activities. We looked at using both the wizards in the 1.2 family and the experts in the 2.0 family to quickly point out potential problems and to identify areas that may require further investigation. Finally, we looked at the network monitor control tool included with Network Monitor 2.0 that can automate some of the day–to-day tasks related for both security concerns and mission-critical network equipment.

IN THE NEXT CHAPTER

We begin our final section of the book by looking at troubleshooting. We first look at some of the more routine problems: slow network, user cannot logon, and the workstation cannot obtain an IP address. We use network monitor to solve all these problems, and we walk away with having gained knowledge in the process. In other words, we do not accidentally solve the problem; rather, we use the problem as a learning tool to reinforce the things we have previously studied.

After we look at the routine problems, we next move into some of the more strange error messages. Once again, our goal is to develop a model for troubleshooting, not just to find the answer to a somewhat obscure problem. Finally, we look at broadcast storms and see how to identify the culprit and to design a strategy for dealing with such a situation.

TROUBLESHOOTING SCENARIOS: A LOOK AT COMMON PROBLEMS

*N*ow *we are ready to find answers to the problems and questions that have been bugging us for a long time. We will see if our knowledge of protocols and the tools to do network monitoring can help us in our attempt to troubleshoot the network.*

Troubleshooting Issues

The problem with connectivity is you either have it or you don't—at least most of the time. There are times when you have intermittent connectivity problems—those are particularly vexatious. What are we talking about when we talk about connectivity? We are talking about computers talking to each other. They need to be able to talk across the wire.

WORKSTATION CANNOT LOG ON

One of the most common connectivity problems on a network occurs when a workstation cannot log onto the domain. Although many things can cause this (protocol configuration, name resolution, NetBIOS name resolution, and permissions), in this section we will look at only a few of them.

Can We Ping the Server?

If the workstation is having problems logging onto the domain, one of the first things to do is to verify connectivity. In order to do this, we will use the ping utility. As shown in the printout below, we first ping by name in order to check name resolution. It comes back with a reply. We next ping by specific IP address to verify that we are reaching the same destination, and lastly, we send a large packet to verify that the large packet sizes can make it to the destination. Ping by default only sends a very small 32-byte packet, which could make it to the destination, when larger logon traffic would not be able to make it across the router.

```
C:\>ping PROX
Pinging PROX [10.0.0.10] with 32 bytes of data:
Reply from 10.0.0.10: bytes=32 time<10ms TTL=128
Reply from 10.0.0.10: bytes=32 time<10ms TTL=128
Reply from 10.0.0.10: bytes=32 time<10ms TTL=128
Reply from 10.0.0.10: bytes=32 time<10ms TTL=128

C:\>ping 10.0.0.10
Pinging 10.0.0.10 with 32 bytes of data:
Reply from 10.0.0.10: bytes=32 time<10ms TTL=128
Reply from 10.0.0.10: bytes=32 time<10ms TTL=128
Reply from 10.0.0.10: bytes=32 time<10ms TTL=128
Reply from 10.0.0.10: bytes=32 time<10ms TTL=128

C:\>ping 10.0.0.10 -1 4048
Pinging 10.0.0.10 with 4048 bytes of data:
Reply from 10.0.0.10: bytes=4048 time<10ms TTL=128
Reply from 10.0.0.10: bytes=4048 time<10ms TTL=128
Reply from 10.0.0.10: bytes=4048 time<10ms TTL=128
Reply from 10.0.0.10: bytes=4048 time<10ms TTL=128
```

If the larger packets do not make it to the destination, but the smaller ones do reach the logon server, then we can edit the registry and specify a smaller packet size as a temporary measure until we can decide whether larger packets can be supported. This is done in the registry as seen below:

ADJUSTING TCP PACKET SIZE

```
Add a value to the following key:
HKEY_LOCAL_MACHINE\SYSTEM\CurrentControlSet\Services\Tcip
ip\parameters_
Name the Value: TcpSendSegmentSize
The type is a Reg_Dword
The default is 1460 bytes
```

Standard warning about editing the registry   This will affect all communication using TCP/IP and should be changed only after much testing. Of course, before making any changes to the registry, make sure that you have a good verified backup and are up to date on your disaster-recovery procedures. At the very least, export the key first (see Figure 10–1). For the purposes of importing and exporting .reg keys, Regedit is the easiest to use (it

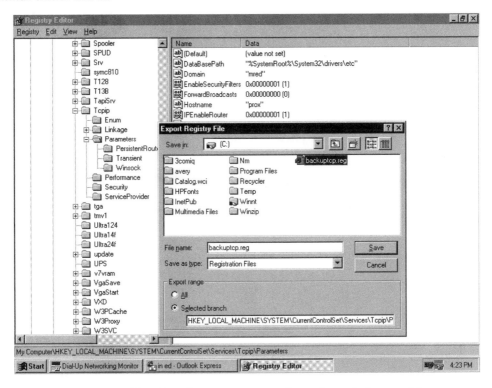

Fig. 10–1 Use Regedit to export registry keys before making changes.

also has the advantage of being able to search the entire registry for a particular value. For registry editing (both local and remote), use Regedt32 because it has a better editor.

Netmon to the rescue   Repeat the pings and perform a Netmon trace selecting only the workstation and the server. In addition to the pings, also try the commands listed below.

- Net view *servername*
- Net use *servername*\ipc$

If these two commands come back with an error message, then we have a significant problem. Let us look at Netmon and see if we can discover the source of our problem. We see that the ping command did in fact work without any problem. This is illustrated in the printout below. We see the ICMP from the source to the destination. It is an echo type of packet. The size is 32 bytes, which is the default ping packet size.

```
ICMP: Echo,      From 10.00.00.60 To    10.00.00.10
     ICMP: Packet Type = Echo
     ICMP: Checksum = 0x2E5C
     ICMP: Identifier = 256 (0x100)
     ICMP: Sequence Number = 7680 (0x1E00)
     ICMP: Data: Number of data bytes remaining = 32
(0x0020)
```

The ICMP echo packet is followed by an ICMP response packet, which we see in the printout below. This packet comes back from our ping destination as an echo-reply packet. It too is 32 bytes. This tells us that we have at least rudimentary communication between our workstation and the server.

```
ICMP: Echo Reply, To 10.00.00.60 From 10.00.00.10
     ICMP: Packet Type = Echo Reply
     ICMP: Checksum = 0x365C
     ICMP: Identifier = 256 (0x100)
     ICMP: Sequence Number = 7680 (0x1E00)
     ICMP: Data: Number of data bytes remaining = 32
(0x0020)
```

We next try a net view*servername* command, which results in a three-way handshake between the workstation and the server. The three-way handshake extends from the workstation to port 139, the NetBIOS session service on the server. It works fine, so let us look at the NBT section of the next frame, which is shown in the printout below. The frame from the workstation to the server looks fine. We see that the packet type is indicated as a session request. It lists the called name of the server, and the calling name of the workstation. The <00> is a NetBIOS unique suffix indicating the workstation service. You would find a <00> registration for this machine in the WINS database mapping it to the IP address of this machine. Registering in the WINS database facilitates NetBIOS communication among machines.

```
NBT: SS: Session Request, Dest: PROX            , Source:
2400          <00>, Len: 68
     NBT: Packet Type = Session Request
     NBT: Packet Flags = 0 (0x0)
        NBT: .......0 = Add 0 to Length
     NBT: Packet Length = 68 (0x44)
     NBT: Called Name = PROX
     NBT: Calling Name = 2400            <00>
```

Since the NBT session request went fine, let us look at the response we get back from the server. This is contained in the printout below. At this point we have some very good information (in a bad sort of way). We have a negative-session response, and the session service error code tells us that the called name is not present. We know now that the problem is not on the workstation but on the server. Other workstations will have the same problem (they just have not called yet). We now need to look at the server and see what is going on there (or not going on as the case may be). But before we do that, let us see whether we can get any more information from the Netmon trace we just made.

```
NBT: SS: Negative Session Response, Len: 1
    NBT: Packet Type = Negative Session Response
    NBT: Packet Flags = 0 (0x0)
        NBT: .......0 = Add 0 to Length
    NBT: Packet Length = 1 (0x1)
    NBT: Session Service Error Code = Called Name Not Pre-
sent
```

We see several queries for the primary domain controller, but we never see a response. These take place as a SMB C transact to \mailslot\ net\netlogon. It is possible that there is a problem with the netlogon service as well.

```
UDP: Src Port: NETBIOS Datagram Service, (138); Dst Port:
NETBIOS Datagram Service (138); Length = 230 (0xE6)
+ NBT: DS: Type = 17 (DIRECT GROUP)
+ SMB: C transact, File = \MAILSLOT\NET\NETLOGON
  NETLOGON: Query for Primary DC
      NETLOGON: Opcode = Query for Primary DC
      NETLOGON: Computer Name = 2400
      NETLOGON: Mailslot Name = \MAILSLOT\NET\GETDC915
      NETLOGON: Unicode Computer Name = 2400
      NETLOGON: NT Version = 1 (0x1)
      NETLOGON: LMNT Token = WindowsNT Networking
      NETLOGON: LM20 Token = OS/2 LAN Manager 2.0 (or later)
  Networking
```

When we look at the event viewer on the workstation, we see this message: "The browser was unable to retrieve a list of servers from the browser master \\PROX on the network \Device\NetBT_E100B1. The data is the error code." This message just confirms that we have a problem on the server. There are now several things we need to check on the server. These are listed below.

- Make sure that the server service is running on the destination computer. Check the services applet in control panel (see Figure 10–2). If the server service is not running, the machine will still respond to a

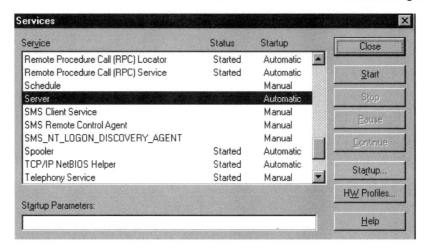

Fig. 10–2 Check the status of services to eliminate potential problems.

ping, but a session cannot be established. If the server service is stopped, start the server service. It does not even require a reboot of the machine. This would also explain the browser error messages in the event log because the computer browser service is dependent on the server service. Additionally, the netlogon service is also dependent on the server service. We saw problems with the netlogon service in the Netmon trace as well. The question, of course, is why is the server service stopped? Some things Netmon just cannot tell you! It may be time to change the administrator password.

• Check whether the destination server is responding. It may have locked up. It is possible for a server to respond to an ICMP echo packet even though a session cannot be established. If the computer is locked up and you cannot regain control through task manager or some other way, then you must tell all your users to save their data and get out cleanly if possible. You can try to shutdown, although depending on what died, you may be forced to (oh no, here it comes) cold boot. If you are lucky, it will come back and recover well. If not, you may be verifying your backup procedures.

• This one is kind of silly, but if license-logging is running, and if you run out of licenses, then the server will respond to a ping, but a session will not be established. Check the licensing applet in control panel and in the event log to see whether you are out of licenses.

• Check whether DNS or a host file is being used. The host name resolution methods are used first by ping to resolve the name. The net commands use NetBIOS name resolution methods (lmhosts, WINS). A ping may work, while a net view may time out.

Now We Have a Case for a Laptop!

The above scenario would have been nearly impossible to solve without using Netmon. If we had the agents installed on the workstation, we could have connected remotely and conducted our traces; however, many companies do not widely deploy the Netmon agents, and of course Netmon 2 requires version 2 agents, which do not work on Windows 9.x machines. In these situations, a laptop with the SMS version of Netmon becomes a mobile sniffer. The laptop does not have to join the domain in order to capture traffic. All it needs is a network connection, and you can troubleshoot networking problems wherever you can get a connection to the network. Of course, the Ethernet card will need to support promiscuous mode, but most modern cards support that functionality.

WORKSTATION CANNOT OBTAIN DHCP LEASE

Although DHCP makes life easier for the administrator, at times a client machine may have problems obtaining a lease. In these situations, information is often scarce. Other than the fact that the workstation did not get an address, there is little to go on. This is where our knowledge of the DHCP process, and Netmon comes in to play.

Look at the Conversation

The first thing to check is whether the machine has been configured to request an address. If the TCP/IP properties box has the "obtain an IP address from a DHCP server" box checked, then it should work. If it does not, we break out Netmon and look at the conversation. Ideally, we should see the four frames listed below.

1. DHCP discover
2. DHCP offer
3. DHCP request
4. DHCP ACK

If these four frames are not present, then DHCP will not work, and the client will not be able to obtain an address. If none are present, then the client is not properly configured to request a DHCP address. Troubleshooting a DHCP problem is a process of looking at the conversation and identifying what is missing from the conversation listed above.

Analyze What Is Missing

Our first step is to look at the trace and see what is missing. We have our DHCP request frame sent using an UDP IP multicast from port 68, the BOOTP client port, to port 67, the BOOTP server port. The magic cookie is ok. This is the four-byte area in a DHCP packet that identifies the start of a special–vendor, specific-options field. If this option field is used, it is marked off by the IP address 99.130.83.99, which shows up in a Netmon trace as 63 82 53 63 hex. The option can list such things as a client identifier, requested address, and other items as well. In our option field, the client identifier is the MAC address of the computer making the request—in this case, KENNY. We also see that the KENNY machine is requesting the same address it had previously owned. If this address is available, it should be able to use it again.

```
UDP: IP Multicast:  Src Port: BOOTP Client, (68); Dst Port:
BOOTP Server (67); Length = 308 (0x134)
        UDP: Source Port = BOOTP Client
        UDP: Destination Port = BOOTP Server
        UDP: Total length = 308 (0x134) bytes
        UDP: UDP Checksum = 0x36C3
        UDP: Data: Number of data bytes remaining = 300
(0x012C)
   DHCP: Request           (xid=05F105F1)
        DHCP: Op Code           (op)     = 1 (0x1)
        DHCP: Hardware Type     (htype)  = 1 (0x1) 10Mb
Ethernet
        DHCP: Hardware Address Length (hlen) = 6 (0x6)
        DHCP: Hops              (hops)   = 0 (0x0)
        DHCP: Transaction ID    (xid)    = 99681777
(0x5F105F1)
        DHCP: Seconds           (secs)   = 0 (0x0)
      + DHCP: Flags             (flags)  = 0 (0x0)
        DHCP: Client IP Address (ciaddr) = 0.0.0.0
        DHCP: Your    IP Address (yiaddr) = 0.0.0.0
        DHCP: Server IP Address (siaddr) = 0.0.0.0
        DHCP: Relay  IP Address (giaddr) = 0.0.0.0
        DHCP: Client Ethernet Address (chaddr) = 00104BEC8DB2
        DHCP: Server Host Name  (sname)  = <Blank>
        DHCP: Boot File Name    (file)   = <Blank>
        DHCP: Magic Cookie = [OK]
        DHCP: Option Field      (options)
            DHCP: DHCP Message Type    = DHCP Request
            DHCP: Client-identifier    = (Type: 1) 00 10 4b
ec 8d b2
            DHCP: Requested Address    = 10.0.0.76
            DHCP: Host Name            = kenny
            DHCP: Parameter Request List = (Length: 8) 01 03 06
 0f 2c 2e 2f 39
            DHCP: End of this option field
```

In the trace below, the requested address is not available because it receives a NACK, which is a negative acknowledgement. If we looked at the IP portion of the frame, we would see the machine that issued this NACK to the workstation. We see in this portion of the packet that it came from port 67, the BOOTP server port, to port 68, the BOOTP client port. Once the workstation receives the NACK, it will not initialize TCP/IP until it obtains an address. If TCP/IP is the only protocol, then the machine will not be able to communicate on the network until a DHCP server is located.

```
UDP: IP Multicast:  Src Port: BOOTP Server, (67); Dst Port:
BOOTP Client (68); Length = 308 (0x134)
     UDP: Source Port = BOOTP Server
     UDP: Destination Port = BOOTP Client
     UDP: Total length = 308 (0x134) bytes
     UDP: UDP Checksum = 0x2D13
     UDP: Data: Number of data bytes remaining = 300
(0x012C)
  DHCP: NACK                 (xid=05F105F1)
     DHCP: Op Code           (op)    = 2 (0x2)
     DHCP: Hardware Type     (htype) = 1 (0x1) 10Mb
Ethernet
```

Since the client machine is sending out DHCP requests, and since it received a NACK from a DHCP server, then we can tell that at least it is communicating. The fact that the machine is sending the requests is encouraging because it is doing all that the client machine is supposed to do. To verify this, we can use the command ipconfig /renew from a CMD box, which will cause the client machine to generate DHCP traffic. This is one way to force the issue without having to reboot the machine. In the Netmon trace, we should be able to see two DHCP frames: a DHCP request and a DHCP ACK.

In our DHCP trace, we found only requests and one NACK. We did not find any other traffic. The next step is to go to the server and look at the DHCP properties. Once there, we may find that the server is out of addresses or that the scope has been deactivated. These seem to be the two most common problems.

WORKSTATION IS SLOW

It certainly is not uncommon for users to complain that the network is slow. This seems to be a complaint that network administrators hear from time to time. It may be followed by certain adjectives that modify slow; rarely do users offer much insight other than the general observation that it is slow. In the old days, the poor administrator would trek to the user's desk, watch the user do something, and either agree or disagree on the accuracy of the observation. That is not the way to do it in the new millennium. We have Netmon to come to our rescue. Let's look at the example below to see how Netmon works.

Can You Define Slow?

The easiest way to define "slow" is to use the average server response time expert included with Netmon 2.0. Before firing up the expert, of course you will need to capture some traffic between the server and the client machine. If you have a version 2 agent installed, it is a piece of cake; if not, you may need to put your laptop onto the same segment as the server and configure a capture filter that isolates traffic between the workstation and the server in question. This should be done after you have checked the workstation to see how many applications are open, how much free space is available on the HDD for paging, and the like. Once you have eliminated all possible workstation issues, then begin the capture.

What Is the Source of Your Discontent?

After you have reproduced the source discontent, load the capture file into Netmon 2.0 and configure the response time expert (see Figure 10–3). Configuring the expert is essential to produce accurate results. If, for example, the user was complaining that POP3 e-mail was really slow, then you would add port 110 to the expert. You can use Appendix A to assist with well-known port

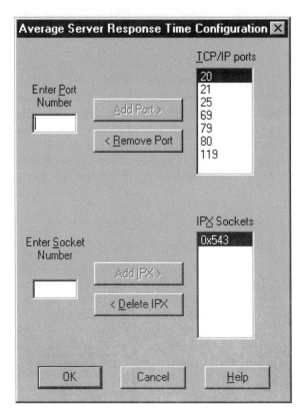

Fig. 10–3 Before running the average server response time expert, it is essential to configure it for the application in question.

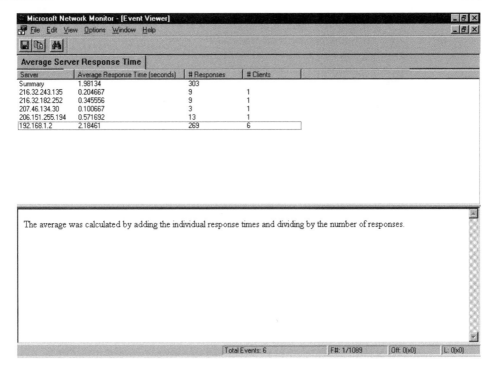

Fig. 10–4 The average server response time report confirms a response time problem.

numbers when adding them to the expert. By modifying the configuration files, the expert can report on most applications running on your network. If you remove all ports but the one application in question, you will get a different reading of performance. The employment of Netmon 2.0 in this arena is nearly unlimited.

The expert produces a report listing the IP address and average response time in seconds as seen (see Figure 10–4). If the results are in line with your baselines, then you may need to look again at the workstation and the particular user's computing habits. If they are in fact slow, then the trace will require further analysis. The protocol distribution report, top users' report, and TCP retransmit expert can offer valuable assistance in troubleshooting the slow network scenario. In addition to viewing on screen, the reports can be saved as text files and printed out, or brought into other documents such as those in Microsoft Word.

LOGON PROBLEMS

As long as people have to log onto the network, there will be logon problems. There are really only a few variables involved in the logon process: the user name, password, and domain. If these are not correct, then the logon will fail.

The server event log can provide valuable information, but you must find the domain controller that received and processed the logon request. In addition, if security logging is not enabled (not a very good idea), then the event log will not help anyway. However, the judicious application of Netmon will be able to assist us in resolving the issue.

I Am Trying to Authenticate, but Where?

Sometimes, the user types in the wrong domain name when trying to logon. This creates a particular problem on Windows 9.x machines because users on these machines must type in the domain name when they log on to the network. On NT-based machines, it is not a problem because they select the logon domain from a dropdown box. On Windows 2000, the entire domain issue is hidden from the user's view, so the users do not know where they are logging in—either onto the workstation, or onto the domain. Whatever is available is where they will connect.

Let us look at a Windows 98 client logging onto the domain. The client types in the user name, password and domain name, and then calls up complaining that it is not getting into the domain. We talk to the client on the phone, and yes, the users are typing in their user name and password. Yes, the domain name is typed in correctly. We have them press the caps lock key a couple of times and check whether the light is now on, now off, now on, now off. We check user manager for domains, and the account disabled is not checked, and the account locked out box is not checked, so we have ascertained that they are not locked out. We look in event viewer, and there are no entries indicating a failed logon attempt. We look at the backup domain controllers, and there is nothing there either. We have the users unplug and plug the patch cable into both the wall and the Ethernet card. We have them confirm that it snapped in place and is not loose. They retry and still are not authenticated—so we have them reboot the machine—but it still does not connect. This is a remote client, and we cannot watch the users log on. What do we do now? We could tell them that the machine is dead and have them ship the computer back to corporate IS so that we can effectively troubleshoot the machine, or we can use a contract service company to go on site and look at the machine, or we can try Netmon.

We tell the user to reboot the machine one more time and fire up Netmon when we hear it beep on the other end of the phone. (This capture is on the CD-ROM named BadDomainLogin.cap.) When the user tell us it still is not working, we stop Netmon and call the user back after we have had a chance to analyze the trace (and yes we are going to do it right now).

We see a DHCP request and a DHCP ACK in the first two frames, so it is not a DHCP issue. The next frame is a gratuitous ARP_RARP, which means that the computer takes the address that is assigned to it and sends out an ARP request for that very address. In this way, if another machine has the address, a duplicate IP address on the network error will ensue. Another feature of the gratuitous ARP_RARP is that machines that have the old IP address in their ARP cache will automatically update their ARP cache when they hear the request. In our trace, we do not see any response to the ARP_RARP, so it is not a duplicate IP problem.

We then see two NBT registration broadcasts. We see a unique NBT broadcast for <00>, which is the workstation service on the computer, and we also see a NBT broadcast for <03>, which is contained in the printout below. This frame is a UDP datagram broadcast to 10.255.255.255 on the network. This broadcast is used for the NetBIOS name service to register computer name with the messenger service. As we see in the record class section, it is a unique NetBIOS name. So far, everything appears as it should. We have confirmed that it is not a wiring problem because the conversation looks perfect.

```
UDP: Src Port: NETBIOS Name Service, (137); Dst Port:
NETBIOS Name Service (137); Length = 76 (0x4C)
        UDP: Source Port = NETBIOS Name Service
        UDP: Destination Port = NETBIOS Name Service
        UDP: Total length = 76 (0x4C) bytes
        UDP: UDP Checksum = 0xF520
        UDP: Data: Number of data bytes remaining = 68
(0x0044)
   NBT: NS: Registration req. for KENNY            <03>
        NBT: Transaction ID = 4 (0x4)
      + NBT: Flags Summary = 0x2910 - Req.; Registration; Suc-
cess
        NBT: Question Count = 1 (0x1)
        NBT: Answer Count = 0 (0x0)
        NBT: Name Service Count = 0 (0x0)
        NBT: Additional Record Count = 1 (0x1)
        NBT: Question Name = KENNY            <03>
        NBT: Question Type = General Name Service
        NBT: Question Class = Internet Class
        NBT: Resource Record Name = KENNY            <03>
        NBT: Resource Record Type = NetBIOS General Name Serv-
ice
        NBT: Resource Record Class = Internet Class
        NBT: Time To Live = 300000 (0x493E0)
        NBT: RDATA Length = 6 (0x6)
        NBT: Resource Record Flags = 0 (0x0)
            NBT: 0.............. = Unique NetBIOS Name
            NBT: .00............ = B Node
            NBT: ...0000000000000 = Reserved
        NBT: Owner IP Address = 10.0.0.76
```

The next frame solves our problem for us. Note the request for a group <00>, which is a domain name. The domain name for which the workstation is looking is NETMO. This is incorrect. It is the wrong domain. Let us see what happens in the rest of the capture file.

```
UDP: Src Port: NETBIOS Name Service, (137); Dst Port:
NETBIOS Name Service (137); Length = 76 (0x4C)
      UDP: Source Port = NETBIOS Name Service
      UDP: Destination Port = NETBIOS Name Service
      UDP: Total length = 76 (0x4C) bytes
      UDP: UDP Checksum = 0x7A22
      UDP: Data: Number of data bytes remaining = 68
(0x0044)
   NBT: NS: Registration req. for NETMO          <00>
      NBT: Transaction ID = 2 (0x2)
    + NBT: Flags Summary = 0x2910 - Req.; Registration; Suc-
cess
      NBT: Question Count = 1 (0x1)
      NBT: Answer Count = 0 (0x0)
      NBT: Name Service Count = 0 (0x0)
      NBT: Additional Record Count = 1 (0x1)
      NBT: Question Name = NETMO          <00>
      NBT: Question Type = General Name Service
      NBT: Question Class = Internet Class
      NBT: Resource Record Name = NETMO          <00>
      NBT: Resource Record Type = NetBIOS General Name Serv-
ice
      NBT: Resource Record Class = Internet Class
      NBT: Time To Live = 300000 (0x493E0)
      NBT: RDATA Length = 6 (0x6)
      NBT: Resource Record Flags = 32768 (0x8000)
         NBT: 1............... = Group NetBIOS Name
         NBT: .00............ = B Node
         NBT: ...0000000000000 = Reserved
      NBT: Owner IP Address = 10.0.0.76
```

The workstation now tries a netlogon broadcast using a UDP datagram to the 10.255.255.255 network. It comes from port 138, the NetBIOS datagram service, and is directed to the NetBIOS datagram service port 138 on the destination machine. The source name is specified Kenny, and the user name is administrator. The Kenny machine is trying to find \mailslot\net\ netlogon for the NETMO domain.

```
IP: ID = 0x3100; Proto = UDP; Len: 253
     IP: Version = 4 (0x4)
     IP: Header Length = 20 (0x14)
   + IP: Service Type = 0 (0x0)
```

```
        IP: Total Length = 253 (0xFD)
        IP: Identification = 12544 (0x3100)
      + IP: Flags Summary = 0 (0x0)
        IP: Fragment Offset = 0 (0x0) bytes
        IP: Time to Live = 128 (0x80)
        IP: Protocol = UDP - User Datagram
        IP: Checksum = 0xF3A5
        IP: Source Address = 10.0.0.76
        IP: Destination Address = 10.255.255.255
        IP: Data: Number of data bytes remaining = 233
(0x00E9)
        UDP: Src Port: NETBIOS Datagram Service, (138); Dst Port:
NETBIOS Datagram Service (138); Length = 233 (0xE9)
        UDP: Source Port = NETBIOS Datagram Service
        UDP: Destination Port = NETBIOS Datagram Service
        UDP: Total length = 233 (0xE9) bytes
        UDP: UDP Checksum = 0x1B35
        UDP: Data: Number of data bytes remaining = 225
(0x00E1)
  NBT: DS: Type = 17 (DIRECT GROUP)
        NBT: Datagram Packet Type = DIRECT GROUP
      + NBT: Datagram Flags = 2 (0x2)
        NBT: Datagram ID = 26 (0x1A)
        NBT: Source IP Address = 10.0.0.76
        NBT: Source Port = 138 (0x8A)
        NBT: Datagram Length = 211 (0xD3)
        NBT: Packet Offset = 0 (0x0)
        NBT: Source Name = KENNY            <00>
        NBT: Destination Name = NETMO            <00>
        NBT: DS Data: Number of data bytes remaining = 143
(0x008F)
  SMB: C transact, File = \MAILSLOT\NET\NETLOGON
      + SMB: SMB Status = Error Success
      + SMB: Header: PID = 0x152F TID = 0xFFFF MID = 0x0101
UID = 0xFFFF
      + SMB: Command = C transact
        SMB: Data: Number of data bytes remaining = 51
(0x0033)
  NETLOGON: LM1.0/2.0 LOGON Request from client
        NETLOGON: Opcode = LM1.0/2.0 LOGON Request from client
        NETLOGON: Computer Name = KENNY
        NETLOGON: User Name = ADMINISTRATOR
        NETLOGON: Mailslot Name = \MAILSLOT\TEMP\NETLOGON
        NETLOGON: Request Count = 1 (0x1)
        NETLOGON: LM20 Token = OS/2 LAN Manager 2.0 (or later)
  Networking
```

The rest of the capture file is a repetition of the above frames we discussed. It took less than an hour to analyze the capture, nor did we have the machine shipped back to corporate to look at and test. We call up the user, have them type in the correct domain name, and they are in. Another happy customer is added to our growing list of fans.

There are rarely times when an application will go haywire to the extent that we need to sniff it out, but when we do need to look at the application conversation, we can gain some very interesting perspective and solve complicated annoying problems with a single bound.

STRANGE EVENT LOG ERRORS

At times there may be some rather strange looking errors in the windows event log. One of them is an event ID 2000 that simply says STATUS_ NO_SUCH_FILE. This event occurs when a network application sends a delete file command to a shared drive and the file has already been deleted. A word in the second line of the data section of the error message will be c000000f, which corresponds to the STATUS_NO_SUCH_FILE.

A Method for Looking at Server Problems

This is clearly an SMB-related problem. Let us first look at a capture file. In order to make it easier, we created a display filter that shows just SMB delete file commands. Figure 10–5 illustrates how this display filter is created. Once we are in display mode, select filter from the display menu. Double-click on the protocol line, and when the selection dialog box appears, disable all the protocols. Select SMB from the list of protocols in the right panel of the dialog box, and then click the enable button. An easy way to get to the "S" section of the protocol list without having to scroll through a long list is to click on the name menu bar and type "S." This will take you to the "S" section, allowing you to find the SMB protocol quickly. Once the SMB protocol is enabled we will need to find the SMB delete command. In order to do this, click on the property tab. Unfortunately, the dialog box is not smart enough to remember which protocol was just enabled, and we are confronted with the same long list of protocols. Typing "S" does not help here, so we are stuck scrolling until we locate the SMB protocol. Click the plus beside SMB and a long list of protocol properties is revealed. Scroll until you can select command from the dialog box. Once command is selected, a list of values is uncovered. Scroll down until you are able to pick delete file and then click ok. This display filter now shows SMB delete commands from any computer.

In looking at the SMB delete frames, we are looking for an error message. Let us look at the conversation. The client machine issues a C delete file to the server. The parameters include the location of the file.

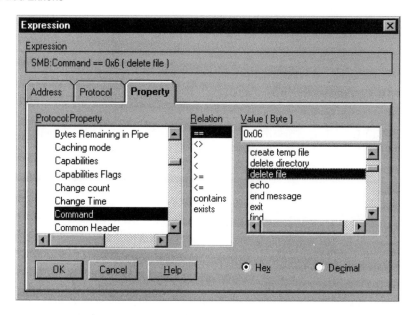

Fig. 10–5 By configuring a display filter, troubleshooting efforts can be focused on a very narrow problem.

```
SMB: C delete file, File = \PROGRAMS\TEMP\tmp1665.aud
    + SMB: SMB Status = Error Success
    + SMB: Header: PID = 0x14E5 TID = 0x0800 MID = 0x6701
UID = 0x0800
       SMB: Command = C delete file
          SMB: Word count = 1
          SMB: Word parameters
        + SMB: File Attributes = 6 (0x6)
          SMB: Byte count = 55
          SMB: Byte parameters
          SMB: File name = \PROGRAMS\TEMP\tmp1665.aud
```

The response from the server comes back in the next frame and is in the printout below. We have an R delete file with no errors reported back. The file was successfully deleted from the server.

```
SMB: R delete file
    + SMB: SMB Status = Error Success
    + SMB: Header: PID = 0x14E5 TID = 0x0800 MID = 0x6701
UID = 0x0800
       SMB: Command = C delete file
          SMB: Word count = 0
          SMB: Byte count = 0
```

We were not able to locate the problem in the first capture. Clearly, this is going to be an annoying culprit to find. We can help ourselves by creating a capture filter to gather just one kind of packet. In order to have the required information we see in Figure 10–6, we must find the pattern and the offset that indicates an SMB delete command. In order to do this, we look at such a frame in the display filter. As we see in Figure 10–7, by selecting the SMB command line in the display panel, it highlights 06 in the hex pane in the 03 offset line. Looking in the status bar of Netmon in the lower right corner, we see that the exact offset is 3e hex. We now have our offset and pattern for a SMB delete capture filter.

Running Unattended

We can get an idea, from the event log as to when the server errors are occurring. Armed with this information, we can run Netmon in an unattended fashion and schedule it by using the AT command. As we are using a very specialized capture filter, and we can specify a rather large capture buffer, we should be able to allow it to run for a fairly long period of time.

In Figure 10–8, we see how to use the scheduler service to automate our unattended Netmon session. In order for this to work, we need to start the schedule service by using the service applet in control panel. Once this is

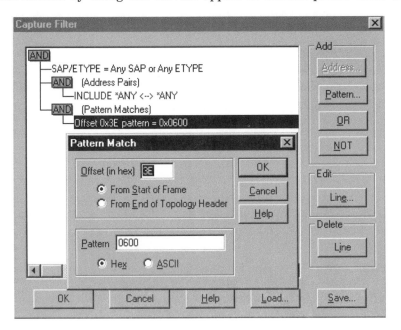

Fig. 10–6   A capture filter that filters out SMB delete commands reduces capture buffer fill problems.

AN UNATTENDED **NETMON** SESSION

using a capture filter
```
    Netmon /autostart /buffersize 10240000 /
capturefilter c:\smbdelete.cf /autostop
```

TYPE THE ABOVE INTO A TEXT FILE AND SAVE AS A .BAT FILE

Use the schedule service to automate the process

---

running, we go to a CMD window and type the desired AT command. In Figure 10–8, we are telling the scheduler to run our .bat file Monday through Friday at 5:00 p.m. The .bat file from above will run until the buffer is full and then stop.

By running the automated Netmon session at the times when we have seen the server problem manifest itself before, we have a good chance of finding the malfunctioning program that is trying to delete a file previously

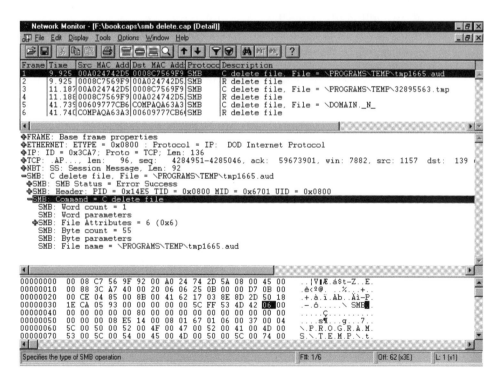

Fig. 10–7 Through careful examination of the hex pane, we find requisite information to create powerful capture filters.

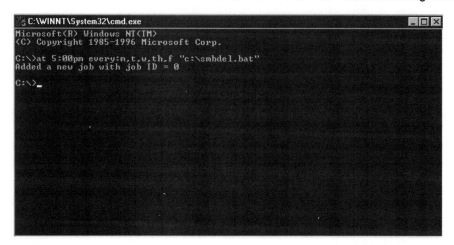

Fig. 10–8   Use the AT command to automate network monitor capture sessions.

deleted. The carefully crafted capture filter will reduce the clutter we must weed through in order to find the problem application. Once we spot the error message, we simply resolve the source address to a user name and find out what program is being run at the time we see the error. In addition, we can switch to time view in our capture file open the event log, and see exactly which frame corresponds to the particular error message in event viewer.

EXCESSIVE BROADCASTS

Broadcasts are always a good thing to monitor because they cause every machine on the subnet to look at the frame. This causes much work for many machines. In addition, when broadcast storms arise, they can have a devastating effect on the entire network. Fortunately, these kinds of problems are very easy to spot, as seen in Figure 10–9, where there can be little doubt we have a problem.

Who Is Doing It?

In looking at broadcast traffic, the first step is to create a broadcast display filter by selecting any broadcast in the display filter box. Once this is done, then examining the broadcasts is relatively straightforward. If a broadcast storm is present, as in Figure 10–9, it will be easy to spot. By running the top user report, it will give you an idea of the impact it can have on the network. The one shown in Figure 10–9 was sending 93 percent of the traffic on a relatively busy network. One would imagine that this user thought the network was really slow on this particular day. This ARP packet gives the IP address and MAC address of the machine causing the storm.

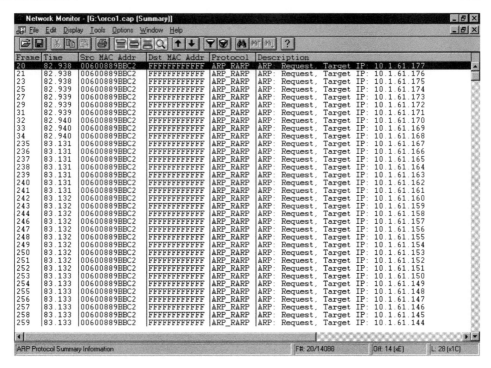

Figure 10–9 Some problems are very easy to spot.

```
ARP_RARP: ARP: Request, Target IP: 10.1.61.176
        ARP_RARP: Hardware Address Space = 1 (0x1)
        ARP_RARP: Protocol Address Space = 2048 (0x800)
        ARP_RARP: Hardware Address Length = 6 (0x6)
        ARP_RARP: Protocol Address Length = 4 (0x4)
        ARP_RARP: Opcode = 1 (0x1)
        ARP_RARP: Sender's Hardware Address = 00600889BBC2
        ARP_RARP: Sender's Protocol Address = 10.1.1.163
        ARP_RARP: Target's Hardware Address = 000000000000
        ARP_RARP: Target's Protocol Address = 10.1.61.176
        ARP_RARP: Frame Padding
```

FINDING THE USER'S NAME

Get the IP address from the frame

```
ping to verify address
      can use ping -a 10.0.0.163 to return host name
      can use arp -a to display ARP cache
      can use nbtstat -a 10.0.0.163 to return NetBIOS remote
machine name table
```

Why Are They Doing It?

This is obviously the question that needs answering in order to fix the problem. In the short term, armed with the information we obtained from using the various command line utilities listed in the box above, we can track down the machine and kill it on our network by pulling the plug from the wall. This will certainly improve response time for the other users on the network.

Now that the problem is not causing a crisis (and the accompanying phone ringing), we have time to investigate the problem. We need to look at the machine and see what software is installed, what protocols are loaded, and what kind of network adapter it is using. Additionally, we need to see whether there are updates for any of this stuff—the applications, drivers, and so forth. Do not forget to check for firmware upgrades for the computer itself.

Since we have discovered the problem, we may want to go back and look at some of our earlier traces to look for broadcasts in them as well. It is possible that we did not run our broadcast filter on the earlier traces. It may be important to see how long the problem has been going on to establish some sort of datum to guide our troubleshooting efforts. If we can determine when the problem began, we may be able to gain insight as to what changed on that day, that is, what was added, deleted, or updated that lead to this problem.

Search the vendor's Web sites, in particular, the ones that support the particular combination found on the machine in question. Go to the support section of the Web site and run a query on ARP broadcast for starters. If this does not help, then going to some of the news groups on the Internet and making a posting about ARP broadcast storms may be beneficial. Of course, before making such a posting, check a news collection service and search the archives to see how many times the question has already been asked. If it were a common problem, then certainly many people would have already seen a symptom such as this. The result of this particular problem was finally traced back to an old version of the Jet Admin software that tried to auto discover every printer in the world by using ARP to query the entire network address space for any nonconfigured printers. This may seem like a good idea, until one realizes that there are nearly 17,000,000 host addresses in a class A network. That is quite a lot of broadcasts. The fix that was finally implemented included: downloading the latest software, finding all the files associated with the old program (it did not have an uninstall program), searching the registry to prune all references to the old program, rebooting the machine, checking whether it had started broadcasting again with Netmon, and finally installing the new software.

CHAPTER REVIEW

In this chapter we looked at some common connectivity issues and how we can employ Netmon to assist in our troubleshooting activities. We looked at a situation where we could ping the server, but where we could not do a net view against the server. In that scenario, Netmon found a NBT session error stating that the service did not exist on the target machine. Next, we looked at a situation in which a DHCP client machine could not obtain a lease. The machine was making the correct requests, but no answer was given other than to disallow his request for an old favorite IP address. Following the successful resolution to that problem, we looked at the age-old generic complaint that the network is slow. Using the Netmon 2 experts, we were able to define how slow the network really was, and we brought additional tools to bear against helping to alleviate the source of slowness. Finally, we solved a logon problem when we were able to verify that the user was not typing in what was represented. This avoided a costly service call from a third-party company, or the hassle and inconvenience of shipping the computer back to the corporate IS department.

IN THE NEXT CHAPTER

In the next chapter, we look at network security. We investigate how to detect and stop rogue DHCP servers using both Network Monitor versions 1.2 and 2.0. We go through the process of capturing the data, analyzing what makes it unique, and designing both a capture trigger, and a capture filter. We then look at setting up a Rogue DHCP server monitor under Network Monitor 2.0 using the included monitor control tools.

We next look at identifying unauthorized sniffers using both Network Monitor versions 1.2 and 2.0. We analyze the traffic patterns related to each, and configure both triggers and capture filters. We look at using the network monitor control tools to stop unauthorized sniffers from accessing the network, and how we can actually stop the sniffer from gathering data.

11

Security Issues

The matter of security is one which must always be on the forefront of every network administrator's agenda. Indeed, securing the network is one of the most important duties of network administration and one of the things that consultants are constantly asked about.

ROGUE DHCP SERVERS

Rogue DHCP servers are unauthorized servers that sit on one's network like a minefield waiting for the wandering arrival of some unsuspecting computer. Although most of these incidents have been caused by naïve users or inexperienced administrators, there are occasions in which sabotage plays a role. Either way, the effect is the same—unrestrained chaos as communication between machines begins to break down. There will be either one of two effects in this scenario. The renegade DHCP server hands out addresses that are valid for the particular network scope thereby resulting in duplicate IP addresses. When this happens, the machine that has had the IP address the longest usually wins when it responds to the gratuitous ARP_RARP sent from the machine receiving the address. The new machine must then release the address. In this scenario, the new machine is unable to communicate with other computers. The other effect is the rogue DHCP server hands out addresses that are invalid for the network, and the new machines are unable to communicate with anyone but themselves. Neither scenario is good.

Have I Got an Address for You?

When a DHCP client machine comes on line, it broadcasts a DHCP request. This request goes to every machine in the network because it has an Ethernet destination of FFFFFFFFFFFF and an IP destination of 255.255.255.255. As we see in the printout below, the UDP datagram is directed to any machine listening on port 67.

```
ETHERNET: ETYPE = 0x0800 : Protocol = IP:  DOD Internet Proto-
col
      ETHERNET: Destination address : FFFFFFFFFFFF
            ETHERNET: .......1 = Group address
            ETHERNET: ......1. = Locally administered address
      ETHERNET: Source address : 00104BEC8DB2
            ETHERNET: .......0 = No routing information pre-
sent
            ETHERNET: ......0. = Universally administered ad-
dress
      ETHERNET: Frame Length : 342 (0x0156)
      ETHERNET: Ethernet Type : 0x0800 (IP:  DOD Internet
Protocol)
      ETHERNET: Ethernet Data: Number of data bytes remain-
ing = 328 (0x0148)
  IP: ID = 0x0; Proto = UDP; Len: 328
      IP: Version = 4 (0x4)
      IP: Header Length = 20 (0x14)
      IP: Service Type = 0 (0x0)
            IP: Precedence = Routine
            IP: ...0.... = Normal Delay
            IP: ....0... = Normal Throughput
            IP: .....0.. = Normal Reliability
      IP: Total Length = 328 (0x148)
      IP: Identification = 0 (0x0)
      IP: Flags Summary = 0 (0x0)
            IP: .......0 = Last fragment in datagram
            IP: ......0. = May fragment datagram if necessary
      IP: Fragment Offset = 0 (0x0) bytes
      IP: Time to Live = 128 (0x80)
      IP: Protocol = UDP - User Datagram
      IP: Checksum = 0x39A6
      IP: Source Address = 0.0.0.0
      IP: Destination Address = 255.255.255.255
      IP: Data: Number of data bytes remaining = 308
(0x0134)
  UDP: IP Multicast:  Src Port: BOOTP Client, (68); Dst
Port: BOOTP Server (67); Length = 308 (0x134)
      UDP: Source Port = BOOTP Client
```

```
        UDP: Destination Port = BOOTP Server
        UDP: Total length = 308 (0x134) bytes
        UDP: UDP Checksum = 0x78C3
        UDP: Data: Number of data bytes remaining = 300
(0x012C)
   DHCP: Discover              (xid=05D105D1)
        DHCP: Op Code          (op)     = 1 (0x1)
        DHCP: Hardware Type    (htype)  = 1 (0x1) 10Mb
Ethernet
        DHCP: Hardware Address Length (hlen) = 6 (0x6)
        DHCP: Hops             (hops)   = 0 (0x0)
        DHCP: Transaction ID   (xid)    = 97584593
(0x5D105D1)
        DHCP: Seconds          (secs)   = 0 (0x0)
```

Any machine that hears this request is free to respond by sending a UDP broadcast with a destination port 68. This is an IP broadcast to 255.255.255. 255. Any machine hearing the DHCP offer is free to request the address.

```
ETHERNET: ETYPE = 0x0800 : Protocol = IP:  DOD Internet Proto-
col
  IP: ID = 0xB71F; Proto = UDP; Len: 328
      IP: Version = 4 (0x4)
      IP: Header Length = 20 (0x14)
    + IP: Service Type = 0 (0x0)
      IP: Total Length = 328 (0x148)
      IP: Identification = 46879 (0xB71F)
    + IP: Flags Summary = 0 (0x0)
      IP: Fragment Offset = 0 (0x0) bytes
      IP: Time to Live = 128 (0x80)
      IP: Protocol = UDP - User Datagram
      IP: Checksum = 0x787B
      IP: Source Address = 10.0.0.11
      IP: Destination Address = 255.255.255.255
      IP: Data: Number of data bytes remaining = 308
(0x0134)
  UDP: IP Multicast:  Src Port: BOOTP Server, (67); Dst
Port: BOOTP Client (68); Length = 308 (0x134)
      UDP: Source Port = BOOTP Server
      UDP: Destination Port = BOOTP Client
      UDP: Total length = 308 (0x134) bytes
      UDP: UDP Checksum = 0x6D2F
      UDP: Data: Number of data bytes remaining = 300
(0x012C)
   DHCP: Offer                (xid=05D105D1)
        DHCP: Op Code          (op)     = 2 (0x2)
        DHCP: Hardware Type    (htype)  = 1 (0x1) 10Mb
Ethernet
```

```
DHCP: Hardware Address Length (hlen) = 6 (0x6)
DHCP: Hops                (hops)   = 0 (0x0)
DHCP: Transaction ID      (xid)    = 97584593
(0x5D105D1)
DHCP: Seconds             (secs)   = 0 (0x0)
DHCP: Flags               (flags)  = 0 (0x0)
    DHCP: 0.............. = No Broadcast
DHCP: Client IP Address (ciaddr) = 0.0.0.0
DHCP: Your   IP Address (yiaddr) = 10.0.0.76
DHCP: Server IP Address (siaddr) = 0.0.0.0
DHCP: Relay  IP Address (giaddr) = 0.0.0.0
DHCP: Client Ethernet Address (chaddr) = 00104BEC8DB2
DHCP: Server Host Name  (sname)  = <Blank>
DHCP: Boot File Name    (file)   = <Blank>
DHCP: Magic Cookie = [OK]
DHCP: Option Field        (options)
    DHCP: DHCP Message Type    = DHCP Offer
    DHCP: Subnet Mask          = 255.0.0.0
    DHCP: Renewal Time Value (T1) = 1 Days, 12:00:00
    DHCP: Rebinding Time Value (T2) = 2 Days, 15:00:00
    DHCP: IP Address Lease Time  = 3 Days,  0:00:00
    DHCP: Server Identifier      = 10.0.0.11
    DHCP: Router                 = 10.0.0.15
    DHCP: Domain Name Server     = 10.0.0.10
    DHCP: NetBIOS Name Service   = 10.0.0.10
```

Due to the broadcast nature of the DHCP protocol, it is imperative that unauthorized DHCP servers not be allowed to operate. One way to control the proliferation of DHCP servers is to configure a trigger with an offset of 2A and a pattern match of 0201. This would detect and alert you to DHCP activity on the network. You could then use the information contained in the captures to track down and eliminate the unauthorized machines present. There is no way easy way, using a trigger, to isolate the response to only unauthorized DHCP servers. This approach is illustrated in Figure 11–1 and is valid on both the 1.2 Netmon and the 2.0 Netmon programs.

With the Netmon 2.0 product, you also have the monitor control tool, which can be configured to create an event when it spots an unauthorized DHCP server. This works in much the same way as the trigger we created in Figure 11–1, but it has the additional intelligence of knowing which DHCP servers are authorized because they are listed when the rogue monitor is configured as in Figure 11–2.

The monitor control tool rogue DHCP monitor still requires checking for events, and it does nothing to the unauthorized server. A better approach would be to initiate a batch file that called the shutdown command from the NT resource kit. Windows 2000 implements a DHCPINFORM broadcast into the DHCP implementation that is designed to check with the active directory before servicing requests from clients. This broadcast occurs even if it does not find a

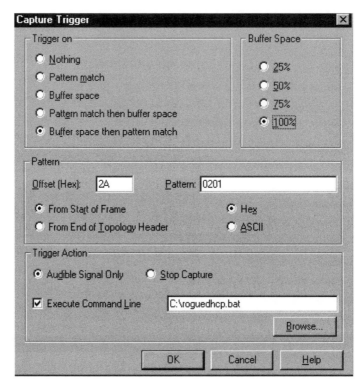

Fig. 11–1   A trigger alerts the administrator when DHCP activity is present.

domain controller. The active directory will continue to probe DHCPINFORM every five minutes even though the DHCP server will begin to run. Once a controller comes onto the network, if the DHCP server is not specifically authorized in the active directory, it will cease to operate as a DHCP server.

Well, Where Are You?

Once we are alerted to the presence of a rogue DHCP server, we can look at the captured DHCP offer, find the server identifier, and then, using utilities such as ARP and NBTSTAT, we can find the server and shut it down.

```
DHCP: Offer                (xid=05D105D1)
      DHCP: Op Code            (op)     = 2 (0x2)
      DHCP: Hardware Type      (htype)  = 1 (0x1) 10Mb
Ethernet
      DHCP: Hardware Address Length (hlen) = 6 (0x6)
      DHCP: Hops               (hops)   = 0 (0x0)
   DHCP: Transaction ID     (xid)    = 97584593
(0x5D105D1)
      DHCP: Seconds           (secs)   = 0 (0x0)
```

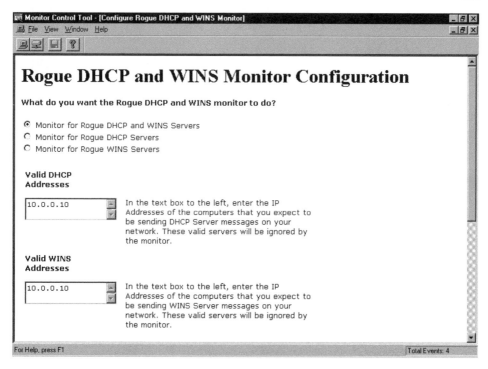

Fig. 11–2 The monitor control tool rogue DHCP and WINS server monitor generates an event when unauthorized servers are detected.

```
DHCP: Flags              (flags)  = 0 (0x0)
    DHCP: 0.............. = No Broadcast
DHCP: Client IP Address (ciaddr) = 0.0.0.0
DHCP: Your   IP Address (yiaddr) = 10.0.0.76
DHCP: Server IP Address (siaddr) = 0.0.0.0
DHCP: Relay  IP Address (giaddr) = 0.0.0.0
DHCP: Client Ethernet Address (chaddr) = 00104BEC8DB2
DHCP: Server Host Name  (sname)  = <Blank>
DHCP: Boot File Name    (file)   = <Blank>
DHCP: Magic Cookie = [OK]
DHCP: Option Field      (options)
    DHCP: DHCP Message Type       = DHCP Offer
    DHCP: Subnet Mask             = 255.0.0.0
    DHCP: Renewal Time Value (T1) = 1 Days, 12:00:00
DHCP: Rebinding Time Value (T2) = 2 Days, 15:00:00
DHCP: IP Address Lease Time  = 3 Days,  0:00:00
DHCP: Server Identifier      = 10.0.0.11
DHCP: Router                 = 10.0.0.15
DHCP: Domain Name Server     = 10.0.0.10
DHCP: NetBIOS Name Service   = 10.0.0.10
```

UNAUTHORIZED SNIFFING

In many respects, unauthorized sniffing is much more of a security threat than is a rogue DHCP server. As we have seen in this book, with Netmon and a proper understanding of the protocols, one can pick up all kinds of information on an unguarded network. This includes the ability to read data that is passed across the wire, such as POP3 and SMTP e-mail, Telnet, FTP, and POP3 passwords, and much, much more! In order to sniff the network, all you need is a laptop computer, a promiscuous mode Ethernet card, and an unguarded network connection. Within a very short time, you can pick up enough information to run completely amok on the network.

First, You Have To Find Them

Netmon 1.2 has the ability to directly identify the driver for the 1.2 sniffers and agents, but it does not inherently identify the Netmon 2.0 sniffer and agent. However, it can filter out the security frame the Netmon 2.0 program sends out. This security frame is illustrated in Figure 11–3. By using an offset of 00 and a pattern of 030000000002, we can configure both display filters

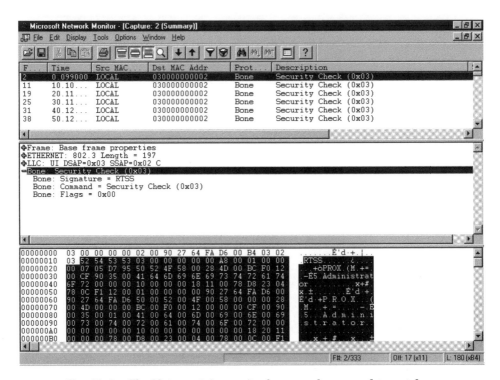

Fig. 11–3 The Netmon 2.0 security frame makes a good target for a trigger.

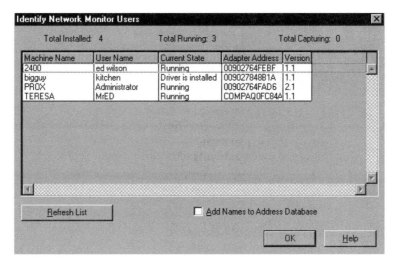

Fig. 11–4 Network Monitor 2.0 can detect both its own driver and the 1.1 driver.

and triggers to isolate the security frame. This can be done from both Network Monitors 1.2 and 2.0.

Network monitor can also use the identify network monitor users feature from the tools menu. The version 2 product is able to detect both the 1.2 driver and the 2.0 driver. Of course, Netmon 1.2 can only detect its own driver. The Netmon 2.0 tool is seen in Figure 11–4.

Then You Give Their Sniffer a Sinus Problem!

The most powerful solution for controlling unauthorized sniffing is the network monitor control tool. Once it is configured, it will allow only authorized sniffing. When one that has not been authorized tries to run, the program is shut down. This only works on network monitor version 2 programs. A 1.2 Netmon will run unabated. To detect its presence, use the identify network monitor users tool.

CHAPTER REVIEW

In this chapter we looked at some of the security issues surrounding networks, protocols, and the tools used for analysis. We looked at some of the things that can happen if a DHCP server is carelessly introduced into the network, and we looked at several methods to detect and remove such a server. We also looked at security surrounding the network monitor tools themselves. We saw that the most powerful weapon we have to guard against a sniffer attack is to use a sniffer to detect and shut down the unauthorized network monitor.

A List of Well-known TCP and UDP Port Numbers

Table A-1   Well-known TCP and UDP port numbers

Decimal	Keyword	Description
0/tcp, udp		Reserved
1/tcp, udp	tcpmux	TCP Port Service Multiplexer
2/tcp, udp	compressnet	Management Utility
3/tcp, udp	compressnet	Compression Process
4/tcp, udp		Unassigned
5/tcp, udp	rje	Remote Job Entry
6/tcp, udp		Unassigned
7/tcp, udp	echo	Echo
8/tcp, udp		Unassigned
9/tcp, udp	discard	Discard; alias=sink null
10/tcp, udp		Unassigned
11/udp	systat	Active Users; alias=users
12/tcp, udp		Unassigned
13/tcp, udp	daytime	Daytime
14/tcp, udp		Unassigned
15/tcp, udp		Unassigned [was netstat]
16/tcp, udp		Unassigned
17/tcp, udp	qotd	Quote of the Day; alias=quote

Decimal	Keyword	Description
18/tcp, udp	msp	Message Send Protocol
19/tcp, udp	chargen	Character Generator; alias=ttytst source
20/tcp, udp	ftp-data	File Transfer [Default Data]
21/tcp, udp	ftp	File Transfer [Control], connection dialog
22/tcp, udp		Unassigned
23/tcp, udp	telnet	Telnet
24/tcp, udp		Any private mail system
25/tcp, udp	smtp	Simple Mail Transfer; alias=mail
26/tcp, udp		Unassigned
27/tcp, udp	nsw-fe	NSW User System FE
28/tcp, udp		Unassigned
29/tcp, udp	msg-icp	MSG ICP
30/tcp, udp		Unassigned
31/tcp, udp	msg-auth	MSG Authentication
32/tcp, udp		Unassigned
33/tcp, udp	dsp	Display Support Protocol
34/tcp, udp		Unassigned
35/tcp, udp		Any private printer server
36/tcp, udp		Unassigned
37/tcp, udp	time	Time; alias=timeserver
38/tcp, udp		Unassigned
39/tcp, udp	rlp	Resource Location Protocol; alias=resource
40/tcp, udp		Unassigned
41/tcp, udp	graphics	Graphics
42/tcp, udp	nameserver	Host Name Server; alias=nameserver
43/tcp, udp	nicname	Who Is; alias=nicname
44/tcp, udp	mpm-flags	MPM FLAGS Protocol
45/tcp, udp	mpm	Message Processing Module
46/tcp, udp	mpm-snd	MPM [default send]
47/tcp, udp	ni-ftp	NI FTP
48/tcp, udp		Unassigned
49/tcp, udp	login	Login Host Protocol

(continued)

Table A-1   *Continued*

Decimal	Keyword	Description
50/tcp, udp	re-mail-ck	Remote Mail Checking Protocol
51/tcp, udp	la-maint	IMP Logical Address Maintenance
52/tcp, udp	xns-time	XNS Time Protocol
53/tcp, udp	domain	Domain Name Server
54/tcp, udp	xns-ch	XNS Clearinghouse
55/tcp, udp	isi-gl	ISI Graphics Language
56/tcp, udp	xns-auth	XNS Authentication
57/tcp, udp		Any private terminal access
58/tcp, udp	xns-mail	XNS Mail
59/tcp, udp		Any private file service
60/tcp, udp		Unassigned
61/tcp, udp	ni-mail	NI MAIL
62/tcp, udp	acas	ACA Services
63/tcp, udp	via-ftp	VIA Systems - FTP
64/tcp, udp	covia	Communications Integrator (CI)
65/tcp, udp	tacacs-ds	TACACS-Database Service
66/tcp, udp	sql*net	Oracle SQL*NET
67/tcp, udp	bootpc	DHCP/BOOTP Protocol Server
68/tcp, udp	bootpc	DHCP/BOOTP Protocol Server
69/ udp	tftp	Trivial File Transfer
70/tcp, udp	gopher	Gopher
71/tcp, udp	netrjs-1	Remote Job Service
72/tcp, udp	netrjs-2	Remote Job Service
73/tcp, udp	netrjs-3	Remote Job Service
74/tcp, udp	netrjs-4	Remote Job Service
75/udp		Any private dial-out service
76/tcp, udp		Unassigned
77/tcp, udp		Any private RJE service
78/tcp, udp	vettcp	Vettcp
79/tcp, udp	finger	Finger
80/tcp, udp	www	World Wide Web HTTP
81/tcp, udp	hosts2-ns	HOSTS2 Name Server
82/tcp, udp	xfer	XFER Utility
83/tcp, udp	mit-ml-dev	MIT ML Device
84/tcp, udp	ctf	Common Trace Facility

Decimal	Keyword	Description
85/tcp, udp	mit-ml-dev	MIT ML Device
86/tcp, udp	mfcobol	Micro Focus Cobol
87/tcp, udp		Any private terminal link; alias=ttylink
88/tcp, udp	kerberos	Kerberos
89/tcp	su-mit-tg	SU/MIT Telnet Gateway
89/udp	su-mit-tg	SU/MIT Telnet Gateway
90/tcp, udp		DNSIX Security Attribute Token Map
91/tcp, udp	mit-dov	MIT Dover Spooler
92/tcp, udp	npp	Network Printing Protocol
93/tcp, udp	dcp	Device Control Protocol
94/tcp, udp	objcall	Tivoli Object Dispatcher
95/tcp, udp	supdup	SUPDUP
96/tcp, udp	dixie	DIXIE Protocol Specification
97/tcp, udp	swift-rvf	Swift Remote Virtual File Protocol
98/tcp, udp	tacnews	TAC News
99/tcp, udp	metagram	Metagram Relay
100/tcp	newacct	[unauthorized use]
101/tcp, udp	hostname	NIC Host Name Server; alias=hostname
102/tcp, udp	iso-tsap	ISO-TSAP
103/tcp, udp	gppitnp	Genesis Point-to-Point TransNet; alias=webster
104/tcp, udp	acr-nema	ACR-NEMA Digital Imag. & Comm. 300
105/tcp, udp	csnet-ns	Mailbox Name Nameserver
106/tcp, udp	3com-tsmux	3COM-TSMUX
107/tcp, udp	rtelnet	Remote Telnet Service
108/tcp, udp	snagas	SNA Gateway Access Server
109/tcp, udp	pop2	Post Office Protocol - Version 2; alias=postoffice
110/tcp, udp	pop3	Post Office Protocol - Version 3; alias=postoffice
111/tcp, udp	sunrpc	SUN Remote Procedure Call
112/tcp, udp	mcidas	McIDAS Data Transmission Protocol

(continued)

Table A-1 *Continued*

Decimal	Keyword	Description
113/tcp, udp	auth	Authentication Service; alias=authentication
114/tcp, udp	audionews	Audio News Multicast
115/tcp, udp	sftp	Simple File Transfer Protocol
116/tcp, udp	ansanotify	ANSA REX Notify
117/tcp, udp	uucp-path	UUCP Path Service
118/tcp, udp	sqlserv	SQL Services
119/tcp, udp	nntp	Network News Transfer Protocol; alias=usenet
120/tcp, udp	cfdptkt	CFDPTKT
121/tcp, udp	erpc	Encore Expedited Remote Pro.Call
122/tcp, udp	smakynet	SMAKYNET
123/tcp, udp	ntp	Network Time Protocol; alias=ntpd ntp
124/tcp, udp	ansatrader	ANSA REX Trader
125/tcp, udp	locus-map	Locus PC-Interface Net Map Server
126/tcp, udp	unitary	Unisys Unitary Login
127/tcp, udp	locus-con	Locus PC-Interface Conn Server
128/tcp, udp	gss-xlicen	GSS X License Verification
129/tcp, udp	pwdgen	Password Generator Protocol
130/tcp, udp	cisco-fna	Cisco FNATIVE
131/tcp, udp	cisco-tna	Cisco TNATIVE
132/tcp, udp	cisco-sys	Cisco SYSMAINT
133/tcp, udp	statsrv	Statistics Service
134/tcp, udp	ingres-net	INGRES-NET Service
135/tcp, udp	loc-srv	Location Service
136/tcp, udp	profile	PROFILE Naming System
137/tcp, udp	netbios-ns	NetBIOS Name Service
138/tcp, udp	netbios-dgm	NetBIOS Datagram Service
139/tcp, udp	netbios-ssn	NetBIOS Session Service
140/tcp, udp	emfis-data	EMFIS Data Service
141/tcp, udp	emfis-cntl	EMFIS Control Service
142/tcp, udp	bl-idm	Britton-Lee IDM
143/tcp, udp	imap2	Interim Mail Access Protocol v2

Decimal	Keyword	Description
144/tcp, udp	news	NewS; alias=news
145/tcp, udp	uaac	UAAC Protocol
146/tcp, udp	iso-ip0	ISO-IP0
147/tcp, udp	iso-ip	ISO-IP
148/tcp, udp	cronus	CRONUS-SUPPORT
149/tcp, udp	aed-512	AED 512 Emulation Service
150/tcp, udp	sql-net	SQL-NET
151/tcp, udp	hems	HEMS
152/tcp, udp	bftp	Background File Transfer Program
153/tcp, udp	sgmp	SGMP; alias=sgmp
154/tcp, udp	netsc-prod	Netscape
155/tcp, udp	netsc-dev	Netscape
156/tcp, udp	sqlsrv	SQL Service
157/tcp, udp	knet-cmp	KNET/VM Command/Message Protocol
158/tcp, udp	pcmail-srv	PCMail Server; alias=repository
159/tcp, udp	nss-routing	NSS-Routing
160/tcp, udp	sgmp-traps	SGMP-TRAPS
161/tcp, udp	snmp	SNMP; alias=snmp
162/tcp, udp	snmptrap	SNMPTRAP
163/tcp, udp	cmip-man	CMIP/TCP Manager
164/tcp, udp	cmip-agent	CMIP/TCP Agent
165/tcp, udp	xns-courier	Xerox
166/tcp, udp	s-net	Sirius Systems
167/tcp, udp	namp	NAMP
168/tcp, udp	rsvd	RSVD
169/tcp, udp	send	SEND
170/tcp, udp	print-srv	Network PostScript
171/tcp, udp	multiplex	Network Innovations Multiplex
172/tcp, udp	cl/1	Network Innovations CL/1
173/tcp, udp	xyplex-mux	Xyplex
174/tcp, udp	mailq	MAILQ
175/tcp, udp	vmnet	VMNET
176/tcp, udp	genrad-mux	GENRAD-MUX
177/tcp, udp	xdmcp	X Display Manager Control Protocol

(continued)

Table A-1 *Continued*

Decimal	Keyword	Description
178/tcp, udp	nextstep	NextStep Window Server
179/tcp, udp	bgp	Border Gateway Protocol
180/tcp, udp	ris	Intergraph
181/tcp, udp	unify	Unify
182/tcp, udp	audit	Unisys Audit SITP
183/tcp, udp	ocbinder	OCBinder
184/tcp, udp	ocserver	OCServer
185/tcp, udp	remote-kis	Remote-KIS
186/tcp, udp	kis	KIS Protocol
187/tcp, udp	aci	Application Communication Interface
188/tcp, udp	mumps	Plus Five's MUMPS
189/tcp, udp	qft	Queued File Transport
190/tcp, udp	gacp	Gateway Access Control Protocol
191/tcp, udp	prospero	Prospero
192/tcp, udp	osu-nms	OSU Network Monitoring System
193/tcp, udp	srmp	Spider Remote Monitoring Protocol
194/tcp, udp	irc	Internet Relay Chat Protocol
195/tcp, udp	dn6-nlm-aud	DNSIX Network Level Module Audit
196/tcp, udp	dn6-smm-red	DNSIX Session Mgt Module Audit Redir
197/tcp, udp	dls	Directory Location Service
198/tcp, udp	dls-mon	Directory Location Service Monitor
199/tcp, udp	smux	SMUX
200/tcp, udp	src	IBM System Resource Controller
201/tcp, udp	at-rtmp	AppleTalk Routing Maintenance
202/tcp, udp	at-nbp	AppleTalk Name Binding
203/tcp, udp	at-3	AppleTalk Unused
204/tcp, udp	at-echo	AppleTalk Echo
205/tcp, udp	at-5	AppleTalk Unused
206/tcp, udp	at-zis	AppleTalk Zone Information
207/tcp, udp	at-7	AppleTalk Unused
208/tcp, udp	at-8	AppleTalk Unused
209/tcp, udp	tam	Trivial Authenticated Mail Protocol
210/tcp, udp	z39.50	ANSI Z39.50
211/tcp, udp	914c/g	Texas Instruments 914C/G Terminal

Decimal	Keyword	Description
212/tcp, udp	anet	ATEXSSTR
213/tcp, udp	ipx	IPX
214/tcp, udp	vmpwscs	VM PWSCS
215/tcp, udp	softpc	Insignia Solutions
216/tcp, udp	atls	Access Technology License Server
217/tcp, udp	dbase	dBASE UNIX
218/tcp, udp	mpp	Netix Message Posting Protocol
219/tcp, udp	uarps	Unisys ARPs
220/tcp, udp	imap3	Interactive Mail Access Protocol v3
221/tcp, udp	fln-spx	Berkeley rlogind with SPX Auth
222/tcp, udp	fsh-spx	Berkeley rshd with SPX Auth
223/tcp, udp	cdc	Certificate Distribution Center
224-241		Reserved
243/tcp, udp	sur-meas	Survey Measurement
245/tcp, udp	link	LINK
246/tcp, udp	dsp3270	Display Systems Protocol
247-255		Reserved
345/tcp, udp	pawserv	Perf Analysis Workbench
346/tcp, udp	zserv	Zebra Server
347/tcp, udp	fatserv	Fatmen Server
371/tcp, udp	clearcase	Clearcase
372/tcp, udp	ulistserv	UNIX Listserv
373/tcp, udp	legent-1	Legent Corporation
374/tcp, udp	legent-2	Legent Corporation
443/tcp	ssl	Secure Sockets Layer used to provide secure communication across the Internet
512/tcp	print	Windows NT Server and Windows NT Workstation version 4.0 can send LPD client print jobs from any available reserved port between 512 and 1023. (See also description for ports 721 to 731.)
512/udp	biff	Used by mail system to notify users of new mail received; currently receives messages only from processes on the same computer; alias=comsat

(continued)

Table A-1 *Continued*

Decimal	Keyword	Description
513/tcp	login	Remote logon like telnet; automatic authentication performed, based on privileged port numbers and distributed databases that identify "authentication domains"
513/udp	who	Maintains databases showing who's logged on to the computers on a local net and the load average of the computer; alias=whod
514/tcp	cmd	Like exec, but automatic authentication is performed as for logon server
514/udp	syslog	
515/tcp, udp	printer	Spooler; alias=spooler; (The print server LPD service will listen on tcp port 515 for incoming connections.)
517/tcp, udp	talk	Like tenex link, but across computers; unfortunately, doesn't use link protocol (This is actually just a rendezvous port from which a TCP connection is established.)
518/tcp, udp	ntalk	
519/tcp, udp	utime	Unixtime
520/tcp	efs	Extended file name server
520/udp	router	Local routing process (on site); uses variant of Xerox NS routing information protocol;alias=router routed
525/tcp, udp	timed	Timeserver
526/tcp, udp	tempo	Newdate
530/tcp, udp	courier	RPC
531/tcp	conference	Chat
531/udp	rvd-control	MIT disk
532/tcp, udp	netnews	Readnews
533/tcp, udp	netwall	For emergency broadcasts
540/tcp, udp	uucp	Uucpd
543/tcp, udp	klogin	
544/tcp, udp	kshell	Krcmd; alias=cmd
550/tcp, udp	new-rwho	New-who

Decimal	Keyword	Description
555/tcp, udp	dsf	
556/tcp, udp	remotefs	Rfs server; alias=rfs_server rfs
560/tcp, udp	rmonitor	Rmonitord
561/tcp, udp	monitor	
562/tcp, udp	chshell	Chcmd
564/tcp, udp	9pfs	Plan 9 file service
565/tcp, udp	whoami	Whoami
570/tcp, udp	meter	Demon
571/tcp, udp	meter	Udemon
600/tcp, udp	ipcserver	Sun IPC server
607/tcp, udp	nqs	Nqs
666/tcp, udp	mdqs	
704/tcp, udp	elcsd	Errlog copy/server daemon
721-731/tcp	printer	Under Windows NT 3.5x, all TCP/IP print jobs sent from a Windows NT computer were sourced from TCP ports 721 through 731. (This is changed for Windows NT Server and Windows NT Workstation version 4.0, which sources LPD client print jobs from any available reserved port between 512 and 1023.)
740/tcp, udp	netcp	NETscout Control Protocol
741/tcp, udp	netgw	NetGW
742/tcp, udp	netrcs	Network based Rev. Cont. Sys.
744/tcp, udp	flexlm	Flexible License Manager
747/tcp, udp	fujitsu-dev	Fujitsu Device Control
748/tcp, udp	ris-cm	Russell Info Sci Calendar Manager
749/tcp, udp	kerberos-adm	Kerberos administration
750/tcp	rfile	Kerberos authentication; alias=kdc
750/udp	loadav	
751/tcp, udp	pump	Kerberos authentication
752/tcp, udp	qrh	Kerberos password server
753/tcp, udp	rrh	Kerberos userreg server
754/tcp, udp	tell	Send; Kerberos slave propagation
758/tcp, udp	nlogin	
759/tcp, udp	con	

(continued)

Table A-1 *Continued*

Decimal	Keyword	Description
760/tcp, udp	ns	761/tcp, udp rxe
762/tcp, udp	quotad	
763/tcp, udp	cycleserv	
764/tcp, udp	omserv	
765/tcp, udp	webster	
767/tcp, udp	phonebook	Phone
769/tcp, udp	vid	
770/tcp, udp	cadlock	
771/tcp, udp	rtip	
772/tcp, udp	cycleserv2	
773/tcp	submit	
773/udp	notify	
774/tcp	rpasswd	
774/udp	acmaint_dbd	
775/tcp	entomb	
775/udp	acmaint_transd	
776/tcp, udp	wpages	
780/tcp, udp	wpgs	
781/tcp, udp	hp-collector	HP performance data collector
782/tcp, udp	hp-managed-node	HP performance data managed node
783/tcp, udp	hp-alarm-mgr	HP performance data alarm manager
800/tcp, udp	mdbs_daemon	
801/tcp, udp	device	
888/tcp	erlogin	Logon and environment passing
996/tcp, udp	xtreelic	XTREE License Server
997/tcp, udp	maitrd	
998/tcp	busboy	
998/udp	puparp	
999/tcp	garcon	
999/udp	applix	Applix ac
999/tcp, udp	puprouter	
1000/tcp	cadlock	
1000/udp	ock	

Command Line Utilities

Table B-1   Useful command line utilities

Utility	Modifiers	Description
Ping	-a	Used to test connectivity between two IP hosts.
ARP	-a	Used to view the ARP cache on a computer.
Nbtstat	-a remote name -A remote IP address	List remote NetBIOS name table.
	-c	Displays local NetBIOS name cache.
	-n	Lists local NetBIOS names.
	-R	Reloads the LMHosts file.
	-r	Lists name resolution statistics.
	-S	Displays both client and server sessions, listing the remote computers by IP address only.
	-s	Attempts to convert the remote computer IP address to a name using the HOSTS file.
Netstat	-a	Lists all connections and listening ports.

(continued)

315

Table B-1　*Continued*

Utility	Modifiers	Description
	-e	Displays Ethernet statistics.
	-s	Displays per protocol statistics.
	-r	Displays contents of the routing table.
telnet	IP address	Used to establish a remote session on another host. Useful for troubleshooting.
FTP	IP address	Used for transferring files across the internet.
Nslookup	IP address of DNS server and target host	Used for verifying DNS resolution.
At	Time and command	Used to schedule a program to run at a certain time.
Rcmd	Name of server	Used to run a remote command on a host.
Netsvc	/query /list /start /stop	Used to remotely stop, start, list, and query the status of a particular service on a particular server.
Ipconfig	/all | more	Used to display IP configuration about a local host.
	/release	Releases the IP address.
	/renew	Renews the IP address.

C

Common NCPs

Table C-1   Common NCP assignments

Type	Field	Meaning
connection NCP	0x2222 23 29	Change Connection State
connection NCP	0x2222 23 254	Clear Connection Number
connection NCP	0x1111	Create Service Connection
connection NCP	0x5555	Destroy Service Connection
connection NCP	0x2222 24	End of Job
connection NCP	0x2222 97	Get Big Packet NCP Max Packet Size
connection NCP	0x2222 23 31	Get Connection List From Object
connection NCP	0x2222 23 26	Get Internet Address
connection NCP	0x2222 23 19	Get Internet Address (old)
connection NCP	0x2222 23 23	Get Login Key
connection NCP	0x2222 23 27	Get Object Connection List
connection NCP	0x2222 23 21	Get Object Connection List (old)
connection NCP	0x2222 19	Get Station Number
connection NCP	0x2222 23 28	Get Station's Logged Info
connection NCP	0x2222 23 22	Get Station's Logged Info (old)
connection NCP	0x2222 23 05	Get Station's Logged Info (old)
connection NCP	0x2222 23 02	Get User Connection List (old)

(continued)

317

Table C-1   *Continued*

Type	Field	Meaning
connection NCP	0x2222 23 24	Keyed Object Login
connection NCP	0x2222 23 20	Login Object
connection NCP	0x2222 23 00	Login User (old)
connection NCP	0x2222 25	Logout
connection NCP	0x2222 33	Negotiate Buffer Size
connection NCP	0x2222 101	Packet Burst Connection Request
connection NCP	0x9999	Request Being Processed
connection NCP	0x3333	Request Processed
connection NCP	0x2222 23 30	Set Watchdog Delay Interval
file system NCP	0x2222 22 39	Add Extended Trustee to Directory or File
file system NCP	0x2222 87 10	Add Trustee Set to File or Subdirectory
file system NCP	0x2222 22 13	Add Trustee to Directory
file system NCP	0x2222 22 33	Add User Disk Space Restriction
file system NCP	0x2222 22 18	Alloc Permanent Directory Handle
file system NCP	0x2222 22 22	Alloc Special Temporary Directory Handle
file system NCP	0x2222 22 19	Alloc Temporary Directory Handle
file system NCP	0x2222 87 12	Allocate Short Directory Handle
file system NCP	0x2222 66	Close File
file system NCP	0x2222 59	Commit File
file system NCP	0x2222 23 244	Convert Path to Dir Entry
file system NCP	0x2222 74	Copy From One File to Another
file system NCP	0x2222 22 10	Create Directory
file system NCP	0x2222 67	Create File
file system NCP	0x2222 77	Create New File
file system NCP	0x2222 22 20	Deallocate Directory Handle
file system NCP	0x2222 87 08	Delete a File or Subdirectory
file system NCP	0x2222 22 11	Delete Directory
file system NCP	0x2222 22 14	Delete Trustee From Directory
file system NCP Subdirectory	0x2222 87 11	Delete Trustee Set From File or
file system NCP	0x2222 68	Erase File
file system NCP	0x2222 22 23	Extract a Base Handle
file system NCP	0x2222 90 150	File Migration Request

Type	Field	Meaning
file system NCP	0x2222 63	File Search Continue
file system NCP	0x2222 62	File Search Initialize
file system NCP	0x2222 87 22	Generate Directory Base and Volume Number
file system NCP	0x2222 71	Get Current Size of File
file system NCP	0x2222 22 35	Get Directory Disk Space Restriction
file system NCP	0x2222 22 31	Get Directory Entry
file system NCP	0x2222 22 45	Get Directory Information
file system NCP	0x2222 22 01	Get Directory Path
file system NCP	0x2222 22 03	Get Effective Directory Rights
file system NCP	0x2222 87 29	Get Effective Directory Rights
file system NCP	0x2222 22 42	Get Effective Rights for Directory Entry
file system NCP	0x2222 22 51	Get Extended Volume Information
file system NCP	0x2222 87 31	Get File Information
file system NCP	0x2222 87 28	Get Full Path String
file system NCP	0x2222 87 26	Get Huge NS Information
file system NCP	0x2222 22 52	Get Mount Volume List
file system NCP	0x2222 22 48	Get Name Space Directory Entry
file system NCP	0x2222 22 47	Get Name Space Information
file system NCP	0x2222 87 24	Get Name Spaces Loaded List From Volume Number
file system NCP	0x2222 87 19	Get NS Information
file system NCP	0x2222 22 41	Get Object Disk Usage and Restrictions
file system NCP	0x2222 22 50	Get Object Effective Rights for Directory Entry
file system NCP	0x2222 22 26	Get Path Name of a Volume-Directory Number Pair
file system NCP	0x2222 87 21	Get Path String From Short Directory Handle
file system NCP	0x2222 90 10	Get Reference Count From Dir Entry Number
file system NCP	0x2222 90 11	Get Reference Count From Dir Handle
file system NCP	0x2222 85	Get Sparse File Data Block Bit Map

(continued)

Table C-1   *Continued*

Type	Field	Meaning
file system NCP	0x2222 22 44	Get Volume and Purge Information
file system NCP	0x2222 22 21	Get Volume Info With Handle
file system NCP	0x2222 18	Get Volume Info With Number
file system NCP	0x2222 22 06	Get Volume Name
file system NCP	0x2222 22 05	Get Volume Number
file system NCP	0x2222 87 02	Initialize Search
file system NCP	0x2222 23 243	Map Directory Number to Path
file system NCP	0x2222 87 35	Modify DOS Attributes on a File or Subdirectory
file system NCP	0x2222 87 07	Modify File or Subdirectory DOS Information
file system NCP	0x2222 22 04	Modify Maximum Rights Mask
file system NCP	0x2222 87 06	Obtain File or Subdirectory Information
file system NCP	0x2222 87 34	Open CallBack Control
file system NCP	0x2222 84	Open/Create File (old)
file system NCP	0x2222 87 01	Open/Create File or Subdirectory
file system NCP	0x2222 87 30	Open/Create File or Subdirectory
file system NCP	0x2222 87 32	Open/Create File or Subdirectory With Callback
file system NCP	0x2222 87 33	Open/Create File or Subdirectory II With Callback
file system NCP	0x2222 22 49	Open Data Stream
file system NCP	0x2222 65	Open File (old)
file system NCP	0x2222 76	Open File (old)
file system NCP	0x2222 90 00	Parse Tree
file system NCP	0x2222 22 16	Purge Erased Files (old)
file system NCP	0x2222 87 18	Purge Salvageable File
file system NCP	0x2222 22 29	Purge Salvageable File (old)
file system NCP	0x2222 87 23	Query NS Information Format
file system NCP	0x2222 72	Read From a File
file system NCP	0x2222 22 17	Recover Erased File (old)
file system NCP	0x2222 87 17	Recover Salvageable File
file system NCP	0x2222 22 28	Recover Salvageable File (old)
file system NCP	0x2222 22 43	Remove Extended Trustee From Dir or File

Type	Field	Meaning
file system NCP	0x2222 22 34	Remove User Disk Space Restriction
file system NCP	0x2222 22 15	Rename Directory
file system NCP	0x2222 69	Rename File
file system NCP	0x2222 22 46	Rename or Move (old)
file system NCP	0x2222 87 04	Rename or Move a File or Subdirectory
file system NCP	0x2222 22 24	Restore an Extracted Base Handle
file system NCP	0x2222 22 30	Scan a Directory
file system NCP	0x2222 22 40	Scan Directory Disk Space
file system NCP	0x2222 22 12	Scan Directory for Trustees
file system NCP	0x2222 22 02	Scan Directory Information
file system NCP	0x2222 23 15	Scan File Information
file system NCP	0x2222 22 38	Scan File or Directory for Extended Trustees
file system NCP	0x2222 87 05	Scan File or Subdirectory for Trustees
file system NCP	0x2222 87 16	Scan Salvageable Files
file system NCP	0x2222 22 27	Scan Salvageable Files (old)
file system NCP	0x2222 22 32	Scan Volume's User Disk Restrictions
file system NCP	0x2222 64	Search for a File
file system NCP	0x2222 87 03	Search for File or Subdirectory
file system NCP	0x2222 87 20	Search for File or Subdirectory Set
file system NCP	0x2222 90 12	Set Compressed File Size
file system NCP	0x2222 22 36	Set Directory Disk Space Restriction
file system NCP	0x2222 22 37	Set Directory Entry Information
file system NCP	0x2222 22 00	Set Directory Handle
file system NCP	0x2222 22 25	Set Directory Information
file system NCP	0x2222 70	Set File Attributes
file system NCP	0x2222 79	Set File Extended Attribute
file system NCP	0x2222 23 16	Set File Information
file system NCP	0x2222 75	Set File Time Date Stamp
file system NCP	0x2222 87 27	Set Huge NS Information
file system NCP	0x2222 87 25	Set NS Information
file system NCP	0x2222 87 09	Set Short Directory Handle

(continued)

Table C-1 *Continued*

Type	Field	Meaning
file system NCP	0x2222 73	Write to a File
print NCP	0x2222 17 01	Close Spool File
print NCP	0x2222 17 09	Create Spool File
print NCP	0x2222 17 06	Get Printer Status
print NCP	0x2222 17 10	Get Printer's Queue
print NCP	0x2222 17 02	Set Spool File Flags
print NCP	0x2222 17 03	Spool a Disk File
print NCP	0x2222 17 00	Write to Spool File
queue management NCP	0x2222 23 132	Abort Servicing Queue Job
queue management NCP	0x2222 23 115	Abort Servicing Queue Job (old)
queue management NCP	0x2222 23 111	Attach Queue Server to Queue
queue management NCP	0x2222 23 130	Change Job Priority
queue management NCP	0x2222 23 123	Change Queue Job Entry
queue management NCP	0x2222 23 109	Change Queue Job Entry (old)
queue management NCP	0x2222 23 110	Change Queue Job Position
queue management NCP	0x2222 23 133	Change to Client Rights
queue management NCP	0x2222 23 116	Change to Client Rights (old)
queue management NCP	0x2222 23 127	Close File and Start Queue Job
queue management NCP	0x2222 23 105	Close File and Start Queue Job (old)
queue management NCP	0x2222 23 100	Create Queue
queue management NCP	0x2222 23 121	Create Queue Job and File
queue management NCP	0x2222 23 104	Create Queue Job and File (old)
queue management NCP	0x2222 23 101	Destroy Queue
queue management NCP	0x2222 23 112	Detach Queue Server From Queue
queue management NCP	0x2222 23 131	Finish Servicing Queue Job
queue management NCP	0x2222 23 114	Finish Servicing Queue Job (old)
queue management NCP	0x2222 23 135	Get Queue Job File Size
queue management NCP	0x2222 23 120	Get Queue Job File Size (old)
queue management NCP	0x2222 23 129	Get Queue Job List
queue management NCP	0x2222 23 107	Get Queue Job List (old)
queue management NCP	0x2222 23 137	Get Queue Jobs From Form List
queue management NCP	0x2222 23 136	Move Queue Job From Src Q to Dst Q
queue management NCP	0x2222 23 125	Read Queue Current Status

Type	Field	Meaning
queue management NCP	0x2222 23 102	Read Queue Current Status (old)
queue management NCP	0x2222 23 122	Read Queue Job Entry
queue management NCP	0x2222 23 108	Read Queue Job Entry (old)
queue management NCP	0x2222 23 134	Read Queue Server Current Status
queue management NCP	0x2222 23 118	Read Queue Server Current Status (old)
queue management NCP	0x2222 23 128	Remove Job From Queue
queue management NCP	0x2222 23 106	Remove Job From Queue (old)
queue management NCP	0x2222 23 117	Restore Queue Server Rights
queue management NCP	0x2222 23 124	Service Queue Job
queue management NCP	0x2222 23 113	Service Queue Job (old)
queue management NCP	0x2222 23 138	Service Queue Job by Form List
queue management NCP	0x2222 23 126	Set Queue Current Status
queue management NCP	0x2222 23 103	Set Queue Current Status (old)
queue management NCP	0x2222 23 119	Set Queue Server Current Status
RPC NCP	0x2222 131 05	RPC Add Name Space to Volume
RPC NCP	0x2222 131 04	RPC Dismount Volume
RPC NCP	0x2222 131 07	RPC Execute NCF File
RPC NCP	0x2222 131 01	RPC Load an NLM
RPC NCP	0x2222 131 03	RPC Mount Volume
RPC NCP	0x2222 131 06	RPC Set Command Value
RPC NCP	0x2222 131 02	RPC Unload an NLM

Troubleshooting Common Network Errors

$$A$$t times you will run across the following terms and wonder what they are and perhaps what causes them. This list has been prepared to help you. This Appendix discusses some of the more common errors you are likely to run into, and offers some quick suggestions for correcting them.

RUNT/LONG FRAMES

Runt frames are frames that are prematurely terminated. They usually occur when a cut-through switch forwards frames that have encountered collisions on the source segment. A long frame occurs when the end of one frame and the start of another are not clearly defined. This can happen when the collision-domain diameter of a segment is outside of specification.

CRC OR FCS ERRORS

Any distortion in a frame can result in a Cyclic Redundancy Check error (also called a Frame Check Sequence error). The transmitting NIC performs a computation on the frame header and data field. The result of the computation is stored in the four bytes after the data field. When the frame reaches the destination, the same computation is performed and compared with the four-byte field. A mismatch is called a CRC or FCS error. Distortions can result from poorly attached connectors on cables, cat 3 cable used for 100-Mb/S Ethernet, electromagnetic noise sources such as transformers and electric motors located near UTP cable, up-cable runs exceeding 100 meters, and many more reasons.

COLLISIONS

Collisions are caused by the interference of transmissions due to two or more NICs sending packets at the same time. Collisions can occur if the NICs are listening and hear nothing so that they decide to transmit at almost the same time. All packets involved in a collision are lost and are automatically retried.

LATE COLLISIONS

The detection of a collision after the first 64 bytes of a packet has been transmitted. The NIC detecting a late collision goes through the normal CSMA/CD jam, bake-off, and retry but also increments the late-collision counter. The danger is that packets close to 64 bytes long can be transmitted before the collision is detected and cannot be retried by the NIC. It will then be up to the computer to wait until the other end does not respond properly and then retry. This can take several seconds or even close down a connection. The cause of late collisions is a network that exceeds the timing constraints of the IEEE 802.3 standard.

NetBIOS Suffixes

Table E-1   NetBIOS suffixes

Name	Number(h)	Type	Usage
<computername>	0	U	Workstation Service
<computername>	1	U	Messenger Service
<\\—__MSBROWSE__>	1	G	Master Browser
<computername>	3	U	Messenger Service
<computername>	6	U	RAS Server Service
<computername>	1F	U	NetDDE Service
<computername>	20	U	File Server Service
<computername>	21	U	RAS Client Service
<computername>	22	U	Microsoft Exchange Interchange(MSMail Connector)
<computername>	23	U	Microsoft Exchange Store
<computername>	24	U	Microsoft Exchange Directory
<computername>	30	U	Modem Sharing Server Service
<computername>	31	U	Modem Sharing Client Service
<computername>	43	U	SMS Clients Remote Control
<computername>	44	U	SMS Administrators Remote Control Tool
<computername>	45	U	SMS Clients Remote Chat

Name	Number(h)	Type	Usage
<computername>	46	U	SMS Clients Remote Transfer
<computername>	4C	U	DEC Pathworks TCPIP service on Windows NT
<computername>	52	U	DEC Pathworks TCPIP service on Windows NT
<computername>	87	U	Microsoft Exchange MTA
<computername>	6A	U	Microsoft Exchange IMC
<computername>	BE	U	Network Monitor Agent
<computername>	BF	U	Network Monitor Application
<username>	3	U	Messenger Service
<domain>	0	G	Domain Name
<domain>	1B	U	Domain Master Browser
<domain>	1C	G	Domain Controllers
<domain>	1D	U	Master Browser
<domain>	1E	G	Browser Service Elections
<INet~Services>	1C	G	IIS
<IS~computer name>	0	U	IIS
<computername>	[2B]	U	Lotus Notes Server Service
IRISMULTICAST	[2F]	G	Lotus Notes
IRISNAMESERVER	[33]	G	Lotus Notes
Forte_$ND800ZA	[20]	U	DCA IrmaLan Gateway Server Service

Domain Controller Startup

Table F-1   Domain controller startup

Frame	Time	Src MAC Addr	Dst MAC Addr	Protocol	Description
1	67.409	2400	*BROADCAST	DHCP	Request (xid=2B1D7FEF)
2	67.467	Prox	*BROADCAST	DHCP	ACK (xid=2B1D7FEF)
3	67.468	2400	*BROADCAST	ARP_RARP	ARP: Request, Target IP: 10.0.0.60
4	67.823	2400	*BROADCAST	ARP_RARP	ARP: Request, Target IP: 10.0.0.60
5	68.823	2400	*BROADCAST	ARP_RARP	ARP: Request, Target IP: 10.0.0.60
6	71.283	Prox	*BROADCAST	BROWSER	Workgroup Announcement [0x0c] MRED
7	72.727	2400	*BROADCAST	ARP_RARP	ARP: Request, Target IP: 10.0.0.10

Frame	Time	Src MAC Addr	Dst MAC Addr	Protocol	Description
8	72.728	Prox	2400	ARP_RARP	ARP: Reply, Target IP: 10.0.0.60 Target Hdwr Addr: 00902764FEBF
9	72.728	2400	Prox	NBT	NS: Registration Req. for 2400 <00>
10	74.214	2400	Prox	NBT	NS: Registration Req. for 2400 <00>
11	75.714	2400	Prox	NBT	NS: Registration Req. for 2400 <00>
12	77.246	2400	*BROADCAST	NBT	NS: Registration Req. for 2400 <00>
13	77.996	2400	*BROADCAST	NBT	NS: Registration Req. for 2400 <00>
14	78.746	2400	*BROADCAST	NBT	NS: Registration Req. for 2400 <00>
15	79.496	2400	*BROADCAST	NBT	NS: Registration Req. for 2400 <00>
16	84.313	Prox	*NETBIOS Multicast	BROWSER	Workgroup Announcement [0x0c] MRED
17	87.283	2400	*BROADCAST	NBT	NS: Registration Req. for 2400
18	88.028	2400	*BROADCAST	NBT	NS: Registration Req. for 2400
19	88.778	2400	*BROADCAST	NBT	NS: Registration Req. for 2400
20	89.528	2400	*BROADCAST	NBT	NS: Registration Req. for 2400
21	90.284	2400	*BROADCAST	BROWSER	Host Announcement [0x01] 2400

(continued)

Table F-1 *Continued*

Frame	Time	Src MAC Addr	Dst MAC Addr	Protocol	Description
22	90.308	2400	*BROADCAST	NBT	NS: Registration Req. for MRED <00>
23	91.044	2400	*BROADCAST	NBT	NS: Registration Req. for MRED <00>
24	91.794	2400	*BROADCAST	NBT	NS: Registration Req. for MRED <00>
25	92.544	2400	*BROADCAST	NBT	NS: Registration Req. for MRED <00>
26	93.295	2400	*BROADCAST	NBT	NS: Registration Req. for MRED <1C>
27	94.044	2400	*BROADCAST	NBT	NS: Registration Req. for MRED <1C>
28	94.794	2400	*BROADCAST	NBT	NS: Registration Req. for MRED <1C>
29	95.544	2400	*BROADCAST	NBT	NS: Registration Req. for MRED <1C>
30	96.297	2400	*BROADCAST	BROWSER	Host Announcement [0x01] 2400
31	96.462	2400	*BROADCAST	NBT	NS: Query Req. for MRED <1B>
32	96.462	Prox	2400	NBT	NS: Query (Node Status) esp. for MRED <1B>, Success
33	96.462	2400	Prox	NETLOGON	Query for Primary DC
34	96.463	Prox	2400	NETLOGON	Response to Primary Query

Frame	Time	Src MAC Addr	Dst MAC Addr	Protocol	Description
35	96.491	2400	Prox	TCP	....S., len: 4, seq: 78400-78403, ack: 0, win: 8192, src: 1025 dst: 139 (NB
36	96.491	Prox	2400	TCP	.A..S., len: 4, seq: 171256-171259, ack: 78401, win: 8760, src: 139 (NBT Session)
37	96.492	2400	Prox	TCP	.A...., len: 0, seq: 78401-78401, ack: 171257, win: 8760, src: 1025 dst: 139 (NB
38	96.492	2400	Prox	NBT	SS: Session Request, Dest: PROX , Source: 2400 <00>, Len: 68
39	96.492	Prox	2400	NBT	SS: Positive Session Response, Len: 0
40	96.493	2400	Prox	SMB	C Negotiate, Dialect = NT LM 0.12
41	96.497	Prox	2400	SMB	R Negotiate, Dialect # = 7
42	96.508	2400	Prox	SMB	C Session Set-up & X, Username = , and C Tree Connect & X, Share = \\PROX\IPC$
43	96.509	Prox	2400	SMB	R Session Set-up & X, and R Tree Connect & X, Type = IPC

(continued)

Table F-1　*Continued*

Frame	Time	Src MAC Addr	Dst MAC Addr	Protocol	Description
44	96.51	2400	Prox	SMB	C NT create & X, File = \NETLOGON
45	96.513	Prox	2400	SMB	R NT create & X, FID = 0x807
46	96.513	2400	Prox	MSRPC	c/o RPC Bind: UUID 12345678-1234-ABCD-EF00-01234567CFFB call 0x1 assoc grp 0x0 xm
47	96.518	Prox	2400	MSRPC	c/o RPC Bind Ack: call 0x1 assoc grp 0x19D9B xmit 0x1630 recv 0x1630
48	96.518	2400	Prox	R_LOGON	RPC Client Call Logon:NetrServer ReqChallenge(..)
49	96.519	Prox	2400	R_LOGON	RPC Server Response Logon:NetrServer ReqChallenge(..)
50	96.52	2400	Prox	R_LOGON	RPC Client Call Logon:NetrServer Authenticate2(..)
51	96.53	Prox	2400	R_LOGON	RPC Server Response Logon:NetrServer Authenticate2(..)
52	96.531	2400	*BROADCAST	NBT	NS: Query Req. for NETMON <1C>
53	96.532	TERESA	*BROADCAST	ARP_RARP	ARP: Request, Target IP: 10.0.0.60
54	96.587	2400	*BROADCAST	BROWSER	Host Announcement [0x01] 2400

Frame	Time	Src MAC Addr	Dst MAC Addr	Protocol	Description
55	96.658	2400	Prox	SMB	C NT Create & X, File = \NETLOGON
56	96.661	Prox	2400	SMB	R NT Create & X, FID = 0x808
57	96.662	2400	Prox	MSRPC	c/o RPC Bind: UUID 12345678-1234-ABCD-EF00-01234567CFFB call 0x0 assoc grp 0x19D9B
58	96.664	Prox	2400	MSRPC	c/o RPC Bind Ack: Call 0x0 Assoc grp 0x19D9B xmit 0x1630 recv 0x1630
59	96.667	2400	Prox	R_LOGON	RPC Client Call Logon:NetrDatabaseDeltas(..)
60	96.674	Prox	2400	R_LOGON	RPC Server Response Logon:NetrDatabaseDeltas(..)
61	96.675	2400	Prox	R_LOGON	RPC Client Call Logon:NetrDatabaseDeltas(..)
62	96.678	Prox	2400	R_LOGON	RPC Server Response Logon:NetrDatabaseDeltas(..)
63	96.683	2400	Prox	R_LOGON	RPC Client Call Logon:NetrDatabaseDeltas(..)
64	96.687	Prox	2400	R_LOGON	RPC Server Response Logon:NetrDatabaseDeltas(..)
65	96.782	2400	*BROADCAST	NBT	NS: Registration Req. for MRED <1E>

(continued)

Table F-1   *Continued*

Frame	Time	Src MAC Addr	Dst MAC Addr	Protocol	Description
66	96.81	2400	Prox	TCP	.A...., len: 0, seq: 80511-80511, ack: 172694, win: 7323, src: 1025 dst: 139 (NB)
67	96.91	2400	*BROADCAST	NBT	NS: Registration Req. for 2400 <03>
68	97.372	2400	Prox	NETLOGON	Query for Primary DC
69	97.374	Prox	2400	NETLOGON	Response to Primary Query
70	97.529	2400	*BROADCAST	NBT	NS: Registration Req. for MRED <1E>
71	97.654	2400	*BROADCAST	NBT	NS: Registration Req. for 2400 <03>
72	98.201	2400	*BROADCAST	NBT	NS: Registration Req. for 2400++++++++++++
73	98.279	2400	*BROADCAST	NBT	NS: Registration Req. for MRED <1E>
74	98.404	2400	*BROADCAST	NBT	NS: Registration Req. for 2400 <03>
75	98.951	2400	*BROADCAST	NBT	NS: Registration Req. for 2400+++ +++++++++
76	99.029	2400	*BROADCAST	NBT	NS: Registration Req. for MRED <1E>
77	99.156	2400	*BROADCAST	NBT	NS: Registration Req. for 2400 <03>
78	99.701	2400	*BROADCAST	NBT	NS: Registration Req. for 2400+++ +++++++++

Frame	Time	Src MAC Addr	Dst MAC Addr	Protocol	Description
79	99.785	2400	*BROADCAST	BROWSER	Announcement Request [0x02]
80	99.79	Prox	*NETBIOS Multicast		BROWSER Local Master Announcement [0x0f]
PROX					
81	99.79	Prox	*BROADCAST	BROWSER	Local Master Announcement [0x0f] PROX
82	99.92	2400	Prox	TCP	....S., len: 4, seq: 81842-81845, ack: 0, win: 8192, src: 1028 dst: 139 (NB)
83	99.92	Prox	2400	TCP	.A..S., len: 4, seq: 171273-171276, ack: 81843, win: 8760, src: 139 (NBT Session)
84	99.92	2400	Prox	TCP	.A...., len: 0, seq: 81843-81843, ack: 171274, win: 8760, src: 1028 dst: 139 (NB)
85	99.92	2400	Prox	NBT	SS: Session Request, Dest: PROX , Source: 2400 <00>, Len: 68
86	99.92	Prox	2400	NBT	SS: Positive Session Response, Len: 0
87	99.922	2400	Prox	SMB	C Negotiate, Dialect = NT LM 0.12
88	99.922	Prox	2400	SMB	R Negotiate, Dialect # = 7

(continued)

Table F-1   *Continued*

Frame	Time	Src MAC Addr	Dst MAC Addr	Protocol	Description
89	99.923	2400	Prox	SMB	C Session Set-up & X, Username = , and C Tree Connect & X, Share = \\PROX\IPC$
90	99.923	Prox	2400	SMB	R Session Set-up & X, and R Tree Connect & X, Type = IPC
91	99.924	2400	Prox	SMB	C Transact, Remote API
92	99.927	Prox	2400	SMB	R Transact, Remote API (Response to Rrame 91)
93	99.928	2400	Prox	SMB	C transact, Remote API
94	99.929	Prox	2400	SMB	R transact, Remote API (Response to Rrame 93)
95	100.094	2400	Prox	TCP	.A...., len: 0, seq: 82509-82509, ack: 171796, win: 8238, src: 1028 dst: 139 (NB
96	100.123	2400	Prox	TCP	....S., len: 4, seq: 82084-82087, ack: 0, win: 8192, src: 1029 dst: 1745
97	100.123	Prox	2400	TCP	.A..S., len: 4, seq: 171282-171285, ack: 82085, win: 8760, src: 1745 dst: 1029
98	100.124	2400	Prox	TCP	.A...., len: 0, seq: 82085-82085, ack: 171283, win: 8760, src: 1029 dst: 1745

Frame	Time	Src MAC Addr	Dst MAC Addr	Protocol	Description
99	100.149	2400	Prox	TCP	.AP..., len: 1, seq: 82085-82085, ack: 171283, win: 8760, src: 1029 dst: 1745
100	100.152	Prox	2400	TCP	.AP..., len: 1129, seq: 171283-172411, ack: 82086, win: 8759, src: 1745 dst: 1029
101	100.31	2400	Prox	TCP	.A...., len: 0, seq: 82086-82086, ack: 172412, win: 7631, src: 1029 dst: 1745
102	100.451	2400	*BROADCAST	NBT	NS: Registration req. for 2400++ ++++++++++
103	100.518	2400	Prox	TCP	.A...F, len: 0, seq: 82086-82086, ack: 172412, win: 7631, src: 1029 dst: 1745
104	100.518	Prox	2400	TCP	.A...., len: 0, seq: 172412-172412, ack: 82087, win: 8759, src: 1745 dst: 1029
105	100.522	Prox	2400	TCP	.A...F, len: 0, seq: 172412-172412, ack: 82087, win: 8759, src: 1745 dst: 1029
106	100.522	2400	Prox	TCP	.A...., len: 0, seq: 82087-82087, ack: 172413, win: 7631, src: 1029 dst: 1745

(continued)

Table F-1   *Continued*

Frame	Time	Src MAC Addr	Dst MAC Addr	Protocol	Description
107	100.921	2400	*BROADCAST	BROWSER	Host Announcement [0x01] 2400
108	101.177	2400	*BROADCAST	BROWSER	Election [0x08] [Force]
109	101.277	Prox	*BROADCAST	BROWSER	Election [0x08] PROX
110	102.278	Prox	*BROADCAST	BROWSER	Election [0x08] PROX
111	103.28	Prox	*BROADCAST	BROWSER	Election [0x08] PROX
112	104.281	Prox	*BROADCAST	BROWSER	Election [0x08] PROX
113	105.288	Prox	*NETBIOS Multicast		BROWSER Local Master Announcement [0x0f] PROX
114	105.289	Prox	*BROADCAST	BROWSER	Local Master Announcement [0x0f] PROX
115	126.562	2400	Prox	NBT	NS: Query Req. for ED1750
116	128.047	2400	Prox	NBT	NS: Query Req. for ED1750
117	129.547	2400	Prox	NBT	NS: Query Req. for ED1750
118	131.063	2400	*BROADCAST	NBT	NS: Query Req. for ED1750
119	131.813	2400	*BROADCAST	NBT	NS: Query Req. for ED1750
120	131.841	2400	*BROADCAST	NBT	NS: Registration Req. for ED <03>
121	131.842	bigguy	*BROADCAST	ARP_RARP	ARP: Request, Target IP: 10.0.0.60
122	132.563	2400	*BROADCAST	NBT	NS: Query Req. for ED1750
123	134.817	TERESA	*BROADCAST	BROWSER	Local Master Announcement [0x0f] TERESA

Opening a Web Page

Table G-1   Opening a Web page

Frame	Time	Source	Destination	Protocol	Description
1	9.525	proxWan	8AA851000101	DNS	0x1:Std Qry for home.microsoft.com. of type Host Addr on class INET addr.
2	9.525	proxWan	8AA851000101	DNS	0x1:Std Qry for home.microsoft.com. of type Host Addr on class INET addr.
3	9.635	8AA851000101	proxWan	DNS	0x1:Std Qry Resp. for home.microsoft.com. of type Host Addr on class INET addr.
4	9.655	8AA851000101	proxWan	DNS	0x1:Std Qry Resp. for home.microsoft.com. of type Host Addr on class INET addr.

(continued)

Table G-1   *Continued*

Frame	Time	Source	Destination	Protocol	Description
5	9.655	proxWan	8AA851000101	ICMP	Destination Unreachable: 206.112.194.65 See frame 4
6	9.655	proxWan	8AA851000101	TCP	....S., len: 4, seq: 241730-241733, ack: 0, win: 8192, src: 3488 dst: 80
7	9.826	8AA851000101	proxWan	TCP	.A..S., len: 4, seq: 142002582-142002585, ack: 241731, win: 8760, src: 80 dst: 3488
8	9.826	proxWan	8AA851000101	TCP	.A...., len: 0, seq: 241731-241731, ack: 142002583, win: 8760, src: 3488 dst: 80
9	9.846	proxWan	8AA851000101	HTTP	GET Request (from client using port 3488)
10	10.136	8AA851000101	proxWan	HTTP	Response (to client using port 3488)
11	10.136	8AA851000101	proxWan	TCP	.A...F, len: 0, seq: 142002909-142002909, ack: 242308, win: 8183, src: 80 dst: 3488
12	10.156	proxWan	8AA851000101	TCP	...R.., len: 0, seq: 242308-242308, ack: 142002583, win: 0, src: 3488 dst: 80
13	10.266	proxWan	8AA851000101	DNS	0x1:Std Qry for www.msn.com. of type Host Addr on class INET addr.
14	10.266	proxWan	8AA851000101	DNS	0x1:Std Qry for www.msn.com. of type Host Addr on class INET addr.

Frame	Time	Source	Destination	Protocol	Description
15	10.417	8AA851000101	proxWan	DNS	0x1:Std Qry Resp. for www.msn.com. of type Host Addr on class INET addr.
16	10.417	proxWan	8AA851000101	TCP	....S., len: 4, seq: 241741-241744, ack: 0, win: 8192, src: 3491 dst: 80
17	10.447	8AA851000101	proxWan	DNS	0x1:Std Qry Resp. for www.msn.com. of type Host Addr on class INET addr.
18	10.447	proxWan	8AA851000101	ICMP	Destination Unreachable: 206.112.194.65 See frame 17
19	10.547	8AA851000101	proxWan	TCP	.A..S., len: 4, seq: 631519114-631519117, ack: 241742, win: 8760, src: 80 dst: 3491
20	10.547	proxWan	8AA851000101	TCP	.A...., len: 0, seq: 241742-241742, ack: 631519115, win: 8760, src: 3491 dst: 80
21	10.567	proxWan	8AA851000101	HTTP	GET Request (from client using port 3491)
22	13.512	proxWan	8AA851000101	HTTP	GET Request (from client using port 3491)
23	13.932	8AA851000101	proxWan	HTTP	Response (to client using port 3491)
24	14.032	8AA851000101	proxWan	HTTP	Response (to client using port 3491)
25	14.052	proxWan	8AA851000101	TCP	.A...., len: 0, seq: 242091-242091, ack: 631522035, win: 8760, src: 3491 dst: 80

(continued)

Table G-1 *Continued*

Frame	Time	Source	Destination	Protocol	Description
26	14.403	8AA851000101	proxWan	HTTP	Response (to client using port 3491)
27	14.423	proxWan	8AA851000101	TCP	.A...., len: 0, seq: 242091-242091, ack: 631523495, win: 8760, src: 3491 dst: 80
28	14.513	8AA851000101	proxWan	HTTP	Response (to client using port 3491)
29	14.644	8AA851000101	proxWan	HTTP	Response (to client using port 3491)
30	14.663	proxWan	8AA851000101	TCP	.A...., len: 0, seq: 242091-242091, ack: 631526415, win: 8760, src: 3491 dst: 80
31	14.844	8AA851000101	proxWan	HTTP	Response (to client using port 3491)
32	14.864	proxWan	8AA851000101	TCP	.A...., len: 0, seq: 242091-242091, ack: 631527875, win: 8760, src: 3491 dst: 80
33	14.935	8AA851000101	proxWan	HTTP	Response (to client using port 3491)
34	15.114	proxWan	8AA851000101	TCP	.A...., len: 0, seq: 242091-242091, ack: 631529335, win: 8760, src: 3491 dst: 80
35	15.244	8AA851000101	proxWan	HTTP	Response (to client using port 3491)
36	15.344	8AA851000101	proxWan	HTTP	Response (to client using port 3491)
37	15.364	proxWan	8AA851000101	TCP	.A...., len: 0, seq: 242091-242091, ack: 631532255, win: 8760, src: 3491 dst: 80
38	15.456	8AA851000101	proxWan	HTTP	Response (to client using port 3491)

Frame	Time	Source	Destination	Protocol	Description
39	15.555	8AA851000101	proxWan	HTTP	Response (to client using port 3491)
40	15.575	proxWan	8AA851000101	TCP	.A...., len: 0, seq: 242091-242091, ack: 631535175, win: 8760, src: 3491 dst: 80
41	15.705	8AA851000101	proxWan	HTTP	Response (to client using port 3491)
42	15.725	proxWan	8AA851000101	TCP	.A...., len: 0, seq: 242091-242091, ack: 631536635, win: 8760, src: 3491 dst: 80
43	15.805	8AA851000101	proxWan	HTTP	Response (to client using port 3491)
44	15.896	8AA851000101	proxWan	HTTP	Response (to client using port 3491)
45	15.896	proxWan	8AA851000101	TCP	.A...., len: 0, seq: 242091-242091, ack: 631539555, win: 5840, src: 3491 dst: 80
46	16.005	8AA851000101	proxWan	HTTP	Response (to client using port 3491)
47	16.106	8AA851000101	proxWan	HTTP	Response (to client using port 3491)
48	16.106	proxWan	8AA851000101	TCP	.A...., len: 0, seq: 242091-242091, ack: 631542475, win: 2920, src: 3491 dst: 80
49	16.186	proxWan	8AA851000101	TCP	.A...., len: 0, seq: 242091-242091, ack: 631542475, win: 8760, src: 3491 dst: 80
50	16.216	8AA851000101	proxWan	HTTP	Response (to client using port 3491)
51	16.346	8AA851000101	proxWan	HTTP	Response (to client using port 3491)

(continued)

Table G-1 *Continued*

Frame	Time	Source	Destination	Protocol	Description
52	16.346	proxWan	8AA851000101	DNS	0x2:Std Qry for msimg.com. of type Host Addr on class INET addr.
53	16.346	proxWan	8AA851000101	DNS	0x2:Std Qry for msimg.com. of type Host Addr on class INET addr.
54	16.366	proxWan	8AA851000101	TCP	.A...., len: 0, seq: 242091-242091, ack: 631545395, win: 8760, src: 3491 dst: 80
55	16.516	8AA851000101	proxWan	HTTP	Response (to client using port 3491)
56	16.536	proxWan	8AA851000101	TCP	.A...., len: 0, seq: 242091-242091, ack: 631546855, win: 8760, src: 3491 dst: 80
57	16.698	8AA851000101	proxWan	HTTP	Response (to client using port 3491)
58	16.797	8AA851000101	proxWan	HTTP	Response (to client using port 3491)
59	16.797	proxWan	8AA851000101	TCP	.A...., len: 0, seq: 242091-242091, ack: 631549775, win: 8760, src: 3491 dst: 80
60	16.897	8AA851000101	proxWan	HTTP	Response (to client using port 3491)
61	16.897	8AA851000101	proxWan	DNS	0x2:Std Qry Resp. for msimg.com. of type Host Addr on class INET addr.
62	16.897	proxWan	8AA851000101	TCP	.A...., len: 0, seq: 242091-242091, ack: 631551235, win: 8760, src: 3491 dst: 80

Frame	Time	Source	Destination	Protocol	Description
63	16.897	proxWan	8AA851000101	TCP	....S., len: 4, seq: 241751-241754, ack: 0, win: 8192, src: 3494 dst: 80
64	16.917	8AA851000101	proxWan	DNS	0x2:Std Qry Resp. for msimg.com. of type Host Add-on class INET addr.
65	16.917	proxWan	8AA851000101	ICMP	Destination Unreachable: 206.112.194.65 See frame 64
66	17.067	8AA851000101	proxWan	HTTP	Response (to client using port 3491)
67	17.207	8AA851000101	proxWan	HTTP	Response (to client using port 3491)
68	17.207	proxWan	8AA851000101	TCP	.A...., len: 0, seq: 242091-242091, ack: 631554155, win: 8760, src: 3491 dst: 80
69	17.247	8AA851000101	proxWan	HTTP	Response (to client using port 3491)
70	17.247	8AA851000101	proxWan	TCP	.A..S., len: 4, seq: 550165240-550165243, ack: 241752, win: 8760, src: 80 dst: 3494
71	17.247	proxWan	8AA851000101	TCP	.A...., len: 0, seq: 241752-241752, ack: 550165241, win: 8760, src: 3494 dst: 80
72	17.267	proxWan	8AA851000101	HTTP	GET Request (from client using port 3494)
73	17.418	proxWan	8AA851000101	TCP	.A...., len: 0, seq: 242091-242091, ack: 631554686, win: 8229, src: 3491 dst: 80

(continued)

Table G-1 *Continued*

Frame	Time	Source	Destination	Protocol	Description
74	17.498	8AA851000101	proxWan	HTTP	Response (to client using port 3494)
75	17.618	proxWan	8AA851000101	TCP	.A...., len: 0, seq: 242091-242091, ack: 550165457, win: 8544, src: 3494 dst: 80
76	18.229	proxWan	8AA851000101	HTTP	GET Request (from client using port 3494)
77	18.319	proxWan	8AA851000101	TCP	....S., len: 4, seq: 241766-241769, ack: 0, win: 8192, src: 3495 dst: 80
78	18.449	8AA851000101	proxWan	HTTP	Response (to client using port 3494)
79	18.449	8AA851000101	proxWan	TCP	.A..S., len: 4, seq:1485616298-1485616301, ack: 241767, win: 8760, src: 80 dst: 349
80	18.449	proxWan	8AA851000101	TCP	.A...., len: 0, seq: 241767-241767, ack:1485616299, win: 8760, src: 3495 dst: 80
81	18.479	proxWan	8AA851000101	HTTP	GET Request (from client using port 3495)
82	18.62	proxWan	8AA851000101	TCP	.A...., len: 0, seq: 242427-242427, ack: 550165671, win: 8330, src: 3494 dst: 80
83	18.73	8AA851000101	proxWan	HTTP	Response (to client using port 3495)
84	18.92	proxWan	8AA851000101	TCP	.A...., len: 0, seq: 242103-242103, ack:1485616512, win: 8547, src: 3495 dst: 80

Frame	Time	Source	Destination	Protocol	Description
85	19.14	proxWan	8AA851000101	HTTP	GET Request (from client using port 3494)
86	19.141	proxWan	8AA851000101	HTTP	GET Request (from client using port 3495)
87	19.381	8AA851000101	proxWan	HTTP	Response (to client using port 3494)
88	19.381	proxWan	8AA851000101	HTTP	GET Request (from client using port 3494)
89	19.381	8AA851000101	proxWan	HTTP	Response (to client using port 3495)
90	19.401	proxWan	8AA851000101	HTTP	GET Request (from client using port 3495)
91	19.691	proxWan	8AA851000101	HTTP	GET Request (from client using port 3491)
92	19.761	8AA851000101	proxWan	HTTP	Response (to client using port 3494)
93	19.821	proxWan	8AA851000101	DNS	0x3:Std Qry for go.msn.com. of type Host Addr on class INET addr.
94	19.822	proxWan	8AA851000101	DNS	0x3:Std Qry for go.msn.com. of type Host Addr on class INET addr.
95	19.852	8AA851000101	proxWan	HTTP	Response (to client using port 3494)
96	19.872	proxWan	8AA851000101	TCP	.A...., len: 0, seq: 243029-243029, ack: 550167891, win: 8760, src: 3494 dst: 80
97	19.872	8AA851000101	proxWan	HTTP	Response (to client using port 3495)
98	19.942	proxWan	8AA851000101	HTTP	GET Request (from client using port 3495)

(continued)

Table G-1 *Continued*

Frame	Time	Source	Destination	Protocol	Description
99	19.942	8AA851000101	proxWan	DNS	0x3:Std Qry Resp. for go.msn.com. of type Host Addr on class INET addr.
100	19.962	proxWan	8AA851000101	TCP	....S., len: 4, seq: 241781-241784, ack: 0, win: 8192, src: 3498 dst: 80
101	19.962	8AA851000101	proxWan	DNS	0x3:Std Qry Resp.
for go.msn.com. of type Host Addr on class INET addr.					
102	19.962	proxWan	8AA851000101	ICMP	Destination Unreachable: 206.112.194.65 See frame 101
103	20.023	8AA851000101	proxWan	HTTP	Response (to client using port 3491)
104	20.222	proxWan	8AA851000101	TCP	.A...., len: 0, seq: 242571-242571, ack: 631554827, win: 8088, src: 3491 dst: 80
105	20.222	8AA851000101	proxWan	HTTP	Response (to client using port 3495)
106	20.222	8AA851000101	proxWan	TCP	.A..S., len: 4, seq: 170783881-170783884, ack: 241782, win: 8760, src: 80 dst: 3498
107	20.222	proxWan	8AA851000101	TCP	.A...., len: 0, seq: 241782-241782, ack: 170783882, win: 8760, src: 3498 dst: 80
108	20.222	proxWan	8AA851000101	HTTP	GET Request (from client using port 3498)
109	20.422	proxWan	8AA851000101	TCP	.A...., len: 0, seq: 243130-243130, ack:1485617155, win: 7904, src: 3495 dst: 80

Frame	Time	Source	Destination	Protocol	Description
110	20.533	8AA851000101	proxWan	HTTP	Response (to client using port 3498)
111	20.643	proxWan	8AA851000101	HTTP	GET Request (from client using port 3498)
112	20.873	8AA851000101	proxWan	HTTP	Response (to client using port 3498)
113	21.023	proxWan	8AA851000101	TCP	.A...., len: 0, seq: 242548-242548, ack: 170784332, win: 8310, src: 3498 dst: 80
114	0	0	0	STATS	Number of Frames Captured = 113

Glossary

Ack A control bit (acknowledge) occupies no sequence space and indicates that the acknowledgment field of the segment specifies the next sequential number the sender of this segment expects, hence acknowledging receipt of all previous sequence numbers.

Bit One or zero.

Byte Eight bits. See also Octet.

Backup Browser Obtains a copy of the browse list from the master browser and hands out the list upon request to computers in the domain.

Connection A logical communication path identified by a pair of sockets.

Datagram A message sent in a packet-switched computer communications network.

Destination Address Destination address, usually the network and host identifiers.

Domain Master Browser Always the primary domain controller; is responsible for collecting announcements for the entire domain, including all TCP network subnets, and network segments.

Fin A control bit (finis) occupying one sequence number. It indicates that the sender will send no more data or control occupying sequence space.

Fragment A portion of a logical unit of data; in particular, an Internet fragment is a portion of an Internet datagram.

FTP A file transfer protocol.

Gratuitous ARP_RARP A broadcast made by a DHCP client prior to using an IP address. The computer takes the address assigned to it by DHCP and sends out an ARP request for that very address. In this way, if another machine has the address, a duplicate IP address on the network error will ensue. Another feature of the gratuitous ARP_RARP is that machines that have the old IP address in their ARP cache will automatically update their ARP cache when they receive the request.

GUID Globally Unique Identifier: another name for a UUID (Universally Unique Identifier), a unique identification string associated with a remote-procedure call interface. Example: 12345678-1234-ABCD-EF00-01234567CFFB.

Header Control information at the beginning of a message, segment, fragment, packet, or block of data.

Host In IP terms, any device with an IP address. This can be a computer, printer, managed hub, switch, or router. In more general terms, it is either a source or destination of messages on the network.

Identification An Internet Protocol field assigned by the sender that aids in assembling the fragments of a datagram.

Internet address A source or destination address specific to the host level. This is an IP address such as 10.0.0.10.

Internet datagram The unit of data exchanged between an Internet module and the higher-level protocol together with the Internet header.

Internet fragment A portion of the data of an Internet datagram with an Internet header.

IRS (Initial Receive Sequence) number. The first sequence number used by the sender on a connection.

ISN Initial Sequence Number. The first sequence number used on a connection (either ISS or IRS). Selected on a clock-based procedure.

ISS Initial Send Sequence number. The first sequence number used by the sender on a connection.

Leader Control information at the beginning of a message or block of data; in particular, in the ARPANET, the control information on an ARPANET message at the host-IMP interface.

Left sequence Next sequence number to be acknowledged by the data receiving (or lowest currently unacknowledged sequence number) that is sometimes referred to as the left edge of the send window.

Local packet Unit of transmission within a local network.

Magic Cookie Four-byte area in a DHCP packet that identifies the start of a special-vendor, specific-options field. If this option field is used, it is marked off by the IP address 99.130.83.99, which shows up in a Netmon trace as 63 82 53 63 hex. The option can list such things as a client identifier, requested address, and other items as well.

Master Browser Responsible for collecting information to create and maintain the browse list, which includes all servers in the master browser domain or workgroup, as well as listing all the domains on the network.

Module Implementation, usually in software, of a protocol or other procedure.

MSL Maximum Segment Lifetime, the time a TCP segment can exist in the internetwork system. Arbitrarily defined to be two minutes.

Nonbrowser Specifically configured to not maintain the browse list.

Octet Eight-bit byte. Somewhat of an anachronistic term today. In the old days, there were ten-bit bytes.

Options May contain several options, each of which may be several octets in length. The options are used primarily in testing situations; for example, to carry timestamps. Both the Internet Protocol and TCP provide for options fields.

Packet A package of data with a header that may or may not be logically complete; more often, a physical packaging than a logical packaging of data.

Port Portion of a socket that specifies which logical input or output channel of a process is associated with the data.

Potential Browser Computer capable of maintaining the network resource browse list. It does not have the list yet and will only maintain the browse list if instructed to do so by the master browser.

Process A program in execution; a source or destination of data from the point of view of the TCP or other host-to-host protocol.

PUSH Control bit occupying no sequence space, indicating that this segment contains data that must be pushed through to the receiving user.

Receive next sequence number The next sequence number the local TCP is expecting to receive.

Receive window The sequence numbers the local (receiving) TCP is willing to receive. Thus, the local TCP considers that segments overlapping the range RCV.NXT to RCV.NXT + RCV.WND - 1 carry acceptable data or control. Segments containing sequence numbers entirely outside of this range are considered duplicates and discarded.

RST Control bit (reset) occupying no sequence space and indicating that the receiver should delete the connection without further interaction. The receiver can determine, based on the sequence number and acknowledgment fields of the incoming segment, whether it should honor the reset command or ignore it. In no case does receipt of a segment containing RST give rise to a RST in response.

RTP Real Time Protocol; a host-to-host protocol for communication of time critical information.

Segment Logical unit of data; in particular, a TCP segment is the unit of data transferred between a pair of TCP modules.

Segment acknowledgment Sequence number in the acknowledgment field of the arriving segment.

Segment length Amount of sequence number space occupied by a segment, including any controls which occupy sequence space.

Segment sequence Number in the sequence field of the arriving segment.

Send sequence Next sequence number the local (sending) TCP will use on the connection, initially selected from an initial sequence number curve (ISN) and incremented for each octet of data or sequenced control transmitted.

Send window Represents the sequence numbers that the remote (receiving) TCP is willing to receive. It is the value of the window field specified in segments from the remote (data receiving) TCP. The range of new sequence numbers that may be emitted by a TCP lies between SND.NXT and SND.UNA + SND.WND - 1. (Retransmissions of sequence numbers between SND.UNA and SND.NXT are expected, of course.)

Socket Address that specifically includes a port identifier, that is, the concatenation of an Internet address with a TCP port.

Source address Usually the network and host identifiers.

SYN Control bit in the incoming segment, occupying one sequence number, used at the initiation of a connection, to indicate where the sequence numbering will start.

TCB Transmission Control Block, the data structure that records the state of a connection.

TCP Transmission Control Protocol, a host-to-host protocol for reliable communication in internetwork environments.

Type of Service An Internet Protocol field which indicates the type of service for this Internet fragment.

UUID Universally Unique Identifier, a unique identification string associated with a remote procedure call interface, also sometimes called a GUID (globally unique identifier). Example: 12345678-1234-ABCD-EF00-01234567CFFB.

URG Control bit (urgent), occupying no sequence space and used to indicate that the receiving user should be notified to do urgent processing as long as there is data to be consumed with sequence numbers less than the value indicated in the urgent pointer.

Urgent pointer Control field meaningful only when the URG bit is on. This field communicates the value of the urgent pointer, which indicates the data octet associated with the sending user's urgent call.

Index

About the CD

On the CD-ROM you will find supplemental material to *Network Monitoring and Analysis: A Protocol Approach to Troubleshooting*. Many of the examples in the book come from items contained here. There are essentially five types of files you will find on the CD-ROM. These items are batch files, Registry entry files, filters, Network Monitor Capture files, and text versions of the more important Network Monitor Capture files. These five types of files are all referred to at the appropriate location with the book.

The batch files provide examples for automatically starting Microsoft Network Monitor with a variety of options. The use of these files is discussed in Chapter Nine. The batch files were written for Windows NT 4.0, however, with some modification it may be possible to start Network Monitor 1.2 on a Windows 95 or 98 machine. The 2.0 version of Network Monitor will not run on the 9.x family of Windows, and therefore the batch files will not work in that manner.

The registry entry files are for use on Windows NT 4.0, and *will not* work on a Windows 9.x machine. They are for illustration only and should not be used without reading Chapters Five, Six, and Seven where the principles that led to the file creation are discussed.

The filters are for use with Microsoft Network Monitor. Two types of filters are included: display filters and capture filters. The display filters will filter out certain types of information to create a custom display of previously captured data. The capture filters are used to limit the amount of data that is actually recorded in Network Monitor. The use and creation of both types of filters are discussed in Chapter Nine. The filters will work will all versions of Microsoft Network Monitor.

The capture files are included for supplemental experimentation and are constantly referred to throughout the book. They will work with all versions of Network Monitor, however, Microsoft's Network Monitor is required. Chapter Nine walks you through the installation of the Network Monitor product (which is included on the NT Server CD-ROM). Once Network Monitor is installed, the capture files can be run either from the CD-ROM or you can copy the files to a directory on your computer and run them from there.

The text version of the capture files do not require Network Monitor and therefore can be opened in any text editor, such as Notepad or Word. This allows you to examine the data without having to install additional software. These files can also be run from the CD-ROM or copied to a directory on your computer.

Technical Support

Prentice Hall does not offer technical support for this software. However, if there is a problem with the media, you may obtain a replacement copy by e-mailing us with your problem at: disc_exchange@prenhall.com